The Analysis of Legal Cases

This book examines the roles played by narrative and culture in the construction of legal cases and their resolution. It is articulated in two parts. Part I recalls epistemological turns in legal thinking as it moves from theory to practice in order to show how facts are constructed within the legal process. By combining interdisciplinary paradigms and methods, the work analyses the evolution of facts from their expression by the client to their translation within the lawyer-client relationship and the subsequent decision of the judge, focusing on the dynamic activity of narrative construction among the key actors: client, lawyer and judge. Part II expands the scientific framework toward a law-and-culture-oriented perspective, illustrating how legal stories come about in the fabric of the authentic dimensions of everyday life. The book stresses the capacity of laypeople, who in this activity are equated with clients, to shape the law, dealing not just with formal rules, but also with implicit or customary rules, in given contexts. By including the illustration of cases concerning vulnerable clients, it lays the foundations for developing a socio-clinical research programme, whose aims include enabling lay and expert actors to meet for the purposes of improving forms of collective narrations and generating more just legal systems.

Flora Di Donato is an Assistant Professor of Philosophy of Law, at the Federico II University of Naples, where she teaches Clinical Legal Education (Formazione Clinico-Legale). Her research focuses on the analysis of the law in real life and the contribution of laypeople in constructing the meanings of the law. In 2010, she was awarded the Annual RCSL Adam Podgórecki (ISA) Prize "for her outstanding achievements as an emerging scholar in socio-legal research". She has been a lecturer, a research fellow and a visiting scholar in several different Italian, Swiss and USA universities.

Law, Language and Communication

Series Editors: Anne Wagner
Université du Littoral Côte d'Opale, France
Vijay Kumar Bhatia
formerly of *City University of Hong Kong*

This series encourages innovative and integrated perspectives within and across the boundaries of law, language and communication, with particular emphasis on issues of communication in specialized socio-legal and professional contexts. It seeks to bring together a range of diverse yet cumulative research traditions in order to identify and encourage interdisciplinary research.

The series welcomes proposals – both edited collections as well as single-authored monographs – emphasizing critical approaches to law, language and communication, identifying and discussing issues, proposing solutions to problems, offering analyses in areas such as legal construction, interpretation, translation and de-codification.

Titles in the series

Synesthetic Legalities
Sensory Dimensions of Law and Jurisprudence
Edited by Sarah Marusek

Legal Persuasion
A Rhetorical Approach to the Science
Linda L. Berger and Kathryn M. Stanchi

International Arbitration Discourse and Practices in Asia
Edited by Vijay K Bhatia, Maurizio Gotti, Azirah Hashim, Philip Koh and Sundra Rajoo

Phraseology in Legal and Institutional Settings
A Corpus-Based Interdisciplinary Perspective
Edited by Stanislaw Gozdz Roszkowski and Gianluca Pontrandolfo

Fiction and the Languages of Law
Understanding Contemporary Legal Discourse
Karen Petroski

For more information about this series, please visit www.routledge.com/Law-Language-and-Communication/book-series/LAWLANGCOMM.

The Analysis of Legal Cases

A Narrative Approach

Flora Di Donato

Routledge
Taylor & Francis Group
LONDON AND NEW YORK

First published 2020
by Routledge
2 Park Square, Milton Park, Abingdon, Oxon OX14 4RN

and by Routledge
605 Third Avenue, New York, NY 10017

First issued in paperback 2020

Routledge is an imprint of the Taylor & Francis Group, an informa business

British Library Cataloguing-in-Publication Data
A catalogue record for this book is available from the British Library

Library of Congress Cataloging-in-Publication Data
Names: Donato, Flora Di, author.
Title: The analysis of legal cases/Flora Di Donato.
Description: Abingdon, Oxon; New York, NY: Routledge, 2019. | Series: Law, language and communication | Includes bibliographical references and index.
Identifiers: LCCN 2018057248 | ISBN 9780415788939 (hardback) | ISBN 9781315223087 (ebook)
Subjects: LCSH: Law—Philosophy. | Sociological jurisprudence.
Classification: LCC K230 .D654 A32 2019 | DDC 340/.115—dc23
LC record available at https://lccn.loc.gov/2018057248

ISBN 13: 978-0-367-72693-5 (pbk)
ISBN 13: 978-0-415-78893-9 (hbk)

Typeset in Galliard
by Apex CoVantage, LLC

This book is dedicated to the memory of Professor Jerome S. Bruner

Sailing through Oceans . . .

Contents

Foreword

Colette Daiute and Ann Shalleck

The two of us come to introduce this important book from different backgrounds, experiences and approaches, both working with narrative in public life, education and leisure. After briefly presenting our connections to this work that adds to the others by Flora Di Donato, we highlight three major contributions, among the many, readers will find here: *critical narrative approach, collaborative lawyering and theory in legal practice.*

1. Colette Daiute

1.1. Narrating legal development as a process of human development

Flora Di Donato offers a brilliant interdisciplinary analysis of clinical legal practice at a time in history when the need for such an analysis is urgent. Participants across the globe, raised in diverse cultures, with diverse resources and painfully (for some) different opportunities to achieve their dreams are increasingly coming in contact via their stories. Some of the most bereft peoples must channel myriad misfortunes through institutional barriers, even after such men, women and children have survived inhuman journeys. These migration processes, technologies and re-organisations of geopolitical power put persons of diverse origins in contact, so no one really escapes these contemporary processes, although only some are protected. This book focuses on the clinical legal narrative process, which could mediate contemporary migration, as well as labour and gender inequalities. This groundbreaking book, *The Analysis of Legal Cases: A Narrative Approach*, by Flora Di Donato, shows how law could develop further as a force for justice by narrating with clients in just ways.

In this preface to this important book, I highlight the major contributions from my perspective as an engaged scholar of the human sciences. I do research integrating a humanities sensitivity into the social sciences, in particular with a focus on narrating social change. As a developmental psychologist working with children, youth and organisations creating positive interventions in extremely challenging and changing circumstances, I study how individuals and collectives use language – especially narrative – to make sense of the world, how they fit, and what they would like to change. My research collaborations analyse oral and written voices of diverse stakeholders in the process of social change in schools, community centres, and policy organisations. Across numerous studies, I have focused on interactions of policymakers, educators, ethnic group leaders, and individuals expressing and negotiating their knowledge, experience and goals. In that process, we hear groups of students/teachers, migrants/policymakers, community organisers/funders, echoing, contradicting and transforming narratives about their shared plights and possibilities (for example, Daiute, 2008; 2014; Daiute et al., 2017). Policy has, thus, been pivotal in the collaborative narration of contentious public and personal issues. Although policy and law have much in common for the development of cultural cohesion, the law has been, in the words of Flora Di Donato, in need of scholarship and practice to "counter the claims to objectivity and self-reference typical of legal positivism, which is still rather dominant, especially in Civil Law systems" (Di Donato, this volume, Introduction p. 1). I am, and we should all be, indebted to Dott. Prof. Di Donato for her rigorous research extending narrative theory to the law as a cultural artefact. Toward that end, this book interprets and extends prior research to forge new insights blurring boundaries between stakeholders in legal cases to increase authorship in the apparently immutable human artefact of the law.

I highlight three major contributions among many of this book. As Di Donato wrote, citing others, "'Narrative' has thus become one of the most overused terms in contemporary scientific language". Di Donato's discourse on narrative is a very different one from the hackneyed reductions. She defines narrating as a relational activity, rather than as representing an authentic individualistic voice. This relational sense is critical because it does not reduce or universalise narrative. Instead, this narrative approach is dynamic, nurtured between and within participants in very different roles in the legal process. Di Donato follows through on that by showing how collaborative legal practice can work in spite of challenges of power relations, time pressures and biases, all processes in legal practice requiring flexibility, patience, insight and humility to achieve new methods. A third contribution is moving theoretical arguments and categories posited by narrative and law pioneers like Bruner, Amsterdam, and others, fully into empirical practice. Advancing theory in practice is no mere step. The priority of practice characterises a new wave of examining institutions through personal, human lenses to social justice goals in troubled times.

I focus on Di Donato's bold contributions setting the scene for the practice of collaborative lawyering including those she refers to as "vulnerable" – migrants, workers, women – who often seem tangential to legal process. What comes across to me, as a scholar working in transdisciplinary ways, are Ms. Di Donato's descriptions of how lawyers in the cases she studied gradually became able to hear and to re-narrate clients' narratives and how judges made sense of counter-narratives in cases. Having worked with thousands of narratives by individuals who are the subjects of policies ("vulnerable and marginalized", in Di Donato's terms), I am less surprised by their ability to narrate, their openness to legal counsel, and their sometimes careful guidance of those in power, than I am by the openness of those in the legal profession as described in this book. Culminating the trio of highlights is Di Donato's exciting extension of theory to practice.

1.2. Critical narrative approach

A critical approach to narrative is dynamic in that it must consider the way a storyteller organises a story (plot, details, etc.) for a specific purpose, to specific interlocutors, in a specific time and location. Considering these dynamics hovering around, within and between any given narrative of experience defies the concept of a single story (Daiute, 2011; 2014), an understanding that Di Donato explains clearly as a construction process.

> Narrating how facts took place is something like piecing a puzzle together, organizing the events as a function of how we generally expect that things happen, on the basis of scripts and categories that are modelled not only by the law, but also by culture. Law and narrations are interdependent and complementary: while the law tends to simplify reality using legal categories (citizen/foreigner) and juridical qualifications (abusive husband/woman as the victim), narrations tend to explore possibilities, making space for human events to have multiple dimensions in specific contexts.
>
> (Di Donato, this volume, Introduction p. 2)

Whereas some narrative theory emphasises "voice" as a possession of individuals, I recognise a more critical approach to narrative inquiry in *The Analysis of Legal Cases*, an approach that understands voices as relational because they are developed, used and transformed in culture. As Di Donato presents in detail in her first few chapters, law involves cultural construction, enacted with narratives – renditions of experience and values – by diverse stakeholders. Culture, as Di Donato explains it in terms of *constructivism*, is interested and power-laden, rather than neutral or universal. Also, critical is the activity-meaning system design of the analysis (Daiute, 2014), that is making sense of the cases from the perspectives of diverse interacting stakeholders. In spite of differences in training, power, stigma and so on, case analysis approaches meaning as an activity to be re-developed not only by the client, who (of course) has much to learn about norms and processes that will prevail in a court of law, but also by the lawyer, who likewise has much to learn from clients' diverse narratives of their experiences, and by the judge.

Many scholars agree that language is action, yet many of those same scholars also tend to study narrative as though it mirrors reality. That is, the *trouble* or *perepetia* inherent in a good story would be discussed as representing the problem in real life, rather than in the way the person sharing the narrative is making sense of events, and thus as salient in the particular time and place of recounting the event. This difference between an assumption that there is one objective plot of a real life event (beginning with a clearly defined initiating action) and the understanding that plot is a cultural literary concept is inherent to the elegant argument in this book. In prior research, we have found, for example, that plot analyses of narratives of the "same" event over time and with different narrative genres (such as first person accounts of experience compared to third person accounts) unfold in different ways across time, collaborative situation, and intended audience (Daiute, 2014). The promise of collaborative narrating offered in this book, thus, relies on such a dynamic literary analysis we can advance from legacies and foundations set forth herein. Implied if not always stated is that collaboration among these diverse stakeholders requires everyone to change at least somewhat, judges, lawyers and clients. Di Donato's re-narration of the cases shows us just how that might occur. A critical analysis – one that allows diversity and tension – is offered in this book.

1.3. Collaborative lawyering

Although institutions have more objective resources, influence, and power, they do not have more objective hold on how events unfold. That, of course, is in the minds of those experiencing the events, making sense of the events and subjected to the events. Institutional narratives hold sway over negotiated norms and processes, but those forms have, after all, been developed through interactions among individuals in daily life. It is in this iterative sense that Di Donato defines construction and its role in the development of legal facts.

> I therefore found this kind of approach well suited to illustrating how what constitutes a judicial fact depends not only on the norm that qualifies the event in legal terms, but also on the perspective and on the roles played by the actors concerned and by the community to which they belong.
>
> (Di Donato, this volume, Introduction pp. 1–2)

Although the power of social and political institutions is assumed in policy studies, education, social welfare, and, as discussed in this book, law, a foundational premise of contemporary human development studies is the interdependent construction of individuals and collectives. The emphasis in narrative inquiry is that this interdependent process occurs via shared engagements with cultural tools, like narrative.

Examining narratives by diverse stakeholders around contentious issues – like inclusion of discriminated minorities, students assumed to be from deficit cultures, and those suffering consequences of violence – has offered surprises about the shared and unshared nature of events, knowledge, and expressive positions of narrators, who are, as Di Donato reviews, those who construct facts. Collaborative policy, education and post-conflict community development from a dynamic narrative perspective have, for example, revealed processes that fell through the cracks of policy monitoring and the limits of autobiographical narrating (Daiute et al., 2017). Those and other insights show that policy studies like legal studies must be more than theoretical. Collaborators must interact, listen as well as speak, and inevitably all change in some way to achieve knowledge and, ultimately, justice; this process comes to life in the cases analysis. As Di Donato shows, open and trusting collaborative lawyering is effortful and developmental by all participants. With an excellent foundation in the legal case analyses presented in this book, Di Donato shows not only that theory requires practice but also that certain premises and narrative steps can be useful for future practice-based inquiry. In brief, we learn that collaborative lawyering is not an abstract endeavour.

Several questions about collaboration emerge from the foundational chapters as the cases unfold and point toward future research. Once lawyering becomes a collaborative process, who is "vulnerable" and in what ways? With what empowerments do those in abject power positions accept the transformations of their personal narratives? With what limits do those in superior power positions admit to learning?

1.4. Theory in legal practice

What does the practice of these ideas about narrative as a dynamic mechanism in legal process reveal about the role of law in the contemporary global world? It's not only in legal theory that knowledge, experience and voices are increasingly democratised but also in systems not previously open to voices of subjects. That there isn't a single narrative but diverse ones situated in time, place, knowledge, goals and power is critical in cultural analysis, which also offers surprising insights when addressed empirically and not only theoretically.

> In the framework of this book, the use of the narrative approach thus has at least three meanings: as a method for analysing legal cases and reconstructing facts in context, i.e. in legal disputes and in cultural contexts; as a method to educate lawyers – to understand the narratives of their clients and their own narratives, both in dialogue with their clients and in the presentation of cases – and as a device to include voices that are silenced or marginalised in the legal discourse.
>
> (Di Donato, this volume, Introduction p. 3)

Complex workshopping of policy narratives by diverse subjects and the effortful analysis of their practices has offered insights about how democratic collaborative processes *could* be. Authoritative as well as uninformed and bigoted voices emerge in social media, whereas the more structured practices like the ones Flora Di Donato presents could purposefully guide deliberate power shifts for democratic justice. Processes like mobbing are ones emerging in practice, clearly making the way for recognising other problematic activities. These moves will be fascinating to continue exploring in collaborative lawyering and scholarship shifting from rigid categories and their relevant scripts – lawyer versus client, correct narrative versus experienced narrative, and so on.

1.5. Conclusion

In his preface to Flora Di Donato's 2012 book, *La realtà delle storie*, Jerome Bruner stated "What I find most striking in this book is its emphasis on 'meaning making' and its combined cultural and personal determinants as means of taking us 'beyond the law,' of humanizing the law" (Bruner, 2012, pp. 9–10). I agree with Bruner, yet seven years later, what I find most striking in *this* book by Di Donato is its progress beyond humanising the law to suggesting a process for changing legal practice and the society around it to open to diverse relevant stakeholders, including clients. After all, once we acknowledge the human nature of narrating, we must also acknowledge that it is the clients who have the most knowledge as well as the most at stake, alongside lawyers, judges, translators, jurists and a broader interested public. Whether and how those diverse stakeholders become collaborative narrators in ways that advance law and society remains an intriguing question that Flora Di Donato's provokes.

References

Bruner, J. (2012). Preface to Di Donato, F. *La realtà delle storie. Tracce di una cultura.* Napoli: Guida.

Daiute, C. (2008). The Rights of Children, the Rights of Nations: Developmental Theory and the Politics of Children's Rights. *Journal of Social Issues.* 64(4): 701–723.

Daiute, C. (2011). "Trouble" in, Around, and Between Narratives. *Narrative Inquiry.* 21(2): 329–336.

Daiute, C. (2014). *Narrative Inquiry: A Dynamic Approach.* Thousand Oaks, CA: Sage Publications.

Daiute et al., (2017). *Minority Teachers – Roma in Serbia – Narrate Education Reform.* Belgrade, Serbia: Institute of Psychology, Faculty of Philosophy at the University of Belgrade and the Association of Pedagogical Assistants.

2. Ann Shalleck

2.1. Narrating law through the relationship of client and lawyer

In combination with her brilliant interdisciplinary analysis, Flora Di Donato offers a superb inquiry into clinical legal theory and practice that brings fresh insights from narrative theory to the enduring subject of how clients and their lawyers participate in the construction of law. People who encounter problems and seek redress through law become actors in the legal system – clients – who interact with lawyers, judges and many other inhabitants of the legal world as they seek to comprehend and solve their problems. Making the operation of law a just and humane human endeavour in solving those problems is an ongoing imperative of building a democratic society. Flora Di Donato brings her full and elegant elaboration of narrative as essential in the construction law to the twin projects of understanding the creation of law and identifying how legal actors can shape law as a just aspect of democratic processes. We see how, through storytelling, law and culture intersect with human aspiration and experience to create law. We learn how, using a narrative approach, lawyers and clients can act together so clients can become legal agents in working toward solution of their problems. We acquire a methodology of research and practice, developed in the context of labour, migration and gender, which could extend to other areas that law has within its ambit. We imagine how a narrative approach could help lawyers and clients develop law as a more just enterprise.

Professor Di Donato, as I have, draws upon the pivotal work of Jerome Bruner and Anthony Amsterdam (Amsterdam and Bruner, 2000) in taking a narrative constructivist approach to understanding and shaping law and legal practice. As a theorist of clinical law and pedagogy, I have extended the narrative frameworks of Amsterdam and Bruner from analysis of court decisions to the creation of a narrative theory of client representation (Ellmann et al., 2009). Both Professor Di Donato and I see a narrative approach as overlapping with and folding into the theory of the client-lawyer relationship developed within clinical scholarship over more than fifty years. In different ways, we both situate the development of narrative theory in the identification and shaping of narrative practices of client representation. My commitment to the interdependent development of theory and practice comes from my daily work as a clinical teacher educating students to represent clients, particularly vulnerable ones, not only skilfully and creatively but, crucially, with an understanding of the context of the clients' lives and the meaning of the representation for them. Through teaching of clinical teachers and the development of clinical law and education as a distinct and transformative form of legal education (Bryant et al., 2014), I have sought to advance a vision of legal practice always attentive to forms of injustice.

Professor Di Donato has deepened our collective understanding of narrative clinical theory and enriched our repertoire of narrative practices through her original and meticulous multi-layered case studies of clients who work, often in collaboration with lawyers, to solve their problems in the situations in which they find themselves. These studies reveal ways that clients find, sometimes inadvertently to address the injustices they encounter. I, like Colette Daiute, am indebted to Professor Di Donato for her rigorous research, which expands prior work, including my own, across disciplinary boundaries enabling us to see how law operates, beginning at the local level, as an essential part of culture. She helps us comprehend how legal actors transform daily events in their local settings into legal stories and deepens our understanding of how clients do and increasingly can, through work with narratively trained lawyers, expand their experience as agents within law. I, along with Colette Daiute, highlight three major contributions of Di Donato's narrative approach.

2.2. *Critical narrative approach*

In Professor Di Donato's constructivist approach, we see narrative as a relational, dynamic activity that occurs through recurring re-narrations, within specific, localised contexts. Di Donato situates her critical constructivist perspective first in the long tradition of narrative theory, particularly in Chapters 1 through 3. She then embeds the approach in multiple detailed contexts, through many levels of analysis, in her three categories of case analysis. She brings critical and transformative insights first to the analysis of the construction of facts in particular cases, in Chapters 4 through 6, then to the analysis of cultural contexts of cases in Chapters 7 and 8, and finally to the analysis of the search of justice through collaborative lawyering in Chapter 9. These three categories of case studies are meant not to differentiate distinctive processes of narrative construction, but rather to reveal interdependent critical features of narrative construction. They are all part of an essential dynamic among law, culture and the actions of individuals working together, through which law gets meaning. In her concluding chapter, Professor Di Donato outlines how this project of integrating fact construction, cultural context and collaborative lawyering to develop understanding of narrative construction of law demands further study, reflection and practice, and she proposes ways to pursue these exciting possibilities.

2.3. Collaborative lawyering

Second, building on her understanding of narratives as a relational endeavour, Professor Di Donato demonstrates through her case studies how the creation of law through iterative re-narrations among participants in legal actions is and increasingly can be a collaborative process. Di Donato describes how lawyers, through a process of reciprocal storytelling with their clients, gradually become able to hear the dynamic development of clients' narratives, to shape collaborative strategies and arguments and to re-narrate clients' narratives to judges. Her accounts of how judges make sense of clients' counter-narratives and can act creatively provide glimpses of how narrative can open possibilities within law for responding to harms to the vulnerable. Clients with lawyers educated in the narrative approach can both recognise and navigate intentionally within the open and imaginative space endemic to the process of narrative construction. Within that space, they can explore narrative possibilities and shape their actions to pursue just outcomes, to increase access to justice, and through specific results achieved in particular contexts, to shape law animated by understandings of justice.

2.4. Theory in legal practice

Third, Professor Di Donato fully integrates the insights of her narrative constructivist approach with the development of practical methods for identifying, analysing and using narrative tools within empirical research and legal practice. In each set of case studies, she pursues related, yet distinctive, empirical methods. In the analysis of fact construction, she deploys methods that emphasise the narrative structure and composition of the dispute, as well as the roles of the legal actors in narrative construction within the specific context of the disputes, emphasising the commonly neglected role of clients. In the analysis of the cultural contexts of narratives, Di Donato continues the methodology, while using new analytic categories that highlight the dynamic between fact construction and cultural context.

By focusing on how legal actors interpret legal meanings as they act in cases, she develops the concept of legal agentivity (Di Donato, this volume, pp. 192–194). This concept provides markers for identifying how clients together with lawyers and other legal actors call on resources in a particular cultural setting to solve their cases. Third, in the analysis of cases involving the search of justice through collaborative lawyering, particularly for vulnerable clients, Professor Di Donato explores practices for the reconstruction of facts when the roles of legal actors, legal documents and evidence do not fit within classical legal processes within which legal storytelling occurs. Significantly, for all three types of empirical methods, she situates her empirical practice in the context of the actions of those engaged in the practice of law, identifies the concrete dynamics through which actors in the legal system construct the law and focuses on the possibilities for the client to be a creative participant in that construction.

2.5. *Implications for clinical narrative law*

These three contributions – critical narrative approach, collaborative lawyering and theory in legal practice – taken individually and together have particular salience for the development of clinical narrative law. Professor Di Donato's approach to understanding how narrative dynamically constructs law is particularly important from the perspective of clinical theory. Clinical theory and practice emphasise the centrality of reciprocal and evolving storytelling within the client-lawyer relationship, as well as attentive listening to those stories. An aspect of storytelling involves the collaborative creation of multiple case theories that integrate facts and law to generate narrative possibilities that frame ways for achieving clients' desires and often challenge legal norms or overcome injustice. The narrative process in case theory development requires recognising how different stories construct facts in multiple, shifting ways. Those possible stories constructed as plots with troubles at their centre, situated in time and place, with causal connections, create frameworks for understanding the development and presentation of facts within different activities within the legal process.

Lawyers, through knowledge of and experience with law and its conventional stories, can devise with clients disruptive or subversive stories in light of the client's situation. These stories, through alternative construction of facts, can challenge or change the law, while maintaining narrative coherence. Through these stories, lawyers can shape the narratives constructed by judges. Responding to the narratives of lawyers in constructing different sorts of judicial narratives, judges can be moved to interact creatively and dynamically with lawyers and perhaps even clients. These stories constructed by clients, lawyers, judges and other actors in the legal system reveal how cultural contexts, including law in its many manifestations with its local practices, matters in each actor's understanding and interpretation of the facts as they each place facts within stories in particular ways.

Professor Di Donato's explanation of the role of factual construction, cultural contexts and collaborative efforts in the construction of a legal dispute deepens our understanding of how clients' narratives of trouble becomes legal narratives seeking redress through the legal process. Her explanation reveals how the routine activities of constructing legal accounts of trouble and redress through the activities of client representation and legal decision-making operate to construct law from the facts, rather than from abstract rules and precepts. Her narrative approach also demonstrates how clients are active participants in each aspect of this process. When helped by lawyers educated in this narrative approach, clients have the potential to be legal actors both advocating on their own behalf and framing the meanings of justice.

In addition to her theoretical and practical contributions, Professor Di Donato's empirical methods for elucidating the construction of narratives contribute to developing educational practices that incorporate narrative understanding of law. The components of narrative – the setting, the plot, the agent with a purpose, the management of time – presented in detail in Chapter 4 provide not just analytic methods but practical tools for deconstructing and constructing possible stories to tell. The characteristic initiatives that clients adopt in the construction of narratives – contesting, alleging, correcting, explaining, confirming – which Di Donato presents in detail in Chapter 5 other ways to mark when and how clients act to influence the course of a dispute. Clinical educators can transform all of these analytic categories into practical lawyering activities that can be transmitted through legal training. Clinical narrative law is at once a theoretical, practical and educational project.

2.6. Conclusion

Flora Di Donato's complex and intricate elaboration of narrative and law takes us from the ordinary regular practices of actors within the legal system to an understanding of how law and culture create meaning through narrative. Her studies of participants in the legal system, most importantly clients ideally acting with narratively trained lawyers, expose how law can be a site for even the most vulnerable to seek and perhaps find through a collaborative narrative process redress for harms they have endured. Her provocative proposal for augmenting the possibilities of intentional narrative processes designed to promote justice for vulnerable people through clinical legal research and practice provides a vision of what narrative theory could achieve.

References

Amsterdam, A.G. and Bruner, J.S. (2000). *Minding the Law*. Cambridge, MA: Harvard University Press.

Bryant, S., Milstein, E.S. and Shalleck, A.C. (2014). *Transforming the Education of Lawyers; The Theory and Practice of Clinical Pedagogy*. Durham, NC: Carolina Academic Press.

Ellmann et al., (2009). *Lawyers and Clients. Critical Issues in Interviewing and Counseling*. St. Paul, MN: Thomson Reuters, American Casebook Series. 139–226.

Acknowledgements

I would like to thank the publisher Franco Angeli for permitting me to publish parts of the book *La costruzione giudiziaria del fatto. Il ruolo della narrazione nel processo* (Milano, 2008). In doing so, I would also like to take this opportunity to clarify that, although I have maintained the original approach in Chapters 1 to 6, I have rewritten them completely, altering both their contents and their structure. For example, Chapter 3 of this volume combines Chapters 3 and 4 of the Italian original, while Chapters 4 to 6 correspond to the original 5 to 7. Chapter 7 furnishes an *ex novo* reconstruction, on the basis of a new theoretical and methodological framework, of some of the cases described in the 2012 volume *La realtà delle storie. Tracce di una cultura* (Napoli, 2012). Chapter 8 is adapted from the volume *La fabrique de l'intégration* (forthcoming), the result of interdisciplinary research financed by the Swiss National Fund (147287). Chapter 9 contains cases analysed in the framework of the course in Clinical Legal Training that I held last year at the Federico II University of Naples (spring semester 2017/2018). My aim here is to furnish a unitary reinterpretation of these various works for the purpose of illustrating the profiles of continuity but also of innovation in the research conducted over the years.

I am infinitely grateful to Anne-Nelly Perret-Clermont, Professor Emerita at the University of Neuchâtel, for having shared my dream of having this book published.

This book has benefitted from the many academic events I have attended, sometimes playing a leading role in them, and from the invaluable suggestions I have received from friends and colleagues. In particular, I would like to thank Professor Colette Daiute (CUNY, New York) for having read the manuscript with passion and enormous care, providing me with invaluable suggestions in both narrative analysis and method. My thanks also go to Professor Ann Shalleck for her invaluable comments which helped me to contextualise clinical lawyering within the European debate. She also hosted me at her university (American University, Washington, DC) in 2016, enabling me to discuss some cases and ideas during a round table organised with her colleagues. I should also like to thank Professors Daiute and Shalleck for having written a joint Foreword, each of them commenting on the book from her own disciplinary perspective. They have been generous companions in this adventure.

My thanks also go to Professor Richard Sherwin, who assisted me in the same way: I have his invitation to thank for having been able to obtain a grant from the University of Neuchâtel (Equal Opportunities Office) in 2016 to travel to the New York School of Law and devote my attention to writing this book and discussing its first developments with him.

My thanks go to all my colleagues at the Federico II Department of Law in Naples for their support and to the National Research Projects Office for helping me learn how to use part of the FFABR 2017/000006_FFABR_2017 research funds allocated to me by the Italian Ministry of Education, University and Research.

I also owe a debt of thanks to the attorney, the social workers and the institutions that permitted me to access the new cases they had dealt with in professional contexts: Luigi Migliaccio for Amenze's case (Chapter 9), and the Dedalus Co-operative for Margaret's case (also Chapter 9). I owe my access to the cases of Charles, Johan, Kirin and Line (Chapter 8) to the institutions of the Swiss Canton of Neuchâtel, in particular to the Department of Justice.

Lastly, my warmest thanks go to my family: my son Giovanni, who is waiting with barely concealed curiosity to hold this new piece of work in his hands, and my husband Antonio, for his boundless patience and encouragement and for always being there to bridge the gaps in my everyday life.

It is in a different vein that I mention the translator/reviewer of this work, Pete Kercher, whom I would like to thank for his lessons in linguistic style and terminological precision.

Introduction

Why adopt a narrative approach to law?

1. Reasons

"Once upon a time . . ." is the classical opening line for every self-respecting story. I am borrowing it to illustrate the timeline of the path I followed in constructing this volume, *The Analysis of Legal Cases: A Narrative Approach*. It is the result of a series of micro-sociological research projects into cases of labour law and migration law, conducted in several different cultural contexts – the south of Italy and north-western Switzerland – between 2004 and 2018.

Originally conceived of as a fresh look at my doctoral book, *La costruzione giudiziaria del fatto. Il ruolo della narrazione nel processo* (Di Donato, 2008), it has since expanded to encompass issues and cases analysed in subsequent works (Di Donato, 2012; Di Donato et al., forthcoming), which I describe anew here in part, in a unitary and updated reinterpretation, from the standpoint of conceptual and methodological frameworks. My original challenge was to identify a paradigm that would enable me to illustrate the socially constructed nature of the facts and of legal reality effectively, so as to counter the claims to objectivity and self-reference typical of legal positivism, which is still rather dominant, especially in Civil Law systems.

The constructivism shaped by a certain part of social and cultural psychology led by authors of the calibre of Jerome S. Bruner – to whom this book is dedicated – has already furnished good results not only in the field of the human and social sciences, but also in that of law, contributing to overcoming a conception of knowledge as reflection (Rorty, 1981), in favour of a conception of knowledge as a quest for meaning (Bruner, 1986; Amsterdam and Bruner, 2000). Indeed, this kind of perspective focuses on the fact that people live in the framework of a history and a culture and act on the basis of meanings that they co-create with their peers in the course of taking part in events and in human actions. This approach also explains the interdependence between law and culture: law's function is to model relations – as well as the individual's behaviour – within the community and we find that it is modelled, in its turn, by the creation of codes that more often than not are internal or implicit to life contexts and have the function of enabling the established order to be maintained, while also being transformed.

I therefore found this kind of approach well suited to illustrating how what constitutes a judicial fact depends not only on the norm that qualifies the event in legal terms, but also on the perspective and on the roles played by the actors concerned and by the community to which they belong, as well as by the context within which the facts take shape. Narrating how facts took place is something like piecing a puzzle together, organising the events as a function of how we generally expect that things happen, on the basis of scripts and categories that are modelled not only by the law, but also by culture. Law and narrations are interdependent and complementary: while the law tends to simplify reality using legal categories (citizen/foreigner) and juridical qualifications (abusive husband/woman as the victim), narrations tend to explore possibilities, making space for human events to have multiple dimensions and meanings in specific contexts.

Moreover, despite being central to American legal realism and to the thinking of many scholars in both Civil Law and Common Law systems, the issue of fact-finding has not yet benefitted from any significant developments, not so much because of any lack of interest on the part of jurists and legal theorists, as because of the lack of suitable methods of investigation, as Jerome Frank himself already pointed out as long ago as the 1930s. As we know, Frank advocated for an accurate factual investigation capable of giving due consideration to the contextual and subjective elements characteristic of the activities of judges, attorneys and witnesses, stressing the artificial nature of the narrations generated by the parties to legal proceedings (Frank, 1930; 1947; 1948). Making use of methods typical of the social sciences to analyse empirical cases – tools such as interviews, observation in context and the documentary analysis of legal records – enabled me to go beyond an analysis of doctrine and jurisprudence, which is generally limited to the decisions handed down by the judges, to their reasoning and to the arguments used, to illustrate how everyday facts are transformed into legal facts in the stories told by clients, attorneys and judges, in a framework that is socially dynamic and interactive, as well as one that is situated culturally, as are legal disputes. These methods from the social science resonate with investigations developed within contemporary work in the New Legal Realism, Law and Society, and clinical theories of lawyering.

Since few publications combine theory and practice in the analysis of cases or pay attention to the role played by narrative, actors and culture in the construction of the facts and solution of the case, the impact of my work in the broader concerned scientific community has been significant.[1] Conscious that fact-finding is of current relevance (Gaakeer, 2017; 2019) and that the law and narrative approach has recently become pervasive (Herman et al., 2008), I decided to focus the attention of a broader scientific community on the results of my research, by translating the work I published in 2008 and subsequent developments into English. In this book, the analysis of cases is extended to take in geographically, anthropologically and legally different contexts, describing the attitude of their

1 See, for example, the international Adam Podgòrecki Prize 2010 I received from the RCSL: http://rcsl.iscte.pt/rcsl_apodgpr10.htm.

protagonists – the clients – towards finding solutions to their legal problems by engaging with lawyers in the process of iteratively narrating their experiences and gradually becoming aware not only of the formal rules, but also of the local meanings of events and of how the law is practised in the respective specific contexts (Di Donato, 2012; 2014; Di Donato et al., forthcoming). It also observes clients who are vulnerable – foreigners, asylum seekers, women who are victims of trafficking – paving the way for a research action that favours the narrative method as a way of including the voices of people who are powerless in society (Di Donato, 2018).

In the framework of this book, the use of the narrative approach thus has at least three meanings: as a method for analysing legal cases and reconstructing facts in context, i.e. in legal disputes and in cultural contexts, as a method to educate lawyers – to understand the narratives of their clients and their own narratives, both in dialogue with their clients and in the presentation of cases – and as a device to include voices that are silenced or marginalised in the legal discourse.

But let's now take a more complete view of some of the reasons why, in my opinion, the combination of law and narrative is valid and pertinent today. The first fundamental reason is epistemological as well as epistemic in nature. Referring to an immanent dimension of knowledge, narration breaks out of the dominion of the humanities where it originated, to move transversally across the various fields of knowledge. As Hayden White wrote, it solves "the problem of how to translate *knowing* into *telling*, the problem of fashioning human experience into a form assimilable to structures of meaning that are generally human rather than culture-specific" (1981, p. 1). In the field of the law, as in others, the narrative approach enables us to achieve a refined understanding of how legal meanings are modelled, which nexuses of cause and time connect events, which characters play the key roles in a story and what role and what actions can be attributed to them in the story. In other words, how knowledge of these elements is translated within the legal and judicial story and for what purposes. The narrative approach partners well with the dimension of legal proceedings where the facts are reconstructed *ex post*, according to the meaning that the events have for the law and from the standpoint of the parties to the conflict. Meanings that are conveyed in narrative form: from the stories told by clients to how they are understood and translated by their attorneys and on to the final decision handed down by the judge or the administrative agent. Establishing the truth in the course of legal proceedings is a complex issue, since due consideration also has to be given to other categories, such as the verisimilitude, coherence, plausibility and probability of the story and the credibility of the narrator. This complexity is particularly acute when the burden of proof on the client is enhanced by the client's vulnerability, as I shall demonstrate in the closing chapters, dedicated to the issue of international protection, where the procedure of the hearing for the asylum seeker rests almost exclusively on the verisimilitude and coherence of the story narrated by the applicant, compared to a framework in which more general information about his or her country of origin in the possession of the authorities dominates.

The second reason is also theoretical in nature: the narrative approach contributes to revealing implicit and instrumental elements that are often left unstated by formal law. As Riessman writes, a narration helps us look beyond the surface of things: "A good narrative analysis prompts the researcher to look beyond the surface of the text" (2007, p. 13; cit. in Daiute, 2014, p. 11). As a result of the artificial and fictive character of legal proceedings, it is not possible to tell the story in its entirety when reconstructing cases: there are parts of the story that are told, others that are eliminated and others that are left unsaid (Baer, 2017). This realisation paves the way to my methodological proposal to reconstruct cases from the standpoint of the narrations furnished by legal actors and legal files, so as to understand which events have been cut out of the construction of the official story, which meanings have been privileged and which left unmentioned; which cultural and implicit meanings model the story and affect the solution to the case and what are the emotions and the agency of the protagonists.

In this way, narration also fulfils another, inclusive function, as mentioned previously. Favouring what is sometimes an unofficial point of view – such as that of the client (a layperson who is often vulnerable) – when reconstructing the facts makes allowance for the other story and for including the other voice, acknowledging their dignity (Delgado, 1989; Luban, 2007) and their possibility of self-making (Bruner, 2003) and self-affirmation (Charon, 2006; Massaro, 1989). This book therefore adopts client narratives – as well as those of the other actors in legal proceedings: attorneys, judges, administrative agents etc. – as its principal lens of observation, illustrating the meanings that events take on in their eyes and how narrations are transformed in accordance with the logic of the law and of legal proceedings and with the roles played by the various actors. As Shalleck (2015) writes, client narrations are a window on the world: they help us understand how the institutions, working contexts and everyday life function.

More generally, narrations incorporate personal and institutional values, making relationships of power and individual motives explicit: people who defend their jobs, others who want recognition for a civic status etc. In this sense, narration also becomes a tool for connecting with other people, mediating with institutions and proposing interpersonal resolution strategies (Daiute, 2014). A narrative analysis of cases enables us to achieve a real understanding of which everyday dynamics may characterise working contexts, what emotions are experienced by victims of mobbing or what strategies of relations can be applied to solve a conflict in the workplace (Chapters 4–7). Or again what it means to have to react to the requirement to integrate in a foreign context, how to establish a dialogue with the institutions and ask for recognition for a civic status such as that of citizenship (Chapter 8) or, lastly, how to tell a story relevantly, so as to obtain recognition of the status of refugee for an asylum seeker or a woman who is a victim of trafficking (Chapter 9).

A fourth good reason for considering making more conscious use of narration in legal practice is related to the recent increase in awareness on the part of academics and lawyers about the implicit use they make of it in the everyday exercise of their functions (Brooks, 2006; Gaakeer, 2017; Aiken and Shalleck, 2016).

A legal narration is actually no different from a literary narration, since every plot comprises a cast of characters and a set of actions, of targets to be reached, of obstacles and of attempts to solve a problem, all in a given context. Some of the key questions for modelling a legal narrative analysis are: how can the basic elements of a narratology elaborated in the framework of the humanities that can also be found in or adapted to a legal framework be identified? Can narration be imagined in terms of a legal category? How do the narrative and cognitive mechanisms that govern the everyday activity of lawyers and practices become conscious?

As recently argued by the judge and expert in law and literature Jeanne Gaakeer (2017, p. 347; 2019), knowledge of how narrative works in law is therefore essential not just for legal theorists, but also for the practitioner, since the way in which the narrative is told often determines the result of the case. The judge is in fact free to choose which stories seem most plausible in a legal context and which do not, to which narratives to attribute legal value and which not, what weight to attribute to individual facts and which pieces of evidence should be valued as sufficient proof and which not. In addition, the way the client's narrative is heard by the lawyer and transformed through narration within the client-lawyer relationship can affect how the client makes meaning through the legal proceeding.

Illustrating this and other aspects that may characterise how a judge, an attorney or an administrative agent reasons is one of the objectives of this book. In addition, I use the analysis of a specific field – that of international protection – to demonstrate how narration plays a vital role and achieves the status of a 'legal category' in certain norms that govern the status of asylum seekers.

2. Trajectories of case analysis: an overview

This book is organised in two main parts. The first part describes the theoretical, epistemological and methodological foundations underlying the case analysis to which the second part is devoted.

The first part comprises Chapters 1–3. In Chapter 1, I propose an interdisciplinary analysis of the nexus between mind, culture and language, highlighting fundamental characteristics of narrative to be translated within the legal discourse. In Chapter 2, I place the discourse within the wider debate on law and humanities, describing such contemporary orientations as the clinical law approach and the lawyering theory as ideal settings for inserting a case analysis capable of harmonising theory and practice. In my attempt to offer stimuli for developing a European debate about legal narratology, I identify possible meanings and uses of narration in law. In Chapter 3, I complete the theoretical and methodological premises that guide case analysis and fact investigation, situating the discourse in a context of Civil Law and in particular in that of the Italian legal order.

In the second part of the book (Chapters 4–9), I develop case analysis along three main paths: a) fact construction; b) narratives in cultural contexts; c) improving justice for vulnerable people.

2.1. Fact construction

In Chapters 4–6, I analyse a first group of cases of labour law that took place in southern Italy, which is framed and defined as follows:

- Dequalification/mobbing – Laura's case;
- Dequalification/revocation of functions – Luciano's case;
- Resignation – Franco's case.

By adopting a standpoint internal to the legal process – which takes the structure and composition of the dispute, the roles played by the parties and the type of controversy into account – the aim of the investigation here is to analyse the outbreak and evolution of the conflict from a dimension that could be described as 'human and inter-individual', as a result of the attempt made by the attorney's client to manage the conflict personally, to one that is legal and institutional, as a result of the intervention first of an attorney and then of a judge. The aim is to understand how the stories told by these various different actors involved interact and contribute to giving the case its shape. Among other aspects, the analysis highlights how the client, whose role is normally ignored in classical analysis, is capable of playing an active role in the construction of her or his own case, thus conditioning the results.

2.2. Narratives in cultural contexts

In continuity with this line of investigation and by adopting the same methodology, Chapters 7 and 8 are framed in a 'law and culture' perspective, whose purpose is to throw light on the relationship between the construction of the facts and the cultural context in which the cases come about and take shape. Here are some of the questions that guide my investigation: how do local cultural meanings model the meaning and application of the law? And how do the legal actors interpret these meanings and contribute to solving cases? To answer these questions, I propose to shape a new socio-legal category – called 'legal agentivity' (Di Donato, 2014) – to highlight the kind of resources (personal, social, professional) that the layperson facing the legal system mobilises when acting in a given legal and cultural context, with the help of a lawyer, friends and volunteer associations, and in co-operation (or not) with the institutions. The clients' narrative – intended as an expression of their experience and also as a way of self-making – is part of this legal agentivity.

In particular, Chapter 7 features a second group of labour law cases – also set in a specific region of southern Italy. They are framed and defined as follows:

- Dismissal/recognition of a higher level of professional qualification – Carlo's case;
- Dismissal/mobbing/sexual harassment – Viviana's case;
- Disciplinary dismissal – Michele's case.

In Chapter 8, this kind of analysis is transferred to a foreign context, so as to analyse how non-native clients interface with the administration in the Canton of Neuchâtel in north-western Switzerland. Cases of naturalisation are described to test the hypothesis already proposed in part for the cases in group two: what form is taken by the relationship between an understanding of the system (legal consciousness) and the actors' ability to find solutions to legal problems (legal agentivity) when the client acts in a foreign context? This third group of cases is framed and defined as follows:

- Naturalisation (approved) – Line's case;
- Naturalisation (refused) – Charles' case;
- Naturalisation (refused) – Kirin's case;
- Naturalisation (approved) – Johan's case.

2.3. Improving justice for vulnerable clients

Chapter 9 illustrates cases concerning particularly vulnerable foreigners: women who had been victims of domestic violence in their countries and are applying for asylum in Italy. This fourth group of cases is framed and defined as follows:

- Application for refugee status – Amenze's case;
- Application for refugee status/violence and prostitution – Margaret's case.

These stories are of particular interest in terms of the reconstruction of their administrative and legal procedures for at least two reasons. The first is that the clients are defended by social workers, working in partnership with other professionals: attorneys, cultural mediators and psychologists. The second is that the reconstruction of the facts is based not so much on legal documents and evidence in the classical sense of the term (as in the cases described in Chapters 4–8), as on the individuals' stories – completed with more general information about their countries of origin – as in the case of asylum seekers. The specific questions that I raise here are: How can laypeople – especially those who are silenced, marginalised or excluded – act successfully within the law and be heard in legal discourse? Can storytelling be an effective tool for self-legal empowerment and if so, how? And for which audiences?

In the last part of the book, Conclusions, I lay the foundations for developing a clinical research programme, one of whose aims is to test possible client collaboration in solving the case. I argue in favour of the creation of a socio-clinical legal space that enables lay and expert actors to meet for the purpose of improving forms of collective narrations. The aim is to explore innovative ways to increase vulnerable persons' consciousness of their rights and agency in legal settings and to promote institutional or professional practices that also take their voices into account. Using research to include the voices of people who sometimes live on the margins of social processes may mean giving serious consideration to diversity and to the alternative values that law risks destroying

(Daiute, 2014, p. 10), contributing to achieving forms of social justice (Block, 2011; Wilson, 2017).

References

Aiken, J. and Shalleck, A. (2016). Putting the "Real World" into Traditional Classroom Teaching. In: Mertz, E., Macaulay, S. and Mitchell, T.W. (Eds.). *The New Legal Realism: Translating Law-and-Society for Today's Legal Practice*. Cambridge, MA: Cambridge University Press. 51–73.

Amsterdam, A.G. and Bruner, J.S. (2000). *Minding the Law*. Cambridge, MA: Harvard University Press.

Baer, S. (2017). Speaking Law: Towards a Nuanced Analysis of "Cases". In: Olson, G. and Reimer, F. (Eds.). *German Law Journal. Special Issue Law's Pluralities*. 2: 271–292.

Block, F.S. (Ed.). (2011). *The Global Clinical Movement*. Oxford: Oxford University Press.

Brooks, P. (2006). Narrative Transactions – Does the Law Need a Narratology? *Yale Law Journal of Law and Humanities*. 2: 201–219. In: Del Mar, M. and Goodrich, P. (Eds.). (2014). *Legal Theory and Humanities*. Surrey: Ashgate. 171–198. Vol. 5.

Bruner, J.S. (1986). *Acts of Meanings*. Cambridge, MA: Harvard University Press.

Bruner, J.S. (2003). *Making Stories*. Cambridge, MA: Harvard University Press.

Charon, R. (2006). *Narrative Medicine*. New York: Oxford University Press.

Daiute, C. (2014). *Narrative Inquiry: A Dynamic Approach*. Thousand Oaks, CA: Sage Publications.

Delgado, R. (1989). Storytelling for Oppositionists and Others: A Plea for Narrative. *Michigan Law Review*. 87(8): 2411–2441.

Di Donato, F. (2008). *La costruzione giudiziaria del fatto. Il ruolo della narrazione nel "processo"*. Milano: Franco Angeli.

Di Donato, F. (2012). *La realtà delle storie. Tracce di una cultura*. Napoli: Guida.

Di Donato, F. (2014). *Narratives in Cultural Contexts: The Legal Agentivity of the Protagonists*. SSRN Scholarly Paper No. ID 2469436. Rochester, NY: Social Science Research Network: http://papers.ssrn.com/abstract=2469436.

Di Donato, F. (2018). How to Increase the Role of Vulnerable People in Legal Discourse? Possible Answers from Law & Humanities and Legal Clinics: Teaching Experiences from Italy & from Switzerland. In: Heritier, P. and Di Donato, F. (Eds.). *Teoria e critica della regolazione sociale. Special Issue on Humanities and Legal Clinics. Law and Humanistic Methodology*. Milano: Mimesis. 35–55.

Di Donato, F. et al. (forthcoming). *La fabrique de l'intégration*.

Frank, J. (1930). *Law and the Modern Mind*. New Brunswick and London: Transaction Publishers.

Frank, J. (1947). A Plea for Lawyer-Schools. *Yale Law Journal*. 56(8): 1303–1344.

Frank, J. (1948). Say It with Music. *Harvard Law Review*. 61: 921–957.

Gaakeer, J. (2017). The Perplexity of Judges Becomes the Scholar's Opportunity. In: Olson, G. and Reimer, F. (Eds.). *German Law Journal. Special Issue Law's Pluralities*. 2: 233–440.

Gaakeer, J. (2019). *Judging from Experience*. Edinburgh: Edinburgh University Press.

Herman, D., Jahn, M. and Ryan, M-L. (2008). Introduction. In: Herman, D., Jahn, M. and Ryan, M-L. (Eds.). *Routledge Encyclopedia of Narrative Theory*. London and New York: Routledge. IX–XI.

Luban, D. (2007). *Legal Ethics and Human Dignity*. Cambridge: Cambridge University Press.

Massaro, T. (1989). Empathy Legal Storytelling, and the Rule of Law: New Words, Old Wounds? *The Michigan Law Review*. 87: 2099–2127.

Riessman, C.K. (2007). *Narrative Methods for the Human Sciences*. Thousand Oaks, CA: Sage Publications.

Rorty, R. (1981). *Philosophy and the Mirror of Nature*. Malden, MA: Wiley-Blackwell.

Shalleck, A. (2015). *Toward a Jurisprudence of Clinical Thought: Investigating the Contours, Urges and Trajectories*. Manuscript on file with the author.

White, H. (1981). The Value of Narrativity in the Representation of Reality. In: Mitchell, T.W.J. (Ed.). *On Narrative*. Chicago and London: The University of Chicago Press. 1–23.

Wilson, R. (2017). *The Global Evolution of Clinical Legal Education More Than a Method*. Cambridge, MA: Cambridge University Press.

Part I

Theoretical and methodological frameworks

1 Culture, narrative and law

With the aim of constructing a theoretical framework for cases analysis, this chapter stresses the works of cultural psychologists, philosophers, anthropologists, literary critics and linguists, contributing to highlighting the nexus between mind, culture and narrative and to the development and improvement of the narrative turn in legal scholarship since the 1980s.

By conducting an extensive analysis of certain characteristics of narrative, such as those advanced by an interdisciplinary array of scholars over the centuries, the chapter proposes a definition of the term 'story' that lends itself to use in conducting a plot analysis in the field of law.

1. What is reality? What is a fact?

I lay no claim to any putative ability to furnish an indisputable answer to a question as complex as this, one involved with the very mystery of the existence of the world and as ancient as the tradition of philosophical thought, from the pre-Socratics to the post-moderns. And yet, as some parts of the human and social sciences have demonstrated, especially since the middle of the twentieth century, the question 'What is reality?' can be broken down tangibly into the question 'How can we know reality?'.

In this way, without denying the difference between what is real and what we can get to know (Putnam, 2012), the question is shifted from one of ontology to one of epistemology. To a significant extent, in fact, it is research conducted by human sciences that has demonstrated the importance of studying the methods whereby reality is constructed by those who inhabit it, in a process that has little or nothing to do with the passive acquisition of information. It has taken centuries of philosophy to debunk the kind of naïve realism that would have us believe that reality is something independent of the act of perceiving it, that it is a given that is situated somewhere, just waiting to be known.

When the question then arises of approaching legal and judicial reality, an analysis that fails to grasp its socially constructed nature may give rise to further observations that turn out to be simplifications and illusory. In particular, with regard to the process of acquiring facts in the course of legal proceedings, although the majority of contemporary legal theorists are prepared to acknowledge a constructed component in this process, rarely does one come across any exhaustive investigations aimed at incorporating theoretical thinking and analyses of legal and judicial practice for the purpose of demonstrating the extent to which what is defined as a "fact" is actually the result of a process of classification of reality. This is a process that is conditioned by apparently objective dimensions – such as the institutional and legal context – and apparently subjective dimensions – such as sometimes diverging perceptions and representations of the reality to which the parties refer in their legal and judicial proceedings.

Thanks to Searle's theories (1969), for example, we have already known for some time that many of the facts that have to be proven in a court of law do not consist in empirical events, but can be classified under the heading of what he calls "institutional facts". Money, the age of majority, marriage and adultery exist as a consequence of legal, political, social and institutional conventions that confer an institutionally significant qualification on events that would otherwise be juridically irrelevant. At the same time, we are less used to thinking that what we call 'natural events' may also be analysed – over and above their empirical existence – as constructions or, maybe more precisely, as reconstructions. We have recent analyses and in particular the narrative turn (Kreiswirth, 2008, pp. 377–382) to thank for our understanding that it is not the material nature of the facts that is involved in legal proceedings, but their nature as linguistic statements, as some have defined them (Taruffo, 2009), or more explicitly as narrations (Amsterdam and Bruner, 2000; Di Donato, 2008). These narrations are constructed *ex post* by the parties as a function of the version of reality that they intend to convey as the truth in the legal dispute in question. They are mediated by a series of factors: by the normative, cultural and institutional context, by the roles played by the parties and by their emotions, perceptions, cultural backgrounds etc.

As I will explain fully in this chapter and in the following one, starting in the 1980s, in fact, the changeover in favour of narrative understandings of the law facilitated the awareness that "to narrate events is not simply to recount them as they occurred, but to impose an order, perhaps to embellish or invent. A narrative is a construction, an artefact" (Binder and Weisberg, 2000, p. 205). This belief is not confined to the literary realm, as narrative is a basic cultural tool whose purpose is to make sense of experience to construct meanings (Bruner, 1990). Furthermore, we have now understood that narrating people's stories and the impact that the application of the law can have on their lives can be considered to be a human strategy and a cure (Charon, 2006). A strategy that is "in no way inferior to, 'scientific' modes of explanation that characterise phenomena as instances of general covering law" (Herman et al., 2008, p. X).

'Narrative' has thus become one of the most overused terms in contemporary scientific language, which is applied in a variety of different fields, such as literature, literary critique, philosophy and legal theory, with a growth of research and teaching activity. It has also generated a host of clichés and, according to some scholars, sometimes "academic cocktail party chit-chat" (Taruffo, 2009, p. 34). In consequence, by adopting the ***distingue frequenter*** method, this chapter sets out to favour a specific approach to studying legal narrations for answering the questions: What is a fact? How can it be perceived and known? How can it be translated in legal proceedings, transforming an everyday event into a judicial fact? This is the approach known as the "narrative construction of reality" (Bruner, 1991), elaborated in a specific field of social and cultural psychology and subsequently applied in the legal field (Amsterdam and Bruner, 2000). Since it is rooted in anthropological, philosophical and psychological conceptions and literary studies, the narrative construction of reality paradigm can help us understand how reality and meanings are constructed, how links of cause and time do not exist in nature, but are created by placing elements of fact in a narrative structure.

As pointed out also by Greta Olson, referring specifically to the theories of Jerome Bruner, theories of the mind are known to have become a key concern in narrative studies in the last thirty years, contributing to developing "perhaps the single most important issue in narratology" (2014, p. 42). Narratology – the attempt to theorise narrative or promote it as an analytical instrument (Kreiswirth, 2008, pp. 379–380) – involves the more general process of how humans make sense of their world through storytelling:

> Narrative studies of law and medicine depart from the insight that humans make sense of their word via stories, a position associated with the work of the psychologist Jerome Bruner (1991). This has led, for instance, to investigations of the role of storytelling in the creation of identity and in psychic and physical healing processes [. . .]. In the field known as *Law and Literature*, narrative elements are used to read or decode legal texts and legal iconography [. . .].
>
> (Olson, 2014, p. 13)

Thus, in an attempt to provide a theoretical grounding necessary for demonstrating how the construction of factual narrations comes about in the framework of a legal process, this chapter first reconstructs Bruner's perspective about mind and culture (par. 2); secondly, it emphasises the functions of language and how it acts as a bridge between human action and the surrounding social context (par. 3); thirdly, it analyses some of the leading characteristics of narration (par. 4), thereby furnishing a definition of a legal story (par. 5) and, finally, it argues that the culturalist approach is thought-provoking for a culturally situated narrative case analysis (par. 6).

2. A constructivist philosophy of mind and culture: Jerome Bruner's perspective

To introduce some topics of Bruner's thinking, I start out from an interview I conducted with him in 2009. A basic question I put to Bruner concerned ways of approaching our knowledge of the world:

Flora: *How do we learn about the world?*

Jerry: I will tell you that what the world does when it impinges upon us is not to deliver reality, but to confirm or disconfirm some hypothesis that we

> are entertaining. This is what we call hypothesis theory – that we are always looking at the world with some hypothesis in mind. The mind is active, not passive. This view is in the European tradition of Act Psychology and of theorists like Heidegger and Husserl. It is not a passive view in the manner of the British associationists, but an active view.
>
> (Except from the interview with Bruner, Di Donato, 2009)

The first thing that emerges from Bruner's answer is that the mind is active. It is not a mere receptor of information, as Descartes (1637) supposed, but frames hypotheses about the world. The main outcome of the sixties cognitive revolution, in which Bruner played a leading role, is thus the assumption that man actively selects and constructs experience. As Bruner than went on to say in the interview:

> It was Tolman who provoked my interest in the purposive nature of cognition. I came increasingly to believe that the development of cognition was in the interest of testing hypotheses about the world, which made one very selective and in need of something to guide your selectivity. So what guides your selectivity? The culture you live in, of course: what you take to be ordinary, and you begin to work to confirm what you take to be ordinary.
>
> (Except from the interview with Bruner, Di Donato, 2009)

What stands out from the very outset in this exchange is the crucial role played by culture in appraising the hypothesis about knowledge of the world. Reality and meaning are created in the framework of pertinent history and culture, not merely 'discovered'. Human beings act on the basis of meanings they give to events or to other people's actions.

It is no coincidence that Bruner (2003, p. 76) detects the first signs of constructivist thinking in Vico (1938), who extended the criterion of *verum-factum* to historical reality, to include the world that is constructed by man. Man is no passive spectator of the world, but can get to know it from the inside, since he himself plays a leading role in it. According to Vico, the individual is always inside history: it is history that produces knowledge (Bruner, 2003, p. 76).[1]

The understanding of the mind as a tool for making the world was then later theorised by the celebrated Harvard philosopher Nelson Goodman, who influenced Bruner's thought.

Drawing on Kant (1781/1855),[2] Goodman (1978; 1984) replaces the *a priori* with a process that witnesses the elaboration of new versions of the world from

1 Even so, Vico's stance can be considered to be isolated for his time: he was the only philosopher in the late seventeenth and early eighteenth centuries who criticised both the empiricists and the rationalists (Löwith, 1989; Otto, 1992). On the contribution made by Vico and other Italian philosophers, such as Cattaneo, to cultural psychology, see Iannaccone and Smorti (2013).

2 In fact it was Kant who developed a form of 'constructivism', whereby what exists is a product of what is thought (Bruner, 2005, p. 119; Ferraris, 2012, pp. 146–147). As we know, Kant

previous versions. He proposes a concept of the mind as a tool for making worlds. There is no such thing as a single real world that pre-exists and is independent of human mental activity and symbolic language. Worlds can be created by an artist's cognitive activity (such as Joyce's *Ulysses*), by that of scientists (such as geocentric theories) or by everyday life (common sense, made up of trains, potatoes and so on). All these worlds are made, but on the basis of data that we have accepted from others. Goodman's approach allows the idea of an unchangeable, definitive world to wane, replacing it with a conception that he calls a "stipulation", i.e. a process of elaboration within a symbolic system. This enables Goodman to account for the extraordinary variety of forms that reality can take, including the one offered by science.

A more radical stance is adopted by Bruner, who acknowledged Goodman's fundamental merit for having contributed to introducing a concept of 'mind' construed as a tool for producing worlds, thus obliging psychology to study:

> How mind and its mental processes transform the physical world through operations on input. The moment one abandons the idea that 'the world' is there once for all and immutably, and substitutes for it the idea that what we take as the world is itself no more nor less than a stipulation couched in a symbol system, then the shape of the discipline alters radically. And we are, at last, in a position to deal with the myriad forms that reality can take – including the realities created by story, as well as those created by science.
>
> (Bruner, 1986, p. 105)

Yet Bruner does not believe in an original reality as a yardstick against which the possible worlds created by human beings can be compared. According to Bruner's outlook, then, 'constructing reality' means knowing the reality that is created as a product of the transformation of a previous reality, which is taken as given. This is a reality that is constructed on the basis of different intentions, of different perceptive experiences or of mediated forms of experience, of the kind typical of social relations.

This kind of conception of the construction of the world takes the version of the world where our reconstruction begins as its starting point: the versions of reality that we generate are not only versions that comply with culture, established and congruent with consolidated beliefs about reality, but versions of the world that might exist one day, that maybe do exist or that we could hope for. Human culture is itself the product of a dialectic between sometimes conflicting ways of 'constructing reality'. Yet this is not a relativist conception: "If there are meanings 'incarnate' in the world (or in the text with which we start) we transform them in the act of accepting them into our transformed world, and that

---

in his turn attributed his intuition to Hume's (1739–1740) discovery that, rather than being attributable to events, certain relationships in the world – the emblematic example being the relationship between cause and effect – are the result of an inductive process.

transformed world then becomes the world with which others start, or that we then offer" (Bruner, 1986, p. 159).

2.1. What, then, is the relationship between the individual and culture?

"There is no such thing as a mind that exists outside of a culture". This is the maxim adopted by Bruner's culturalist approach since the teachings of the American anthropologist Clifford Geertz, who opined that, without culture's formative role, we would be no more than "incomplete or unfinished animals who complete or finish ourselves through culture – and not through culture in general but through highly particular forms of it: Douban and Javanese, Hopi and Italian, upper-class and lower-class, academic and commercial" (Geertz, 1973, p. 49). Borrowed from Weber's sociology, this kind of conception refers to the web of everyday relationships that constitute social fabric:

> The concept of culture I espouse, and whose utility the essays below attempt to demonstrate, is essentially a semiotic one. Believing, with Max Weber, that man is an animal suspended in webs of significance he himself has spun, I take culture to be those webs, and the analysis of it to be therefore not an experimental science in search of law but an interpretive one in search of meaning. It is explication I am after, construing social expressions on their surface enigmatical.
>
> (Geertz, 1973, p. 5)

Geertz construes culture as a 'network of meanings', created by participants through their actions. The meaning of these actions has to be grasped from within, through observation, referring to rules implicit to the context. As I shall illustrate more concretely in some of the chapters of case analysis (7, 8 and 9), these cultural meanings are not written, but incarnate in actual behaviours and in the communicative practices that regulate the interaction between participants. Since culture is made up of implicit dimensions, it is still hard to say exactly what it is 'once and for all'. It is no coincidence that culturalist psychologists use such metaphors as "fish and water" to describe the imperceptible interdependence between man and culture, or the "elephant in the room" when talking about how hard it is to identify the traces of a culture that is apparently invisible and yet at the same time pervasive (Mantovani, 2003).

So is the vital issue at stake that of *understanding how people construct the world, how they give it meaning?*

It is by means of negotiation that individuals create new meanings that regulate their relations with each other: man is not "an island complete in itself", but a member of the culture he inherits and then recreates (Bruner, 1992, pp. 173–174). This is an active interpretation of culture as the "product of action and condition of action" undertaken by its members, with a seamless passage from an individual to an inter-individual dimension.

What seems to be beyond question is that the concept of culture always has to be rewritten in terms of the system that a society uses to interpret and achieve common meanings, so that the central nucleus for an investigation that starts out from the concept of culture is an understanding of the meanings that the classical culturalist perspective treats as inevitably 'local', even if only in part. In this sense, when Geertz emphasises the local dimension of meanings, he is also talking about 'local knowledge', proposing a conception of culture and meaning as interpretative learning processes that take place *in situ*. There is no universal essence underlying human nature that determines human behaviour. On the contrary, says Geertz (1983, pp. 233–234): "We need, in the end, something more than local knowledge. We need a way of turning its varieties into commentaries one upon another, the one lighting what the other darkens."

Influenced by anthropologists (such as Geertz), linguists and by psychologists, in particular by Vygotsky,[3] Bruner made the practically revolutionary statement that "culture shapes our minds":

> Our minds are shaped in a remarkable degree by the widely accepted banalities of the worlds around us – the 'realities' of conversational exchange, mass media, occupational habits and the like. Our psychodynamics, indeed, probably lurk in the background – like some sort of 'need to conform'. But the shaping of our 'psychic realities' for all that, is largely from the outside in, strikingly public and cultural in origin and with minimum resistance.[4]

Regardless of culture's symbolic-material and local-global connotations, the most demanding task for the scholar who decides to embark on the adventure of trying to define it is understanding how individuals come into contact with each other in a relationship mediated by symbolic, material and institutional tools (including law), in a dynamic complex generally defined as a construction of meanings.

Then the next question I would ask as a socio-legal scholar actively involved in the study of law and culture is: *How do we interact with culture?*

Mediating between Kroeber's super-organic conception, which considers culture as a whole and that of Geertz, who interprets culture as 'a way for the individual to depict reality with an inevitably local dimension', Bruner reaches the conclusion that it is impossible to explain reality without referring to the institutional nature of the cultural complexity of which reality is only a manifestation.[5] Being a member of a culture means constructing what is ordinary together with others, an ordinariness framed and supported by institutionalised forms made

3 As Bruner also says in the interview (Di Donato, 2009): "What I liked particularly about Vygotsky was that he appreciated the intersection of mind and culture and how mind internalised culture".

4 Cf. Bruner, *Culture, Mind, and Narrative*, unpublished Manuscript, on file with the author, p. 2.

5 About this, see Bruner (2008). For the comment on Bruner's essay, see Di Donato (2007, pp. 181–187).

necessary for the purpose of promoting a society's systems of exchange according to a principle of intersubjectivity.[6]

The keywords for Bruner are therefore ordinariness and intersubjectivity, and they are closely related: "ordinariness [is] supported by cultural habits, what they had come to expect in ordinary life" (except from the interview with Bruner, Di Donato, 2009). It is intersubjectivity that makes ordinariness possible in everyday life and to some extent it has a local dimension:

> Indeed, culture itself, in the words of the gifted anthropologist, Clifford Geertz, seems always local. Nobody ever lives in the whole of it, and when we invoke cultural generalities to justify our acts, we do so with reference to the local scene. To use Pierre Bourdieu's expression, we each shelter ourselves in a restricted habitus with its unique rules and norms – as waiters, lawyers, mothers, New Yorkers, fruit-stand operators, prostitutes, professors, or some combination thereof. Yet, despite our localness, we somehow sense (however implicitly) that we are part of some larger whole, even when we are divided by such potentially divisive forces as the division of labour or gender differences.[7]

In the culturalist-interactionist perspective, the 'world' is not an immutable given, but is constructed, or it might be better to phrase it 'co-constructed', by human beings in the course of their relations with each other. In this sense, what we call the 'world' is not reality tout court, but the meanings that human beings give to it. This process is not individual: it takes place within a community whose members can communicate and act together, a fact that presumes the presence of a common ground of understanding that emerges from social intercourse (on the basis of scripts, stereotypes and common sense).[8]

If we start out from this representation of 'reality as a social construction', then, the issue becomes one of understanding how individuals manage to share the visions of the world that they have constructed and to live in a shared dimension. This is possible thanks to the so called categories. Categories are the result of a process of 'cultural construction': they represent our way of theorising about reality in ways that enable us to verify our theories.

Bruner's answer to the question "where do categories come from?" is then that it is culture that provides us with the rules we use to build our awareness

6 See Bruner (2008, especially pp. 35–36). In the perspective of Berger and Luckmann (1995, pp. 12–14), for example, the subjective experiences of meaning undergo a sort of 'intersubjective' re-elaboration when they come into contact with the heritage of experiences and schemes of actions belonging to the social context in which we live. A crucial role is played in creating and stabilising meanings both by traditions and by the institutions of society and of power (such as working organisations) that regulate individual actions, creating hierarchies in social relations.

7 Cf. Bruner, *Culture, Mind, and Narrative*, unpublished Manuscript, on file with the author, pp. 5–6.

8 At the same time, however, as Matusov (1996) points out, the construction of intersubjectivity implies neither the homogenisation nor the cancellation of individuality and of differences.

of reality. Categories are the product of a 'cultural construction' and constitute our approach to theorising about reality in such a way that they are found to be verifiable (Amsterdam and Bruner, 2000, pp. 18–53).

While the function of the categories from a cognitive standpoint is 'practical' and one of mental economy,[9] from the social standpoint it is to create and promote social cohesion. Obeying the same rule, having the same habits and recognising the same way of seeing things gives social groups a powerful bond, as well as a unique identity. This is because the categories themselves are deeply rooted in institutional and linguistic practices and in our mindsets. When a certain element is included in a given category, it acquires a meaning that comes from its being placed in a particular context of ideas.

This operation of constructing meaning takes place in a 'public' context, as an expression of the community's perception of events and of their relevance at a given moment in time. This is no arbitrary process, but one that is constructed by means of interactions and in relation to a given worldview that is not individual, but collective. Yet participation in culture – construed as practices or symbols – does not imply 'subjectivism' but 'public and agreed meaning': "Our culturally adapted way of life depends upon shared meanings and shared concepts, and depends as well upon shared modes of discourse for negotiating differences in meaning and interpretation [. . .] We live publicly by public meanings and by shared procedures of interpretation and negotiation" (Bruner, 1990, p. 29).

The relationship between the individual and society is one of intrinsic reciprocal belonging, so that the one models the other, from within, supplying it with the possibility and the condition for its existence. As highlighted by Rijsman with a brilliant example about the socially constructed dimension of knowledge: "A transition takes place from an individual dimension to a social dimension of knowledge: all we know about the stars (or any other object) is ultimately none other than a common narrative, a mode of collective discourse that co-ordinates the different points of view expounded" (1996, p. 148).

In short, categories are 'made' and not 'found' in the world.

3. Language as a bridge between mind and culture

Culture is construed by Bruner (as well as by Geertz) as something dynamic, a repertoire of responses to individual actions: it must enable its members to do something with their acquired knowledge (Barth, 1991). It must enable them to develop a form of 'agentivity', an action aimed at targets under the control of those who act (Bruner, 1990). This can be achieved using language that is functional to the action and constitutes a bridge between mind and culture.

9 A person can be included or excluded from the category of 'electors', for example, on the basis of such data as age, place of residence and criminal record, enabling millions of people to be classified incontrovertibly on polling day (Amsterdam and Bruner, 2000, p. 34).

The intuition that thought and language are tools for programming and implementing action can be traced back to the historical and cultural school first and then to pragmatists of language. According to the Soviet psychologist Vygostky (2012), the function of language is not restricted to transmitting cultural history, nor to the communication traditionally attributed to it. Language is a way of putting order into our thoughts about reality, while thought, in its turn, is a way of organising our perception and action.

The linguistic changeover is known to have caused the migration from a conception of language as neutral, non-evaluative and above all construed as a representation, to a conception of language as action: *saying* is always also *doing* (Austin, 1962). The function of words is not only to describe what is true or false, but also to promise, threaten, marry or declare war.

To apply Austin's fundamental intuition, most of the things that one individual communicates to another would be incomprehensible if subjected to nothing but the rules of grammar, dictionary definitions and codes of formal logic. The fact that we understand them derives more from an activity of interpretation, which is influenced by the nature and specific circumstances of the communicative setting.[10]

As we know, Austin and the theorists of linguistic acts who came after him (Searle in particular) distinguished three dimensions of every linguistic expression. Every linguistic act has a *locutory* dimension (it states how things are: "Tom drinks a glass of gin every day") and a *perlocutory* dimension (it aims to influence the individual and, through him, the world). On the basis of this second dimension, every proposition depends on the context, in the sense that it cannot be understood outside the context in which it is conceived and pronounced (e.g. stating that Tom drinks produces different effects according to who is hearing the utterance: it could be Tom's wife or a confession between friends in the middle of a desert).

At the hub of Austin and Searle's interest is the illocutionary act: the utterance "I shall send you a letter" may have different effects, according to whether the utterance expresses a promise, a threat, or a simple statement. Understanding the type of illocutionary act implemented is far from straightforward: indicators include the tone of voice, the mood of the verb, any particular lexicon used or, in the case of a written text, the punctuation and the word order. Another important element is non-verbal body language (gestures, posture, movements of the head and body). Lastly, due consideration must also be given to the context in which the words are uttered, the relations between the speakers (e.g. relations of power), expectations and intentions (Searle, 1969). In fact, by virtue of the *illocutionary* dimension, the meaning of any discourse is intersubjective, i.e. it does

10 We know that the performative conception of language came about as a critical response to the claim of logical positivism to specify a set of conditions so that every 'human pronouncement' could be judged to be true, false or meaningless. Austin in fact holds that a great many discourses would actually be meaningless on the basis of these criteria.

not belong to the utterer and to his intention to be transmitted subsequently to a recipient, but is constructed contextually, in the here and now of the communicative relationship. A communication is interpreted starting from the situation in which we find ourselves, assigning a meaning to the specific relationship, to the task being carried out and to what is considered relevant and opportune in the given circumstance. As Duranti explains:

> For Austin, we can demonstrate that 'saying is doing' through a study of the purposes and conventional effects of speaking. What we should focus on, then, will no longer be (only) the conditions of truth of a given utterance (an aspect tackled by the semantics adopted by logical neo-positivism), but the contextual conditions that make it function for the purpose that the speaker wants to achieve.[11]

So language is a constituent element of human agency: language is considered to be "like a code that is simultaneously dependent on the context of its use and constituent of it".[12]

Driven by the theorists of the linguistic act, scholars of the mind – Bruner included – have thus focused their efforts on attempting to bring the communicative context back into the framework of treating the concept of "meaning". Language is no longer considered to be independent of any particular or private meaning. In this way, we pass from a conception of language as transparent and neutral to one of language as a field of action, transiting from a conception of language as a description of reality and of knowledge as a 'reflection' to a constructivist (post-analytical) conception, that adopts the thesis of language as social practice. In this case, the metaphor used is that of the mind not as a 'mirror', but as a 'reflector': every description of reality presupposes an evaluative assumption on the part of the scholar, who chooses the vantage point from which (s)he will describe reality. The result of the subsequent cognitive activity will depend on this first choice.

Anyway, in accordance with the culturalist approach to which I subscribe, language should be considered not in its analytical, but in its broader holistic dimension, as something complete that structures the meanings that each participant in a dialogue gives to events while interacting, thus forging relationships between them and their context.

11 Our translation. The "contextual conditions of an utterance", already identified by Austin (1962), are also listed by Duranti (2007, p. 91; see also p. 120).

12 Ultimately, and unlike structuralist conceptions, the ethnopragmatic approach makes an effort to go back "to the social fabric that gives rise to language, precedes, supports and follows it, constituting it by means of meetings that take place in all sorts of different situations and all sorts of different communications. This is the material that gives rise to the 'experience' that we call 'meaning'. Or, to put it another way, interaction *per se* (doing-with and doing-for others) is the material that gives codifiable meanings to words uttered (or to those implied)" (Duranti, 2007, p. 22, our translation).

4. The narrative gives form and meaning to reality. The characteristics of the narrative

According to the perspective that sees language as 'action', language is not restricted to conveying reality, but actually 'constructs' it. As Bruner states: "it is not just language per se that is 'reality creating', but rather one particular power that language makes possible the power of narrative, the power to create and to comprehend stories. Without that gift of narrative, without some virtually innate access to it for shaping the world, there is no reality of fiction" (Bruner, 2005, p. 56). Bruner suggests that there is a natural tendency to organise events narratively. Language, construed as 'narrative forms', gives shape to the real world: events, people and objects are not located in an 'indifferent' world, but in a narrative world. Language mediates in the relationship of knowledge between the subject and the object, between the subject and the world, organising experience in a narrative form, structuring it and creating a nexus between occurrences. Narrative models not only the world, but also the minds that attempt to give it meaning:

> The main way that our minds and our realities are shaped by everyday models of life is by the stories we tell, we hear and we read – whether true or false. We become active participants of our culture above all through the narratives we share, which fulfil the function of giving meaning to what is happening around us, to what has happened and to what might happen. We model our realities on the basis of these narratives.[13]

Narrative is thus a principle that organises experiences and knowledge: to tell a story is tantamount to seeing the world as it is incarnated in the story (Bruner, 2003). In fact, at the core of his thought is the idea that language shapes the mind within a cultural framework: to tell a story is, for Bruner, to shape reality.

As Bruner and others point out, as a matter of fact, even the etymology of the word 'narrative' comes both from the Latin *narrare* and from the Latin *gnarus*, which means 'one who knows in a particular manner'. We can deduce that storytelling implies both a way of knowing and a way of narrating, in an inextricable blend. It follows that narrative is not so much a way of reflecting or representing meanings that already exist, as a way of constructing unprecedented meanings and coaxing them out to make them explicit. In this activity of cultural modelling of meaning, human action plays a crucial role, as I shall explain as follows, emphasising individuals' actions in solving legal cases, for example.[14]

That is how a narrative constructed around a culture's predetermined or canonical expectations and around the mental elaboration of deviations from

13 Bruner, ***Culture, Mind, and Narrative***, unpublished Manuscript, on file with the author.

14 Polkinghorne adopted a similar stance, defining narrative as the fundamental plan for connecting events and human actions in correlated aspects of a comprehensible whole and meaning as the mental operation of establishing a link between two things and another (Polkinghorne, 1998).

those expectations is represented as the main tool for constructing and negotiating meanings: "The 'negotiated meanings' discussed by social anthropologists or culture critics as essential to the conduct of a culture are made possible by narrative's apparatus for dealing with canonicality and exceptionality" (Bruner, 1990, p. 47).

Although Bruner proposed drawing an initial distinction between paradigmatic or scientific thinking and narrative thinking, holding that scientific thinking ought to 'restrain' narrative thinking by means of verifiable hypotheses and subjecting them to examination, he later came to the conclusion that the distinction was somehow mistaken or in any case unnecessary.[15] This is how he used the story of Antigone to explain how logic can very often appear to be contrary to the human dimension, so seem to be per se inconsistent, generating sometimes disastrous effects:

> Yes, a paradigmatic mode of thought relies on the verification of well-formed propositions about how things are. And yes, the narrative one is also directed toward the world, not toward how things are but toward how things might be or might have been. The paradigmatic mode is existential and declarative: there is an x of property y such that its orbit has the property z. The narrative one is normative and its mode subjunctive: Creon should have let Polynices be buried, and his refusal to do so brought unfathomable disaster on everyone, including those he most loved. How can we translate from one world of mind to the other?
>
> (Bruner, 2003, p. 101)

According to this approach, then, narratives constitute a version of reality that is conventionally acceptable, plausible and constructed in accordance with the laws of narrative, rather than with empirical verifiability and logical correctness. Bruner identifies the following eleven characteristics of narrative in particular:

1 *Narrative diachronicity*: The story is an exposition of events that recur in time: by its nature, it has a duration. The time taken by the story is not the abstract time of the clock, but a time that derives its meaning from the events and how they are placed in the plot. Each story has a beginning (before), a development (during) and an epilogue

15 Scientific thinking tends to constitute the ideal of a system of formal or mathematical description. It is based on logic and underpins such disciplines as mathematics and the sciences. Narrative thinking, on the other hand, focuses more on intuition and less on logic. It consists in using the most sophisticated tools of narration, by constructing stories that are not necessarily 'logical', but consistent with what is happening, for example, in judicial proceedings and with what the actors involved expect. While logic reasons on the basis of a principle of cause and effect, human events are distinguished by intentions and responsibilities cannot necessarily be traced back to any 'logical' reasoning. See Bruner (2003).

(afterwards).[16] Exactly what the beginning, the central part and the end represent is defined by the story itself. The sequence of the facts and events does not exist in nature, but is created by means of the story: it is the result of our activity of reconstructing meaning, adapted to the demands made on it by our story. The narrative's time frame contrasts with a method of thinking of the kind "if p, then q" (Amsterdam and Bruner, 2000, pp. 124–127).

2 *Consequentiality:* Bruner identifies the leading characteristic of narrative as its extrinsic 'consequentiality': a narrative is made up of a particular sequence of events, mental states and occurrences that involve human beings as characters or as actors. Nevertheless, these components have no life or meaning of their own. Their meaning is triggered by their being placed in the general framework of the entire sequence, the plot. The act of understanding a narrative is thus dual in nature: the interpreter has to capture the main plot in order to understand its components' meaning and relate it to the plot. In its turn, the plot's form must be abstracted from the sequence of events (Bruner, 1992).
3 *Particularity*: A story line is pieced together by descending into the details. The narrative deals with events and questions that are not general or abstract, but specific, concerning people.
4 *Intentional state entailment*: This characteristic is related to the previous one. Stories are concerned with human actions, so with the intentions of the people who operate in a situation, starting from states of intention, beliefs, aspirations, theories and values.
5 *Hermeneutic composability*: The events that make up a story can only be understood in relation to the context. The protagonists and events that constitute a narrative are selected and shaped as the ingredients of a putative story or plot that contains them, in accordance with a circular relationship between parts and the whole. This 'hermeneutic property' opens the narrative up to interpretation, both in its construction and in its comprehension. The stories do not exist in some real world, waiting to be veridically mirrored in a text. The act of constructing a narrative is rather more complex

16 Ricoeur considers the event to be like a "narrative component". According to him, the most relevant narrative unit is the plot: "a story is made up of events to the extent that the plot makes events into a story. The plot, therefore, places us at the crossing point of temporality and narrativity: to be historical, an event must be something more than a single recurrence, a single happening" (Ricoeur, 1980–1981, p. 167). According to Ricoeur, the common character of human experience that is expressed through the act of storytelling is its temporal character. The experience of time cannot be explained without referring to the narrative: "everything that is told happens in time, takes time and occurs temporally; and what occurs temporally can be narrated. It may be said that every temporal process is only recognised for what it is to the extent that it can be narrated, in one way or another. This supposed reciprocity between narrative and the time frame is the theme of Time and Narrative". Our translation. Cf. Ricoeur ([1986] 1991, p. 12). Cf. also Ricoeur ([1983, 1984, 1985] 1988).

than selecting events and placing them in an appropriate sequence. As a result, every text can be interpreted, even when it does not seem to have any ambiguous characteristics.

6 *Canonicity and breach*: Not every sequence of events gives rise to a narrative text. The object of the story must in fact be a description of how an implicit canonical script has been breached or deviated from, as a result of the 'trouble' or the event that triggered it. The other essential characteristic of the narrative is thus its capacity to establish bonds between the 'exceptional' and the 'ordinary'.[17]
7 *Referentiality*: In the narrative, realism should be construed as a literary convention. As already mentioned, the appraisal of the truth is based on plausibility, not on verifiability: 'the narrative constructs reality'.
8 *Belonging to a genre*: In addition to constituting a way of constructing human situations, the narrative genre also provides us with a guide for using the mind. This is because the use of the mind is guided by the use of language that makes it possible.
9 *Normativeness*: A narrative is necessarily 'normative': a narrative's 'tellability' as a form of discourse rests on a breach of conventional expectation, i.e. on a breach of legitimacy. A breach presupposes a norm. In terms of Burke's pentad, the play's driving force is the imbalance of one of the elements of the pentad itself, because of a disturbing factor known as 'trouble'.[18]
10 *Context sensitivity and negotiability*: The narrative is a tool for negotiating meanings in everyday life.
11 *Narrative accrual*: Narrative accrual is generally given the name of 'culture', history' or 'tradition'. Consider, for example, the use made of precedent in law. There are also such institutional principles as *stare decisis* that guarantee this tradition, establishing that, once a case has been interpreted in a given

17 For Bruner, the ordinary is what people take for granted. For the meaning of 'ordinary', he refers to Barker, who stated that there is a social rule that says that people are expected to behave "according to situations" and on the basis of their own roles, political opinions etc. When people go to the post office, they adopt a 'post office' mode of behaviour (Barker, 1978). This 'situational rule' applies both to verbal behaviour and to behaviour that takes the form of actions. But if someone behaves in a way that is exceptional for the context, for example by waving a flag in the post office, then we start to theorise a series of potential explanations, a series of versions that are 'made to measure' to give meaning to that exceptional behaviour, implying both a state of intention (a belief or aspiration) on the part of the person who waves the flag and certain canonical elements of the cultural context (national day, fan, nationalism, extremist etc.). And so, according to Bruner (1990), the function of the story is to mitigate a canonical cultural model or at least makes a deviation from it comprehensible. And that is what gives the narrative its plausibility.

18 The balance between the elements of the pentad is defined as a *ratio* determined by cultural convention. When this *ratio*'s balance is disturbed and expectations are breached, disorder is created. Cf. Bruner (1991, p. 32). V. *amplius* par. 6.

way, any other cases similar or identical to the first one will be decided in the same way. In this case, we say that the legal system imposes an 'orderly process of narrative accrual'.

Starting out from this form of classification of the characteristics of narrative proposed by Bruner (1991, p. 38), the next aim is to describe how narrative shapes human experience in the particular context of the law and makes the creation of legal meanings possible.

5. Where do legal stories come from? A definition of story

What are the origins of a (legal) narrative, and what phases does a 'human story' pass through in order to evolve into a 'legal story'?

According to the definition of narration furnished by Amsterdam and Bruner (2000, pp. 113–114), a story starts from a breach of the legitimate order of things and its function is to re-establish the breached order or create a new one. The heart of every narration is represented by the occurrence of a 'trouble' that derives from a collision between the *telos* – i.e. the purpose that the subject wants to achieve – and the obstacles in its path, provoking an imbalance between the five constituent elements of the narrative (and of the pentad) and of the world's canonical order (the way things should be), giving rise to *peripateia*. Amsterdam and Bruner use the metaphor of Burke's Pentad to describe the composition of a narrative plot.[19] Five elements make up the Pentad (agent, action, purpose,

19 Bruner traces the dawn of literature about narrative to Aristotle's *Poetics*. According to Bruner's reconstruction (2003, chapter 1, footnote 1), Aristotle was interested in understanding how literary forms imitate life, in the process known as mimesis. Later on, Renaissance and Enlightenment rationalism tended rather to cast a shadow over the interest in narrative. It was the Soviet scholar Propp, influenced by the formalism of Russian linguistics, who realised that the structure of the narrative was not just a question of syntax, but "reflected men's efforts to come to terms with the unpleasant and unexpected things in life". Later, developing on Aristotle's thinking, Burke (1945) saw humanity's ability to tackle human difficulties reflected in the drama of narrative. In the fifties, Claude Lévi-Strauss considered legends and stories to be manifestations of a culture "that comes to terms with the conflicting requirements of life in a community". In the sixties, which were dominated by the cognitive revolution and by artificial intelligence, there was no flourishing of studies of narrative, except for those of Labov, whose primary interest was in the language of narrative. Labov considered the story to be a medium for understanding the unexpected. In the last two decades, there has been a revival of interest in narrative, still considered to be a way of modelling our concepts of reality. In the Anglo-American area, the invitation to go back to narrative storytelling came from scholars like Hayden White (1980–1981); in Europe, it was the legacy of the French structuralism (in particular Barthes and Bremond), who emancipated narrative from literature and from fiction. But interests in narrative also ended up expanding into many other fields: for example, American anthropologists (Mead, etc.) started discussing how human beings create meaning in the context of their culture. Geertz showed how local narratives are part of a process of making meaning. Writings about narrative that have left a

agency and scene): an actor (construed as a human being) undertakes actions that have intentionality, so as to achieve a purpose, holding beliefs and having feelings (Amsterdam and Bruner, 2000).

Their thesis is that every story's plot has its own characteristics (the ones listed previously, par. 4) and offers some kind of answers to five questions: what was done ('act'), when or where it was done ('scene'), who did it ('agent'), how (s)he did it ('agency') and why ('purpose'). Although the interchangeability of the Pentad's elements makes the narrative into a flexible, variable tool, the authors believe that there is a degree of constancy in how the agents of the pentad interact to pursue their aims within the temporal framework of the setting. This constancy is a characteristic of what Amsterdam and Bruner call the *plot*. According to them, a story thus requires:

1 an initial steady state grounded in the legitimate ordinariness of things;
2 that gets disrupted by a trouble consisting of circumstances attributable to human agency or susceptible to change by human intervention;
3 in turn evoking efforts at redress or transformation, which succeed or fail;
4 so that the old steady state is restored or a new (transformed) steady state is created;
5 and the story concludes by drawing the then-and-there of the tale that has been told into the here-and-now of the telling through some coda – say, for example, Aesop's characteristic moral of the story.

(Amsterdam and Bruner, 2000, pp. 113–114)

The psychologist Daiute, in turn, provides a definition of the plot as "dynamic":

> (The) plot is the structure of narrative, including characters (which may be human or otherwise), an **initiating action** or problem (sometimes also referred to as the 'trouble'; Bruner, 2003), **complicating actions** that rise to a **high point** (climax, conflict, or turning point), attempts to resolve the problem, **resolutions of the problem** and sometimes a moral of the story or the coda.[20]
>
> (Daiute, 2014, p. 115)

Daiute breaks the plot down into an initiating action or problem (trouble); a complicating action that rises to a high point (climax, conflict or turning point); an attempt to solve the problem, the resolution of the problem, and sometimes the moral of the story, or coda.

---

mark include collections of articles by eminent historians, psychoanalysts and philosophers, such as Ricoeur, and literary critics.

20 The bold is of the author.

Integrating the definition of story suggested by Amsterdam and Bruner with Daiute's specifications about the plot, I suggest the following definition for analysing a legal story:

1 An initial steady state grounded in the legitimate ordinariness of things;
2 that gets disrupted by a trouble – the initiating action that marks the break with the steady state – attributable to human agency or susceptible to change by human intervention;
3 in turn evoking efforts at redress or transformation, which succeed or fail – under the form of complicating actions that rise to a high point (climax, conflict or turning point);
4 so that the old steady state is restored or a new (transformed) steady state is created;[21]
5 and the story concludes by drawing the then-and-there of the tale that has been told into the here-and-now of the telling through some coda – say, for example, Aesop's characteristic moral of the story.

According to the provided definitions, the actor or the agency are two key elements in the narration oriented towards pursuing an objective.[22] As Propp already taught (1958/1968), the characters are vehicles for action within the plot.[23] It is by virtue of the meanings of their actions and their roles that their function within the plot can be identified (Brooks, 1984).[24] There are always two or more people involved in the narrative: it is, in fact, the contrast between visions – the conflict – that enables a story and, in particular, a 'legal story' to be constructed.

21 This often takes several steps in naturalistic stories, so Daiute (2014, p. 115) refers to them as 'resolution strategies'.

22 Bruner's idea of individuals who characterise the scene of the comedy or tragedy is in fact inspired by Aristotle: the drama is triggered by the character who acts in an incident dominated by restrictions set by a particular situation. Cf. Bruner (1986).

23 Propp's (1968) analytical perspective in particular, later taken up by Brooks (1984), reconstructs stories' narrative plots starting out from an analysis of the roles and actions played out by the characters within the events narrated. The characters' function is not identified by virtue of their characteristics and their attributes, but of their completed actions and the meanings they acquire as events unfold. Ultimately, this conception has the merit of inducing us to think about narration as a structure of actions and about the character's dynamic role within the plot. In turn Ricoeur writes: "Let us say that a story describes a series of actions and experiences made by a number of characters, whether real or imaginary. These characters are represented either in situations that change or as they relate to changes to which they then react. These changes, in turn, reveal hidden aspects of the situation and of the characters and engender a new predicament that calls for thinking, action, or both. The answer to this predicament advances the story to its conclusion" (1981, p. 170).

24 Brooks, in his turn, defines the plot as the dynamic of its hermeneutic order, so as something more than the mere structure that puts the elements of the narration into order, as it is construed by structural conceptions. Cf. Brooks (1984). Both Ricoeur and Brooks in fact share the concept of the plot as a dynamic element of the narration, as a 'whole' that governs a sequence of events in a story, thus throwing light on the interface between the temporal dimension and the narrative. The plot's function is to enable a link to be forged between the events and the story.

Normally the characters of a story initiate an action to attain a goal that may be complicated by obstacles. The purpose of the 'narrative action' is to restore the canonical state of things or to create a new one: normally it takes shape while respecting culture and tradition. Thus, (legal) narrative is intended to be the means which eliminates or reduces ruptures by neutralising the discordances inherent in the potential conflicts between different views (Bruner, 2003).

A breach of canonicity may correspond simply to a violation of a cultural script[25] which, for example, has to deal with normal behaviour or what we imagine to be normal when we are at the post office or the restaurant, or (more probably) may have to deal with the violation of a rule of law. For example, X does not stop at a red traffic light; Y has been unfaithful to his wife; Company X has given inferior duty to Miss Y, rather than the one stipulated in her contract. It is easy to observe that, either in the case of a breach of a rule of behaviour, such as queuing at the post office, or in the case of the violation of a rule of law – like the reciprocal fidelity obligation (set out in Article 143 of the Italian Civil Code) – we are dealing with meanings that we assume to be prescribing rules in the context of a culture.

Not every trouble that disturbs the legitimate order of reality is able to start a legal narrative (Amsterdam and Bruner, 2000, pp. 129–131). As I shall explain in Chapter 3, violations of the law can be determined only with reference to the rules of law within a specific legal system: the trouble – meant as an everyday life problem – needs to be translated into a recognisable legal problem to become a relevant issue of fact.

Let's consider a typical plot of a (legal) story, that of Nunzio.[26] Nunzio has achieved some important professional goals, only to find himself replaced by a colleague at the whim of his immediate boss. The decision is based on the deterioration of working relations in the professional context and a series of behaviours taking place in the professional context that are tolerated socially, although they are detrimental to Nunzio's rights:

1 *An initial steady state grounded in the legitimate ordinariness of things*:
In 1999, a dear friend and colleague, whom I met while working as an intern in an important Neapolitan office, invited me to come and work as a manager of monitoring and accounting of the management of European Funds. He introduced me to the general director of the 'territorial agreements' (drawn

25 In continuity with the discourse about the relationship between exceptional and ordinary, Bruner (1990) clarifies that the 'script' (i.e. the plot) embodies legitimate expectations and ordinary practices in a culture. Its purpose, when it is told, is to 'tame' these breaches, increasing cultural solidarity by adopting some shared vision of reality. When scripts are consolidated, they constitute the background to narratives and are often tacit rather than explicit. The first rule for anyone who intends to go deeper than the surface of a narrative is to try to understand what norm is incorporated in the script, what events would derail the script and what consequences follow if it is derailed.

26 Nunzio's story was originally told in Di Donato (2011).

up between the council and the province) and we started to collaborate on managing these funds. **In the space of two years, we managed to spend eight hundred million funded by the European Union without wasting any public money. In a very closed environment, we became 'market-leaders'.** We received calls from everywhere [in our region], even from very difficult contexts in the province of Naples. It was informally organised, we were four professionals: a general director, an administrative director, **I was appointed general co-ordinator**.

2 *that gets disrupted by a trouble* – made of initiating action, complicating action, high point, resolution strategies – *consisting of circumstances attributable to human agency or susceptible to change by human intervention:*

a. *initiating action*: The relationships [among colleagues] that were also highly emotional eventually started to deteriorate. **The time came when the administrative director wanted to take over as the general director (the boss): he was bored with being the number two**.
b. *complicating action:* In the meantime, a fifth person had entered the group, a woman, who was having an extra-marital affair with number two.
c. *high point:* **Number two lost his head** – notwithstanding my insistence and requests for more sober behaviour – he bought a €50,000 car, holidays, jewellery. In particular, he violated the pact to make no deals with local politicians. **Last year, on 24 July, by complete surprise, he called the six partners of the firm together and obtained the unjustified dismissal of number one, being subsequently appointed in his place.**
d. *climax:* I was replaced.

3 *in turn evoking efforts at redress or transformation which succeed or fail:*

e. *resolution strategies*:
On 25 July, as part of my duties as secretary of the meeting held on 24 July, I faxed a copy of the minutes of the meeting to all the partner agencies, as well as to the President of the Board of Administration, and invited the mayors as well as the President "to give any opinions . . . with the aim of not prejudicing the rights of the partner agencies".

4 *so that the old steady state is restored or a new (transformed) steady state is created:*
The organisational set-up was subsequently modified, I was assigned an exclusively internal role, which I was not interested in. I was also asked to be more flexible, to meet the needs of politics. **I was also literally asked "to behave". Obviously, I didn't accept. All my duties were subsequently taken away**.

5 *and then story concludes [. . .] with a 'coda':*
I do not know how to be dishonest.[27]

27 From this point onwards, I shall use bold type to draw attention to certain passages in the stories.

The articulation of Nunzio's story, according to the definition of plot proposed previously, highlights how a narration is made up of a particular sequence of events in which human beings are the protagonists who behave as 'actors', with 'intentions': Nunzio and his colleagues. The events and characters that exist in reality acquire specific meanings within the narrative plot: the protagonists (the antagonists) are described by Nunzio as "number one", "number two", according to their hierarchical positions in the professional context and their specific aim of having a successful career. The story is triggered by the violation of the legitimate initial situation. In this case, it is the violation not only of the rules of law, but also of the rules of behaviour among the protagonists (rule of loyalty and fair play in relationships between colleagues). The narration is an attempt to restore the status quo: the mediation between Nunzio and his colleagues is not enough; they have to go to a lawyer.

Nunzio's story and the others that I shall examine in the second part of the volume illustrate how the (legal) narrative is actually part of a more extensive process of making meanings that is functional, in its turn, to maintaining a culture's consistency. In this function of cultural taming, legal rules in their turn fulfil the essential function of stabilising a socially constructed reality that is universal, but at the same time also particular and typical of a given community. Nunzio's narration contains an example of how things can change in the context of the client's life and activities. Nunzio and his colleagues proved themselves capable of successfully managing European funding, becoming a yardstick both for their local and a broader community. Unfortunately, the resulting social change was not carried through and Nunzio's future in the company was jeopardised by locally focused thinking, to which he nevertheless refused to give ground, preferring to resign his position.

More generally, Nunzio's story shows how stories, narrated in both daily and institutional contexts (such as legal and judicial ones), enable legal meanings to be created (Bruner, 1990; 2003). This process is not automatically imposed as 'top-down' by the state and other institutional representatives (judges, lawyers, professors), but is 'bottom-up' (Cover, 1983–1984), deriving from ordinary people, human beings, all those who have an "active" role in the construction of the social and legal reality of which they are part (Ewick and Silbey, 1998). Naturally, meanings negotiated and given by individuals to their world become patterned, established, objectified in virtue of the rules, the role of the institutions (courts, legal offices, schools, laws, codes and so on).

According to a well-known metaphor by Robert Cover (1983–1984), *Nomos and narrative* are interrelated (unavoidable). Every prescription has to be placed in a discourse, in a broader universe made up of legal institutions, social conventions, rules and principles and every narrative, in its turn, requires elements of prescription. Once it has been included in the context of the narrative that gives it its meaning, the law stops being just a system of rules that have to be obeyed, becoming the world in which we live. In this normative world, law and narrative are connected inseparably.

Legal narratives then build a bridge between the initial reality, intended as cultural visions, and the 'possible' and 'alternative' social and cultural constructions of reality. A conception of the law as a 'system of forces' is flanked by another, of the law as a 'system of meanings'.[28]

6. Conclusions

Now that I have reached the conclusion of this analysis of the culturalist approach – which by preference refers only to some of the authors who have nourished this line of thinking (Bruner above all) – I would like to clarify the extent to which it lays the foundation for my work, what I have learned from it and how it can be of use for bringing law together with reality.

The most important thing I have learned from my reading and from frequenting cultural psychologists is that man is an animal impregnated with culture. Culture should be construed not as static, but as dynamic, as a web of relationships and a set of codes that have to be deciphered to enable individuals to adapt to their surroundings. Starting from this basic premise, which enables me to suggest more precise hypotheses – from Chapter 3 onwards about how the facts are constructed in the course of a legal dispute – my first priority is to illustrate how meanings related to the legal process are modelled and negotiated by the parties in the course of their various communication exchanges.

The adoption of the narrative lens highlights how diverging narrations about the same events reflect the divergent interests, experiences and representations of the world, according to the roles played by the narrators – the client, the attorney and the judge – in a given context (Chapters 4–9). In the three chapters where these roles are analysed (Chapters 4–6), the definition of story provided in par. 5 (this Chapter) is used to analyse the structure of the stories told by clients, attorneys and judges. While this type of analysis remains restricted to a dimension internal to the legal dispute in the first part of the book (Chapters 4–6), culturalist teaching – further embellished by other perspectives – plays and expanded role from Chapter 7 onwards, where the cases are analysed in relation to their contexts of origin. I shall focus on this aspect from Chapter 7, where clients involved in controversies of labour law are capable of interpreting events and of reaching solutions to their situations, as a result of their ability to look deeper than the appearances of reality and interpret the implicit meanings that provide the backdrop to the events in question. On the basis of this understanding, they gradually become capable of interacting with the institutions and the local network for the purpose of achieving the results to which they aspire. Although foreign clients experience something similar – this is the subject of Chapter 8 – they have to tackle greater obstacles in achieving interaction with the institutions in their host country. This leads spontaneously to the question raised in Chapter 9 – which analyses cases of particularly vulnerable foreign clients – of understanding how narration can be

28 As Cover (1983–1984, p. 18) writes: "There is a radical dichotomy between the social organization of law as power and the organization of law as meaning".

used to help reduce the gap between the client and the institutions and mediate their positions with regard to society, putting them on a par with everyone else.

References

Amsterdam, A.G. and Bruner, J.S. (2000). *Minding the Law*. Cambridge, MA: Harvard University Press.

Austin, J.L. (1962). *How to Do Things with Words*. Oxford: Oxford University Press.

Barker, R.G. (1978). *Habitats, Environments, and Human Behaviour*. San Francisco: Jossey-Bass.

Barth, B.M. (1991). Avant-propos. In: Bruner, J.S. (Ed.). *Car la culture donne forme à l'esprit*. Paris: Retz. 5–12.

Berger, P. and Luckmann, T. (1995). *Modernity, Pluralism and the Crisis of Meaning*. Munich: Bertelsmann Foundation.

Binder, G. and Weisberg, R. (2000). *Literary Criticism of Law*. Princeton, NJ: Princeton University Press.

Brooks, P. (1984). *Reading for the Plot*. Cambridge, MA: Harvard University Press.

Bruner, J.S. (1986). *Actual Minds, Possible Worlds*. Cambridge, MA: Harvard University Press.

Bruner, J.S. (1990). *Acts of Meaning*. Cambridge, MA: Harvard University Press.

Bruner, J.S. (1991). The Narrative Construction of Reality. *Critical Inquiry*. 18(1): 1–21.

Bruner, J.S. (1992). A Psychologist and the Law. *New York University Law Review*. 37: 173–174.

Bruner, J.S. (2003). *Making Stories*. Cambridge, MA: Harvard University Press.

Bruner, J.S. (2005). The Reality of Fiction. *McGill Journal of Education*. 40(1): 55–64. (Paper Presented to the Le Monde Annual Forum, Paris, 10.04.2004).

Bruner, J.S. (2008). Culture and Mind: Their Fruitful Incommensurability. *Ethos*. 36(1): 29–45.

Bruner, J.S. (Unpublished MS). *Culture, Mind and Narrative*. Manuscript in file with the author.

Burke, K. (1945). *A Grammar of Motives*. Berkeley and Los Angeles: University of California Press.

Charon, R. (2006). *Narrative Medicine*. New York: Oxford University Press.

Cover, R. (1983–84). The Supreme Court, 1982 – Term-Foreword: Nomos and Narrative. *Harvard Law Review*. 97: 4–68.

Daiute, C. (2014). *Narrative Inquiry: A Dynamic Approach*. Thousand Oaks, CA: Sage Publications.

Descartes, R. (2004) [1637]. *A Discourse on Method: Meditations and Principles*. Translated by Veitch, John. London: Orion Publishing Group.

Di Donato, F. (2007). Liaisons Dangereuses. Un incontro interdisciplinare su mente e cultura. *Sociologia del diritto*. XXIV(2): 181–187.

Di Donato, F. (2008). *La costruzione giudiziaria del fatto. Il ruolo della narrazione nel processo*. Milano: Franco Angeli.

Di Donato, F. (2009). Conversing in the Garden on Psychology, Culture, Law, and Narration: An Interview with Jerome Bruner. In: Faralli, C. and Mittica, M.P. (Eds.). *ISLL Papers. The Online Collection of the Italian Society for Law and Literature*. 3–19. doi:10.6092/unibo/amsacta/5572.

Di Donato, F. (2011). Constructing Legal Narratives. Client-Lawyer Stories. In: Wagner, A. and Cheng, L. (Eds.). *Exploring Courtroom Discourse*. Surrey: Ashgate. 111–131.

Duranti, A. (2007). *Etnopragmatica. La forza nel parlare*. Roma: Carocci.

Ewick, P. and Silbey, S. (1998). *The Common Place of Law. Stories from Everyday Life*. Chicago and London: The University of Chicago Press.

Ferraris, M. (2012). *Manifesto del Nuovo Realismo*. Roma-Bari: Laterza.

Geertz, C. (1973). *The Interpretation of Cultures. Selected Essays*. New York: Basic Books.

Geertz, C. (1983). *Local Knowledge. Further Essays in Interpretive Anthropology*. New York: Basic Books. III ed.

Goodman, N. (1978). *Ways of Worldmaking*. Indianapolis and Cambridge: Hackett Publishing Company.

Goodman, N. (1984). *Of Mind and Other Matters*. Cambridge, MA: Harvard University Press.

Herman, D., Jahn, M. and Ryan, M-L. (2008). Introduction. In: Herman, D., Jahn, M. and Ryan, M-L. (Eds.). *Routledge Encyclopedia of Narrative Theory*. London and New York: Routledge. IX–XI.

Hume, D. (1739–1740). *A Treatise of Human Nature*. London: John Noon.

Iannaccone, A. and Smorti, A. (2013). Editoriale. *Psicologia Culturale*. 1.

Kant, I. (1781). *Kritik der reinen Vernunft*. [Engl. Transl. (1855). *Critique of Pure Reason*. London: Bohn].

Kreiswirth, M. (2008). Narrative turn in the Humanities. In: Herman, D., Jahn, M. and Ryan, M-L. (Eds.). *Routledge Encyclopedia of Narrative Theory*. London and New York: Routledge. 378–379.

Löwith, K. (1989). *Significato e fine della storia*. Milano: Il Saggiatore.

Mantovani, G. and Spagnolli, A. (Eds.). (2003). *Metodi qualitativi in psicologia*. Bologna: Il Mulino.

Matusov, E. (1996). Intersubjectivity Without Agreement. *Mind, Culture and Activity: An International Journal*. 3(1).

Olson, G. (2014). Narration and Narrative in Legal Discourse. In: Huhn, P., Meister, J.C., Pier, J. and Schmid, W. (Eds.). *Handbook of Narratology*. Berlin and Boston: De Gruyter. 371–383.

Otto, S. (1992). *Gian Battista Vico. Lineamenti della sua filosofia*. Milano: Guida.

Polkinghorne, D.P. (1998). *Narrative Knowing and the Human Sciences*. New York: State University of New York Press.

Propp, V. ([1958]1968). *Morphology of the Folktale*. Austin: University of Texas Press.

Putnam, H. (2012). Realismo e senso comune. In: De Caro, M. and Ferraris, M. (Eds.). *Bentornata realtà. Il nuovo realismo in discussione*. Torino: Einaudi. 5–20.

Ricoeur, P. ([1980] 1981). Narrative Time. In: Mitchell, W.J.T. (Ed.). *On Narrative*. Chicago: The University of Chicago Press. 165–187.

Ricoeur, P. ([1983, 1984, 1985] 1988). *Time and Narrative*. Chicago: The University of Chicago Press. 3 Vols.

Ricoeur, P. ([1986]1991). *From Text to Action: Essays in Hermeneutics II*. Evanston: Northwestern University Press.

Rijsman, J. (1996). Le panorama intellectuel et technologique de la scène piagétienne. In: Barrelet, J-M. and Perret-Clermont, A-N. (Eds.). *Piaget et Neuchâtel. L'apprenti et le savant*. Lausanne: Editions Payot. 7–11.

Searle, J. (1969). *Speech Acts. An Essay in the Philosophy of Language*. Cambridge: Cambridge University Press.

Taruffo, M. (2009). *La semplice verità. Il giudice e la costruzione dei fatti*. Roma-Bari: Laterza.

Vico, G.B. (1938). *Scienza Nuova*. [Pagine scelte da Augusto Guzzo]. Napoli: Luigi Loffredo Editore.

Vygostky, L.S. (2012). *Thought and Language*. Cambridge, MA: MIT Press. Revised ed.

White, H. (1980–1981). The Value of Narrativity in the Representation of Reality. *Critical Inquiry*. 7(1): 5–27.

2 The narrative turn in the legal field

In continuity with Chapter 1, this chapter analyses the narrative turn in the legal field. It begins by describing the interpretative turn that started taking place in Europe in the 1940s. It then emphasises the revolt against legal formalism conducted in particular by certain exponents of American realism, enforcing the idea that the study of law has to be integrated with the study of the social sciences, so as to analyse the impact of the law in people's everyday lives and promote a perspective of observation 'from the bottom up'. Then, by reconstructing contemporary developments in legal studies, such as Clinical Legal Education, Lawyering Theory and Law and Humanities, it illustrates the evolutions of the Law and Narrative Movement within the contemporary debate. Finally, in order to propose new pathways for the development of a law and narrative approach with a European matrix, the chapter ends by outlining some uses of 'narrative in law', as I have experienced myself in recent years, in different fields of law and in different cultural contexts.

1. The interpretative community

If we now shift the debate about the ways of accessing reality to legal environs, we find ourselves dealing with a path parallel to the one described in Chapter 1, whose turning point is located in the constructivist and linguistic turn. In fact, in opposition to the rationalist tendency typical of modernity to organise legal knowledge into a system, using coherent, verifiable propositions and creating an autonomous method – based on deduction, analogy and precedent[1] – postmodern jurists came to refute the underlying theories and interpretations based on belief in universal truths.[2] Even before this, legal theory experienced an interpretative turn featuring a flourishing new interest in the possibility to replace underlying theories, transcendental values and neutral conceptions with a contextual discourse about the law:[3] this is what has come to be defined as the 'interpretative turn'.

1 For a critical approach to the changeover from modernity to post-modernity, see Vogliotti (2008).
2 For an overall view of postmodern theories of law, cf. Minda (1995).
3 Ibid.

As we know, this interpretative turn started taking place in Europe with the advent of Gadamer's hermeneutics and the revival of studies of the practical rationality of language and of action, when the focus of investigation shifted from the nexus between truth and validity to that between truth and interpretation. According to the German philosopher, it is not logical and scientific verification procedures that guarantee that the truth will be achieved, but the processes of mediation and interpretation conducted using language between the given historical horizon and that of the interpreter (Gadamer, 1960).[4] In the new epistemological horizon to which this leads, 'reason' is not considered to be a uniform faculty in the entire human race, but is more of a social construct, situated within local practices and discourses. In this context of interpretation, judicial syllogism, for example, construed as the mechanical deduction of a decision based on given premises, is subjected to criticism. Attention is focused on the factual premises of the judicial decision that are not 'given a priori', but constitute the result of a process of interpretation that involves not so much the norm to be applied as the facts to be evaluated (Canale, 2018, p. 7; Taruffo, 2018, p. 29).[5] This interpretation is also culturally oriented, since a natural event can also acquire a meaning that depends on the culture of the person who observes it (Nappi, 2018, p. 72).

By virtue of the role of interpretation, objectivity is thus perceived as the result of a process of discovery and not as a given, as an incontestable starting point (Papaux, 2006, p. 166). At the beginning of the eighties, legal theorists operating in the United States highlighted the existence of a dimension of judicial interpretation that is not generated by an isolated subject, but represents an expression of the social, legal and political benchmark context, an expression of the community. The term 'community' is construed here to include the sense of a limit to the possible subjectivist aberrations related to recognising the judge's real interpretative and creative function.[6] Thus Fiss, for example, has pointed out that judicial decisions should not be considered acritically as the result of a syllogistic procedure of applying the law to the case, but as the product of 'disciplinary rules' set by the 'interpretative community' of the legal system. Fiss imagines that judges' operations are limited by the legal culture's established rules, customs and conventions prevailing in society (Fiss,

4 Cf. also Ferraris (1986).

5 The main limit to this criterion is that it takes what it ought to explain for granted. The syllogistic operation is not restricted to 'identifying' a correspondence, but aims at 'constituting' a correspondence between fact and norm, such that it could be said that, through a process of interpretation, the norm in question qualifies the fact legally. Cf. Taruffo (1992, p. 48 ff).

6 The Italian legal philosopher Pariotti emphasises that "[t]he introduction of the interpretative community eliminates [for Fish] the very possibility of reading the practice of interpretation in the light of the categories of objectivity and subjectivity [. . .]. In fact, the interpretative community constitutes a parameter both subjective – since it represents a set of interests, aims and point of view that, as such, are always particular – and at the same time objective, to the extent that the interpretation product it attains does not derive from an isolated individual, but from a public and conventional point of view." See Pariotti (2000, p. 126).

1982). The 'community' is construed here as "the set of those who recognise these rules and, in so doing, give them their authoritative character" (Pariotti, 2000, p. 127). Disciplinary rules, together with social and cultural rules, fulfil the function of orienting the creative activity of the judge who, despite being impartial by definition, comes together with the parties to constitute an interpretative community that is both contingent and temporary (Di Donato, 2009; Viola, 2018, p. 26). In his turn, Fish illustrates how a text's 'authority' is none other than the expression of the interpretative community's constituted power. A text's meaning is created by the community of interpreters who share "social and aesthetic practices". What is in the text is a function of the traditions, the practices and the customs of an 'interpretative community' (Fish, 1980). Last but not least, in his *Laws' Empire*, Dworkin (1986) uses narrative theory to promote a liberal account of the law. Substantially criticising modern legal positivism, the American philosopher discusses the judge's "interpretative attitude" by stating that legal practice always consists in an "exercise of interpretation". In particular, it is recourse to literary interpretation that enabled Dworkin to demonstrate that a legal norm is an expression of a story written by a political society, an expression of an attribution of meaning by the community. Dworkin considers literary interpretation to be the model for legal interpretation, comparing the judge with a writer in a chain of authors, where each must guarantee in his turn that the narration continues: each writer in the chain interprets the chapters written by those who preceded him and composes a new one that is added to the others; the next writer then receives it all, interprets it, writes his piece and passes it all on again. Each one is tasked with writing his own chapter so that the novel gets the best possible structure. Just as the writer cannot create without interpreting, so cannot write a single word without first having decided what it will be, so the judge must lean on his predecessors' decisions, not to try to discover what their state of mind was, but to determine what has been achieved collectively in the history of a law that resembles a chain held together by a multitude of decisions. For Dworkin, then, as for Fiss and Fish, a legal norm – as a result of a procedure of interpretation – turns out to be the expression of a history written by a community that shares social and political practices and values.[7] These authors definitively criticised a narrow positivistic philosophy of law that saw law as a science of rules, stressing the fundamental nature of principles and rights.

These positions, which I have quoted by way of example, enable us to illustrate how legal theory shifted, in the second half of the twentieth century, from an attempt to find an objective foundation for the law to the opinion that the law's

7 According to Pariotti (2000, p. 149), as Dworkin explains things, an individual judicial decision's consistency depends on its "being the best possible expression of a given community's values", a community that is connoted "ethically rather than ontologically" and identified on the basis of certain main principles, compliance with which, in the case of legal interpretation, ought to express the law's potential integrity.

interpretation and application depend to a considerable extent on the perspective of the 'analyst' as a 'tangible individual' who is reasonable, predisposed to deliberation and inserted in a community with ideas and values determined by its history.

To complete this paradigm change and bring it up to date, it is worth remembering that the same philosophers who were already associated with post-modernism, talking about 'post-modern incredulity' with regard to meta-narrations[8] from the beginning of the eighties, have recently expressed the need for a comeback of the Enlightenment, or at least of what has been called New Realism (Ferraris, 2012, p. 106). For some theorists of New Realism (Searle, Putnam, Eco, Ferraris etc.), a movement launched in Europe in 2012 with the organisation of a symposium with the same title, the postmodernist fashion of sustaining the existence of multiple truths has partly produced paradoxes not only in philosophy, but also in other areas of science, reverberating above all on the issue of truth and on its relationship with external reality (Taruffo, 2009, p. 74 ff.). New Realism's main thesis can be summarised in the words of Searle, who has stated that realism should be construed as the idea "that a reality exists that is wholly independent of our representations" (Searle, 2012, p. 169). What New Realism – which maintains the critical and deconstructive principle typical of post-modernism – sets out to do is to distinguish between an unadorned and objectively unamendable reality, comprising facts that exist autonomously and independently of conceptual or cognitive schemes, i.e. so-called ontological truth, and a so-called epistemological truth concerned with how this reality is accessed (Ferraris, 2012, p. 43 ff.).[9]

Although accepting this thesis, which leads to a greater emphasis being put on the distinction between reality and truth, enables us to clarify definitively that such a thing does exist as an objective reality, independent in its ontological existence of every cognitive claim of external agents, it nevertheless leaves the question that gave rise to this work unanswered: how does reality, how do facts, enter into court proceedings?

To this question, another can be added: what methodological as well as theoretical tools can be used to analyse how reality and truth evolve during a legal dispute? The issue at stake here is in fact not merely one of establishing whether or not the fact happened (or how it actually happened): as I shall highlight from Chapter 3 onwards, the context of a legal dispute is substantially a discursive context in which the facts must first and foremost be 'described', using the various different categories of communication (linguistic, visual etc.), then 'understood' and 'shared'. All this can be done in hermeneutic (Ubertis, 2018, pp. 59–60) as well as in narrative proceedings, where each actor attributes a meaning to what (s)he is called upon to deal with within a situation of conversation (Di Donato, 2009).

8 See Litowitz (1997, pp. 10–12).

9 See also De Caro and Ferraris (2012).

Bearing these distinctions in mind, in the following paragraphs I shall highlight the contribution of legal philosophical currents, such as American legal realism, which played a crucial role in the contextualisation of research and teaching, advocating for the interpenetration of social science methods with the analysis of law in action, thereby creating the bases for the proliferation of contemporary legal scholarship aimed at bringing together technical dimensions of law with humanistic ones (par. 2). In particular, I shall emphasise contributions about law and narrative that, in addition to challenging law's autonomy as a rational system, look very useful for bridging the divide between theory and practice in legal analysis (par. 3). Finally, in order to trace new paths for analysing legal cases and support legal-judicial practices, I shall analyse some functions of narrative in law that I have experienced over the years as a researcher in the field of law, humanities and social sciences (par. 4), highlighting the many ways in which a narrative and culturalist approach can help us to contextualise legal discourse and frame human interactions in legal settings (par. 5).

2. From the case method to the clinical law approach and lawyering theory

While the postmodern turn in legal studies was favoured in Europe by the rise of hermeneutic trends, in the Anglo-American context it can be considered a direct consequence of legal realism, which came about and developed in reaction to legal formalism. In the early twentieth century, there was a tendency both in the United States and in Europe to see law as a science based on general, abstract concepts and categories, so as to make it less easily influenced by politics and more responsive to expectations of certainty and stability, by creating an autonomous system of legal reasoning based on deducing general principles, armed with unquestionable logical certainty. One of the most pregnant manifestations of late nineteenth- and early twentieth-century American legal formalism is the case method proposed by Langdell and adopted as a pedagogical model in most American law schools. Drawing its inspiration from the logic of 'law in books',[10] the case method was based on identifying and mechanistically applying a series of landmark cases and precedents as capable of having an influence on the life of the law. This method was resisted by the sociological jurisprudence advanced by Holmes, Pound and Cardozo and by the American legal realists, whose battle cry was Holmes's statement that "the life of the law has not been logic, it has been experience" (Holmes, 1881, p. 1).

10 On the distinction between law in books and law in action, see Pound (1910). Pound spoke out against the degeneration of legal science, arguing that it had become too technical, incapable of relying on principles to adapt its rules to real cases and detached from the pragmatist matrix proposed by Dewey, characterised by a refutation of dogmatism and alert to tangible experience.

The realists attacked law's claims to autonomy typical of formalism and agreed with the idea that the law ought to be brought back into touch with social reality, using the methods of social sciences. In particular, the exponent of the radical wing of fact sceptics of American realism, Jerome Frank,[11] criticised the pedagogical reductionism advocated by Langdell, intended to neglect "[t]he lawyer-client relation, the numerous non-rational factors involved in persuasion of a judge at a trial, the face-to-face appeals to the emotions of juries, the elements that go to make up what is loosely known as the 'atmosphere' of a case" (Frank, 1933, p. 908).

According to Frank, the case method previously interpreted by Langdell, mainly as a study of precedents, should be based on the study not only of judicial decisions, but of all the trial documents, from the compilation of the first paper to the application made to the higher court. One of the main objectives is for the student to see how a legal practitioner thinks at each step and deals with troubled people and raw facts.[12]

Drawing up a well-known comparison of the law schools and medical schools, Frank believed that, in addition to analysing true legal case-books, "law students should be given the opportunity to see legal operations", like doctors in medical schools: "Our law schools must learn from our medical schools. Law students should be given the opportunity to see legal operations. Their study of cases should be supplemented by frequent visits, accompanied by law teachers, to both trial and appellate courts" (Frank, 1933, p. 916).

In a way that was revolutionary for the times, Frank proposed a pedagogical method that he called "clinical". Rather than operating deductively by applying general abstract principles, it was inductive, attentive towards fact-finding, open to the client's needs and allied with the methods of social sciences in the study of professional practices and the interaction between law and society.

> The law student should be taught to see the interactions of the conduct of society and the works of the courts and lawyers. [. . .] Knowledge of the other social disciplines will help the lawyer to be useful to his clients. Moreover, it will enable him to take his place as a constructive member of the community. As draftsman of legislation, as lobbyist, as a member of a legislative body, as advocate, as judge, as statesman, the lawyer should be adequately 'socialised'.
>
> (Frank, 1933, pp. 921–922)

The desired outcome of this model of education was to have students trained not as mere technicians but as people conscious "of the possible values of a rich and well-rounded culture in the practice of law", as "the practice of law and the

11 An exponent of the moderate wing and of the rule of scepticism was Llewellyn. Cf., for example, Llewellyn (1930, 1935).

12 This method was further developed by Bradway (1934, 1958)

deciding of cases constitute not sciences but arts – the art of the lawyer and the art of the judge" (Frank, 1933, p. 923). Frank's proposal moved definitively towards experimenting with abstract principles of doctrine in real cases, so as to enable students "to see, among other things, the human side of the administration of justice" (ibid., p. 918). This is how he described his model of legal clinic:

> The student must at one and the same time learn the technique of scientific method, which he can acquire only through 'sampling', and he must acquire a vivid sense of the existence of breaks, gaps, and problems. The clinics I am now discussing carry him from the patient in the bed to the point beyond which at the moment neither clinical observation nor laboratory investigation can carry him.
>
> (Frank, 1933, p. 920)

Apart from giving law students the opportunity to learn the interaction of legal theory and legal practice (Wizner, 2002) and see how the law is practised in everyday life and in real contexts (court activities, lawyers' offices), clinical legal education has aimed to make justice accessible to all people, particularly the most marginalised (Bryant et al., 2014).[13] Clinical legal education has in fact been based primarily on cases of clients who are marginalised, partly to make up for the lack of legal aid (Bradway, 1934) and partly because clinics perceive that analysing cases by seeing them through the eyes of a powerless client can pave the way to new perspectives, as we shall see in greater detail in Chapter 4.[14]

However, there were only a small number of law school clinics in the first half of twentieth century. Clinical legal education increased in the period of social and political activism, from the mid-sixties and through the seventies, as an expression of clinical teachers' commitments to social justice (Grossman, 1973–1974; Wizner, 2002). Increasing the understanding of "the ways that the law reinforces oppressive systems and the ways that it can be used to challenge them" (Shalleck, 2015) was at the core of the work of such pioneers as Anthony Amsterdam (1984) and Gary Bellow (1973),[15] who engaged in advocacy for social change:

> As founders of a movement to change legal education, clinicians wanted to bring those commitments within the law school. To do this, they began

13 According to Frank, "Six months properly spent on one or two elaborate court records, including the briefs (and supplemented by reading of text-books as well as upper court opinions) will teach a student more than two years spent on going through twenty of the case-books now in use" (Frank, 1933, p. 916).

14 For a brilliant reconstruction of this movement, see Perelman (2014).

15 See also Bellow and Moulton (1978). The two scholars proposed organising a neighbourhood clinic based on the model of law and organising, in which collaboration between attorneys and clients would be fundamental and geared to highlight critical elements arising from the practice of the law, in particular the relationships of power that can develop between client and attorney. For criticisms of this mode, see also Piomelli (2016).

> creating educational experiences that reflected their desires to combat inequality, poverty, exclusion and subordination, to make access to justice a reality for all and to make the vision of the lawyer who pursues justice present to law students.
>
> (Shalleck, 2015)

As we shall see again in Chapter 3, these pioneers were very critical towards legal education, since they thought that the practice in American law schools was disengaged from the world and social facts and from lawyers' responsibilities toward their clients. The call for social justice was a central issue in their discourse, fighting against inequality, challenging discrimination or giving voice to the excluded. Providing representation to indigent clients and asserting the dignity and autonomy of clients who suffered injustice were thus at the core of clinicians' emerging vision.[16]

This work of reflexion or reflexivity about the art of lawyering – which started with American Legal Realism and continued with clinicians – was to produce a new movement, dubbed 'lawyering theory', which was much discussed in the New York University Lawyering Theory Colloquium from the early 1990s.[17] As a continuation of American Realism, the lawyering theory approach invites the study of the concrete details of cases, inverting the methodology: discarding the effort to construct abstract models as a starting point and then analysing 'what law ought to be': when lawyering theorists apply law, they tend to 'look first at what happens in practice'. The idea is that legal meanings are not created in judges' decisions alone, but also in the activities that precede or are in any case external to such institutional contexts, such as attorneys' chambers. Attention is focused on local situations, on what is the usual practice in a given community and on the local dimension of the conflicts, in an effort to harmonise the generalisation of the law with the particular nature of tangible meanings (Davis, 1992). Lawyering theory investigations aim to reveal the models that we take for granted, the prototypes and structures that underpin legal practices, so as to understand how shared meanings use conventional discursive practices to create and maintain a dominant legal regime in specific contexts and structures. It follows that one of the ways of conducting this kind of investigation in practice is to ask what kind of stories and narrations have been used by the attorneys, the judges and everybody else operating in the legal system. Starting from the motto of "making the already familiar strange again" (Amsterdam and Bruner,

16 For an up-to-date overview of clinical legal education (from its origins to the present day), see Wilson (2017).

17 The New York University Lawyering Theory Colloquium is "an interdisciplinary collaboration of students and faculty interested in the analysis of lawyering as a means to a deeper understanding of law. It involves a sustained effort to develop more formal methodologies for exposing the processes by which troubles and aspirations in the world become, or fail to become, 'matters' or 'cases' and move to formal or informal resolution through lawyering or judging". See Davis (1992, p. 187).

2000, p. 1), lawyering theorists look beyond the logical structure of legal texts to expound the possibility of structuring official discourses in alternative ways (Davis, 1991, pp. 1635–1681).

The questions typical of a lawyering theory investigation are therefore: how does legal culture operate within specific contexts and what tools does it use? How are meanings created in everyday practice in court, in attorneys' chambers, in universities and everywhere else? How are meanings conveyed from one generation to the next in this day and age? To answer these questions, lawyering theory has adopted Bruner's theory that states that reality and meaning are narratively constructed. In Sherwin's words:

> The cultural turn that takes us beyond modernist rationalism leads us from narratives made up of 'objective' truths and 'universal' categories of 'natural' reason to a path of reflection about how meanings emerge in the first place. This path invites us to explore a distinct set of issues, such as: (1) how various narratives construct or obscure meaning in everyday legal practices; and (2) how dominant legal discourses frame our experience and judgments, telling us what is there (what the relevant facts are, or what a 'fact' is in the first place), what norms apply, and what goals should be pursued by what methods in a given context.
>
> (Sherwin, 1992, p. 23)

Law itself constitutes an example of socially constructed reality: 'doing law' is considered to be a way of experiencing and constructing the world, a practice that is not distinct from other ways of living, despite efforts to isolate its specific nature (Amsterdam and Bruner, 2000).

The construction of legal meanings in everyday life is also the topic of New Legal Realism. As I wrote in par. 2, since the time of Legal Realism, the idea has been that the study of law was going to be integrated with the study of the social sciences, so as to analyse the impact of the law in people's lives and promote a perspective of observation from the bottom up (Kruse, 2011–2012). Nowadays, by partially pursuing the project of Legal Realism, New Legal Realism (NLR) emphasises "the way law works for the average citizen, in daily practice".[18] In order to capture the impact of reality on law and achieve a bottom-up analysis – moving from the law in books to law in action, from everyday life to the highest courts – New Legal Realists propose complementing empirical research using ethnography, psychology and qualitative research, so as to understand how laypeople relate their experience of the law in order to understand the real law. As

18 This approach has also been called studying "law in action" or "law on the ground": www.newlegalrealism.org/about.html. The aim is to understand "how law affects everyday life, or it could mean studying how legal processes pan out for people who wind up in courts or lawyers' offices. It could push us to ask how well-meaning changes in administrative and bureaucratic practices work out for the workers or the public".

New Legal Realists have pointed out that cross-disciplinary socio-legal partnerships, and especially new interpretative turns, have not influenced the broader legal academy as much as many had originally hoped, they aspire to repackage the cutting-edge insights of socio-legal research, amplify their significance and revitalise their impact for law school teaching and research. Thus NLR scholars follow the original Realists in pushing to complement social science with study and research about law in action, thereby exploring new directions in both research and teaching (McCann, 2016, XIII–XXI). In order to reach this goal, they "bring together legal theory and empirical research to build a stronger foundation for understanding law and formulating legal policy" (Erlanger et al., 2005, p. 2), preferring bottom-up research that prioritises individuals' experience over abstract theories.

My work also goes in this direction, bringing together paradigms and methods borrowed from the humanities and the social sciences for the purpose of elaborating a narrative methodology as a basis for a research action that starts out from human beings' stories and views their social inclusion as its ultimate goal (see Chapter 9).[19]

3. Law and humanities and the narrative turn

American Legal Realism was to lead the way not only to subsequent developments in the clinical law approach, but in some sense also to the humanistic turn in legal scholarship and in particular the Law and Literature and more widely the Law and Humanities movements.

The origins of the Law and Literature Movement in the United States can be traced back to two early twentieth-century essays: one by Wigmore, entitled "A List of Legal Novels" (Wigmore, 1907–1908); the other by Cardozo, entitled "Law and Literature" (Cardozo, 1925).[20] This line of investigation, which considers literature to be an important part of lawyers' training and ethical conscience, was taken up anew by Frank with two mid-century essays entitled "Words and Music: Some Remarks on Statutory Interpretation" (Frank, 1947) and "Say It with Music" (Frank, 1948). In these two essays, Frank compared law with music, so as to develop the thesis that the activity of interpreting the law is not a science – in the sense of a set of impersonal rules beyond the reach of the human emotions and behaviour – but an art. The judge's activity of interpreting the law can accordingly be compared to that of someone performing a piece of music: "judges, when applying (and therefore interpreting) statutory or other legal rules, may be compared with musical performers when playing (and therefore interpreting) musical compositions; that, perforce, judges, like musical performers, are to some extent creative artists" (Frank, 1948, p. 921). The creativity of the judge is thus considered to be functional to interpreting

19 About action research, see Reason and Bradbury (2001).
20 Cf. also Cardozo (1931).

and completing the work of the legislator with equity (Faralli, 2018). This issue was subsequently taken up by James Boyd White, the thinker recognised for giving start to the second phase of the Law and Literature Movement. In 1973 he wrote *The Legal Imagination* (White, 1973) and then a trilogy that includes the books *When Words Lose Their Meaning* (White, 1984) and *Heracles' Bow* (White, 1985). In these and other works, White criticised the cultural and legal currents of the mid-1950s which forced legal education into a technical mould and gave the impression that law is separated from other languages and the humanities at large. For White, literature should be part of the judge's ethical training: both law and literature emphasise the dramatic aspects of individuals' existence (Gearey, 2008, p. 272).

It was in this climate that a debate was rekindled in the United States in the seventies about the relationship between law and the system of values and the social and cultural context in which it is embedded – a debate that also took up the question of what tools of critical analysis to provide law students with (Faralli, 2018).[21] Law and Literature and Clinical Legal Education became part of those tools, albeit with different perspectives and methods, contributing to the revolt against legal formalism and projecting towards a policy of protecting the rights of minorities, following in the footsteps of Critical Legal Studies (CLS), of Feminist Theory and of Critical Race Theory,[22] all movements that to a considerable extent shared a deconstructivist approach to the study of law and an interest in individuals' stories.

In fact, while Law and Literature was founded with the aim, on the one hand, of giving jurists a literary and humanistic sensitivity (law *in* literature) and, on the other, of inviting them to make a critical reading of the law through the use of literary techniques and philological means for the interpretation of legal texts (law *as* literature), in a more recent phase, it has been orientated towards the consideration of Law as Narrative (Binder and Weisberg, 2000, p. 201 ff.). In fact, one of the main purposes of the Law & Literature movement is to bring to the attention of scholars the relationship between the legal text and the narrative process through which the law itself is originated as a human and cultural experience.

According to Robert Cover's famous definition (already mentioned in Chapter 1), narrative enables the bridge between individuals and institutions to be built: "Law may be viewed as a system of tension or a bridge linking a concept of a reality to an imagined alternative – that is, as a connective between two states of affairs, both of which can be represented in their normative significance only through the devices of narrative" (1983–1984, p. 9). Cover's approach stresses that law is always located in a social text, the material world that he defines as a *nomos:* "A nomos, as a world of law, entails the application of human will to an

21 As both Faralli (2018) and Buono (2018) testify, there was a comparable trend afoot in Italy at that time, moved by such jurists as Carnelutti (1935), who suggested introducing flesh-and-blood clients into the study of law in universities.

22 For a reconstruction of these events, their differences and similarities, see Minda (1996).

extant state of affairs as well as toward our visions of alternative futures. A nomos is a present world constituted by a system of tension between reality and vision" (ibid., p. 9). Narration is concerned with what is possible and with the use of the subjunctive:

> The codes that relate our normative system to our social constructions of reality and to our visions of what the world might be are narrative. [. . .]. To live in a legal world requires that one know not only the precepts, but also their connections to possible and plausible states of affairs. It requires that one integrate not only the 'is' and the 'ought', but the 'is', the 'ought', and the 'what might be'. Narrative so integrates these domains.
>
> (Cover, 1983–1984, p. 10)

As has recently been argued, this enables the individual case to meet with general law: "law does not simply demand its supporting narrative, but also becomes itself a narrative of multiple possible worlds of ends and means; not simply nomos and narrative, but nomos as narrative and narrative as nomos" (Condello, 2017, p. 41).

Thus, since Cover's works, narrative has become a "category of sociological importance", as it can provide phenomenological insights into law's construction and ordering of the social world (Gearey, 2008, p. 275). In addition to contributing to repairing the breach in order, legal narratives have a broader function of contributing to processes of constructing the identity of the community, for example of the nation state, drawing on founding myths, popular imagery etc. In fact, narrating is a cultural tool: stories serve the purpose of enables society to develop and imagine new possibilities, thereby contributing to achieve the imagined community by creating a legal order and establishing legal categories and qualifications (citizens/foreigners; honest/dishonest) to exclude those who are not part of it. In this way, Cover contributed significantly to the narrative and cultural turn, suggesting the benefits of a narratological literate approach to legal discourse (Olson, 2014).

The narrative turn (Kreiswirth, 2008, pp. 377–382) is specifically identified with the organisation of an important symposium "On Narrative", in 1980.[23] Distancing himself from a classical theoretical perspective (primarily structuralism), the literary critic Hayden White recognised narration as a sort of 'impulse' rooted in human nature and a 'solution' to the more general problem of how knowledge is translated into the story, "how to translate knowing into telling" (1981, p. 1). For White, it was clear that inserting events into a narrative structure meant giving them a 'meaning', rather than making it possible to draw up a mere chronological listing, which is what would result from an orthodox, historical or scientific perspective: "every narrative, however seemingly 'full', is constructed on the basis of a set of events which *might have been included but were*

23 See the special issue of *Critical Inquiry on Narrative* (Mitchell, 1980).

left out; and this is as true of imaginary as it is of realistic narratives" (White, 1980–1981, p. 10).[24]

Bruner, whose approach I reconstructed in detail in Chapter 1, has similarly shown how narrative contributes to the construction of the autobiographic self:[25]

> Self making is a narrative art, and though it is more constrained by memory than fiction is, it is uneasily constrained, a matter to which we shall come presently. Self-making, anomalously, is both from the inside and the outside. The inside of it [. . .] is memory, feelings, ideas, beliefs, subjectivity. [. . .] But much of self-making is from outside in – based on the apparent esteem of others and on the myriad of expectations that we early, even mindlessly, pick up from the culture in which we are immersed.
>
> (Bruner, 2003, p. 65)

Finally, ethnographic approaches to narrative followed Geertz's metaphor of culture as text to focus on epistemological problems connected with the production of ethnographic texts (Clifford and Marcus, 1986).

The narrative turn in the humanities has thus highlighted that "Narrative is [. . .] not confined to the literary realm but rather appears as a basic cultural tool used to make sense of experience" (Erll, 2008, p. 89).

Since its inception, the study of narrative in law has ended up becoming a field in its own right and with its own nature, both a method for investigating legal reality in legal discourse, inside and outside formal tribunals, and a tool for combatting the dominant élite, for example by constituting the way for a woman to tell her own story, the way for an individual to belong to an ethnic group, the way for an individual to seek vindication or recognition etc.[26]

In 1981, Bennett and Feldman carried out a study that for the first time introduced the theory – not without criticism – that the effective representation of a case in court depends above all on the storytelling ability of the legal actors (accused, lawyers, witnesses). In their view, jurors tend to base their decision on an evaluation of the "overall narrative plausibility"[27] and "coherence" of the stories narrated, as well as considering them on the whole rather than on the basis of the verification of individual elements of the story. They also found that the structure of a story had a considerable impact on its credibility.

24 This vision is not so far from that of Bruner (1991), who explained how reality is represented in the act of learning about it through the narration that constitutes it. Bruner himself acknowledged that he was indebted to White's theories.

25 Cf. also Bruner (1997). Similarly, Charon (2006, p. 65 ff) stresses the importance of stories in defining a patient's pathology.

26 Gearey (2008) proposes four categories to identify the reception of narrative theory in the legal field: 1) the use of narrative insights for the adjudicative process; 2) a law and literature approach where literary narratives are studied for their relevance to the law; 3) the use of philosophical accounts to provide general jurisprudential accounts of law; 4) the use of narrative construction of identity in feminism, critical race theory and post-colonial theory.

27 For a critical reappraisal of this theory, see Jackson (1996).

In 1989, the University of Michigan dedicated a symposium and a special issue to Legal Storytelling. It was an event that scholars judged significant, considering it to be an indication of the opening of the Law School to a different approach to law.[28] The main lesson learned through the symposium was that, in addition to highlighting 'diversity' (e.g. feminist legal theories, race-related issues and sexual difference), stories narrated in a legal dispute have the power to communicate the 'truth', even though they constitute only one of the possible ways of observing the world. Stories are always descriptions made from different points of view and are informed by their narrators' different cultural backgrounds. In one of the contributions to the symposium, for example, its author Scheppele highlighted how stories' underlying structures always make their way to the fore, despite all the variations in content, style and tone. The 'judicial narrative' is no less structured than any other narrative genre, since it is incorporated into a broader institutional structure that "reduces its solutions to routine and plays up the value of regularity" (Scheppele, 1988–1989, pp. 2073–2075). In his contribution, meanwhile, Delgado highlights the function of 'community building' typical of stories, basing those communities on a shared culture of agreed meanings. They "can open new windows into reality, showing us that there are possibilities for life other than the ones we live" (Delgado, 1989, p. 2414).

In 1996, Brooks and Geewirtz published a collection of essays about law's stories, showing how academics' interest in literature and narration is related to overcoming the idea of objective truth and accepting the awareness that reality is socially constructed. The scholars believe that the narrative turn is of the 'politically reformist' type, evidence of a greater public dimension of law, with a realisation that the traditional models of judicial analysis are somehow connected to maintaining the status quo and do not respond sufficiently to the interests of certain local and social groups (such as minorities and women) (Brooks and Geewirtz, 1996).

At the same time, Ewick and Silbey (1998) collected stories about law from everyday life, showing an interest in understanding the connections between everyday human consciousness of legal problems and the practices of law. Moving the focus of investigation from legal texts to everyday legal practices, the two scholars made a significant contribution to the postmodern awareness that the law should give more definite consideration to the 'life of the people' it aims at.

Subsequently, by considering the law as "a storytelling enterprise thoroughly entrenched with culture", the noteworthy work of Amsterdam and Bruner,

28 The symposium featured several different contributions, conveying 'unconventional' messages, mostly the product of the authors' own experiences. Some of these authors, such as Mari Matsuda, David Luban and Milner Ball, reported the official versions of stories that had been the subjects of decisions, illustrating how the stories selected by the courts have the 'power of truth', even though there might be other versions suitable for leading to other conclusions. See the minutes of the *Legal Storytelling Symposium* in *The Michigan Law Review*, 87, 1988–1989; in particular, cf. Cunningham (pp. 2459–2494); Delgado (pp. 2411–2444); Luban (pp. 2152–2224); Massaro (pp. 2099–2127); Scheppele (pp. 2073–2098); Winter (pp. 2225–2279).

Minding the Law, published in 2000, became a turning point in the application of the narrative turn to the law (Brooks, 2006). Starting out from different backgrounds (legal and psychological), the authors bring their vast knowledge of narrative theory to bear to explain how understanding narrative helps us decipher how lawyers persuade courts, how courts construct their understanding of law and how these stories shape our collective lives. By examining the judicial opinions of the American Supreme Court, the authors aim to explore the underlying relationships between the court's decisions and the American culture of which they are considered expressions.

It is in this perspective, i.e. that of identifying a methodological value in the approach of law as narrative, that the study conducted by Binder and Weisberg (2000, pp. 232 ff.) belongs, listing at least five uses of narration in legal scholarship: 1) as a source of practical wisdom; 2) epistemological insights; 3) moral improvement; 4) political subversion and 5) psychological integration. With the aim of refuting the common misconception that narrative is reduced to revealing the authentic subjectivity that law suppresses, the two scholars call attention to the fact that narration is an indispensable element in the process of constructing legality, of which the stories of individuals, both as individuals in themselves and as communities, are part.

The study of "legal narrativity" was subsequently presented by Brooks (2002, p. 2) as a useful enterprise. As an eminent scholar in this field, he argues that narrative should be considered as a legal category with a crucial role in the process of legal adjudication and in the construction of legal reality:

> If the traditional supposition of the law was that adjudication could proceed by 'examining free-standing factual data selected on grounds of their logical pertinency', now increasingly we are coming to recognise that both the questions and the answers in such matters of 'fact' depend largely upon one's choice (considered or unconsidered) of some overall narrative as best describing what happened or how the world works.
>
> (Brooks, 2002, p. 1)

Obviously, in recognising the potential of legal narrative as an autonomous field, Brooks is aware of the possible resistances and the suspicion of legal scholars, who might consider narratology a threat to law's autonomy and hermeticism.

Although this list lays no claim to being exhaustive, the works mentioned previously constitute significant contributions to the turn to narrative in the law and the storytelling enterprise. In fact, with time, the law as a narrative approach has thus ended up becoming a tool for making a critical analysis of the law, contributing to revealing particular, implicit and often instrumental elements that are often left unstated by formal law, including grass-root requests – the voices of the more vulnerable parts of society – and paving the way for other forms of expressiveness typical of the humanities. The recent transition from the label of Law and Literature to the broader one of Law and Humanities marks the determination to harmonise the study of law with that of other forms of human expression (literature, films, theatre, painting), so as to reduce the technicality of the law and include other cultural dimensions of experiential life in legal discourse, as a possible bond for a life in common inspired by principles of empathy and acknowledgement of others as underlying principles of modern democratic societies (Nussbaum, 2010; Sarat et al., 2010; Manderson, 2018).

On the other hand, legal narrative has been employed with practical wisdom as a tool for lawyering and especially fact construction and lawyer-client relationships. Thus, for example, moving from a dimension of theoretical analysis to a practical one, the first conference on Applied Legal Storytelling, organised in 2007, illustrated the birth of a new movement interested in "the use of stories – and of storytelling or narrative elements – in law practice, in law-school pedagogy" (Rideout, 2015, pp. 247–264). Some of the participants were teachers of legal writing programmes in law school clinics. In fact, as argued by Robbins, "storytelling is the backbone of the all-important theory of the case, which is the essence of all good lawyering".[29] She also notes that the Applied Legal Storytelling Movement shares common ground with the Law & Literature Movement, for example the theories that underlie legal storytelling (narrative, rhetoric or semiotic), the ethical implications of legal storytelling and the presence of legal themes in literary works. Other participants, such as Kiernan-Johnson, propose shifting the focus of AppLS from story, narrative and storytelling to narrativity, arguing that narrativity is both more inclusive and more accurate than storytelling, with the ability "to capture the breadth of material falling within AppLS's purview. [. . .]. AppLS [. . .] seeks to add something new. The legal texts and performances it focuses on are those likely to be encountered in actual legal practice: real legal briefs, real oral arguments, all marked, to some degree, by narrativity" (Kiernan-Johnson, 2012, p. 94).

Shifting from the American academic panorama to the European one, Gaakeer (2017)[30] – co-founder of the European Network for Law and Literature[31] – then proposed reflecting on the elaboration of a legal narratology with a European matrix. In fact, when expounding on an interest that is both theoretical, as a legal scholar and expert in law and literature, and at the same time practical, as a judge, in addition to being conscious of the role played by narration in selecting facts and in determining the outcome of a case, this scholar also considers the narrative

29 Cit. in Rideout (2015, p. 248).

30 On the concept of Narratology, see Fludernik (2009), Prince (1982/2012).

31 In 2007, the EURNLL was established with the aim "to reflect on and thematise possible differences between European Law and Literature work and that of Anglo-American scholars and related legal cultures". The EURNLL is also linked to the European Narratology Network (ENN), an association of individual narratologists and narratological institutions, whose focus is on narrative representation in literature, film, digital media etc. in all European languages and cultures. In 2008, the University of Bologna held the first national conference of the Italian Society for Law and Literature (ISLL), which was inaugurated by Jerome Bruner. The ISLL is devoted, among other fields, to the exploration of the binomial of law and narrative. See Mittica (2015, p. 22).

approach to be the most suitable way for achieving cultural access to the study of law. Starting out from the realisation that when the narrative turn is presented as an antidote to juridical formalism and to the excess of technicality, it remains purely academic and is not absorbed by practitioners, she suggests that judges should develop a narrative ability and knowledge as parts of a legal methodology (Gaakeer, 2017, p. 337 ff).

Acting on Gaakeer's invitation to judges to increase their awareness about the narrative mechanisms characteristic of the interpretative process, I shall focus on this issue in greater detail in Chapter 6.[32] Before that, starting with Chapter 4, I invite practitioners (attorneys, mediators) to learn how narration can be employed to support not only their everyday professional practices, but also their client's capacity to act as an agent and participant in the solution of the case (Chapters 7–9).

On a more general level, I should mention that two international symposia were recently organised in Italy and Europe for the purpose of responding to this need to harmonise theoretical and practical dimensions in the study of law and humanities, illustrating both the shared humanistic roots of law and humanities and legal clinics and the possibility to find in narration a potential tool for linking these two perspectives and including the participation of laypeople in juridical discourse.[33] To achieve this goal, I personally argued for a research programme to be conducted "with people rather than on people, starting out from the client's needs and working together, also in collaboration with institutional and local actors, in order to increase social justice programmes and ensure that their voice is heard in decision making" (Di Donato, 2018). I shall develop on this proposal more fully in Chapter 9 and in my conclusions, by designing a socio-clinical space shared by both clients (laypeople) and expert actors, with the aim of increasing legal knowledge and awareness about how the law operates in specific legal systems (in daily life, in administrative practices and in court proceedings).

Continuing in this European-inspired direction towards research in legal narratology and narrative practices, the next step will be the organisation of a special workshop on the topic of Law and Narrative entitled "Dignifying and Undignified Narratives in and of (the) Law", during the 2019 World Congress of the International Association for the Philosophy of Law and Social Philosophy (IVR). This workshop will bring together researchers from the Italian Society for Law and Literature, the European Network for Law and Literature and the

32 In addition to European projects, there is also one national research project deserving of attention. "On stories and storytelling as a basic cultural condition underlying the Norwegian criminal process" is directed by Frode Helmich Pederson in Norway: www.uib.no/personer/Frode.Helmich.Pedersen.

33 See the volumes of the Proceedings of the conference organised in Naples in 2015 entitled *Clinical Teaching in Italy and the Rest of Europe: Theoretical Roots and Practical Dimensions* (Di Donato and Scamardella, 2016) and of the Special Workshop entitled *Law & Humanities and Legal Clinics* (at the XXVIII World Congress of the *International Association for the Philosophy of Law and Social Philosophy* (IVR) – Lisbon, July 17–21, 2017, *Peace based on Human Rights*) (Di Donato and Heritier, 2018).

Lucernaiuris[34] for the purpose of developing on the idea that narration can be considered as a legal category, a tool for analysing the law and a practical device.[35]

4. Toward a legal case analysis: uses of narratives

While Gaakeer thus used her experience as a judge to furnish a positive response to Brooks' question – whether law needs a narratology (Brooks, 2006) – and to increase awareness of the function of narration in law, my aim is to elaborate a narrative methodology for legal case analysis. I will do this by means of a sequence of steps: by proposing research hypothesis and methodological frameworks (Chapter 3); by showing how narrative works in practice in constructing legal reality within the interactions between clients and attorneys (Chapters 4–5); by highlighting that even judicial decisions take narrative forms (Chapter 6); by clarifying that legal narratives are culturally situated (Chapters 7–8), and finally by proposing a socio-clinical devices for solving cases collaboratively that includes clients' voices (Chapters 9 and conclusions).

Thus, in addition to identifying the characteristics of narrative listed in Chapter 1 (par. 4), I for my part am also suggesting a preliminary step that consists in describing some possible uses or features of 'narrative' that I have experienced in recent years in different fields of law (such as labour law, family law and immigration law) as lenses for case analysis. I shall dwell in particular on the function of modelling reality and interactions that is typical of narration, as well as on its inclusive, analytical and clinical function. While the following listing cannot be considered exhaustive, it can serve to identify some ways to approach the study of narratives in law.

4.1. Storytelling is a way of shaping the world

As I have been explaining since Chapter 1, sociocultural psychologists, cultural anthropologists, literary critics and medical scholars point out the aptitude of human beings to organise the knowledge of reality through narration (Bruner, 1991; Brooks, 1992; Charon, 2006; Herman, 2002; Kafalenos, 1999; Mink, 1978; White, 1980–1981). This is not a descriptive approach: narrative is a mode of thinking, "the mode that relates to the concrete and particular as opposed to the abstract and general" (Ryan, 2008, p. 345). The famous sentence "Stories construct facts that comprise them" (Amsterdam and Bruner, 2000, p. 41) summarises the passage from a deductive to a constructive logic of human knowledge, also in the context of the law. By adopting a narrative approach, we can thus analyse how facts are shaped within a legal dispute, by whom and by what means. This is the type of analysis that I shall propose from Chapter 4 onwards.

34 *Lucernaiuris* is the Institute for Interdisciplinary Legal Studies which will host the IVR 2019 Conference.

35 See the Call for Papers at the following link: www.ivr2019.org/special-workshops.

4.2. It brings together facts, human agency and places

In a socio-constructivist approach, events, actors, time and location acquire meanings through a narrative structure – a plot – that organises them in causal, temporal and emotional terms (Bal, 2009; Charon, 2006, pp. 48–51), in everyday discourses as well as in legal discourse. The plot is 'dynamic', bringing together facts and (human) agency (Daiute, 2014). As I wrote in Chapter 1, in a legal story, as in a literary novel, we can thus identify the plot, the characters and the setting as the key elements that make up a narrative (Brooks, 1992; Kafalenos,[36] 1999; Propp, 1968; Ricœur, 1980–1981). Every narrative plot contains a 'theory' of the events, the actions, the emotional states, the function of the characters etc., and is inevitably constructed starting from the narrator's point of view.[37] Plot analysis enables us to develop a sophisticated tool for understanding how a legal story is constructed, as I shall illustrate in Chapters 4–6 and later in Chapters 7 and 8.

4.3. It is a relation tool

Storytelling makes the bridge between minds and cultures possible, linking individuals to society (Bruner, 1986). People use it to do things, to connect with other people, to deal with social structures, echoing, resisting and transforming institutional discourses (Daiute et al., 2015). Narrating is a tool "for managing (mediating) self-society relationships" (Daiute, 2014, p. 19). This aspect of narration will emerge in Chapters 4 and 7, in particular where the individuals in question have to cope with dynamics of relationships in their working contexts. I shall show that conflicts very often originate in breaches of norms of good behaviour and good faith in interpersonal relations. It is by managing relationships (thus filtering the application of the law) that solutions are reached. Because of its relational nature, "narrating can be a means of social inclusion", a way to include and empower voices of a minority by mediating situations, relations and purposes (Daiute and Kreniske, 2016). This aspect comes to light primarily in cases of integration (Chapters 8 and 9), where the issue is one of allowing due space for the foreigner's story so that it can mediate her or his position with regard to the institutions of the host country.

Legal narratives may have both a conservative and a subversive or transformative value of the social order (Ewick and Silbey, 1998; Andrews et al., 2008):[38] people may use them to conform to preferred narratives in society, but also to express

36 Kafalenos proposes a comparison between the actions of the characters in a story and the actions of individuals. In both cases, there will be actions generated from information available that produces events that will be interpreted and will produce new actions. Characters and actions, individuals and events are held together by the narrations. For a reconstruction of the structuralist approaches, Cf. Andrews et al. (2008, p. 23 ff).

37 This definition can be attributed to the anthropologist and linguist Ochs (1997, pp. 185–207).

38 On the subversive power of stories, cf. Ewick and Silbey (1995, spec. p. 199 ff).

counter-conforming experiences and ideas. Thus court decisions and lawyers' narrations may or may not deal with the hegemonic culture in society, in 'maintaining' a given order or in subverting it, in shaping collective representations of the law and social life.[39] Using a detailed analysis of the role played by the attorney and the judge (Chapters 5 and 6), I intend to show that the attorney's narration may also be subversive in nature, while that of the judge tends to be conservative.

4.4. A social and cultural process

Stories are the product of individual and collective experience (Bruner, 1986; László, 2008; Sammut et al., 2012) and are constructed according to cultural scripts: tools such as films, novels, tales, myths or visual images circulating in society (Smith and Joffe, 2013; Sherwin and Wagner, 2012) are bearers of values and visions of the world (Jovchelovitch and Bauer, 2000). The use of collective references provides a common base from which to share experience (Levasseur, 2014) and maintain a culture's consistency. Legal meanings and representations of the truth depend on the context, on a knowledge that is culturally constructed and embedded in local and interpretative practices (Geertz, 1973). Public legal narratives (constitutional texts, parliamentary discourses, laws, administrative decisions), for example, are essential for producing legal knowledge and achieving an imagined community, determining who belongs and who does not (Cover, 1983–1984; Daiute et al., 2015; Olson, 2015). This, for example, is what I demonstrated in my individual work (Di Donato, 2016) and the collaborative effort (Di Donato and Mahon, forthcoming a); reconstructing the meanings of the term 'integration' in the Swiss legal order. A reading of the messages issued by the Swiss Federal Council and the confederation's legislative instruments enabled me to illustrate how the question of naturalisation in Switzerland has been an element of the means used to manage society since the last century.

4.5. A site for action

In an ethnographic approach, legal narratives may be considered in their dynamic dimension, located within social practices and the contexts of specific actions (business, organisational etc.).[40] They constitute a way of acting or more accurately of 'inter-acting', since one of the main functions of narrative activity is building relations between the members of one and the same culture (Ochs and Capps, 2001). An ethnopragmatic approach then especially takes into account the interactive and relational dimensions of narratives that deal with communicative

39 The reference is primarily to what is known as the sociology of narration, as proposed, for example, by the scholars Ewick and Silbey (1998, p. 30), for whom "[sociology] recognises that narratives are social acts performed within specific contexts that organise their meanings and consequences".

40 Regarding narratives and contexts, Ochs and Capps (2001) conceptualise 'conversational narratives' in order to emphasise the interactive and collective nature of narration.

exchanges. This contextual dimension of the narrative analysis – still not sufficiently developed by legal scholars – deals with a dimension of inter-activity between human beings.[41] This is the approach that I have basically adopted to reconstruct stories in Chapters 7 and 8, by highlighting the tangled web of relationships and the implicit cultural codes that govern the solution of a case.

4.6. . . . for lawyering and adjudication

Storytelling is a tool for lawyering, especially for engaging with clients and developing a lawyer-client relationship. Leading clinical scholars have sought to identify how narrative theory can yield narrative practices that help lawyers develop a better understanding of their clients' lives and their clients' desires in seeking help through lawyers (Elmann et al., 2009, p. 139 ff). In their view, telling the story is the 'cure' for silenced or powerless voices to be heard (Delgado, 1989).

Narrative as a tool for mediating in lawyer-client relationships – much as in the case of doctor-patient relationships – will be analysed in Chapters 4 and 5. Narrative is obviously also an essential part of legal decision-making, as I shall show in Chapter 6, and a sophisticated tool for conducting in-depth analyses of the relationships of power that provide the backdrop to legal disputes, as I shall illustrate in Chapter 7. The issue of educating lawyers to take clients' narrative 'seriously' will be raised in Conclusions.

4.7. . . . and for visualising

The integration of narrative approaches with visual studies may help to consider how the visual element is central to the cultural construction of social life in contemporary societies, as social categories are not natural, but constructed, and these constructions can take visual form. Institutions mobilise certain forms of visuality to order the world and in imposing specific visions of how society functions (Haraway, 1991, pp. 5, 188). As argued by Sherwin (2012/2013, p. 15): "images do not merely add to words. They are transformative, both qualitatively and quantitatively [. . .] both in the terms of the content that they display and the efficacy of emotion and belief that they evoke. Much of the power of the image derives from the way it performs its function – how we mind the image for meaning's sake".[42] Thus 'the agency of the image' can be considered as a part of a broader story about clients' specific legal paths, as I shall show to some degree in Chapter 8.

At the end of this reconstruction, I should also like to clarify that, despite the many definitions of story, narrative and narrating that abound, I shall use 'story' and 'narrative' as synonyms. I construe 'story' to mean not a single event, but a

41 Among the works that ethnography devotes to analysing the judicial discourse, see for example Conley and O'Barr (1988, pp. 467–508).

42 See also Sherwin (2012/2013, pp. 192–212) and the more recent work edited by Manderson (2018) on the intersection between legal and visual discourses.

chain of events linked together by a plot. Similarly, I understand 'narrating' and 'storytelling' as synonyms that refer to the act of narrating.

5. Conclusions

With its reference to hermeneutic thinking, but also to American realism and more recently to neo-Realism, this chapter further clarifies the epistemological and methodological premises for a narrative case analysis, as sketched out in part in Chapter 1. Having clarified the distinction between ontology and epistemology, it specifies that it is the use of the latter that is more likely to help us answer the question: how does reality, how do facts enter into a legal dispute? For a constructivist and narrativist epistemology, this option does not in fact constitute an alternative to the idea of truth, but aims at creating the premises for an ever-increasing precision of experience, examining the various different points of view that contribute to modelling reality in the legal process. Hence the interest in analysing some of the many dimensions that can be investigated in law by means of narration.

In the following chapters, by combining most of the dimensions described previously (par. 4), I adopt a case-study approach, showing the potential of narrative as a tool for legal case analysis and fact construction and a device for supporting legal actors' performances/actions.

References

Amsterdam, A.G. (1984). Clinical Legal Education. A 21st Century Perspective. *Clinical Law Review*. 34: 612–619.

Amsterdam, A.G. and Bruner, J.S. (2000). *Minding the Law*. Cambridge, MA: Harvard University Press.

Andrews, M., Squire, C. and Tamboukou, M. (Eds.). (2008/2013). *Doing Narrative Research*. London: Sage Publications.

Bal, M. (2009). *Narratology. Introduction to the Theory of Narrative*. Toronto: University of Toronto Press.

Bellow, G. (1973). On Teaching the Teachers: Some Preliminary Reflections on Clinical Education as Methodology. *Clinical Legal Education for the Law Students*. 374: 375–386.

Bellow, G. and Moulton, B. (1978). *The Lawyering Process: Materials for Clinical Instruction in Advocacy*. Mineola, NY: Foundation Press.

Bennett, W.L. and Feldman, M. (1981). *Reconstructing Reality in the Courtroom. Justice and Judgment in American Culture*. New Brunswick: Rutgers University Press.

Binder, G. and Weisberg, R. (2000). *Literary Criticism of Law*. Princeton, NJ: Princeton University Press.

Bradway, J. (1934). Some Distinctive Features of a Legal Aid Clinic Course. *The University of Chicago Law Review*. 1(3): 469–479.

Bradway, J. (1958). *The History of a Lawsuit*. Durham, NC: Carolina Academic Press.

Brooks, P. (1992). *Reading for the Plot*. Cambridge, MA: Harvard University Press.

Brooks, P. (2002). Narrativity of the Law. *Law and Literature*. 14(1): 1–10.

Brooks, P. (2006). Narrative Transactions – Does the Law Need a Narratology? *Yale Law Journal of Law and Humanities*. 2: 201–219. In: Del Mar, M. and Goodrich, P. (Eds.). (2014). *Legal Theory and Humanities*. Surrey: Ashgate. 171–198. Vol. 5.

Brooks, P. and Geewirtz, P. (1996). *Law's Stories.* New Haven: Yale University Press.

Bruner, J.S. (1986). *Actual Minds, Possible Worlds.* Cambridge, MA: Harvard University Press.

Bruner, J.S. (1991). The Narrative Construction of Reality. *Critical Inquiry.* 18(1): 1–21.

Bruner, J.S. (1997). A Narrative Model of Self-Construction. In: Snodgrass, J.G. and Thompson, R.L. (Eds.). *The Self Across Psychology: Self-Recognition, Self-Awareness and Self-Concept.* New York: New York Academy of Sciences.

Bruner, J.S. (2003). *Making Stories.* Cambridge, MA: Harvard University Press.

Bryant, S., Milstein, E.S. and Shalleck, A.C. (Eds.). (2014). *Transforming the Education of Lawyers: The Theory and Practice of Clinical Pedagogy.* Durham, NC: Carolina Academic Press.

Buono, E. (2018). "Our Forgotten Tradition". The Neglected Role of Continental Legal Culture in the Parallel. In: Di Donato, F. and Heritier, P. (Eds.). *Humanities and Legal Clinics. Law and Humanistic Methodology. Special Issue of Teoria e critica della regolazione sociale.* 17–26. Vol. 2.

Canale, D. (2018). Presentazione. Ars Interpretandi. *Special Issue on Ermeneutica e diritto processuale.* 23(1): 7–12.

Cardozo, B. (1925). Law and Literature. *Yale Law Journal.* 14: 699–718.

Cardozo, B. (1931). *Law and Literature.* New York: Harcourt, Brace & Co.

Carnelutti, F. (1935). Clinica del diritto. *Rivista di Diritto di Procedura Civile.* 12(1): 169–175.

Charon, R. (2006). *Narrative Medicine.* New York: Oxford University Press.

Clifford, J. and Marcus, G.E. (1986). *Writing Culture: The Poetics and Politics of Ethnography: A School of American Research, Advanced Seminar.* Berkeley, Los Angeles and London: University of California Press.

Condello, A. (2017). *Between Ordinary and Extraordinary the Normativity of the Singular Case in Art and Law.* Leiden and Boston: Brill.

Conley, J.M. and O'Barr, W.M. (1988). Fundamentals of Jurisprudence: An Ethnography of Judicial Decision Making in Informal Courts. *The North Carolina Law Review.* 66(3): 467–508.

Cover, R. (1983–1984). The Supreme Court, 1982 – Term-Foreword: Nomos and Narrative. *Harvard Law Review.* 97: 4–68.

Cunningham, C.D. (1989). A Tale of Two Clients: Thinking About Law as Language. *Michigan Law Review.* 87: 2459–2494.

Daiute, C. (2014). *Narrative Inquiry: A Dynamic Approach.* Thousand Oaks, CA: Sage Publications.

Daiute, C. and Kreniske, P. (2016). Hopes, Misunderstandings and Possibilities of Narrating for Inclusive Education. In: Surian, A. (Ed.). *Open Spaces for Interaction and Learning Diversities.* Springer. 53–67: https://link.springer.com/chapter/10.1007/978-94-6300-340-7_5.

Daiute, C., Todorova, S. and Kovacs-Cerovic, T. (2015). Narrating Participation and Power Relations in a Social Inclusion Program. *Language & Communication.* 45: 46–58.

Davis, P.C. (1991). Contextual Legal Criticism: A Demonstration Exploring Hierarchy and "Feminine" Style. *New York University Law Review.* 66: 1635–1681.

Davis, P.C. (1992). Law and Lawyering: Legal Studies with an Interactive Focus. *New York School Law Review.* 37(185): 185–207.

De Caro, M. and Ferraris, M. (Eds.). (2012). *Bentornata realtà. Il Nuovo Realismo in discussione*. Torino: Einaudi.

Delgado, R. (1989). Storytelling for Oppositionists and Others: A Plea for Narrative. *Michigan Law Review*. 87(8): 2411–2441.

Di Donato, F. (2009). La comunità processuale come contesto attivo di interazione tra clienti, avvocati e giudice. *Ars Interpretandi*. 1: 187–206.

Di Donato, F. (2016). *L'integrazione degli stranieri in Svizzera. Genesi ed evoluzione dei significati giuridici*. Milano: Mimesis.

Di Donato, F. (2018). How to Increase the Role of Lay and Vulnerable People in Legal Discourse? Possible Answers from Law & Humanities and Legal Clinics: Teaching Experiences from Italy and from Switzerland. In: Di Donato, F. and Heritier, P. (Eds.). *Humanities and Legal Clinics. Law and Humanistic Methodology. Special Issue of Teoria e critica della regolazione sociale*. 2: 35–55.

Di Donato, and Heritier, P. (Eds.). (2018). Humanities and Legal Clinics. Law and Humanistic Methodology. *Special Issue of Teoria e critica della regolazione sociale*. 2: 35–55.

Di Donato, F. and Mahon, P. (forthcoming a). Retracer la notion d'intégration: histoire du droit. In: Di Donato, F. et al. (Eds.). *La fabrique de l'intégration*.

Di Donato, F. & Scamardella, F. (2016). *Diffusione dell'insegnamento clinico in Italia e in Europa: radici teoriche e dimensioni pratiche*. Napoli: ES.

Dworkin, R. (1986). *Law's Empire*. Cambridge, MA: Harvard University Press.

Elmann, S., Dinerstein, R., Cunning, I.R., Kruse, K. and Shalleck, A. (2009). *Lawyers and Clients. Critical Issues in Interviewing and Counseling*. St. Paul, MN: Thomson Reuters, American Casebook Series.

Erlanger, H.S. et al. (2005). Foreword. Is It Time for a New Legal Realism? *Wisconsin Law Review*. 335–363.

Erll, A. (2008). Cultural Studies Approaches to Narrative. In: Herman, D., Jahn, M. and Ryan, M-L. (Eds.). *Routledge Encyclopedia of Narrative Theory*. London and New York: Routledge. 88–93.

Ewick, P. and Silbey, S.S. (1995). Subversive Stories and Hegemonic Tales: Toward a Sociology of Narrative. *Law & Society Review*. 29: 2.

Ewick, P. and Silbey, S.S. (1998). *The Common Place of Law. Stories from Everyday Life*. Chicago and London: The University of Chicago Press.

Faralli, C. (2018). American Realism's New Proposals for Legal Education: Legal Clinics and Law & the Humanities. In: Di Donato, F. and Heritier, P. (Eds.). (2017). *Humanities and Legal Clinics. Law and Humanistic Methodology. Special Issue of Teoria e critica della regolazione sociale*. 2: 11–17.

Ferraris, M. (1986). *Storia dell'ermeneutica*. Milano: Bompiani.

Ferraris, M. (2012). *Manifesto del Nuovo Realismo*. Roma-Bari: Laterza.

Fish, S. (1980). *Is There a Text in This Class? The Authority of Interpretative Communities*. Cambridge, MA: Harvard University Press.

Fiss, O. (1982). Objectivity and Interpretation. *Stanford Law Review*. 34: 739–763.

Fludernik, M. (2009). *An Introduction to Narratology*. London and New York: Routledge.

Frank, J. (1933). What Constitutes a Good Legal Education? *American Bar Association Journal*. 19: 723–728.

Frank, J. (1947). A Plea for Lawyer-Schools. *Yale Law Journal.* 56(8): 1303–1344.
Frank, J. (1948). Say It with Music. *Harvard Law Review.* 61: 921–957.
Gaakeer, J. (2017). The Perplexity of Judges Becomes the Scholar's Opportunity. In: Olson, G. and Reimer, F. (Eds.) *German Law Journal. Special Issue Law's Pluralities.* 18(2): 233–440.
Gadamer, H.G. (1960). *Wahrheit und Methode.* Tübingen: J.C.B. Mohr (Paul Siebeck).
Gearey, A. (2008). Law and Narrative. In: Herman, D., Jahn, M. and Ryan, M-L. (Eds.). *Routledge Encyclopedia of Narrative Theory.* London and New York: Routledge. 271–275.
Geertz, C. (1973). *The Interpretation of Cultures. Selected Essays.* New York: Basic Books.
Grossman, G.S. (1973–1974). Clinical Legal Education: History and Diagnosis. *Journal of Legal Education.* 26(162): 162–193.
Haraway, D. (Ed.). (1991). *Simians, Cyborgs and Women: The Reinvention of Nature.* London: Free Association Books.
Herman, D. (Ed.). (2002). *Narrative.* Cambridge: Cambridge University Press.
Holmes, O.W. (1881/1991). *The Common Law.* New York: Dover Publications.
Jackson, B. (1988). *Law, Fact and Narrative Coherence.* Liverpool: Deborah Charles Publications.
Jovchelovitch, S. and Bauer, M. (2000). Narrative interviewing. In: Bauer, M., Martin, W. and Gaskell, G. (Eds.), *Qualitative Researching with Text, Image and Sound: A Practical Handbook.* London: Sage Publications. 57–74.
Kafalenos, E. (1999). Not (Yet) Knowing: Epistemological Effects of Deferred and Suppressed Information in Narrative. In: Herman, D. (Ed.). *Narratologies. New Perspectives on Narrative Analysis.* Columbus, OH: Ohio University Press. 33–65.
Kiernan-Johnson, D.H. (2012). A *Shift* to *Narrativity. Legal Comm. & Rhetoric: JAWLD.* 9: 81–98.
Kreiswirth, M. (2008). Narrative turn in the Humanities. In: Herman, D., Jahn, M. and Ryan, M-L. (Eds.). *Routledge Encyclopedia of Narrative Theory.* London and New York: Routledge. 377–382.
Kruse, K.R. (2011–2012). Getting Real About Legal Realism, New Legal Realism, and Clinical Legal Education. *New York Law School Law Review.* 56: 659–681.
László, J. (2008). *The Science of Stories: An Introduction to Narrative Psychology.* London and New York: Routledge.
Levasseur, E. (2014). *Les objets du quotidien: une négociation mémorielle. – Approche psychosociale de l'articulation des traces mémorielles et matérielles dans la transmission de l'expérience d'une inondation.* Thèse de doctorat en psychologie sociale. France: Université de Lyon.
Llewellyn, K. (1930). Realistic Jurisprudence – The Next Step. *Columbia Law Review.* 30(4): 431–465.
Llewellyn, K. (1935). On What Is Wrong with So-Called Legal Education. *Columbia Law Review.* 35: 651–678.
Litowitz. D.E. (1997). *Postmodern Philosophy of Law: Rorty Nietzsche Lyotard Derrida Foucault.* Lawrence, KS: University Press of Kansas.
Manderson, D. (Ed.). (2018). *Law and the Visual: Representations, Technologies, Critique.* Toronto: University of Toronto Press.
Massaro, T. (1989). Empathy Legal Storytelling, and the Rule of Law: New Words, Old Wounds? *The Michigan Law Review.* 87: 2099–2127.

McCann, M. (2016). Preface. In: *The New Legal Realism*. New York: Cambridge University Press. XIII–XXI. Vol. I, II.

Minda, G. (1996). *Postmodern Legal Movements. Law and Jurisprudence at Centuries' End*. New York and London: New York University Press.

Mink, L. (1978). Narrative Form as a Cognitive Instrument. In: Canary, R.H. and Kozicki, H. (Eds.). *The Writing of History: Literary Form and Historical Understanding*. Madison: University of Wisconsin Press.

Mitchell, T.W.J. (Ed.). (1980). *On Narrative*. Chicago and London: The University of Chicago Press.

Mittica, M.P. (2015). Cosa accade al di là dell'Oceano? Dirittto e Letteratura in Europa. *ANAMORPHOSIS – Revista Internacional de Direito e Literatura*. 1. 3–36: http://rdl.org.br/seer/index.php/anamps/article/view/29.

Nappi, A. (2018). Interpretazione e giudizio di legittimità: norme, contratti, fatti. *Ars Interpretandi. Special Issue on Ermeneutica e diritto processuale*. 23(1): 71–86.

Nussbaum, M.C. (2010). *Not for Profit: Why Democracy Needs the Humanities*. Princeton, NJ and Oxford: Princeton University Press.

Ochs, E. (1997). Narrative. In: Van Dijk, T. (Ed.). *Discourse as Structure and Process. Discourse Studies*. London: Sage Publications. 185–206.

Ochs, E. and Capps, L. (2001). *Living Narratives. Creating Lives in Everyday Storytelling*. Cambridge, MA: Harvard University Press.

Olson, G. (2014). Narration and Narrative in Legal Discourse. In: Huhn, P., Meister, J.C., Pier, J. and Schmid, W. (Eds.). *Handbook of Narratology*. Berlin and Boston: De Gruyter. 371–383.

Olson, G. (2015). Futures of Law and Literature: A Preliminary Overview from a Culturalist Perspective. In: Hiebaum, C., Knaller, S. and Pichler, D. (Eds.). *Recht und Literatur im Zwischenraum/Law and Literature In-Between: Aktuelle inter- und transdisziplinäre Zugänge/Contemporary Inter- and Transdisciplinary Approaches*. Bielefeld: Transcript. 37–69.

Papaux, A. (2006). *Introduction à la philosophie du "droit en situation"*. Zurich, Bâle and Genève: Schulthess.

Pariotti, E. (2000). *La comunità interpretativa nell'applicazione del diritto*. Torino: Giappichelli.

Perelman, J. (2014). Penser la pratique, théoriser le droit en action: des cliniques juridique et des nouvelles frontières épistémologiques du droit. *Revue interdisciplinaire d'études juridiques*. 72(2): 133–153.

Piomelli, A. (2016). Rebellious Heroes. *Clinical Law Review*. 23: 283–310.

Pound, R. (1910). Law in Books and Law in Action. *American Law Review*. 44: 12–36.

Prince, G. (1982/2012). *Narratology: The Form and Functioning of Narrative*. Berlin, New York and Amsterdam: Mouton Publishers.

Propp, V. (1958/1968). *Morphology of the Folktale*. Austin: University of Texas Press.

Reason, P. and Bradbury, H. (2001). *Handbook of Action Research*. London: Sage Publications.

Ricoeur, P. ([1980] 1981). Narrative Time. In: Mitchell, W.J.T. (Ed.). *On Narrative*. Chicago: The University of Chicago Press. 165–187.

Rideout, C.J. (2015). Applied Legal Storytelling: A Bibliography. *Legal Communication & Rhetoric: JALWD*. 12: 247–264.

Ryan, M.L. (2008). Narrative. In: Herman, D., Jahn, M. and Ryan, M-L. (Eds.). *Routledge Encyclopedia of Narrative Theory*. London and New York: Routledge. 344–348.

Sammut, G., Tsirogianni, S. and Wagoner, B. (2012). Representations from the Past: Social Relations and the Devolution of Social Representations. *Integrative Psychological and Behavioral Science*. 46(4): 493–511.

Sarat, A., Anderson, M. and O. Frank, C. (Eds.). (2010). *Law and the Humanities: An Introduction*. Cambridge: Cambridge University Press.

Scheppele, K.L. (1988–1989). Forward: Telling Stories. *The Michigan Law Review*. 87: 2073–2098.

Scheppele, K.L. (1989). Legal Storytelling. *Michigan Law Review*. 87(8): 2073–2098.

Searle, J. (2012). Prospettive per un nuovo realismo. In: De Caro et al. (Eds.). *Bentornata realtà*. Torino: Einaudi.

Shalleck, A. (2015). *Toward a Jurisprudence of Clinical Thought: Investigating the Contours, Urges and Trajectories*. Manuscript on file with the author.

Sherwin, R.K. (1992). Lawyering Theory: An Overview, What We Talk About When We Talk Law. *New York Law School Law Review*. 37: 9–51.

Sherwin, R.K. (2012/2013). Law's Life on the Screen. In: Priska, G., Borella, S. and Wiedmer, S.C. (Eds.). *Intersections of Law and Culture*. 192–212.

Sherwin, R.K. and Wagner, A. (2012). *Law, Culture & Visual Studies*. New York and London: Springer. Vol. 1–2.

Smith, N. and Joffe, H. (2013). How the Public Engages with Global Warming: A Social Representations Approach. *Public Understanding of Science*. 22(1): 16–32.

Taruffo, M. (1992). *La prova dei fatti giuridici*. Milano: Giuffrè.

Taruffo, M. (2009). *La semplice verità. Il giudice e la costruzione dei fatti*. Roma-Bari: Laterza.

Taruffo, M. (2018). Ermeneutica, prova e decisione. *Ars Interpretandi. Special Issue on Ermeneutica e diritto processuale*. 23(1): 29–42.

Ubertis, G. (2018). Dialettica probatoria e terzietà del giudice. *Ars Interpretandi. Special Issue on Ermeneutica e diritto processuale*. 23(1): 57–70.

Viola, F. (2018). Una teoria deliberativa della giurisdizione? *Ars Interpretandi. Special Issue on Ermeneutica e diritto processuale*. 23(1): 13–28.

Vogliotti, M. (2008). *Tra fatto e diritto. Oltre la modernità giuridica*. Torino: Giappichelli.

White, H. (1980–1981). The Value of Narrativity in the Representation of Reality. *Critical Inquiry*. 7(1): 5–27.

White, J.B. (1973). *The Legal Imagination: Studies in the Nature of Legal Thought and Expression*. Boston: Little, Brown and Company.

White, J.B. (1984). *When Words Lose Their Meaning*. Chicago: University of Chicago Press.

White, J.B. (1985). *Heracles' Bow: Essays on the Rhetoric and Poetics of the Law*. Madison, WI: University of Wisconsin Press.

Wigmore, J.H. (1907–1908). A List of Legal Novels. *Illinois Law Review* 2: 574–579.

Wilson, R. (2017). *The Global Evolution of Clinical Legal Education More Than a Method*. Cambridge, MA: Cambridge University Press.

Winter, S.L. (1989). The Cognitive Dimension of the Agon Between Legal Power and Narrative Meaning. *The Michigan Law Review*. 87: 2225–2279.

Wizner, S. (2002). The Law School Clinic: Legal Education in the Interests of Justice. *Fordham Law Review*. 70: 1929–1937.

3 Fact construction

Contexts, roles and methods

Continuing along the path laid down in Chapters 1 and 2, this chapter completes the definition of the theoretical and methodological premises that provide the backdrop for case analysis. It describes some of the various different lines of research that have developed around the issue of fact investigation in both Common Law and Civil Law contexts since the second half of the twentieth century, ranging from a theoretical to a practical dimension. Incorporating suggestions derived from a variety of disciplinary areas, including the theory of law, procedural law and the sociology of law, it opts to locate case analysis within the sociological perception of legal proceedings as a dynamic place of interaction between legal actors. Finally, in order to illustrate my thesis that facts are constructed in the course of the legal process, the chapter fully describes a methodology based on tools typical of the social sciences that I have experienced over the years, so as to analyse cases and the interactions between the various legal actors: clients, lawyers and judges.

1. A plea for fact investigation: Jerome Frank as a pioneer

The issue of fact investigation has a long history, and yet is extremely pertinent today. In legal theory, fact investigation has a long history, dating back to American legal realism, in which the legal philosopher Jerome Frank questioned whether facts were objectively reconstructed in the framework of a trial. Expressing an opinion that was revolutionary for the time, Frank stated that facts are not "data", they are not "found" and are not waiting around somewhere to be discovered. Instead, he argued that facts are "made" – that is, created by the court on the basis of subjective reactions to the witnesses' stories:

> Considering how a trial court reaches its determination as to the facts, it is most misleading to talk, as we lawyers do, of a trial court 'finding' the facts. The trial court's facts are not 'data', not something that is 'given'; they are not waiting somewhere, ready-made, for the court to discover, to 'find'. More accurately, they are processed by the trial court – are, so to speak, 'made' by it. On the basis of its subjective reactions to the witnesses' stories.
>
> (Frank, 1949, pp. 23–24)

Frank thus drew attention to the point that subjective dimensions (such as opinions, perceptions and cognitive bias) are part of the process of construction of legal reality (Paul, 1959, p. 77), with regard not only to judges, but also to witnesses, who in turn are also 'fallible', as they may have misunderstood or mistaken what they saw, or simply be unreliable, so that their evidence is biased:[1]

> Most legal rights turn on the facts as 'proved' in a future lawsuit, and proof of those facts, in contested cases, is at the mercy of such matters as mistaken witnesses, perjured witnesses, missing or dead witnesses, mistaken judges, inattentive judges, biased judges, inattentive juries, and biased juries. In short a legal right is usually a bet, a wager, on the chancy outcome of a possible future lawsuit.
>
> (Frank, 1949, p. 27)

Frank's scepticism is not to be equated with some form of absolute relativism. One of his contributions was to draw attention to certain critical aspects of fact-finding – the possibility that mistakes might be made, the role played by subjectivity in perceptions and representations – and the impossibility of perceiving these aspects as a result of logical deduction and reasoning. With the aim of shedding light on certain critical passages in the process of ascertaining facts, Frank thus advocated for an accurate factual investigation rooted in social science methods, bringing together the generalities of the law, interpretive frameworks and social and individual representations to contextualise and analyse law in action, i.e. the law that is created by the activity of judges, of attorneys etc. (Frank, 1930, 1947, 1948).

Although we now find Frank's intuition to be obvious as well as pertinent, the issue of fact-finding, as I mentioned earlier, requires far greater exploration. In general, two trends can be identified in the area of fact-finding. On the one hand, scholars focus their discussion on the acquisition of truth, in accordance with a specific legal theory or legal epistemology (Jackson, 1988; Samuel, 2016; Twining [1990, 1994], 2006; Taruffo, 2009). On the other hand, the use of storytelling in law (Amsterdam, 1984; Sheppele, 1988–1989; Sherwin, 1994) has opened new perspectives in socio-legal research and in clinical legal education, highlighting how legal reality and legal facts are not recounted by narrative but constituted by it (Amsterdam and Bruner, 2000; Di Donato, 2008; Aiken and Shalleck, 2016; Berger and Stanchi, 2018).

Following this dual trend, the next paragraph (par. 2) describes some positions of relevance in the recent debate. The chapter then continues with reconstructions of a selection of contemporary approaches to fact-finding, placing this thinking in the Civil Law context of Italy and dwelling in particular on the theory of the construction of factual utterances proposed by the Italian proceduralist

1 For a more detailed reconstruction of Frank's sceptical conception and the criticism levelled at him, see Twining ([1990, 1994], 2006, p. 99 ff).

Michele Taruffo (par. 2.1). Using this theoretical background as a starting point for a critical discussion, it analyses my own proposal for a culturally located narrative process of fact construction (par. 2.2), specifying certain premises for investigations, such as the definition of the context (par. 3), of legal dispute (par. 3.1.) and the role played by the parties in shaping the dispute (par. 3.2). Lastly, it illustrates in detail the method used in this book to reconstruct cases (par. 4), arguing for the usefulness of an analysis in context (par. 5).

2. A dual trend: from theory to practice

Starting out from a perspective of legal epistemology and writing in the framework of a more extensive work dedicated to legal reasoning and to legal method, Geoffrey Samuel believes it was counterproductive to reduce knowledge of the law to mere norms, without considering the facts. At the same time, he stresses that knowledge of the facts is mediated in any case by legal categories and institutional dimensions: institutions and concepts "act as bridges between the worlds of law and social fact" (2003, p. 173). Samuel argues that even science does not treat facts as 'real', since science aims at constructing models of the real world, which it then uses to explain and forecast the phenomenon thus modelled. He suggests that this approach could be applied directly to the law, which does not operate directly on the facts, arguing that it is lawyers who build bridges between the social and the legal world. He then concludes that, given the process of construction and reconstruction to which they are subjected before being formally assigned to a 'stable' legal category, the facts in a legal dispute are not real, but virtual facts.

From a legal theory perspective, it is worth remembering that, in a series of essays that led to his well-known book *Rethinking Evidence* ([1990, 1994], 2006), William Twining builds on a vision that he describes as "contextualist" or "realist", the premise that "reality is a social construction and not something out there waiting to be found" (ibid., p. 15). He considers that rules, institutions, trials and legal methods can only be understood if they are located in a broader context, rather than in isolation: "rules are important – indeed a central feature of law – but for the purposes of understanding, criticising, or even expounding the law, the study of rules alone is not enough. Rather, legal rules, institutions, procedures, practices and other legal phenomena need to be set in some broader context" (ibid., p. 167).

Conscious of the limits of a study that is not contextualised in adjudication, one of the crucial theses of his essays "relates to the uses and limits of 'reason' in fact determination" (ibid., p. 6). In *Taking Facts Seriously* in particular, Twining argues that "questions of fact deserve as much attention as questions of law" as questions of fact, along with the questions of law, represent the key phase of the transformation of "daily events" into "legal stories" (ibid., p. 7).[2] In fact, it has been noted ever since the time of Jerome Frank "that an imbalance exists between

2 For further information about this issue, see Chapters 5 and 6.

the amount of attention devoted to disputed questions of law in upper courts and the amount devoted to disputed questions of fact in trials at first instance" (ibid., p. 15). Evidence, proof and fact-finding do not seem to be accepted generally as integral and focal elements in jurists' training, nor in general of legal research, legal literature or law reforms (ibid., p. 16).[3] Lastly, another issue has traditionally been neglected by legal theorists: the role played by narrative in legal discourse. Although Twining challenges the idea that "constructing stories is 'the central act of the legal mind'" (ibid., p. 287), in his essay *Lawyers' Stories*, he recognises that narrative plays a central role in legal discourse. Lawyers use narration as a tool to shape fragments of information and single elements of proof within an ordered meaning that has a significant relevance for the law.

In his turn, in a semiotic perspective of the law as a form of communication rooted in the work of structuralist semiotics, Bernard Jackson argues that narrative is an essential part of legal decision-making. His thesis is that "'narrative coherence' structures the intelligibility of both fact and law in the adjudicatory process" (1988, p. 1), pointing out that narrative coherence is used as a primary principle for organising and manipulating factual reconstruction of events within the legal dispute. Despite the fact that legal reasoning tends to represent itself as scientific, it makes use of narrative forms: "Narrative structures inform not only the content but also the manner in which stories are told. Events may be brought out in testimony in a sequence different from that in which they are claimed to have occurred" (ibid., p. 11).

To some extent breaking away from the analytical approaches mentioned previously, contributions with a more revolutionary impact have amply demonstrated the pertinence of a narrative approach to fact-finding.[4] Continuing seamlessly from Frank's teachings, yet without discerning a thread common to the various schools of thought, clinicians in particular have continued practising a sort of fact scepticism. As Shalleck recently wrote:

> Clinical scholars are the inheritors of many intellectual traditions that have challenged the givenness of facts. What is surprising, however, is that so much legal thought has failed to take the broad and deep intellectual critiques of the stability and certainty of factual accounts of the world seriously. These critiques have been treated largely as beside the point. Clinical scholars have brought these insights into the realm of legal theory.[5] As in their

3 The most significant objection tackled by Twining when proposing the introduction of what he calls "fact-handling" as an autonomous discipline is that it would be superfluous to teach it, since how a fact is constructed is something that is learned in practice.

4 The reference is primarily to the theories of Bernard Jackson (1988), Neil MacCormick (1984) and Ronald Dworkin (1986). The approaches proposed by these authors are largely inspired by rules of consistency internal to legal texts or by the application of rules, such as those governing *stare decisis* in Common Law systems.

5 Milstein, *Clinical Education, Indeterminacy and the Reform of the Law School Curriculum*. Manuscript on file with the author.

> conflicting understandings of lawyering, clinical scholars differ significantly in their understandings of facts. Nonetheless, across all the schools of clinical thought, clinical jurisprudence makes factual inquiry and knowledge a central component of an understanding of what the law is and how it operates.
>
> (Shalleck, 2015)

Clinical scholars have thus problematised the issue of fact investigation, developing approaches that combine both theory and practice, taking into account the significance attributed to legal rules in the contexts and interpretative activities of the attorneys who engage in understanding their clients' stories, presenting them to the world in other forms (Amsterdam, 1984; Miller, 1994; Ellmann et al., 2009).

> The notion of applying the law to the facts, an activity replicated daily throughout legal education, is deeply problematic and seems almost fanciful after thinking about and teaching the process of framing any legal matter, whether an individual case or a multi-faceted community lawyering project, in the context of clinical method. Certainly, other critical legal theories since the advent of Legal Realism have challenged various aspects of the idea that law is simply applied to facts.[6] The contribution of clinical method to these critical projects has been to identify, question and inquire deeply into the complex, embedded practices through which legal rules and doctrines take on meaning in the world through the interpretive activities of lawyers as they engage with clients in understanding and shaping their stories, in presenting them to the world, or in reshaping them as they assume new forms or enter into new relationships.
>
> (Shalleck, 2015)

As I mentioned in Chapter 2, curricula in clinical legal education were developed beginning in the early eighties in the wake of the drive of such jurists as Anthony Amsterdam, whose article *Clinical Legal Education – a 21st Century Perspective* (1984) criticises the limits of traditional legal education. In fact, traditional legal education cuts those (attorneys, judges etc.) who are involved on an everyday basis in the task of applying the law out of its teaching. In practice, Amsterdam identified the development of effective techniques for learning the law as a function of twenty-first century law schools, starting out from practical experience. Along with the four strands of analytical thinking traditionally taught in law faculties – the use of precedent (*stare decisis*) for solving cases, the analysis and application of doctrine, the organisation of legal categories and institutions, and logical conceptualisation and criticism – Amsterdam identified at least three typical mindsets to be thematised: 1) reasoning in terms of aims and objectives,

6 These movements include Critical Legal Studies, Feminist Jurisprudence, Critical Race Theory, and Law and Economics. See Minda (1995).

i.e. presenting a factual situation theorising how it could be solved and the objectives achieved; 2) formulating hypotheses for the purpose of acquiring pertinent information; and 3) decision-making based on considering risks and cost-benefit factors.[7]

The current-day pertinence of this approach to teaching is confirmed in many fields of law and on a global scale (Bartoli, 2016; Block, 2008, 2011; Wilson, 2017). Specific programmes are devoted to the issue of fact-finding – in the field of human rights, for example – illustrating the crucial importance of compiling evidence, while also attracting attention to the impact of reality on people's lives. Once again, the tendency here is to criticise such traditional principles as 'objectivity', 'coherence' and 'truth', showing how facts are not a prior given, but the effect of a discovery and that 'those who seek the facts' play an active role in constructing social reality.[8] This calls for a certain degree of awareness on the part of fact-finders (attorneys, Courts, NGO and so on).

2.1. *The theory of the construction of factual utterances: a truth-oriented perspective*

Systematic theories about fact investigation have been proposed in the last ten years in the European and more particularly the Italian context. These can be ascribed to the dual trajectory described previously: the legal theory of the legal process and the socio-clinical approach to law.

The first of these includes the proposal launched by the civil proceedings lawyer Michele Taruffo (Taruffo, 2009), which, while remaining true to an analytical perspective, pays due attention to the latest theoretical input from the narrativist and culturalist trends originating in the United States. My own research conducted in Italy and Switzerland (Di Donato, 2008; 2012; Di Donato et al., forthcoming) can be classified under the heading of the second.

Considering that the ideal aim of a trial is to discover the truth – as tends to be the case typically of civil law systems – as a principle of juridical civilisation and a basis for creating a relationship of trust between the individual and the institutions, Taruffo suggests using pure epistemology to analyse facts as the subject matter of proof.[9] This means that he opts for a 'correspondentist' conception of truth, according to which "external reality exists and constitutes the yardstick, the criterion of reference that determines the truth or falseness of the utterances

7 On the issue of how to teach fact-finding and bringing the real world into the lecture room, see also Aiken and Shalleck (2016).

8 For example, to stress the importance of a correct fact-finding procedure in the human rights field, guidelines have been provided, by the International Bar Association and the Raoul Wallenberg Institute, to "improve accuracy, objectivity, transparency and credibility in human rights fact-finding", in order to contribute to good practice in the conduct of fact-finding visits and in the compilation of reports by the NGO. See Weissbrod and McCarthy (1981–1982).

9 Cf. Tuzet (2013).

that deal with it" (2009, p. 78).[10] The subject matter of the determination of the evidence in the trial is thus the factual utterances as linguistic constructs forged by the parties and by the judge, on the basis of such different standards as rules of language, institutional factors, categories of thought, ethical and social values and so on. Taruffo identifies some of the factors that give rise to what he calls a "linguistic construction". In this first place, this is a "selective construction": of all the infinite possibilities available for describing a fact as true or false, only those are selected that are useful to its description and that may of course vary at different times in the course of the legal proceedings.

On the basis of which criteria are these factual utterances chosen? The first criterion of choice is the selection of the norm that is presumed to apply to the fact and that acts as a filter (Taruffo, 2009, p. 42). It is the reference to the abstract case in hand that enables the circumstances to be determined, which must then be indicated in such a way as to construct a description of the specific fact (the *konkreter Tatbestand*) that corresponds to what is covered by the norm. The norm indicates not only to which fact the plaintiff must allude, but also which aspects of what actually happened must be described and which ones should be omitted. In other words, a norm acts both as a criterion of inclusion and as a criterion of exclusion.

In addition, utterances are constructed by making use of so-called categories, such as causality and temporality. Taruffo agrees with Amsterdam and Bruner that it is categories that supply conceptual tools for interpreting reality, enabling an utterance to be located in a particular context of ideas (2009, p. 54). The reference here is primarily to the nexus of causality, which enables a connection to be established between two or more events: take the nexus of cause and effect, for example. Not all connections between events exist in nature. Of course, it has already been demonstrated extensively in literature that it is not natural causality that is detected in a legal process.[11] Instead, the dominant role is played by a linguistic and cultural dimension that enables a negotiation of meanings attributed to apparently relevant events.

Another category employed by Taruffo is that of time. Yet while Amsterdam and Bruner talk about a narrative dimension of time, in the sense that events find a 'significant' organisation in time, Taruffo holds that continuous linear time (measured in seconds, minutes and hours) is essential for establishing a chronological sequence between events, so as to establish a before and an after. He also takes the

10 This conception is criticised by Ubertis (2018, p. 58), who holds that the judge does not necessarily have to espouse any specific notion of truth in order to check whether a decision is fair. A decision is fair when its factual base has been verified in the course of evidence and when the norms have been interpreted as a function of the facts, which have been reconstructed as a function of the norms.

11 On the concept of the causal nexus, see Richardson (2008, p. 48), who focuses in particular on Hume's discovery that it is impossible to demonstrate the causal relationship between events in nature, while the relationship between cause and effect can only be reconstructed in terms of probabilities. On this issue, see also Chapter 1.

distinction between objective time and subjective time into account, i.e. the fact that the different individuals involved in an event have different perceptions of it (the different evidence they give in court is a good example). As I shall illustrate by means of case analysis, in particular that of Laura (Chapters 4–5–6), time takes on a narrative dimension in legal disputes: events acquire a different meaning in terms of time, depending on who recounts them, the client, the attorney or the judge.

The cultural dimension also constitutes a further criterion in the selection of utterances of fact. Taruffo suggests a conception of culture construed as "knowledge of the world",[12] i.e. as an accumulation of different ethical, religious, ethnic and customary points of view that influence how the fact is represented, selected and described, bearing the multicultural dimension typical of contemporary society in mind, among other things. I shall demonstrate this when discussing the case of Carlo (Chapter 7), who felt that the version of the facts suggested to him by his superiors by way of justifying his disciplinary dismissal was surreal, like something borrowed from a story by Kafka, as he himself wrote in his reply to his superior. Likewise, Michele's case (Chapter 7) illustrates how the client's view of work management and interpersonal relations in the working context did not coincide with those of his colleagues.

Another element necessary for constructing utterances of fact is language, construed not only as the correct use of categories of grammar and syntax in the trial, so from the standpoint of the function of expression and description it fulfils, but also from the standpoint of the use of strictly technical terminology, since this – the legal process – is a highly specialised context.[13] We shall see this in the cases of Line and of Kirin (Chapter 8), who gradually adopt the conventional language of the law and of administration, abandoning the everyday language of emotion that they use in the early phases of their interactions with administrative officials.

Individual factual utterances about individual factual circumstances, based on the elements described previously and in relation to an abstract legal forecast, are not located atomistically in legal proceedings, but give rise to a composition that Taruffo compares to a mosaic.[14] The fact is represented by an event, by a set of circumstances

12 Taruffo (2006), *Judicial Narratives*, Manuscript on file with the author, p. 23. With this in mind, Taruffo suggests distinguishing between 'scripts' and 'stereotypes', borrowing the latter concept from Schauer (2006). While for Amsterdam and Bruner (2000) 'scripts' constitute the plot of the narration, for example the script of the good cop and the bad cop, 'stereotypes' constitute the typical mode of behaviour and are concerned with constructing characters in specific settings, for example the stereotype of the Islamic terrorist. Stereotypes are variable cultural elements that may or may not come into play, according to the situation. For Taruffo, both scripts and stereotypes constitute tools for constructing the mosaic of the narration (ibid., pp. 23–29).

13 The descriptive function of language is countered by its evaluatory function. Descriptions are often accompanied by evaluations (e.g. the qualification of the intolerability of cohabitation). Individual appraisals are naturally of no relevance, unless they are accompanied by the descriptive construction of facts (those same facts that complement the details that make the cohabitation intolerable).

14 The model of the mosaic conveys the idea of an open structure, unlike that of the puzzle, which implies a pattern.

and behaviours. Together, they constitute the 'construction of a story' (e.g. the story of the legal separation between two people) and not the random combination of utterances. What we have, then, is a plurality of stories: the raw, everyday story as told by the client, the one that has been modelled by the attorney in accordance with legal categories and lastly the one espoused by the judge. In other words, the utterances are organised in a narrative context that gives them an overall meaning.[15] The utterances can of course be combined in many different ways, but the possibilities are neither infinite nor random: random combinations of utterances would not lead to a narration. A story is not a random assembly of facts.

The author describes this model as 'realistic narration': "facts are narrated that are located in a certain space-time sequence with the criterion of narrative coherence", in which he explains that 'narrative coherence' means the "correspondence of a story to the models of narrative existing inside the 'stock of knowledge' representing the contents of that culture".[16] This is what culturalists also call 'scripts'. Lawyers and judges normally take these scripts into account when compiling the legal definition of events, but lawyers may also suggest subversive narrations (Ewick and Silbey, 1998). This is what happened in the cases of Line and Kirin, for example (Chapter 8).

Realistic narrations are created – for different purposes and starting out from different points of view – by the actors in the legal proceedings, whom Taruffo identifies in the classical roles of attorneys, witnesses and judges. The attorney is considered to be a storyteller by definition: (s)he narrates the facts as a function of her/his aim to safeguard the client's interests. This means that the attorney is under no obligation to reveal the truth in the strict sense. The author considers that a greater obligation to reveal the truth, which he describes as 'reinforced' or 'strong', is incumbent on the witness, who is in fact obliged 'to tell the truth' and is threatened with penal sanctions if he makes false or reticent statements (Taruffo, 2009, pp. 49–51). As for the role played by the judge, he may just act as a 'referee', choosing the best narration from among the ones offered to him, or as an 'author' of a narration of his own (at least, in those systems where this is allowed, as for example in civil law countries). His position is – and must be – a detached one, as is unanimously acknowledged by all doctrine. In his role as guarantor of the epistemic function of the legal proceedings, the judge thus has the task of "minimising the parties' tendency to distort the truth" (ibid., pp. 168, 172 ff.). The final decision that ought to guarantee that the truth has been ascertained is thus based on the facts proven in accordance with a logical approach that looks something like this: $W = E \rightarrow H$, where W = warrant, E = available evidence and H = hypothesis in question (ibid., p. 208 ff.). The facts that become known on the basis of the evidence acquired during the trial contribute to the final decision, which comprises "an orderly series of factual utterances, each of which has

15 It is in this sense that Taruffo interprets the statement made by Amsterdam and Bruner (2000, p. 19) to the effect that "stories construct the facts that comprise them".

16 Taruffo, *Judicial Narratives*, Manuscript on file with the author, p. 23.

obtained from the available evidence, rationally appraised, a sufficiently strong degree of evidence-based confirmation" (ibid., p. 225), so that such utterances can be construed as acquired as true because they accord with the reality of the facts that took place.[17]

The epistemic model proposed by Taruffo thus shifts the question of the ascertainment of the truth onto a purely logical plane, vesting with meaning the role of the judge, to whom it ascribes the function of reducing the risks of uncertainty and of any manipulations that may be perpetrated by the parties in the phases leading up to the legal proceedings. Despite these premises, it leaves the background of the narrative, cultural, linguistic and causal dimensions that he himself acknowledges to be integral parts of the construction of the facts. This model is distinguished from the one proposed by Haack, for example, which, while also having recourse to epistemology and to the role of evidence in ascertaining the truth, puts greater emphasis on the contextualisation of the trial and of any irrational factors that may govern the decision. Since he questions the validity and the absolute degree of certainty offered by science, the epistemologist holds that an epistemological approach to the trial must be capable of combining the objective elements of evidence with a subjective perspective activity derived from the reconstruction of the facts, from the context, from social reality and from all the subjective elements of appraisal (the judge's reasoning and that of the attorneys, but also the parties' beliefs and behaviours) (Haack, 2012, p. 222).

Taruffo's model is also distinguished from the one proposed by Chase (2006), who examines both the conflict-solving methods typical of Common Law systems, such as the ADR, and the rituals typical of specific populations, such as the Azande. This population uses the *Benge*, or 'poison oracle', to determine whether or not a crime has been committed. This kind of comparison illustrates that the purpose of the legal proceedings for these legal orders is that of solving the conflict rather than establishing the truth.[18] By adopting an anthropological and cultural lens to analyse legal processes, Chase's studies thus have the merit of illustrating how different contexts use different techniques and methods to determine the truth and, more generally, how a culture shapes the law and determines its structures and its rituals, including the form of legal proceedings. With the result that an absolute validation of a model for ascertaining the facts and the truth, a model that separates law from culture or that does not take this combination into sufficient account, risks leading to only partial results.

17 Taruffo (2009, pp. 173–179) identifies the tools available to the judge from time to time in the various legal orders for guaranteeing his function: from the power to order that means of evidence be taken into consideration to the power to invite the parties to produce evidence that (s)he (the judge her/himself) considers relevant (this is typical of German and English judges, while the Spanish judge has less power to do this).

18 The trial conducted by the Azande people, described by Chase, takes the form of a ritual in which a chick is fed poison (hence the name of the 'poison oracle'). The validity of the accusation thus depends on whether the chick lives or dies.

2.2. *A theory of narrative fact construction: a culturally oriented perspective*

Despite the different analytical, socio-constructivist and clinical matrices of the concepts characteristic of the dominant theories in the field of fact-finding described previously, there now seems to be a consensus on at least two premises:

- the legal process is a social construct, shaped by rules, rituals and roles that can only be understood if they are situated in a rather broad context of ideas and in a specific legal culture (Chase, 2006; Haack, 2012; Taruffo, 2009; Twining [1990; 1994], 2006);
- narratives are the main tool by means of which objective constraints (places, dates, names) can be modelled as 'facts' in the legal process and in institutional contexts (administrative procedures) (Amsterdam and Bruner, 2000; Di Donato, 2008).

It is nevertheless worth pointing out that, while taking the distinction between fact and law that must necessarily be drawn in the context of the legal process into account, the narrative dimension is not limited to the reconstruction of the facts, but is concerned with the construction of the case as a whole (Ellmann et al., 2009). The role played by the narration is in fact that of providing a form for dates, places and actions, but also normative meanings. There is a place and a significance for norms and evidence in the story: as Cover (1983–1984) taught us, no complex of legal prescriptions and institutions exists in isolation from the narrations that place it and give it meaning (see Chapter 1).

This method of putting facts and law together in a narrative framework also corresponds to what clinicians call the case theory.[19] The process of developing a case theory is an iterative one, a spiral – to a degree reminiscent of a hermeneutic circle – that goes back and forth from facts to norms and vice-versa, devising possible ways to tell the story to different audiences. In my own perspective, case theory is then constructed starting from the perspective of the narrator, according to the role (s)he plays in the legal proceedings. I am not only referring to institutional roles, as in the case of the lawyer, the judge and the witness as proposed by Taruffo (2009). I also consider the informal roles, such as that of the client who collaborates with his or her lawyer in (re) constructing the facts of the case.[20]

19 Miller (1994, p. 486) defines case theory as "an explanatory statement linking the 'case' to the client's experience of the world. Is serves as a lens for shaping reality, in light of the law, to explain facts, relationships, and circumstances of the client and other parties in the way that can best achieve the client's goals. The relevant reality combines the perspective of the lawyer and the client with an eye toward the ultimate audience – the trier of fact".

20 For a case theory that focuses specifically on the role of the client, see the work of Murray (1995), Thomas (2008) and, in more extreme terms, of Chavkin (2003), who discusses the client's theory with reference to the work of Bellow and Moulton (1978).

In fact, as I shall show in the next chapter (4), the first stage of constructing a legal story involves the story proposed by the client to her or his lawyer. An examination of different cases will highlight how the client (whose role is completely ignored in classical analysis) is capable of playing an active part in the construction of her or his own case, thus conditioning the results. The client is not a mere information giver but is capable of taking initiatives and executing strategies agreed upon with the lawyer, particularly during the phase that precedes the actual legal proceedings.

The next step – which will be analysed in Chapter 5 – is the translation of live events into legal events: how do laypeople understand the law and how do they learn to narrate it within legal frameworks? Lawyers are involved in the process of translation of non-legal knowledge. How do they filter the story of a case and how do they translate clients' representations?

In turn, on the basis of what criteria and/or parameters does the judge evaluate the case and choose between the narrations proposed by the parties or maybe construct a new one? This issue is tackled in Chapter 6.

By way of answering some of these questions and drawing my inspiration from a cultural-narrativist approach of the kind I explored extensively in the previous two chapters, as well as from the approaches to fact investigation that I have reconstructed in this chapter, I shall now expound on the results of research conducted subsequently and in a variety of cultural contexts, for the purpose of throwing light on:

- How reality is shaped in the legal process and how the meanings of events are negotiated in the exchanges between legal actors: the client, the attorney, the judge and administrative agents, considered in their mutual interactions (Di Donato, 2008). Narrative interaction between legal actors will be analysed in greater detail in Chapter 4–6, but will also be found again in Chapters 7 and 8.
- The role played by the context in modelling the meanings of events and orienting the activities of the actors who have to deal not just with formal rules, but also with implicit or customary rules, in order to solve the case and obtain the recognition of their rights (Di Donato, 2012; 2014; 2015; Di Donato and Garros, forthcoming). This issue will furnish the background in particular to the analyses conducted in Chapters 7–9.

To summarise my research hypothesis, I would suggest that the fact is reconstructed in the narrative interactions between the actors: it is the parties who construct it and reconstruct it, starting out from the 'roles' they play and 'negotiations' in specific situations, according to the information they possess and taking the social practices common to a given community into account. Specific premises of the hypothesis mentioned previously guide my investigations.

- By opting for a 'constructivist' approach, I am referring to a series of scientific positions, emphasising the 'meanings' that may be attributed to the events in the ethical and cultural mindsets of the various participants in the dialogue. These positions enable me to hypothesise that, although a reality external to the individual exists and can be perceived (Ferraris, 2012), it is hard to decipher a direct access to it, especially in an artificial context like that of a legal process. Constructivism's underlying assumption is that knowledge is right or wrong in the light of the perspective chosen, as it is never point-of-viewless. My work thus aims to focus on the process of construction of legal meanings by various legal actors.

- As I showed in Chapter 1, studies of the relationship between mind and culture, including anthropological observations about the situated dimension of knowledge, have enabled us to assume that the reproduction or reconstruction of reality is not independent of its context of analysis. My culturalist approach, then, is that a certain degree of awareness of the cultural dimension of reality – construed as knowledge of the social context in the broad sense – on the part of legal actors (natives/foreigners) makes a decisive difference in whether or not their legal actions are successful, conditioning their perception of the facts and their agentivity in the course of administrative or judicial proceedings. As I shall illustrate in Chapters 7 and 8, clients end up winning or losing according to their ability to handle both formal rules and those that are implicit in the context where they act.
- The individual's access to reality is mediated by symbols and the language they infer in the forms that provide the narration with its structure. It is in the narration that the events that happen in the world acquire 'meaning'. Stories are not just containers of facts: they are structuring forms that organise events. In this sense, it is the facts themselves that are 'constructed' by means of and with the characteristics typical of narration explored in Chapter 1 (normativity, temporality etc.).
- The relevant fact for the law is selected by virtue of a norm, as already explained by Taruffo (2009): it is the norm that tells us which elements are relevant for identifying the concrete case in hand. Norms, however, do not tell us how to identify the elements that are 'juridically relevant'. As we shall see in the case of Laura (Chapters 4 and 5), for example, it is often possible for the interpreter (the attorney) to choose between several cases in hand (for example, mobbing/dequalification), according to the result he sets out to achieve and the extent to which success is possible in the judgement. The rules of evidence contain no indications governing how the information to be proven is selected (cf. Chapter 7). Even the evidence itself, acquired by virtue of the elements selected by the parties, is liable to be interpreted differently by the parties and by the judge.[21]

21 Chase (2006) suggests that trust in the evidence and in the truth, as essential elements in ascertaining the fact, are no more than a cultural product, not unlike the way the Azande have recourse to the *Benge*. The use of such methods in Western cultures is considered to be 'natural' or 'logical'. In reality, what is paradoxical, according to Chase, is that this requirement is profoundly cultural and contingent.

- In general, in the selection and presentation of the factual elements and of the results of the evidence, a role is played by debate and rhetoric. The activities of the parties are all aimed at getting to know the fact and making it knowable, so as to persuade the judge about what happened.[22] I shall illustrate this aspect in particular in Chapter 5.
- Institutional contexts and rules of procedure also influence the parties' actions and limit the possibilities of choice available to the decision maker: statutes of limitations, forfeiture, irrebuttable presumptions and decisive oath are mechanisms that make a rigid or an elastic contribution (the latter in the case of witness evidence) to constructing the fact by 'establishing it'.[23]
- The context of fact construction is not just that of the decision, as Taruffo maintains, but also the more extensive one of the 'legal process', construed sociologically as the set of social interactions that takes shape through the roles played by the parties (Abel, 1974, pp. 226–227), from the client's meeting with the attorney to the final decision handed down by the judge.

3. Fundamental definitions in a multidisciplinary perspective: context, dispute and the role of the parties

As mentioned previously, I interpret the legal process as the context of fact construction in broader sociological terms rather than in narrow procedural terms. In fact, as clearly defined by Abel, the legal process, in its most basic meaning as a dispute, is none other than a form of social interaction, a stage of evolution through which any interaction may pass (Abel, 1974, pp. 226–227).[24] Abel's definition of the dispute as a 'dynamic' place, made of social relationships that require a kind of 'normative domestication', seems to deal perfectly with a definition of narration as a 'tool' to shape human interactions, through negotiations of meanings that are rooted in everyday life, as well as in legal contexts (Bruner, 1986; Daiute, 2014).

Starting from this premise, I intend to be more specific about the meanings of context, dispute and the role played by the parties in the dispute, relating these definitions to the types of cases analysed in the chapters that follow.

22 For a basic meaning of rhetoric, intended as the capacity to seek audience adherence to a claim through persuasion, see Perelman and Olbrechts-Tyteca (1969). For a contextualisation of the meaning of rhetoric in the issue of legal persuasion, see Berger and Stanchi (2018). These scholars provide an original study that combines theory and case analysis to show that the capacity to persuade the audience depends on the capacity of "making and breaking mental connections". See also Tigar (1999).

23 See Ferrari, *Quelques raisons du relativisme juridique*, Manuscript on file with the author.

24 How disputes are handled through the role played by the parties was investigated by Abel. Starting with a study conducted in 1973 into a particular legal system, that of Kenya, Abel concludes that it is the roles played by the people who intervene in a dispute that characterise the structural differences in disputes between one system and another. Cf. Abel (1974, pp. 221–224, 226, 303).

3.1. *The notion of 'context': the legal dispute as the context of fact construction*

The first step, then, is to introduce a definition of 'context' as practised by the human and social sciences in recent decades, in accordance with the approach known as 'situated research' or 'research on the ground' (O' Reilly. 2005).

In general, the notion of context is cited by social scientists to indicate that "a given action or a given event may not be appropriately understood except by taking into consideration some other aspect of the environment, of the situation or of the event in which it is inserted" (Mantovani and Spagnolli, 2003, p. 22). In a perspective of social constructionism, for example, Perret-Clermont is of the opinion that considering the activities within the context in which they take place means considering that the events with which individuals confront one another have a character that is at one and the same time objective, subjective and intersubjective; that events are seldom completely new, but are more likely to share points with known events and are organised in accordance with certain rules or practices that enable individuals to give meaning to what they are experiencing. Moreover, since intellectual activity always belongs in a context of intentions and interpretations, every activity, including legal activity, is not only the application of a procedure, but is also accompanied by a parallel activity of interpretation "of the meaning of the situation, of the task, of the roles and of the responsibilities of the partners, of their intentions, of the validity of their responses, of the nature of the knowledge involved, of their past and of their pertinence to the moment. [. . .] These interpretations concern not only the cognitive aspect, but also the meaning that the content has for the individual, as well as its meanings in social and identity terms".[25]

In an ethnopragmatic perspective, then, the notion of context acquires greater plasticity, since the 'interactive fabric' is taken as the basis for defining the context. In fact, it is not imagined as a 'fixed, unchangeable framework', but as the product and changeable background of our knowledge, our emotions, our actions and our communications:[26]

> intersubjectivity constitutes the social world, considering that the context is fundamentally the meeting with others [. . .]. Subjectivity itself can be seen as the result (if not even the 'residue') of intersubjectivity, i.e. of our being with and being for others [. . .]. When giving meaning to our actions, we have to take others into consideration and are therefore obliged to adopt their point of view, if not actually their social aims. This is a type of activity whereby we

25 Translated by this volume's translator from the French text of Perret-Clermont (2001, I, pp. 65–82).

26 Cf. Duranti (2007, pp. 59 ff our translation). In one of his latest interviews, Bruner talks about 'we-go', to stress the irrepressible dimension of relations that face us and without which we would have no social dimension: www.repubblica.it/cultura/2015/04/16/news/jerome_bruner-112104846/.

> transfer our knowledge, our feelings and our ethical and aesthetic preferences to others.
>
> (Duranti, 2007, p. 59)

In this sense, the context is also said to expand as our demands for the recognition of experiences, intentions and aspirations expand and is the result of negotiations about the potentially infinite, locally constructed and negotiated meanings to attribute to reality.

In a more technical sense, the context of fact construction comprises the process. In a socio-legal perspective, the context can be defined as "the totality of factors that influence the dispute and contribute to defining it in social interaction" and in turn the process as "the totality of the social actions addressed to treating the dispute, until the decision or decisions that settle it more or less contingently or definitively" (Ferrari, 1993, p. 345).[27] The 'context of the legal process' can be further connoted as a 'conflictual' context, although the function of the law is not just that of solving conflicts, but also of preventing them by means of transactional matters where parties anticipate conflict and possible resolution strategies: in some sense law and conflict are considered to be coessential. The law intervenes for the purpose of treating[28] conflicts ex post facto that have already become manifest, in the form of incompatible claims. These are 'declared', 'public' conflicts (Ferrari, 1987, p. 157), articulated by means of the representation of at least one claim expressed publicly in normative terms, where 'normative' is construed as the attitude of the party insisting on his own claim despite the other's opposition, generally by citing a norm (belonging to any system whatsoever, including one that may be alternative to the legal order acknowledged to be in force) that justifies or legitimises it (Ferrari, 1993, p. 344).

Generally in my investigation, the context is construed to include the different meanings listed previously, as a real and at the same time symbolic place where the interactions between the parties come to life and take shape, modelling the narrations that give the dispute its structure. In particular, from a narrative-centred perspective, context is the both implicit and explicit discursive interaction between stakeholders in the relevant system of relations. Within the narrative analysis of legal cases, the notion of context gives due consideration to the broader context where the story of the client originates. Thus, to study the proceedings in court interactively and in their context means to examine not only the dispute itself, but also its origins and the inter-individual and social relationships in which it was unleashed, so that the proceedings can be considered as a variable of the context.[29]

27 Ferrari (1993, p. 345, our translation; 1987).

28 Following Ferrari's (1987) examples, I use the verb "to treat" rather than "to solve", since the law intervenes in conflicts without necessarily solving them, but often only making them worse (the law invoked by the victor is often perceived as arbitrary by the loser).

29 Ferrari holds that talking about disputes is reductive. In this legal sociologist's opinion, the term 'dispute' carries too many minimalistic and individualistic connotations. Declared

This issue of the interaction between the context and the legal dispute will emerge more explicitly in the cases analysed in Chapter 7 (labour law). Moreover in Chapters 8 and 9, for example, clients are considered to be vulnerable not only because of their legal story, but also because of their immigration status, prior history, religious believes etc. As I will show in the cases of Line and Charles, or Amenze and Margaret, these stakeholder discourses include histories of unjust treatment, circumstances of interaction with the local institutions and the prejudices to which the individuals in question feel they are subject as non-citizens.

3.2. *The legal dispute as a form of social interaction*

As Abel sees it, characterising a conflict as a common stage of evolution in every relationship means stressing that it is not a question of an example of deviance. A conflict can be transformed into a dispute if the claims are stated publicly, if their incompatibility is communicated to anyone and if they are justified in terms of a norm that could satisfy them. Moreover, as already mentioned, disputes are classified as having either a dyadic or a triadic structure, according to whether or not the parties involve a third-party intervenor.[30] If they do, we talk about a 'case' or a 'controversy'.

Naturally enough, as Abel points out, although a dispute may presuppose a conflict and a conflict an interaction, the chronological sequence is neither inevitable nor irreversible: the contact may not lead to a significant interaction (e.g. bumping against another passenger on a bus), the interaction may not lead to a conflict (one party may immediately offer an apology), and the conflict may never evolve into a dispute. The evolutionary sequence can also be reversed, of course: a dispute may be reduced to a mere conflict if one of the parties stops stating its claim publicly. This is what happened in Laura's case (Chapter 4), for example, where the case was solved after the court of first instance by a settlement between the client and the firm.

The conflict may disappear from an interaction if one party stops believing it has a right, while a significant interaction may be limited to a mere physical contact and the contact itself may stop.

Every society is of course characterised by a relatively limited number of patterns that are institutionalised as recurrent patterns of disputes (Abel, 1974, pp. 227–229). The simplest structure of the dispute, in terms of numbers of elements, is the one in which every party plays the role of audience to the claims

---

conflicts, to whose treatment law contributes, are not restricted to those taking place between individual subjects. Every kind of dispute can be nudged into juridical channels and related to normative models, as long as it is declared.

30 Aubert also classifies the questions subject to the conflict as "disputes of value" and "disputes of interest": the former tending to reconstruct the rights and wrongs and to understand what happened, the latter tending to regulate the relationship in the future, focused on establishing what must happen later. The former tends characteristically to have a dyadic structure, the latter a triadic structure (Aubert 1963).

stated by the other. In this case, the study is limited to the roles plays by the disputers and to their reciprocal relationships.[31] A dispute with a more complex structure is one where a third party intervenes.

The additional characteristics that might define this situation are the presence of an audience that acknowledges the parties' requests, in addition to the parties themselves, who listen to their own reciprocal claims and intervene in the dispute in some way. Disputers commonly bring their claims before a third party, whose response is seldom entirely passive.[32] The role played by the third party in the conflict is variable, nor do all conflicts culminate in a judicial decision.[33]

As mentioned before, there are two variables to how a conflict becomes a dispute. One of these concerns the claimant, who asserts a claim, whether (s)he does so personally or through a representative, to whom the claim is addressed and above all in what forum. Once the dispute has started, its scope is defined in terms of three dimensions: the number and scope of grievances, the number and identity of the parties involved and the historical depth in which the controversy is explored.

Disputes also differ in terms of the results towards which they tend: some expect no fixed result, while others drive towards a specific result. This result can be imposed unilaterally on one party or a more or less important effort may be made to achieve an agreement between them through a variety of meanings. This is the trend I observe in most of the labour law cases analysed (Chapters 4–7): the trend to reach a settlement based generally on a claim expressed by one of the parties. The remedy may be expressed in sanctions that are repressive or restitutive, positive or negative, diffuse or organised. The judge's decision may be pronounced as final or such finality may be consciously avoided; in both cases, there may be opportunities for revision or reinterpretation. And of course, there will be variations in how subsequent behaviour is impacted by the decision.[34] Lastly, the term 'decision' – as we shall see in Chapter 6 – refers to a choice between alternatives; a decision may also be the result of an agreement between the parties.

When the abstract model of dispute described previously is set in a specific legal order, such as Italy's – which is comparable to the majority of civil law orders – it is structured in such a way that a 'neutral' subject (a court, a judge or a jury) that considers the case will identify the problem, learn the facts of the case and the relevant rules of law and thus pronounce a judgement. The parties to the conflict

31 With this is mind, Abel cites Evans Pritchard, whose study of the Nuer demonstrates, for example, that the structural distinction between particular disputers impacts significantly on the evolution of the dispute (Abel, 1974, p. 246).

32 Abel takes advantage of the role played by the third party to explain the characteristics of disputes (for example, whether the form is by judge or by jury; ibid. p. 244–251).

33 It is perfectly possible, for example, that the parties abandon the conflict or reach a settlement through the legal procedure, via the simple mediation of a third party or submitting the case to arbitration for a decision. At least in the case of civil proceedings, this option is freely available.

34 Ibid, pp. 229–232.

are authorised to present their own opposing versions of the case, in accordance with a dialectic and adversarial procedure, so that the final judgement will also originate in opposing presentations.

In terms of narration, the legal proceedings start with a narration (fact pleading) proposed by the plaintiff, based presumably on complete, detailed facts. The defendant can then contest all or part of the plaintiff's narration and proceed in his turn to present his own complete and detailed narration of the relevant facts. Both parties have the burden to prove the facts they narrate.

Given the public nature of the legal proceedings, it is not free competition between the private parties that governs how they function, but, in terms of procedural law, it is the judge who must ideally guarantee the legitimacy and justice of the decisions. As a result, in civil law systems, the judge may not restrict himself to choosing between opposing narrations, as is generally the case in Common Law systems, but may formulate his own autonomous reconstruction of the facts of the case when the narrations offered by both parties are not considered to the truthful or credible (Taruffo, 2009, p. 47).[35]

In general, the cases analysed in Chapters 4–7 share the characteristic of a 'triadic dispute', starting with the involvement of a judge. Only in one of these cases, that of Laura, is the dispute scaled back to the previous stage of 'conflict' as a result of the parties' decision to submit to a negotiated procedure to solve the controversy.

3.3. *The role played by the parties in negotiating the dispute*

The public nature of the conflict ensures that the parties play formal roles, channelling their actions within preconstituted limits: those of the plaintiff and the defendant (Ferrari, 2004, p. 77). Legal conflictual interaction nevertheless involves other subjects who may not necessarily participate in the dispute, such as a party who fails to appear in court or also, for example, and in a broader sense, all those employees who are affected by the interpretation of a norm contained in a contract of employment resulting from collective bargaining etc. This is the case of Viviana, for example (Chapter 7), who managed to organise a co-ordinated

35 With regard to the power to take an independent investigative initiative, Italy is aligned with the trend that prevails in the legal orders of the majority of European countries, which attributes an active role to the judge in the process of discovering the truth of the facts, giving him the power to act on his own responsibility to order the acquisition of relevant evidence that was not supplied by the parties, thus plugging any gaps left by the evidence offered in their own initiatives. It should be pointed out, however, that the version of this approach to configuring the powers of the judge adopted in Italy is rather weak: only the judge in the employment tribunal – which thus applies to my context of investigation – has the right to issue such an autonomous order to acquire every kind of evidence, while the judge in the ordinary civil courts only has the power to order the acquisition of certain kinds of evidence, not including witness evidence, confessions, decisive oaths and the exhibition of documents.

reaction among her colleagues in her work context against such illicit practices as fake pay packets.

Nor are these necessarily parties who play the role of one of the parties or that of a judge. There are parties who, from a sociological standpoint, "conflict de facto for and on behalf of others and subjects who act from outside, in an attempt to influence the dispute because they are interested in its solution", as I will show in the case of Line (Chapter 8), whose husband was part of what I would define as her legal agentivity. There are also subjects who participate in a thoroughly passive manner, as an audience, for example, but who may have the effect of influencing the action by somehow orienting the behaviour of the active participants (Ferrari, 1987, p. 162).[36] This is the case of Carlo (Chapter 7), where public opinion – and the trade unions in particular – played a decisive role in solving the case from outside.

This naturally "absolutely includes those who flank the parties in the conflict, i.e. in the typical judicial dispute: the attorneys and other counsellors" who translate the parties' questions into the formal language of the courts, who treat them to make them compatible with the rules of the game (Ferrari, 2004, p. 78). That is what happened classically in the cases of Laura and Luciano (Chapters, 4, 5 and 6), as well as of Carlo, Michele and Viviana (Chapter 7). Some features are similar, and some are different in the cases analysed in Chapters 8 and 9, in which the attorney or the judge only intervened occasionally, where recourse was had to the judge to contest the decision handed down by the administration.

It is a typical trait of court proceedings that the subjects' interaction is hardly ever direct, but is channelled through the intervention of other subjects, who mediate with functions relevant to the procedural communications. According to the model proposed by Abel (1974, pp. 254–255), but also by Mather and Yngvesson (1980–81, p. 776), the roles played by the individuals who intervene feature significantly among the elements that contribute to defining the structure of a dispute. Disputing can be seen as a process of negotiation, in which the object of the dispute and the normative framework to be applied are negotiated step by step, as the dispute proceeds. Disputes are modified in response to the interest of the participants: for example, the presentation of the facts on the basis of the result hoped for. Disputes can in fact expand by adding new issues, thus broadening the area under discussion or increasing the number and type of active participants. Since the dispute is not a static event, subjects have different interests and different outlooks. In this sense, a vital role is played by the agent of transformation, e.g. the participation of the audience or the intervention of a third party, the judge, just as a relevant role is played by the presence of the parties' supporters (attorneys and other speakers). According to Felstiner, Abel and Sarat, the agents of transformation who play the most important role are the attorneys. A classical vision holds that 'lawyers exercise considerable power over

36 Ferrari endorses the example of the role played by the trade union and the company union representation in the proceedings arising from Art. 28 of the Italian Labourers' Statute (Statuto dei Lavoratori).

their clients'. They are capable of controlling their clients, orienting the dispute in order to fit their own interests rather than those of their clients: they can refuse to provide assistance, thus stopping the dispute from developing any further; they can inform their clients about the consequences of their choices and help them identify, explore and negotiate their problems, furnishing emotional support, social support etc. (1980–1981, pp. 645–647).

As I shall explain at greater length in Chapter 5, the attorney translates her/his client's claims into a legal key, on the basis of a model with a normative appearance. This is a variable role, however: one that on some occasions disappears behind the client, on some others modifying her/his version in the client's interest, in that of the state or in her/his own interest (Cain, 1979).[37] Acting as an advisor and 'filter' who intervenes in relationships between private individuals or between them and the power of the institutions, the attorney is at one and the same time the accredited interpreter of a system of legal rules, a factor that restricts her/his freedom of movement, and the representative of interests that clash with the interests of others.[38] According to Ferrari, the ambivalence of the attorneys' role is a catalyst of tensions that involve the attorney vis-à-vis the client (s)he represents even before the other party or the judge. It is nevertheless true that advocacy has developed cultural mechanisms that enable it to take these tensions in its stride, outlining a sort of free space within which the attorney can and must move to protect private interests: a space that encompasses on the one hand both the organisation and/or the reconstruction of the facts and, on the other, the identification of the norm applicable to those facts (Ferrari, 2004, pp. 140–146).

4. The reconstruction of cases in the following chapters

On the basis of the sociological model of the legal dispute in the broad sense, as described previously, as a form of social interaction within which the conflict between two or more parties takes shape, the chapters that now follow focus on the roles played by the parties (the client, the lawyer, the judge, the administrative agent/civil servant and social workers) in 'constructing' the facts primarily during the proceedings of first instance (for cases of labour law; Chapters 4–6 and 7) or in the course of administrative procedures (for cases of migration law; Chapters 8–9). The choice of these fields of research is partly justified by the scarcity of investigations and of attention paid to law in action in these areas of civil proceedings, especially to labour law. In the case of migration law, existing studies tend to focus mainly on ethnographic analyses of administrative contexts or of court activities (Eule, 2014; Jubany, 2017). This therefore means that it is a new

37 Cf. Cain (1979).

38 When translating the client's story, the attorney offers also "a sort of 'local knowledge', of familiarity with people and conventions", among other things because the system's functioning depends on a sort of idiosyncrasy of its key characters, as well as on local practices and conventions (Levi and Walker, 1990).

approach to look at the protagonists of migration, defined in the broad sense as 'clients' (Di Donato et al., forthcoming; Di Donato and Garros, forthcoming), above all in the area of asylum.

4.1. Data collection: legal files and interviews

The construction of the cases is based on combining two classical qualitative tools: interviews and the analysis of documents. To depict laypeople acting in the law in contexts and to analyse how legal narratives evolve from one phase to another of the dispute, I start with individuals' stories, by interviewing and listening to them, and then comparing their narratives with the interviews of other legal actors and the documents contained in the administrative and legal files.

4.1.1. Legal files

For the first two series of cases (Chapters 4–7) the material analysed includes official documents of court proceedings: the document instituting the proceedings, memoranda for and against, notes for the defence, the ruling, minutes of the hearings and other documents appended by the parties or provided *ex officio.* These may be documents created, collected and made available by the law office, either with the client's consent or created directly by the client her- or himself. In that case, they will be private documents that will not become part of the official proceedings. I have also taken into account notes sometimes taken by the client, at the attorney's request, containing the 'narration' of the facts. For both groups of cases, the study also pays due attention to correspondence between attorney and client, when there is any. The analysis of documents and of aspects of the cases that are not tackled in the official proceedings threw revealing light on aspects and events that would otherwise have passed in silence, because of the limits set by the legal rituals and by the need to channel the conflict legally (see Chapter 3), or as a consequence of the strategic decisions made by the attorney, as in Carlo's case, for example, where the political substance underlying the case was never mentioned explicitly (Chapter 7).

For the third group of cases (Chapter 8), I shall proceed in like manner to examine the legal files created by the candidate for naturalisation or by the administration. These contain the originals or copies of correspondence exchanged with the administration services or with the attorneys and concern progress being made with the procedure, detailing requests for additional information, advance notice of decisions made by the various different authorities involved in the procedure, internal communications and correspondence between the administrative services. My attention is focused here both on the content of the document and on the form it takes, e.g. the use of capital letters in the text to emphasise certain passages (Chapter 4), or the organisation of an information data sheet (Chapter 7).

For the fourth group of cases (Chapter 9), I have been able to draw on the administrative and/or legal dossier, whose type varies according to the cases in question and to the institutional actors involved in them, as a function of the different procedures in use in Italy.

This analysis of the documents called for several stages. The content of the dossiers was scanned in its entirety, after which the documents were classified in chronological order. The dossiers were then read and interpreted as a group, i.e. as a set comprising a variety of different elements tracing the route followed by a judicial or administrative application. The construction and the analysis of these legal stories sometimes illustrated different representations and the meanings that the clients attributed to events and how they acted or reacted, but also the constraints of the framework in which their applications took shape. As announced in Chapter 2, and as we will see in Chapter 8, the specific forms of the documents furnished by the clients are used as elements for constructing the story and tools to develop legal agentivity.

4.1.2. Interviews

This study of documents is accompanied by an analysis of the contents of interviews about the cases, conducted separately with clients, attorneys and administrative agents. An exception to this rule is made for the cases tackled in Chapter 9, where the delicacy of the issues involved precluded the possibility of interviewing the clients. In one of the cases (Margaret), I was able to benefit from attending and observing the meetings between the client and the NGO responsible for identifying her.

For interviews with clients, their attorneys and other institutional actors, I used a semi-directive type of interview that nevertheless took the methods of narrative interviewing into account as a starting point. The use of this latter is justified not only by the cross-referencing of data pertinent to the legal path taken by the candidate for naturalisation or to more precisely autobiographical elements (as in the cases belonging to the third group) and more in general by its relevance to the study of stories and of legal storytelling. Inevitably reflecting certain characteristics of narration (Atkinson, 1998), the narrative interview is conducted implicitly or explicitly, taking such canons into account as the definition of a scenario, of the characters, of the problem, of the peripatetic interactions between the protagonists, the coda etc.

A characteristic trait of the interview is the 'active role of the interviewer', starting from her or his competence as a researcher, with respect to the field and the object of the investigation. Further such traits are the duration and the intensity of the interaction: the interview may take several hours to conduct, or it may be conducted on successive occasions. Lastly, it is the interviewer who defines 'the subject matter' of the interview, including it specifically in what is asked of the interviewee, who is asked to narrate significant episodes of her or his life, with reference to the object of the research, commenting on documents in support of the story, as in the specific case of this research. Ultimately, in the narrative interview, the researcher/interviewer herself experiences being the active party, interacting with the interviewee, not manipulating the content of the interview, but orienting the story towards the object of the research and overcoming the barrier of the external observer. To a certain extent, the resulting narration constitutes the object of a negotiation, of a co-construction of meanings, enriched, modified and interpreted in the exchange of opinions. In line with a clinical approach, the 'client' is not an object of study, but in a certain sense the protagonist-actor of how her/his case is reconstructed. For every client, a history of her/his case has thus been reconstructed.

On the basis of these premises, the interview grid was designed in the form of open questions, adapted every time to the relative themes tackled. This grid functioned as something of a general canvas rather than as a sequence of questions following a strict order. This facilitated personal stories and approaches on the part of the clients. All the formal interviews were recorded and were subjected to transcription.

4.2. Involving clients and other legal actors

The majority of meetings with clients was generated by contacts with attorneys or with managers of offices with clients. After a first contact had been established, several people were approached, who were identified on the basis of the pertinence of their cases to the object of the research, so as to ask them if they would agree to provide their co-ordinates and be contacted by the researcher.

In its turn, the contact with the attorneys – for the cases in the first and second groups – was made possible as a result of private acquaintances deriving from my previous experience as an attorney working in the area of labour law. Meanwhile, the contacts with institutional actors (civil servants and social workers) – for the third and fourth groups – were forged by directly addressing the competent institutions (e.g. the Canton Neuchâtel Department of Justice, during my research stay at the University of Neuchâtel)[39] or voluntary associations (such as Dedalus),[40] explaining the reasons behind the research to them. Whenever possible, attorneys and institutional actors were interviewed, in their turn, about the stories told to them by their clients, so as to hear another version of the story.

The client interviews were conducted in their attorneys' law offices or in public places chosen by the clients. In general, there is only one interview per client, but some individuals were interviewed again, both to complete the information, by compiling dossiers, and when the candidates wanted to be part of the progress made by their cases. Similarly, the interviews with attorneys and with institutional actors were held in their workplaces: law offices, public offices or association headquarters.

4.3. Data analysis: following the narrative evolution of the dispute

On the basis of these data, cases were reconstructed as legal stories (Delgado, 1989; Luban, 2007; Massaro, 1989; Somers, 1994) that leave space for values,

39 http://p3.snf.ch/Project-147287.

40 See Chapter 9 for an explanatory note about this organisation.

for subjective features and for emotions. In the reconstruction of all these cases, although the interview – which contains the client's point of view – is the starting point for detecting the main thread of the story and constructing a narrative plot, it was the official documents that guided me in the chronological reconstruction of the events. The analysis of documents catered for a variety of requirements: it enabled the facts that were narrated to be put into a context and the manner in which the 'reality of the stories' took shape in the documents and in written records to be established. Finally, it enabled the practices of attorneys, judges and administrative agents to be elucidated, together with the representations associated with them.

This kind of reconstruction has a dual purpose: on the one hand, to highlight the interactive mechanism and the narratives at the basis of how law is modelled and, on the other, to illustrate the link between the construction of the law and the historical, cultural and human context in which the case originated.

The link between documents and legal and cultural meanings is very strong, since documents contribute to the construction of social and institutional reality. Sociology and ethnology aim to achieve the result of tracing and objectivising culture, in part by studying documents, which are examined, among other things, in the light of the social context in which the juridical phenomenon to be analysed takes place, and in part by making use of testimonies (collected from surveys, interviews etc.) that humanise field research (Ferraris, 2013; Latour, 1995).[41]

In order to throw light on the different points of view that give rise to a story, multiple perspectives are taken into consideration, according to the cases in question: the perspective of the client, the perspective of the attorney and the perspective of the administration. The aim is to understand how the stories told by the various different actors involved interact and contribute to giving the case its shape.

For the cases of labour law (the first and second groups), the clients were asked to tell their stories, framing it both in the context of their work and in the broader one of their lives. The aim was to understand what meanings could be hidden behind a request for an individual to tender resignation or be transferred to another workplace or to change qualification, for example.

- The stories told in Chapters 4–6 (first group) are analysed as follows: in Chapter 4, I have based my work on the transcription of interviews with the clients, so as to understand how the plot is articulated in their stories and how they perceive and represent what happened. I then analyse written notes addressed by the clients to their attorneys, so as to glean certain aspects of their interaction and the type of initiatives they are capable of taking in order to solve their cases. In Chapter 5, I analyse the story from the point of view of the attorney, using both interviews and dossiers. The aim in this case is to understand how

41 'Documentality' is the thesis expounded by Ferraris (2013), who identifies in the traceability of signs the approach for passing from nature to culture (and from concrete to abstract), culminating in the manifestation of documents as the top-down expression of an institutionally defined social construction.

the representation of the events evolves, how they are transformed from one phase to another of the legal process and how they are translated by the attorney. In Chapter 6, I analyse the decision made by the judge, focusing on the motives that persuade her/him to support the story advanced by one party or the other or to construct a new narration of her/his own.

- In Chapter 7, I move on to analyse the cases in the second group (labour law). Here, the story is proposed as a whole (without dismantling it analytically): it is reconstructed highlighting the setting, the characters, their agentivity and the solutions found by the actors in the context of the social and cultural relations of which they are part. The purpose of the analysis, conducted in a 'law and culture' perspective, is to understand how local cultural practices model how the law is applied and orient how legal actors act to solve the cases.

For the cases of migration law (the third group), I have reconstructed the legal trajectory of the protagonists in the framework of a more extensive story about their life experiences.[42]

- In Chapter 8, the stories describe how foreigners arrived in Switzerland, the procedures they went through to obtain a residence permit and apply for naturalisation and the obstacles they encountered along the way. They also shared their opinions about Switzerland as the country where they live, but also their relationships with the law and its procedures. As in the cases in the first and second groups, with my colleagues, I was able to interview the officials of the administration who were dealing with their cases, acquiring information of use for understanding how a certain view of integration oriented them in their decision about whether or not to grant naturalisation to the clients interviewed.
- Lastly, for the cases in the fourth group (Chapter 9), I have reconstructed their administrative and legal developments, using the official documentation provided by the voluntary associations who dealt with the cases in Italy. In one of these cases (Margaret's case), I had the opportunity to attend the interview conducted by the social workers with the person applying for asylum in Italy. These interviews are functional to reconstructing the route she followed from Nigeria and to demonstrating that the conditions necessary for her status as a refugee to be recognised really exist.

The stories proposed in this book are told anonymously (the names of the people involved, places and dates etc. have all been changed), in the interest of respecting the privacy of the client in question, of the attorneys and of the

42 As I shall explain in Chapter 8, these stories are extrapolated from a more extensive interdisciplinary research project whose purpose was to analyse legal trajectories as segments of the foreigners' life experiences: http://p3.snf.ch/Project-147287.

institutions that treated their cases, although the stories are all publicly defined and real. Some of the pseudonyms used here were chosen to maintain a link with the initial of each individual's name, so as to avoid sacrificing every last trace of the authenticity and uniqueness of the person's story to the requirement for abstraction that is sometimes a feature of such research.

5. Conclusions

Intervening in a debate rooted in American realism and of extreme relevance today, in both Civil Law and Common Law contexts, in this chapter I have sketched out a possible trajectory that combines theory and practice in analysing fact construction.

Starting from some of the mainstream theoretical positions on the topic, I opted to adopt a constructivist and culturalist model of analysis that gives due consideration not only to legal categories, but also to contextual dimensions when reconstructing and qualifying the events. The importance of considering the context will be clear not only when determining whether a client has been the victim of dequalification, mobbing or retaliatory dismissal – as in the cases of labour law (Chapters 4–7), for example – but also when establishing whether there have been any human rights infringements (Chapter 9), considering that the concept of human rights protection is not a given and varies from one context to another.

From a standpoint of the theory of disputing, I have defined the legal process in sociological terms as a dynamic place where the various people taking part in the conflict for different reasons orient its solution from within or from outside. As a result, the other element on which I have focused is the active role played by legal actors – first and foremost the clients – in defining the facts and constructing a theory of the case, partnering with the attorney. How and why do the facts acquire different meanings for different actors? In what contexts? How can these different meanings be harmonised in solving the case? How do they differentiate or come into conflict?

Since the fictional nature of the legal dispute ensures that it is impossible to reconstruct the entire story when reconstructing the facts (some parts are told, other parts are left out and others again remain merely implicit), the narrative interdisciplinary approach that I propose – based on the story told by the actors and on the documents – aims at reconstructing which events have been left out of the official narrative, which meanings are at the root of the story and orient the solution to the case and which emotions and actions orient the protagonists.

The point of view of the client, analysed as the starting point and the key for interpreting the story (Chapter 4), is bolstered by at least two other points of view: that of the attorney (Chapter 5) and that of the judge (Chapter 6). The points of view of other legal actors (i.e. administrative agents, cultural mediator, social workers) will be also taken into account in Chapters 8 and 9.

The legal story that derives from the process of reconstructing some of the voices that give shape to the case, in addition to documentary materials (legal and judicial files, newspapers, journals, images), is the outcome of different narratives in which the case takes shape as the result of a polyphonic discourse about it.

References

Abel, R.L. (1974). A Comparative Theory of Dispute Institutions in Society. *Law & Society Review*. 8(1): 217–347.

Aiken, J. and Shalleck, A. (2016). Putting the "Real World" into Traditional Classroom Teaching. In: Mertz, E., Macaulay, S. and Mitchell, T.W. (Eds.). *The New Legal Realims: Translating Law-and-Society for Today's Legal Practice*. Cambridge, MA: Cambridge University Press. 51–73.

Amsterdam, A.G. (1984). Clinical Legal Education. A 21st Century Perspective. *Clinical Law Review*. 34: 612–619.

Amsterdam, A.G. and Bruner, J.S. (2000). *Minding the Law*. Cambridge, MA: Harvard University Press.

Atkinson, R. (1998). *The Life Story Interview*. Thousand Oaks, CA: Sage Publications.

Aubert, V. (1963). Competition and Dissensus: Two Types of Conflict and of Conflict Resolution. *Journal of Conflict Resolution*. VII(1): 26–42.

Bartoli, C. (2016). Legal clinics in Europe: For a Commitment of Higher Education in Social Justice. *Special Issue of Diritto e Questioni pubbliche*. 1: 1–27.

Bellow, G. and Moulton, B. (1978). *The Lawyering Process: Materials for Clinical Instruction in Advocacy*. Mineola, NY: Foundation Press.

Berger, L. and Stanchi, K.M. (2018). *Legal Persuasion. A Rhetorical Approach to the Science*. London and New York: Routledge.

Block, F.S. (2008). Access to Justice and the Global Clinical Movement. *Washington University Journal of Law & Policy*. 28: 111.

Block, F.S. (Ed.). (2011). *The Global Clinical Movement*. Oxford: Oxford University Press.

Bruner, J.S. (1986). *Acts of Meanings*. Cambridge, MA: Harvard University Press.

Cain, M. (1979). The General Practice of the Lawyer and the Client: Towards a Radical Conception. *International Journal of the Sociology of Law*. 7: 331–354.

Chavkin, D.F. (2003). Spinning Straw into Gold: Exploring the Legacy of Bellow and Moulton. *Clinical Law Review*. 10(1): 245–280.

Chase, O.G. (2006). *Law, Culture and Ritual*. New York and London: New York University Press.

Cover, R. (1983–1984). The Supreme Court, 1982 – Term-Foreword: Nomos and Narrative. *Harvard Law Review*. 97: 4–68.

Daiute, C. (2014). *Narrative Inquiry: A Dynamic Approach*. Thousand Oaks, CA: Sage Publications.

Delgado, R. (1989). Storytelling for Oppositionists and Others: A Plea for Narrative. *Michigan Law Review*. 87(8): 2411–2441.

Di Donato, F. (2008). *La costruzione giudiziaria del fatto. Il ruolo della narrazione nel "processo"*. Milano: Franco Angeli.

Di Donato, F. (2012). *La realtà delle storie. Tracce di una cultura*. Preface by J.S. Bruner. Napoli: Guida.

Di Donato, F. (2014). *Narratives in Cultural Contexts: The Legal Agentivity of the Protagonists*. SSRN Scholarly Paper No. ID 2469436. Rochester, NY: Social Science Research Network. http://papers.ssrn.com/abstract=2469436.

Di Donato, F. (2015). Making in-Justices Visible. The Blindness of Bureaucracy. *Visiocracy, Special Issue of Teoria e critica della regolazione sociale*. 57–77.
Di Donato, F. and Garros, E. (forthcoming). Agir avec la loi: récits et actions. In: Di Donato, F. et al. (Eds.). *La fabrique de l'intégration*.
Di Donato, F. et al. (forthcoming). *La fabrique de l'intégration*.
Dworkin, R. (1986). *Law's Empire*. Cambridge, MA: Harvard University Press.
Duranti, A. (2007). *Etnopragmatica. La forza nel parlare*. Roma: Carocci.
Ellmann, S. et al. (2009). *Lawyers and Clients. Critical Issues in Interviewing and Counseling*. St. Paul, MN: Thomson Reuters, American Casebook Series.
Eule, T. (2014). *Inside Immigration Law*. London and New York: Routledge.
Ewick, P. and Silbey, S. (1998). *The Common Place of Law. Stories from Everyday Life*. Chicago and London: The University of Chicago Press.
Felstiner, W.L.F., Abel, R.L. and Sarat, A. (1980–81). The Emergence and Transformation of Disputes: Naming, Blaming, Claiming. . . . *Law and Society Review*. 15(3–4): 631–654.
Ferrari, V. (1987). *Funzioni del diritto. Saggio critico-ricostruttivo*. Roma-Bari: Laterza.
Ferrari, V. (1993). Teorie e metodo nell'analisi sociologica della litigiosità. In: Galgano, F. and Bin, M. (Eds.). *Contratto e Impresa*. Padova: Cedam. 1, 342–354.
Ferrari, V. (2004). *Diritto e società. Elementi di sociologia del diritto*. Roma-Bari: Laterza.
Ferrari, V. *Quelques raisons du relativisme juridique*. Manuscript on file with the author.
Ferraris, M. (2012). *Manifesto del Nuovo Realismo*. Roma-Bari: Laterza.
Ferraris, M. (2013). *Documentality*. New York: Fordham University Press.
Frank, J. (1930). *Law and the Modern Mind*. New Brunswick and London: Transaction Publishers.
Frank, J. (1947). A Plea for Lawyer-Schools. *Yale Law Journal*. 56(8): 1303–1344.
Frank, J. (1948). Say It with Music. *Harvard Law Review*. 61: 921–957.
Frank, J. (1949). *Courts on Trial*. Princeton, NJ: Princeton University Press.
Haack, S. (2012). The Embedded Epistemologist. Dispatches from the Legal Front. *Ratio Iuris*. 25: 206–235.
Jackson, B. (1988). *Law, Fact and Narrative Coherence*. Merseyside: Deborah Charles Publications.
Jubany, O. (2017). *Screening Asylum in a Culture of Disbelief*. Cham: Springer.
Latour, B. (1995). The Pedofil of Boa Vista. A Photo-Philosophical Montage. *Common Knowledge*. 3: 147–187.
Levi, J.N. and Walker, A.G. (1990). *Language in the Judicial Process* New York: Springer.
Luban, D. (2007). *Legal Ethics and Human Dignity*. Cambridge: Cambridge University Press.
MacCormick, N. (1984). *Legal Reasoning and Legal Theory*. Oxford: Clarendon Press.
Mantovani, G. and Spagnolli, A. (Eds.). (2003). *Metodi qualitativi in psicologia*. Bologna: Il Mulino.
Massaro, T. (1989). Empathy Legal Storytelling, and the Rule of Law: New Words, Old Wounds? *The Michigan Law Review*. 87: 2099–2127.
Mather, L. and Yngvesson, B. (1980–81). Language, Audience, and the Transformation of Disputes. *Law & Society Review*. 15(3–4): 775–821.
Miller, B. (1994). Give Them Back Their Lives: Recognizing Client Narrative in Case Theory. *Michigan Law Review*. 93(3): 485–576.

Milstein, E. *Clinical Education, Indeterminacy and the Reform of the Law School Curriculum.* Manuscript on file with the author.

Minda, G. (1995). *Postmodern Legal Movements. Law and Jurisprudence at Centuries' End.* New York and London: New York University Press.

Murray, P (1995). *Basic Trial Advocacy.* Portland: Maine Law Book Company.

O' Reilly, K. (2005). *Ethnographic Methods.* London and New York: Routledge.

Paul, J. (1959). *The Legal Realism of Jerome N. Frank. A Study of Fact-Skepticism and the Judicial Process.* Herausgeber: Green, Leon.

Perelman, C. and Olbrechts-Tyteca, L. (1969). *The New Rhetoric: A Treatise on Argumentation.* (Engl. Trans.). London: University of Notre Dame Press.

Perret-Clermont, A.-N. (2001). Psychologie sociale de la construction de l'espace de pensée. In: Ducret, J-J. (Ed.). *Actes du colloque. Constructivisme: usages et perspectives en éducation.* Genève: Département de l'Instruction Publique. Service de la Recherche en Education. 65–82. Vol. I.

Richardson, B. (2008). Causality. In: Herman, D., Jahn, M. and Ryan, M-L. (Eds.). *Routledge Encyclopedia of Narrative Theory.* London and New York: Routledge. 48–52.

Samuel, G. (2016). *Epistemology and Method in Law.* London and New York: Routledge.

Schauer, F. (2006). *Profiles, Probabilities, and Stereotypes.* Cambridge, MA: Harvard University Press.

Shalleck, A. (2015). *Toward a Jurisprudence of Clinical Thought: Investigating the Contours, Urges and Trajectories.* Manuscript on file with the author.

Sheppele, K.L. (1988–1989). Legal Storytelling. *Michigan Law Review.* 87(8): 2073–2098.

Sherwin, R.K. (1994). The Narrative Construction of Legal Reality. *Vermont Law Review.* 18(681).

Somers, M.R. (1994). The Narrative Constitution of Identity: A Relational and Network Approach. *Theory and Society.* 23(5): 605–649.

Taruffo, M. (2006). *Judicial Narratives.* Manuscript on file with the author.

Taruffo, M. (2009). *La semplice verità. Il giudice e la costruzione dei fatti.* Roma-Bari: Laterza.

Thomas, K.A. (2008). Sentencing: Where Case Theory and the Client Meet. *Clinical Law Review.* 1(15): 187–210.

Tigar, M.E. (1999). *Persuasion: The Litigator's Art.* Chicago: American Bar Association.

Tuzet, G. (2013). *Filosofia della prova giuridica.* Torino: Giappichelli.

Twining, W. ([1990, 1994,], 2006). *Rethinking Evidence. Exploratory Essays.* Cambridge, MA: Cambridge University Press.

Ubertis, G. (2018). Dialettica probatoria e terzietà del giudice. *Ars Interpretandi. Special Issue on Ermeneutica e diritto processuale.* 23(1): 57–70.

Weissbrod, D. and McCarthy, J. (1981–1982). Fact-Finding by International Nongovernmental Human Rights Organizations. *Virginia Journal of International Law.* 22(1): http://scholarship.law.umn.edu/faculty_articles/281. (Website consulted on 12.09.2018).

Wilson, R. (2017). *The Global Evolution of Clinical Legal Education More Than a Method.* Cambridge, MA: Cambridge University Press.

Part II

Trajectories of case analysis

4 Rediscovering the role of the client

Citing several pioneering works in the field of the client-lawyer relationship, this chapter describes the role played by the client in solving the case, reconstructing three cases situated in the area of labour law. Taking its starting point from the story told by the clients – Laura, Luciano and Franco – it offers three types of analysis. The first is a plot analysis, whose purpose is to identify the story's contents and determine the extent to which they can be considered to be typical or recurrent also in other stories. The same story is then re-analysed, so as to understand how the client perceives the events (names, blames, claims) that give rise to the case and how everyday occurrences gradually come to take on the form of legal stories. Lastly, in a theoretical framework that considers the evolutions in client-lawyer relationships, which are framed more in terms of collaboration than of asymmetries, the analysis stresses the initiatives taken by the client in the reconstruction of the facts and in developing strategies agreed upon with the lawyer to resolve the case, particularly during the phase that precedes the legal dispute.

1. The client-lawyer relationship in recent works

Having examined the possible structure of the dispute and identified the formal as well as the informal roles that the parties may play in it (Chapter 3), the next step is to analyse clients' stories and to sketch out some profiles of interaction between lawyer and clients in fact construction.

From the perspective of clinical legal education, giving space to the client's story ideally means making that client into a participant in possible social change, as an individual or as a member of a community. Thus, by sharing a "rebellious vision" of clinical legal education – promoted, among others, by three leading contributors and pioneers, Gerald López (1992; 1996; 2004; 2005; 2009; 2017), Lucie White (1987–1988) and Anthony Alfieri (Alfieri, 1987–1988) – I support the idea of recentralising clients' stories to enhance their "power to act independently and collectively upon the laws and legal institutions", by restoring the integrity of their voices and stories in legal settings (Alfieri, 1990–1991, p. 2146). To this end, I engage with clients' stories, considering them as the vehicle through which otherwise silenced voices may be heard (Bandes, 1996;

Brooks and Geewirtz, 1998; Delgado, 1989), and highlighting some profiles of their participation in the legal process.

Before moving on to the analysis of clients' real stories (par. 2) and then to certain aspects of the client-attorney interaction in constructing the case (par. 4.2), I call attention once again to part of the literature that highlights how the study of this relationship evolves over time (Scamardella and Di Donato, 2012). In contrast to the traditional 'lawyering-centered' approach, which assigns a passive and 'invisible' role to clients and to their stories (Alfieri, 1990–1991), the client/lawyer-centred approach promotes the client's autonomy, based on the idea that the client is in a better position than that of the lawyer to evaluate alternatives and consequences (Ellmann et al., 2009). According to this view, clients are actively involved in the choice of which story to tell and in the development of a "case theory" that links the legal case to their personal story (Miller, 1994). In fact, the late 1980s and early 1990s saw the emergence of an extensive literature highlighting the importance of a more egalitarian collaboration between attorneys and (lower-income) clients. In this context, the client becomes important to understanding the law and the case, starting from the specific experience of which (s)he is the bearer, as an individual or as a member of a group or institution (Shalleck, 2015). The new model's primary concern is to ensure that clients play the central role not only in setting ultimate objectives and offering details of their experiences, but also in making important decisions (Zulack, 1994–1995).

From the perspective of "rebellious lawyering", López, White and Alfieri – whom I referenced previously – promote a vision exhorting lawyers to involve clients directly in individual and collective efforts to speak and act against their own oppression (Piomelli, 2016). Manifesting concerns about a litigation-centred model that tends to reinforce clients' feelings of powerlessness and to reinforce the dominant position of lawyers – a dynamic that often impedes social change – these scholars challenge the client's traditional subordination with the novel antidote of the model of the client's autonomy (Cummings and Eagly, 2001). In particular, while López (2004) argues that lawyers, clients and other community members should work together in a non-hierarchical relationship to challenge the existing system of power, taking the local, sociocultural context of the lawyering process into account, White (1994–1995; 1997) looks for the "ideal context" to facilitate a conversational process between lawyers and clients, and to empower clients to articulate their own lives and to transform themselves into more potent political actors. In turn, Alfieri stresses the potential of (poor) clients' stories as a means of social change, despite lawyers' "attitude to silence clients' voices" and representations (1990–1991). He highlights how lower-income and subordinated people are not completely powerless or helpless. In his view, clients possess skills and knowledge that enable them to recount "alternative stories", resisting the dominant elites' views in society. As such, he urges that attorneys should not simply work for clients, but with clients as lay allies (ibid; 2016).

In these scholars' views, lawyering, construed here as the task of problem-solving, risks being abstract or generic, disconnected from context and "denying who we are" (López, 1992). Thus López, in particular, proposes a more collaborative and community-engaged approach to problem-solving. To shape client roles and lawyer-client and client-community relationships, he urges "multiple, experimental forms of lawyer, client and community collaboration, inclusion, intervention enforcement, evaluation and innovation" (Alfieri, 2016, pp. 14–15).[1] In Alfieri's comment, these experimental forms include "(1) collaboration with individual, group and community clients; (2) inclusion of diverse client perspectives in framing and resolving problems; (3) encouragement of client-generated alternative approaches to community intervention and problem-solving; (4) community-erected monitoring and enforcement strategies; (5) joint client-lawyer outcome measurement and impact evaluation, and (6) innovative organisational management and delivery system design" (ibid., p. 15).

In synthesis, Lopez's rebellious lawyering reconceives the standard subject-object roles and hierarchical dominant-subordinate relationships of client-centred lawyering. The client is neither a powerful subordinate 'object' controlled by the disciplining discourse and view of a dominant lawyer, nor a sovereign 'subject' controlling the means and ends of a purely instrumental lawyer agent. Instead, in this alternative conception, clients are complex, multidimensional and ever-changing, inhabiting a range of subject-object roles and negotiating a variety of dominant-subordinate relationships, while situated in local networks of family, school, work, religion and community.

Behind the translatability of those ideals in practice, the client-centred vision does not escape criticism. As Rubinson argues (1999), clients' capacity to participate in the solution of the case should be the result of a co-operative and constructive relationship between lawyer and client. Contemporary scholars thus prefer to speak of client-lawyer relationships, wherein both parties co-operate in the case according to their specific competences (Ellmann et al., 2009, pp. 139–140).

The analyses that follow in this chapter and those that follow (Chapters 7, 8 and 9) confirm that, under certain conditions, the client is found to be capable of taking initiatives in solving the case, either independently or in partnership with the attorney. (S)he can be an active agent in many aspects of the lawyering process: from asking questions about how the case fits into the framework of a given legal field to making decisions and executing strategies in partnership with the attorney.

2. Telling stories from the client's perspective

In the paragraphs that follow, I shall analyse three stories in the area of labour law: those of Laura, Luciano and Franco. Franco's story will only be analysed in part. It will be reconstructed primarily because of its characteristic initiatives

1 One fertile field for client partnership is, for example, the area of proposing policies for integrating foreigners, where the client can make a contribution of information, as well as following information. Daiute et al. (2017) offer the example of the Roma community: as a result of the intervention of pedagogical assistants, this community has taken part in education reform activities in the former Yugoslavia, providing mediation between its own positions and those of society.

(par. 4.1.4). Laura's and Luciano's stories, on the other hand, will be subjected to three kinds of analysis.

The first of these to be studied is the human and social background of the story, which is collected by means of a post-factum interview with the client, then analysed for the purpose of verifying whether there is a plot that could be considered to be somehow 'typical' of the stories proposed (par. 2.1.). Then this same story is analysed again, to investigate how the client perceives for her/himself the narrative of how the 'trouble' came about that then developed into the conflict with the other party, then conveys this narrative to the attorney (par. 3). For this purpose, I make use of the sociological categories of "naming, blaming and claiming" (Felstiner et al., 1980–1981) to analyse the state of the conflict's evolution, from what I can call the preliminary phases (naming and blaming), which concern how client interacts with the counterpart, as well as, to a certain extent, with the attorney, to phases when the conflict has become public (claiming) and has acquired the characteristics of the dispute. The aim is to discover how the story was first described by the client and to study and identify the phases through which a human story evolves into a legal story. Lastly, I analyse both the interviews and the notes written by the client about the case, as well as all the correspondence between the client and the attorney (par. 4). The aim here is to detect elements that are more strictly relevant to the client-attorney interaction and to examine the 'initiatives' taken, so as to verify the kind of engagement in the client's narrative construction of the case.

For this purpose, I shall expand on the theoretical framework of the client-lawyer relationship (reconstructed previously) by reviewing some socio-psychological positions about symmetries or asymmetries in terms of power and the distribution of space. I shall then use case analysis to show how clients' participation in solving their cases depends on complex dynamics and factors, such as the cultural background of the clients and their professions (Di Donato and Garros, forthcoming), for example.

In Chapter 5, the same stories will then be constructed in the perspective of the lawyer and on the basis of the legal files, in order to compare the two stories: the one of the client and the other of the lawyer. Plot analysis will follow the same criteria and the same structure in both chapters.

2.1. Plot analysis

To analyse the interview with the client, I propose a plot analysis. The plot is one of the most difficult elements of the narration to identify. As we saw in Chapter 1 (par. 6), some definitions found in literature focus on the temporal sequence, others on the cast of characters and on actions, others again on the dynamic interaction between the various elements of the narration. The plot contains the structure of the narration and provides us with the lens for reading a story, helping us understand its implicit meanings. It is functional to the creation of causal and temporal connections between different events and to giving significance to the actions, the characteristics of and the roles played by the different characters.

This also applies in the case of legal stories: litigants' stories are plot-driven and protagonist-centred and are written to justify a predetermined or desired outcome (Meyer, 2014, p. 9). This is confirmed at a more general level by Daiute, who points out that "without always being aware, narrators know which stories are worth sharing, which details to include, how to organise details to capture the attention of the audiences, and which stories are gripping or fun rather than boring" (2014, p. 114).

Thus, following Amsterdam and Bruner's approach as well as Daiute's illustrations of the plot, I use the definition of story explained in Chapter 1 (par. 5) to identify the basic structure of a narrative, answering questions about the 'what', 'where' and 'when', 'who' and 'why' relative to a story's content in terms of the legal process and allowing for comparison and consideration of how clients use the plot.

2.2. *Laura's and Luciano's stories*

Laura's and Luciano's stories are used as paradigmatic stories of fact construction. The two summaries that precede the plot analysis reiterate the gist of the legal story, while also anticipating its epilogue. While they are based on the interview with the client, they also consider the legal file and the point of view of the attorney, which is reconstructed in greater detail in the following chapter. The data acquisition method used (e.g. interviews, and the reconstruction of legal files) was illustrated in Chapter 3. It should be pointed out, moreover, that the norms mentioned in relation to the cases quoted here and as follows are always those that were in force at the time when the dispute in question was being tackled.

2.2.1. *Laura's story: 'from project leader to stop-gap'*

Laura is a white-collar worker whose job description designates her as a 'project leader', working in a multinational corporation with offices in several countries, including cities in Italy. After Laura has been working happily at her job for several years, the company's management is reorganised and she finds herself having to tackle a series of changes in the company's structure. Her new boss refuses to accord her a higher job description that she believes she has come to deserve as a result of years of training and experience with the firm. At the same time, Laura is obliged to ask for several days' leave so that she can undergo a cycle of therapeutic treatments against infertility. The management interprets her absences as a reduction in her working efficiency, culminating in an invitation to Laura to tender her resignation. Laura refuses this invitation to resign and takes the issue to her lawyer, who first advises her to negotiate privately with her employer, then steps into the case directly.

The first step that the attorney takes is to caution Laura's employers against continuing to hold her client in a state of inactivity, inviting them to acknowledge the higher professional qualification she has developed. At a later stage, after the company has taken the step of assigning Laura to a position of responsibility that involves moving to another city, the attorney applies for an injunction, of the kind regulated by Art. 700 of the Italian Code of Civil Procedure,[2] asking for the transfer to be blocked.[3] The attorney considers the decision to be 'illegitimate' because of a lack of motive or because the motives cited are unreasonable, in accordance with Art. 2103 of the Civil Code. According to the attorney, there are no reasons why Laura should be transferred to another city. He also believes that the company's behaviour is 'retaliatory' and a consequence of the employee's request for leave. Speaking through its own attorney, the company defends its action, declaring that the contested provision is not a 'transfer', but a temporary 'assignment' in another city. The judge rules against Laura, refusing to accord recognition to the need for urgency (which had been justified by the *fumus boni iuris*, or likelihood of success on the merits of the case, and the *periculum in mora*, or the danger implicit in a delay) necessary for a precautionary ruling. The judge thus accepts the thesis advanced by the company, ruling that the 'assignment' is "contemplated as a normal hypothesis in the contract of employment".

In the subsequent appeal lodged by virtue of Art. 669.13 of the Italian Code of Civil Procedure,[4] Laura's attorney complains that her client has been allotted the formal description of project leader, but is in fact assigned to tasks of a lower standing, which thus breaches the obligations deriving both from the contract of employment and from the principles of "fairness" and "good faith" enshrined in Art. 2103 and Art. 2087 of the Civil Code.[5] The company's attorney then tries to deny that Laura has been assigned to tasks inferior to those for which she had been employed, even going so far as to complain about her presumed "negligence" in executing previous projects. Nevertheless, just before the appeal is due to be heard, the company's legal representative suggests to Laura that they might have recourse to a 'transaction', instead of taking the issue before the judge for a

2 Art. 700 of the Italian Code of Civil Procedure reads: "Conditions for concession. Outside the area of cases regulated in the previous sections to this heading, anyone who has a well-founded reason for fearing that, during the time necessary for her/his right to be invoked in ordinary proceedings, that right is threatened by an imminent and irreparable prejudice, may apply to the judge for an injunction (Art. 669.3, 669.4, 669.5) that, according to the circumstances, appears to be the most suitable for temporarily ensuring the effects of the decision on the substance."

3 Cf. Art. 2103 of the Italian Civil Code: "Job performance. The employee shall be designated to the tasks for which (s)he was employed or to those corresponding to the superior category that (s)he shall have attained subsequently. i.e. to tasks equivalent to the latest actually executed, without any reduction in salary." Deliberating about this, the Italian Court of Cassation (Labour Section, Decision N° 1530 in 1998) has clarified that "the employer has the obligation not only of not assigning him to inferior tasks (Art. 2103 Civil Code), but also of not keeping him in enforced inactivity without assigning any concrete functions to him, as work constitutes a means not only of earning a living, but also of manifesting her/his personality."

4 Art. 669.13 "Appeal against precautionary provisions. A party may lodge an appeal against the ruling whereby a precautionary provision has been made before the beginning or in the course of the discussion of the substance of the case, in the terms provided for in Art. 739, section 2."

5 Art. 2087 of the Italian Civil Code reads: "Safeguarding working conditions. The employer shall adopt such measures in the exercise of her/his enterprise as are necessary, in accordance with the particular nature of the work, experience and technique, to safeguard the physical integrity and moral personality of her/his employees (Art. 37 Constitution)."

decision, trebling the economic offer that had initially accompanied the proposal to Laura to tender her voluntary resignation. Laura accepts the proposal.

Then, from the point of view of the evolution of the 'conflict', after a first phase of internal negotiations, which are first managed autonomously, then with the aid of an attorney, Laura's story evolves into a legal case, leading to public proceedings, in the form first of a hearing in accordance with Art. 700 of the Italian Code of Civil Procedure, then of a subsequent appeal. The initial conflict is thus transformed into a 'dispute', before reverting once again to the status of a mere 'conflict', as a consequence of the transaction proposed by the company and accepted by Laura.

In the following paragraph, Laura's personal narration is pieced together on the basis of the definition of 'story' identified previously (Chapter 1, par. 5).

2.2.2. Conducting plot analysis

In an initial state that can be defined as legitimate, because of a regular working relationship whereby Laura works as a 'project leader' in a multinational company, with an excellent annual budget, a series of benefits (such as the use of a company car) and public acknowledgement, a case of 'trouble' comes about. A change in the company's management ends up progressively derailing the relationship of trust between Laura and the company. The trouble takes the form of tension between the company management (the 'agent') and Laura (the 'recipient') culminating in an invitation to Laura to tender her voluntary resignation. The conflict develops in particular between Laura's intention to safeguard both her professional status (hence her request for recognition in her current role or a superior one) and her personal status (hence her request, for example, for several days' leave for medical attention), and the company's implied intention to free itself of its employee. The erosion of a relationship of trust between the firm and its employee evolves into a gradual deprivation of functions or dequalification[6] and the consequent development of a company strategy (the 'action') that aims (the 'purpose') at excluding Laura from the firm (the 'setting'), first in the form of an invitation to tender her resignation, then in the request to her to transfer to another city. It is this particular interaction between the elements of the Pentad (in particular, between the divergent aims of Laura and the company) that determines the breach of an initial stable condition, causing the 'trouble' to come about.

I. *An initial steady state grounded in the legitimate ordinariness of things*: **"I have been working at XAS since 1997**. In the first two years, I worked

6 The term 'dequalification', like that of mobbing, which occurs immediately afterwards, refers to a strictly Italian context. 'Dequalification' is defined as the downgrading of a worker to responsibilities that are lower in the working hierarchy than the ones for which (s)he was previously employed, unless the law makes allowance for this.

with a continuous collaboration contract, so I was a freelancer, then I was taken on by 2000 as an employee. **Until 2003, everything went very well**".

II. *That gets disrupted by a trouble – the initiating action that marks the break with the steady state – attributable to human agency or susceptible to change by human intervention:*

a. Initiating action:

More or less suddenly, when my immediate boss was changed, there was a complete reorganisation [. . .]. From that moment on, let's say that **I started having my first problems at work** [. . .] **Before that, I was a project leader** [. . .]**. Then suddenly I found myself doing that and also working as something of a stop-gap;** in other words I was doing practically any task that needed to be done by somebody [. . .].

III. *In turn evoking efforts at redress or transformation, which succeed or fail, in the form of complicating actions that rise to a high point (climax, conflict or turning point)*:

b. Complicating action:

After that, I started being assigned to projects but, let's put it this way, only on paper [. . .]. In addition to being put under pressure with a form of horizontal mobbing,[7] **I suffered by being deprived of my functions.** [. . .] **"Obviously we are offering you a sum, an incentive handshake of € X0,000 gross' – they told me one day – so, if you sign, you can feel free already as of tomorrow not to come into the office any more, actually from today**: if you like, you can leave your desk, **that's not your desk any more**. If you like, you are quite free to go home, in fact, **we'd prefer it that way, because we'd like this to stay between us, we wouldn't want you to talk about it with anyone else"**.

c. High point/turning point:

When I talked about this with my attorney, we decided that the first thing to do was to rid ourselves completely of this invitation to tender my resignation [. . .]. **We decided to send this e-mail, in which I said officially to the personnel manager and the managing director that I had been underused for two years**, that

7 According to a definition framed in Article 6 of the national collective employment contract for Italian civil servants dated 28 February 2003, mobbing is defined as "moral or psychological violence on the occasion of work, practised by the employer or by other employees and characterised by acts, attitudes or behaviour that are repeated over time with aggressive, disparaging or vexatious connotations".

I had brought this to the notice of my immediate superiors and that nothing had changed.

d. Resolution strategies:

At this stage, we had recourse to Art. 700 of the Code of Civil Procedure to challenge what we called the transfer to Milan, because there were no real reasons why I of all people should go to Milan (that city is covered by my colleagues from the head office in Milan, among other things for a question of costs; in addition, it was far from clear what functional role I was to be given, or in actual fact it seemed to be little more than the role of a secretary!). **We described all this as a relationship of cause and effect like this: I ask for some days off for medical treatment and they suggest I resign.** [. . .] **We revealed all this as a series of retaliations that the company always put up against any request of mine, so one of these was this proposal of a transfer** [. . .] at this stage, after the ruling against me, we decided to lodge an appeal.

IV. *So that the old steady state is restored or a new (transformed) steady state is created:*[8]

this strategy proved to be a winner, because in the end they were afraid that the appeal would go against them and it was then that they came out into the open **and offered to negotiate so that the whole business could be closed** . . .

V. *And the story concludes by drawing the then-and-there of the tale that has been told into the here-and-now of the telling through some coda – say, for example, Aesop's characteristic moral of the story:*

I am so relieved . . . all I should have said was said . . . **the documents show that I did not rush to sign the first thing they put in front of me, but I tried to react and put them on the spot**. That's what gives me the greatest sense of achievement . . . anyway, ***I managed it***, because that agreement would never have been made if we had not gone through the whole process together with my lawyer.

(these passages are taken from the interview with Laura, July 2006)

An analysis of Laura's story, reconstructed on the basis of the interview, highlights the narrative tension that generates a conflict between the parties, i.e. the company and its employee. This tension derives from the fact that they have opposing purposes that fail to be achieved because of the obstacles set in their path by one side or the other: wanting to get rid of Laura, the firm suggests that

8 This often takes several steps in naturalistic stories, so Daiute (2014) refers to them as 'resolution strategies'.

she sign a false letter of resignation. When she refuses, it then orders her transfer to another town. Realising that this behaviour is illicit, Laura goes to an attorney and together they piece together a strategy designed to enable her to unmask the company's intentions.

The analysis of the plot in Laura's narration enables us to understand that the story's high point was when Laura shaped the strategy to be followed in concert with her attorney: "we decided that the first thing to do was to rid ourselves completely of this invitation to tender my resignation". It is this passage that turns the narrative authoritatively, by means of an interplay of actions and reactions agreed with the attorney and carried out to a great extent by Laura herself. The use of the pronoun "we" tells us that we are witnessing an example of collaborative lawyering and of narrative construction in the client-attorney relationship.

The moral of the story is then summarised in the following statement (see excerpt provided): "I managed it!"

2.2.3. Luciano's story: 'a prisoner in a gilded cell'

Luciano, a top-level executive in a local bank, is invited to take over responsibility for a service company that the bank is about to establish. The future company will have less than fifteen employees and its establishment is part of a commercial expansion strategy declared by the bank. What actually happens is that, within a few months after Luciano has left his position as an executive with the bank to start working as managing director of the new company, the bank's project is altered, depriving Luciano's role of all its functions and making it impossible for the now ex-executive to negotiate a transfer back to the bank where he had worked until then. The result is a human drama generated by the erosion of Luciano's relationship of trust with his employer, by the dequalification of his role and by his progressive inactivity. In order to preserve his dignity as a person, Luciano decides to tender his resignation. He goes to a lawyer, who can only help him lay claim to a contractual restoration (the recognition of the position he held in the bank before being transferred, also with retroactive effect) and to lodge a request for damages.

From the point of view of the legal qualification of the 'facts', the attorney argues that the service company where Luciano is employed is actually fictitious in nature and that the employment relationship between Luciano and that company is in reality null and void, since it is really attributable to the bank. There is thus a joint liability between the bank and the service company, consequent upon the illegitimate revocation of Luciano's mandate as managing director, which is reflected in an obligation to make good his damages, pay the difference in his salary etc.[9]

9 Essentially, Luciano's attorney considers that this case can be classified under the heading of 'fictitious intermediation', which is prohibited by Art. 1 of Italian Law N° 1369/60. Section 1

In its defence, the bank justifies the unilateral modification of Luciano's contractual conditions, including the revocation of his position as managing director, with the statement that Luciano's position was not one that had been defined contractually, but a "delegation of functions" practised by the bank's own Board of Directors. It then also calls on the thesis of the exercise of the employer's discretion to justify the change in the company's structure following what it describes as a period of crisis. The judge of first instance rules against Luciano, finding that the bank is justified in the decisions it has made with respect to its employee and accepting that the hypothesis of the company crisis is sufficient to explain the change in the very nature of the service company's activities.

From a point of view of the evolution of the proceedings, this is another case of a public conflict, one whose characteristics are those of a dispute with a triadic structure. Unlike the first story, the expectation in the normative sense of the term, which gives rise to the judicial conflict, only takes place after the working relationship has been terminated.

2.2.4. *Conducting plot analysis*

Acting in a 'legitimate initial condition' (Luciano's professional position – that of an executive – is defined by contract), the bank (the 'agent') applies a commercial strategy that leads it to outsource (to an 'agency') the figure of the employee (the 'recipient'). The 'purpose', according to what Luciano declares in his interview, is to isolate him as a person, since he probably no longer caters for the bank's requirements, by moving him to an external company (the 'setting'). The conflict between the bank and its employee comes about as a result of the collision between Luciano's telos, or objective, i.e. to achieve the professional position for which he was employed, and the obstacles set in his way by the bank, leading up to the point when he is forced to tender his resignation.

I. *An initial steady state grounded in the legitimate ordinariness of things*:

> I was a top-level executive with the X bank. At that time, the bank was organised as a credit group, so had two instrumental service companies towards which at a certain point in time I was transferred as managing director.

of this article (the law was repealed by Art. 85, s. 1, ss. c of Italian Legislative Decree N° 276, dated 10 September 2003), prohibits entrusting to a contract, a subcontract or any other form, including that of a co-operative, the execution of the mere performance of work by means of using labour employed and paid by the contractor or by the intermediary, whatever the nature of the function or the service to which the performance refers.

II. *That gets disrupted by a trouble – the initiating action that marks the break with the steady state – attributable to human agency or susceptible to change by human intervention*:

a. Initiating action:

In practice, the nature of this project was suddenly altered after my transfer: **what emerged was more of a company strategy to isolate me as a person and my position outside the bank, imprisoning me in the gilded cage** that was this company with three or four employees.

III. *In turn evoking efforts at redress or transformation, which succeed or fail – under the form of complicating actions that rise to a high point (climax, conflict or turning point)*:

b. Complicating action:

So within a short while – I don't know all the motives underlying the other party's moves – **I found myself with a transfer, in a position that made it impossible for me to renegotiate it after six months and with my powers eroded after two months. So everything that had been agreed to achieve a strong, interested corporate business strategy**, which this service company was supposed to develop, **was immediately drained of all content because the bank had lost all interest. My contractual position was tampered with unilaterally so that, since the bank had concluded a personal contract** with me for my position, **it believed it could alter that contract, downscaling it, introducing economic changes and also inserting other contractual elements**.

c. High point/turning point:

It was from that point that the motivations for my resignation also started, because I tried to get back into the bank on several occasions, but it was never possible.

As I did not want to downgrade my professionalism, I started considering, however unwillingly, the idea of taking early retirement.

d. Resolution strategies:

The result of the case was quite a surprise for everyone: for me, for my attorney and maybe also for the other party's attorney [. . .]. **Although I still hold to what is called the 'free conviction of the judge' [. . .] I believe that the judge was superficial . . . I think he distorted the nature of the professional, human, political and trade union element, imagining that I was trying to instrumentalise it**. [. . .] also because I did not leave the bank to earn more, but I actually earned less by leaving the bank, **so from**

that standpoint the judge decided not to give any weight to the psychological and human drama [. . .]. **I believe that the judge brought a mental prejudice to my case**, because the result of his motivations tells me as much: he did not deny the facts, but he did deny the conclusions.

IV. *So that the old steady state is restored or a new (transformed) steady state is created:*[10]

e. Resolution ending:

My case was described as one that would be difficult: if we were to hope that the judge would reach a valid, positive ruling in my favour about the contractual injustice suffered over the period, the professional isolation I suffered had to be described very well to him, as well as the union discrimination and the absence of safeguards, which in practice.[11]

The result of the court of first instance did not recognise as relevant the bank's practice of isolating the client.

V. *And the story concludes by drawing the then-and-there of the tale that has been told into the here-and-now of the telling through some coda – say, for example, Aesop's characteristic moral of the story:*

I hope that greater justice can be done. I am confident [. . .]. I am optimistic, because I know that the work we have done so far has been done very well . . . so what I hope is this: that everything that has been done can be re-examined with calm judgement by someone who is without prejudice **[. . .]**. ***What I hope is that I will find a judge who will read the papers carefully and not with a prejudice that is, shall we say, of a cultural order.***

(these passages are taken from the interview with Luciano, May 2006)

Luciano's story has some similarities with Laura's, since what is concealed behind the proposal made by the bank to entrust the management of a new company to its employee was in fact the intention to remove him from his functions. Nevertheless, since the bank's action was taken in a situation of apparent legitimacy, it was hard for Luciano, unlike for Laura, to perceive immediately that he was the victim of injustice, so to draw up suitable strategies for avoiding

10 This often takes several steps in naturalistic stories, so Daiute (2014, p. 115) refers to them as 'resolution strategies'.

11 Translator's note: The protection accorded to employees by employment legislation in Italy is significantly weaker when the individual is employed in a firm with fewer than fifteen employees.

the almost irreparable damage consequent on the situation. What we have here, however, is not real problem-solving strategies agreed with the attorney, as in Laura's case. Luciano tendered his resignation on his own initiative before he spoke to a lawyer.

The analysis of the plot as recounted by Luciano enables us to get a closer understanding of the client's decision-making process and how the story progresses from normal life to the legal trouble. The high point is found in this passage: "It was from that point that the motivations for my resignation also started, because I tried to get back into the bank on several occasions, but it was never possible". As in Laura's case, on the one hand we can observe the process of the client's gradual realisation that there was a strategy behind the employer's actions that called for legal defence. On the other, we watch as the story's construction and resolution progresses through gradual stages, building on complications, then turns inevitably into a court action. Once the legal action had started, the judge was in a position to detect only some of the breaches suffered by Luciano, nor did he prove to be capable of going any further than a literal narration in his interpretation of what happened. The result is that this seems to be the moral of this story: "What I hope is that I will find a judge who will read the papers carefully and not with a prejudice that is, shall we say, of a cultural order" (Luciano, May 2006).

2.3. *The first kind of analysis: conclusions*

The application of the definition of narration drawn up by Amsterdam and Bruner (2000) as well as by Daiute (2014) to the reading of the facts as narrated by the clients – in particular Laura and Luciano – made it possible to verify that narrations can certainly also be interpreted in the light of a common plot that is articulated in legal terms with at least five elements. Each time, the narration starts out when an imbalance or tension takes place among the differently articulated elements of the *Pentad* (agent, action, recipient, setting, purpose), because of the occurrence of what is known as a 'trouble', that generates the narration containing the facts.

As emerged from a reading of the clients' stories, what determines a trouble's origins is something that breaches an original condition of legitimacy shared by the clients participating in the issue. The first element to be determined with regard to the birth of a 'legal story', then, is that the original condition was indeed 'legitimate': a contract, an agreement between the bank and the employee etc.

The definition of the 'trouble' in legal terms proceeds in step with the identification of the relevant norm, not only to establish what the problem is all about, but also to understand how to solve it. Starting from a norm or from conditions that are legitimate in the broad sense of the term, and taking the specific circumstances of the case into account, the existence of a 'trouble' may be determined thus: for a trouble to come about, there has to be a breach of the norm in question. This means that the norm acts as a criterion of selection with respect to the trouble, consistent with the operation of legal qualification. The focus of the clients' story orbits around the attempt to identify and define this trouble: what does it consist of? How did it come about? To whom can it be attributed? Does it correspond to a breach of a norm, or not?

3. Naming, blaming, claiming the trouble: the client-attorney relationship compared to the doctor-patient relationship

Returning to the examination of the interviews with the clients about the two stories examined, the next step is to verify how the client names, blames and claims the trouble and to what extent her/his representation changes as a result of having recourse to an attorney.

The analysis of the plot of Laura's and Luciano's narratives shows that the central focus of the legal construction of the client's story orbits around the attempt to define the 'trouble' that gave rise to the story in the first place. By espousing the hypothesis that the way that 'trouble' is represented in the evolutionary stages of dispute may be completely or partly different within the relationship with the attorney (and the judge), a second kind of analysis of the client's role is therefore proposed, so as to verify whether and to what extent the client's representation of the 'trouble' can be modified as a result of her/his having employed an attorney.

In a perspective whereby disputes are socially constructed, Felstiner, Abel and Sarat show how disputes indeed evolve through the dynamic states of *naming*, *blaming* and *claiming* (1980–1981).[12] When studying and analysing how disputes emerge and are transformed before they are channelled towards a legal process, these scholars provide a framework for studying the developments whereby 'injurious experiences' "are perceived or go unnoticed and how people respond to the experience of injustice and conflict" (ibid., p. 632).[13] In particular, they argue that 'naming' constitutes the first stage of transformation: telling yourself that a particular experience was injurious. When 'perceived' and 'named', an injurious experience may be transformed into a case of 'blaming'. 'Blaming' is in fact the transformation of the experience that has been perceived to be injurious into a grievance: a person attributes an injury to another physical person or to a legal person. The term 'claiming' is used, on the other hand, when the party that perceives the injury addresses the other person or organisation it believes to be responsible and lays claim to a remedy. A 'claim' then evolves into a dispute when the claim is refused in part or in full. According to this interpretation, the attorney come onto the scene at the moment of 'claiming' or of 'disputing'.

In the cases examined here, naming, blaming and claiming are found to be recursive process. They continue within the lawyer-client relationship as they

12 The studies conducted by Conley and O'Barr (1998, 1990) also highlight how disputes are constantly transformed in interaction: these are not entities that come ready-packaged already before the court proceedings. The result of those proceedings is the joint product of the interaction between the parties, the rules of the law and the institutional, social and cultural context.

13 The two scholars assert that this is an aspect that is neglected by sociologists of law.

repeatedly reconstruct the story of what happened. In the process that begins with telling the story to the lawyer and then progresses through identifying multiple case theories that intertwine law and facts (see Chapter 5), clients feel new injurious experiences that they may not have recognised in initial naming. When the time then comes to make strategic decisions with or without the lawyer, clients can incorporate the new names they have attached to these injurious experiences.

What emerges from an analysis of the interviews conducted with Laura and Luciano is especially their emotional difficulty with accepting the injustice and/or talking about their trauma. Drawing a comparison with narrative medicine, what we have here is what Charon (2006, pp. 30–33) describes when discussing the doctor-patient relationship and the feeling of shame, humiliation and guilt that patients sometimes feel when describing the symptoms of their illnesses to doctors. These are emotions that sometimes keep patients (who in such cases are the clients) away from doctors (and presumably in a similar way from lawyers), complicating the process of identifying the illness and so the therapy. We shall come across this phenomenon once again in particular when reconstructing the case of Margaret (Chapter 9), who, as a victim of trafficking, was reluctant to tell her story.

3.1. . . . in Laura's story

The first thing that emerges from Laura's narration is the client's sensation of shame, since she sees the company's proposal to pay her a lump sum to persuade her to resign as a consequence of her own inability. To begin with, Laura tries to identify any mistakes she may have made at work, accepting that she herself is responsible for what is happening to her.

A. 'Naming': the trouble as Laura's perception of shame.

> **I told myself about it as though it were true.** In other words, I thought that if the human resources manager told me: **'nobody in the firm sees you as capable'** – because that's what he told me during the meeting, nobody sees you as capable of doing anything –, maybe I failed as a project leader but could do something else. . . . 'but no, nobody sees you as capable of doing anything' . . . **that's why I regretted not having taken a recording device, because something like that, I think now that I see it more clearly, is something you would not even say to someone who joined the firm yesterday** and whom you do not know to be completely incapable, **what I mean is that I worked there for ten years . . . is it possible that I suddenly can't do anything any more!?**
>
> [. . .] **In other words they really made me feel. . . [that] suddenly that was not my office any more, but I actually had to hide, because the mere fact that you could see it on my face that something traumatic had happened**, that I had spoken to the personnel manager and come

out upset . . . could annoy someone. [. . .] **This person had told me some incredibly serious things, but who would have imagined it? I would never have imagined it**. [. . .] Then I realised everything afterwards, because as long as you stay there, yes, you know that you feel bad, but **in actual fact you have no really clear idea that you are the object of persecution**, something that is actually part of a strategy. You see, **that's something that I would never have imagined**.

I then started feeling persecuted, not just by him [the human resources manager], **but by the whole working context. I started reappraising all the working relationships I had had on various projects with various colleagues** . . . 'I probably made a mistake here or there, they probably thought they were doing the right thing to tell the human resources manager about everything that I had been incapable of doing' . . . so that was my idea. . .

Laura represents the breach of trust experienced in her workplace to herself (naming) in the form of a difficulty (humiliation) that she perceives to be personal before she perceives it to be legal. The intuition that a potential breach of rights has taken place that is serious enough to call for legal safeguards is subordinated to the feeling that she has been through a trauma or heard something of such "terrible and unimaginable gravity" as to make her understand that she is on the receiving end of a "persecution" or a "strategy".

Laura's representations (naming) change and the stage of 'blaming' comes about with the aid of an attorney: Laura's sense of discomfort reveals a company strategy.

As a result, **I stayed very cool during the interview: I tried to take notes about what they said to me in detail, about the conditions attached to this agreement, and then I spoke about it with Federico** [Laura's husband] **and we agreed that I would talk to an attorney, because I clearly needed to be protected from that moment on.**

[. . .] **I had no idea what to do: the only thing I knew with any certainty was that I would never have signed that thing, that was one small certainty! But I wanted to find out what my rights were, how far I could push things. So I went to the lawyer, who immediately gave me a clear impression that the way things were being described had to be revised completely. In other words, he immediately gave me the impression that there was a strategy, that it was obvious** . . . that everything that they were telling me was not what they were thinking, but was **the result of a strategy, because they are the things that are usually said in contexts like this, when you want to force someone into a corner and force them to resign** . . . [. . .] but he adopted this other approach: using a different and particular pair of spectacles to interpret the affair . . . ***he marked the path on the basis of our indications.***

The breach of trust in a human 'agency' (in the act of 'blaming'), as well as the definition of facts in legal terms, in this case aimed at a precise company strategy, is thus attributed in Laura's case with the aid of the attorney, who is defined during the interview as the one who is "marking the path". The lawyer also helps Laura achieve an understanding that the "harassments suffered" and the "deprival of her tasks" correspond to a phenomenon that is fairly common in professional environments, taking place somewhere on the borderline between an attempt at dequalification and mobbing.

B. Specialists help define the 'blaming': "**I started applying for anti-mobbing certification: . . . I went through a series of psychological and psychiatric interviews and these, too, gave me positive results** [. . .]. What emerged was that there had already been a situation of uneasiness and difficulty at work for years and it had also had effects on me psychologically".

Laura's sense of uneasiness at work is also confirmed by certificates issued by anti-mobbing centres, which provide a documentary record of the situation of alienation and difficulty that Laura experienced for years. In this way, Laura's uneasiness and the definition of the trouble started to acquire objective outlines.

C. The stage of 'claiming'.

> My attorney never actually spoke about mobbing. **Let's say that he gave me to understand that mine was certainly a question of dequalification . . . above all of dequalification that had in itself caused harm to my professional image** . . . the fact that I had not been able to work for two years and had not been able to keep up to date was already in itself harmful to my professionalism.
>
> [. . .] **My request was to stop these acts of harassment and to acknowledge the duty to pay two years of social security contributions for the two years that I worked as a freelance. I had worked for them**, but I had not asked them for anything, but at this stage my lawyers said: **'let's put it all together, that way they will understand that we mean this seriously . . . you have a whole series of rights to be respected'.**
>
> In our writ, we showed another card in our hands, **the card of the mobbing certificates, which we had never mentioned before then. In this case, too, I discovered that the attorney was leading me to show my hand a little at a time . . . In other words, we had our whole strategy clear, right from the start, but the way we put it across was very gradual**, because he always kept the main aim of the transaction in mind. That's something that I understood afterwards. So what counted for him was making the other party understand that we had many things in hand, but without giving them any information about exactly what we had.
>
> (These passages are taken from the interview with Laura, July 2006.)

Laura becomes completely aware that she is a victim of dequalification during her meeting with the attorney. It is in this phase of requesting the firm to remedy the situation (the stage of the 'claim') that Laura's strategies are agreed in close liaison with her attorney: "I started contesting everything they told me [. . .]. The first mail I sent asking for clarification about the two years of dequalification was actually already a way to push them to make a mistake . . . and that's how it was from that moment on" (ibid.).

An analysis of Laura's story conducted on the basis of the categories of naming, blaming and claiming illustrates the progressive evolution of the client's representations: from a personal sense of unease to the awareness of being a victim of mobbing and of having suffered a breach of her rights. The interventions of the attorney and of the anti-mobbing centre are significant for the purposes of the naming as well as the more technical legal qualification (claiming) of what happened and for attributing responsibility to somebody's agentivity (blaming), that somebody being the company. The collaborative relationship established between the client and her attorney enables Laura to orient her behaviour in the working context towards achieving a precise aim.

3.2. . . . in Luciano's story

As in Laura's case, Luciano experiences the occurrence of a 'trouble' in his professional life as a difficulty that affects him as a human being, as a 'drama'.

A. Naming: "a human drama".

> **What developed was a human drama that was triggered by my inactivity** [. . .]. **Who am I today? I didn't recognise myself any more** . . . I was not experiencing a process of achievement, nor one of professional growth. And I was made even more bitter and resentful by the fact that the bank informally never allowed me to go back to the bank. **So in the end I realised that, if I did not want to degrade my professionalism, I had to look, however unwillingly, at the idea of taking retirement.**

Here again, as in Laura's case, in a first phase, the client attributes the crisis in his working life to his own inabilities, with the consequence that he questions the nature of his own professional role and his real ability to fulfil it. What makes matters worse is the realisation that he is not growing professionally in the firm where he works. Hence Luciano's decision to accept a degree of defeat and consider retirement.

B. Naming/Blaming.

> **The logic at work here is underhand . . . let's say something between isolation and a clear list of this kind of behaviour that goes from the deprivation of tasks to taking away functions and revoking the managing director's powers without stating any reason,**

> **downgrading him to secretary of the Board of Directors, again without any reason.**

It eventually dawns on Luciano that the whole performance staged by the firm corresponds to a clear strategy that was designed to harm courageous employees.

C. Claiming.

From the unsuccessful requests to be taken back on in the bank, made by Luciano on his own initiative, to his recourse to an attorney, who puts the entire affair onto a legal footing:

> ***My lawyer asked me to write a memo about the affair:*** **I drew up a very detailed, accurate report of everything that then became the overall package of evidence for the affair. Then I gave him the papers, the letters and also let's say the internal company documentation that made it crystal clear how the company's actions contradicted its strategic decisions. [. . .] I asked for my qualifications to be recognised, also with retroactive effect, and for my damages to be paid.**
>
> (These passages are taken from the interview with Luciano, May 2006.)

In Luciano's case, unlike that of Laura's, the effect of the attorney's intervention is not so much to reveal the responsibility of the bank (blaming), nor to define the problem (naming and blaming), but to cast light on the consequences of the actions taken by Luciano to defend himself against the ones taken by the bank (claiming). In both cases, the definition of trouble also incorporates the client's activity of writing notes and searching for information about the case.

3.3. The second kind of analysis: conclusions

This analysis of the interviews (with the clients) using the sociological categories of naming, blaming and claiming highlights the fact that the clients' representation of the injury (the 'name') in the stories illustrated tends to be 'human' in nature, accompanied by nothing more than a sometimes belated intuition of being the victim of a breach of rights. In a first phase, the client has a naïve/human representation of the injury, which is perceived more as a personal disturbance (maltreatment, humiliation, trauma and personal drama) that is not related immediately to somebody's action or to the possibility of a legal remedy, but more to the client's own inability. It is then the attorney who helps the client reformulate this representation to illustrate the breach of rights. While in Laura's story, for example, the client's immediate perception of injury means that she does not accept the invitation to tender her resignation, in Luciano's story the injury is only perceived when he turns to a lawyer, this being the moment when he is confronted by the complete isolation of his role and the deprivation of its contents, plus the impossibility of returning to the situation as things stood previously.

In the two cases of Laura and Luciano, on the other hand, it is the client who attributes the injury, or 'blame', to the 'agency' of somebody (the employer). In particular, while the manifestation of the grievance comes about autonomously in the case of Luciano, in Laura's case the role played by the lawyer makes a decisive difference, helping her client to make the link between her situation of feeling uneasy at work and not any inability of her own, but an implied 'company strategy'. Acting as a constant throughout both stories are the steps taken by the attorney to ask for a remedy – making a 'claim' – from the body that first brought about the occurrence of the conflict (the firm, the bank).

The attorney's assistance seems therefore to be crucial, basically for the purpose of establishing the extent to which the client's grievance is attributable to somebody's 'agency'. Then it seems clear that it is only by referring to a norm and verifying the existence of conditions that are legitimate in the broad sense of the term (the existence of a contract, for example), as well as by taking the specific circumstances of the case into account, that it is possible to determine whether or not the actions suffered constitute a 'trouble' for the client and if so, which of those actions. "In other words for a 'trouble' to occur that may have judicial relevance, there must be a breach of the norm".[14] The norm – as I explained before (Chapter 3) – acts as a criterion for establishing the existence of the trouble.

The conclusion that could be reached might therefore be that the 'legal story' only starts when the client (with or without the aid of an attorney) represents or attributes (by blaming or claiming) her/his 'trouble' to the action of 'somebody'. In the cases examined, this happens with the aid of an attorney.

4. From asymmetries in the analysis of conversations to clients' initiatives

This section is devoted to analysing client-attorney relations characterised in terms of symmetries/asymmetries, so as to illustrate the evolution of this kind of interaction, drawing in particular on certain studies of language. Since the 1970s, studies on 'law and language' have been investigating how language is used in the reality of institutions: courtrooms, lawyers' offices and police offices (Säljö et al., 1990).

Specifically, studies of asymmetries[15] are interested in understanding the role played by the institutions in constructing social reality.[16] In Sweden, for example,

14 Bruner, Personal note to the author, Reenogrena, July 2006.

15 In a psychological perspective, both symmetries and asymmetries are constructed by interagents. Nevertheless, in the case of asymmetries, one of the speakers tries to force her/his point of view on the other, in an attempt either to persuade her/him, or to impose her/his own power. In any case, according to Marková, for example, there is a need for certain agreed parameters, such as a common language, the culture in which both interagents cohabit and certain basic assumptions about the other interagent. Marková's thesis is that asymmetry itself can only derive from mutuality, construed as a basic element of communication. Cf. Marková et al. (1995) and Marková and Foppa (1991).

16 The first studies in this field were conducted in the field of forensic medicine, for example to investigate the doctor-patient relationship. Cf. Aronsson, Larsson, Säljö (1990).

social psychologists (Jönsson and Linell, 1991) have examined thirty cases of police questioning that reveal asymmetries in the dialogue, deriving from the different roles played by the respective parties. On the one hand is a representative of justice, the policeman, while on the other is an individual who is under the suspicion, if not the certainty, of having committed a crime. The process that aims to bring out memories of what happened is therefore guided strictly by the party who is doing the questioning, who frames the questions in search of clarification and information. The memory coaxed out of the party being questioned is not spontaneous. The investigating officer sometimes offers a direct suggestion of what might have happened, so as to help the construction of a more detailed, consistent story. This means that the resulting memory cannot be considered to be an internal, private product, so much as a product of the interaction between the representative of the institution and the suspect. It is as though the function of the person doing the questioning is to obtain a version of the facts from the point of view of the 'suspect', even though the entire reconstruction of the facts, starting from the version proposed by the 'suspect', is made using legal terminology and in accordance with the rules in force in the type of institution in question. The police officer has a sort of 'operating plan' that he has picked up in the course of practice and to which he tries to make the 'facts' correspond. As a result, even in the way that it is organised, the questioning procedure complies with the objectives, the procedures and the practices of the institution. The final version of the facts drawn up during the verbal interaction is the product of a form of negotiation between the narrative produced by a person who may have broken the rules and the police officer. The person who manages the questioning therefore plays the role of the 'representative' of the institution that makes the rules and sets the conditions for the activities that take place in this context. This is what Perret-Clermont (2001) describes with the expression of "guardian of the framework".

A similar study was conducted in the United States by Troutt who, in *Koon v United States*, demonstrated the prevalence of cultural models of narrative in police practices, drawing an analogy between how the Koon case was portrayed by the government and perceived by public opinion and another similar case, *Screws v United States*. In general, cases of police brutality are related to instances of racial discrimination. But then every person of colour who is a victim of police persecution knows very well that the decay in race relations is partly the product of such practices: the explanation given to a coloured person about why he has been beaten up by the police is not that he was punished for being "a bad guy" (which he can contest), but because he is despised as a person of colour (which he cannot change).[17]

17 "Because now he is not necessarily being beaten 'as a bad guy' (which he can contest), but because he is despised as a person of colour (which he cannot change)" (Troutt 1999, p. 102).

Such cases show that the prevalence of cultural models of persecution of crime is 'camouflaged' by narrative strategies that tend to mask institutional forms of racism.

4.1. *The literature concerning asymmetries in client-attorney relations*

Moving from the socio-psychological field to the legal field, a substantial part of research into interactions in the last twenty years has concentrated, moreover, on asymmetries in dialogues in audiences, in client-attorney interactions (Sarat and Felstiner, 1986) and on restrictions or prohibitions on contributions from the accused or from witnesses. In particular, attention has been focused on how questions put together in a certain way induce a certain type of answer, on controlling turns in conversation,[18] on distributing interactive spaces and argumentation (Atkinson and Drew, 1979) and on the techniques of storytelling and of linguistic style.

What has emerged mostly is that many linguistic characteristics of discourse in court, the questions asked by the judge or by the attorneys, the answers given by the accused or by witnesses and the system of conversations controlled by the judge are the main tools used by the court to fulfil its institutional functions. It has been demonstrated that linguistic strategies are used to achieve the power exercised by the attorney over her/his client in practices of interaction. Conley and O'Barr (1998, 1990), in particular, investigate how the form of the questions asked is used to restrict the possible range of answers and how the attorney channels the topics under discussion in the direction (s)he wants to pursue. The crucial points of these studies appear to be the 'suppression' of the client's role and the fact that the client ends up being dominated by the attorney.

The way that the relationship between attorney and client is constructed for the purpose of obtaining technical and legal support has been studied by Hosticka[19] in terms of the dynamics of control practised by the two partners in the relationship in the course of their interactions. An analysis of their interaction (in this case of conversations) illustrates that, after the first formalities of recording personal information have been completed, these conversations typically have a

18 Studies conducted into asymmetries in legal spheres, especially by sociologists of law, have been rather latecomers compared to those conducted in the field of forensic medicine, for example. According to Sarat and Felstiner (1995), research in this specific field has been "frustrated" by the routines of excessively busy lawyers and by the difficulty encountered in convincing them of the need for research into client-attorney conversations About this, see the study conducted by Danet (1980). One of the main obstacles found was the 'doctrinal' conception of the privileged client-attorney relationship.

19 This research was conducted in a city in the United States, where a group of lawyers offers free legal aid to deprived people. The study examined 50 first meetings between an attorney and her/his client, using as indices of the action of control exercised by each individual the number of times that each one interrupted what the other was saying. Hosticka (1979, pp. 599–610).

phase in which the general intention of illustrating the facts, (i.e. what actually happened) is soon transformed into the client's intention (i.e. what happened to *me*), which is what the attorney is interested in discovering. The attorney's dominant position with respect to her/his client has been highlighted, in terms of the conversation, by the high frequency of the times when (s)he interrupts the client's storytelling and the high rate of questions and requests for explanation whose formulation already suggests the answers (s)he expects to receive. For the client's part, the commonest form of behaviour seems to be one of acquiescence with respect to the attorney, which comes across as short answers that confirm what the lawyer has suggested with her/his questions, with a very low rate of spontaneous questions and requests for explanation about what the attorney has said. The other attitude detected is that of the 'hostile' client, who tends to take over from the attorney and want to control the conversation by interrupting and changing the topic under discussion.[20]

Generally speaking, these research studies find that the legal problem is defined primarily by the attorney, who tends to classify every new case in a specific legal and juridical category, corresponding to a routine of professional behaviour that derives from her/his experience, or what Engeström (1996, pp. 1999–2032) has described as the attorney's expertise.

This is what happened in Laura's case, for example, where the attorney focused more on the dimension of dequalification than that of mobbing, because it was easier to define in terms of the legal circumstances, despite the sensation of humiliation and maltreatment perceived by the client, which is typical of mobbing.

The study conducted by Sarat and Felstiner into client-lawyer interactions – in cases of divorce – constitutes a break with traditional sociological studies about the legal professions, which portray professional practices as dominated by the lawyer or the client. They describe lawyers as playing the role of intermediaries between their clients and the legal system, acting as an important source of information about their rights and helping their clients to connect legal rules to their personal problems and to introduce their clients to how court proceedings operate (Sarat and Felstiner, 1986). In this study, Sarat and Felstiner explore how the client and the attorney 'negotiate' their different points of view about the law and legal proceedings and how their negotiation influences the decisions they make about the routes to be prioritised for achieving the ruling they seek. Unlike what (s)he may be expecting, the client is introduced to a system of routines, with a personal, random modus operandi. The attorney's function is primarily to legitimise some parts of the human experience and deprive others

20 An interesting example of asymmetry was outlined in the field of gender studies in an experiment conducted by Peggy Davis (1991). This scholar demonstrates the role played by the male-female difference of gender in the asymmetry between client and attorney. One of the results that emerges is that the role played by a female attorney in her interactions with her client is not one of being 'powerless', to use a term dear to Conley and O'Barr, but on the contrary is characterised by a series of potentialities with regard to the future of the legal representation in question.

of their relevance. The model most frequently found is that of the attorney who tries to persuade her/his client to agree to a negotiated out-of-court settlement. In the case of a divorce, the attorney focuses in particular on inviting the client to avoid confusing emotions and financial issues with legal issues. These are negotiations in which the parties have different kinds of knowledge, different models, different expectations and different requirements. In brief, the attorney teaches her/his client to socialise with her/his role and with the characteristics of legal proceedings. The authors describe this as the "legal construction of the client". A subsequent study conducted by Sarat and Felstiner in 1995 reveals that the relationships of power between client and attorney are not so oppressive and static, as the power in question is not something that can be 'possessed' once and for all, but something that is continuously being exercised and re-exercised, constituted and reconstituted. This is what is demonstrated by the cases examined in this chapter (and developed further in Chapter 5).

More recent studies, conducted using the ethnographic method and longitudinal approach, with the purpose of 'measuring' the internal change and the development of practices in a Finnish court district, illustrate the active role played by the client in 'constructing the case' and the tendency for the client to 'expand' her/his initiatives,[21] thereby seeking to influence the dispute and its construction during the proceedings. In fact, the traditional approach, before Finland reformed its court proceedings, considered the parties to be 'judicial actors' and not 'principal actors': the main assumption was that the parties were represented above all by their defending counsel. The client was defined in procedural law by her/his judicial role as the plaintiff or the defendant, in terms of her/his rights and duties in the proceedings, in addition to being described as an important "supplier of information".[22] What was highlighted in the debate about the reform, and through this research, was how the client's role could be made more active, going beyond the limit of the source of information.[23] One of the key questions is "what is the task of the client in the negotiation?". The result of the research is that the client is an *actor* by whom the judicial case is constructed in the proceedings by means of the negotiation: the client is not one of the judicial actors (according the classic roles of plaintiff and defendant), but someone who may take an active part in the transformation of the dispute.[24]

The results of these studies are rather distant from the traditional conception of the position of the client, which consider her/him to be a mere informer: the

21 I refer here to the doctoral thesis written by Haavisto (2002a). The data collected was comprised of videotapes and transcriptions of interactions in court. The author analysed the client's interventions, including the number of questions asked, the answers given and interruptions made.

22 Finnish Government Bill 15/90, pp. 13, 28, 35.

23 Haavisto's research focuses on the contribution made by the client in constructing the case (2002b, pp. 399–409).

24 The main 'initiatives' taken by the client are identified as the 'explanation', which pairs with the 'confirmation' to characterise her/his actions during the hearing.

initiatives (s)he takes have an impact on the organisation and result of the proceedings, while the very relations between client and attorney have undergone change. This is confirmed by an analysis of the majority of the cases examined in this and the following chapters (5, 7, 8, 9). In particular, in the cases of Laura and Franco, client participation in constructing the case takes the form primarily of initiatives, as I shall show in the next paragraph.

4.2. Client initiatives

By taking Haavisto's study and the others analysed previously into account, my investigation attempts to illustrate the initiatives taken by the client in the specific cases analysed previously, on the basis of written texts. These are notes drawn up by the client in response to a request voiced by the attorney, for the purpose of obtaining a more detailed version, and probably one that is also as 'mature' as possible, of the facts pertaining to the case for which the attorney has been engaged. These notes are quite extensive: in some cases, they even have a title that indicates their internal structure, such as *quadro normativo* (normative framework), *situazione giuridica* (legal situation) or *situazione scolastica* (educational situation). I will show how the salient characteristics of the client's initiatives may emerge through the narration of events and elements of her/his history.

Using Haavisto's work as a starting point, I consider the client's initiative to be the key tool for analysing the attempts made by the client to take part in the negotiation and 'transform' the dispute. No statistical evaluations are offered here, only some elements of analysis of the content taken from the notes. Building on the example provided by Haavisto and on the notes analysed, the term "initiative" is construed in terms of linguistics to encompass the following distinctions: contesting, alleging, correcting, explaining, confirming and stating. Initiatives are distinguished from one another according to how the client wants to influence the dispute. When the initiatives in question are capable of influencing how the dispute has been discussed, suggesting new topics (or putting an end to old ones), the distinctions noted are those of expanding, enlarging, questioning and restricting. Each category of initiatives tends to recur several times.

In an attempt to focus on some of the initiatives taken by the client that contribute to constructing the facts, the cases examined previously are now subjected to a fresh analysis. As I will show – case by case – the client does rather more than just supply information about the dates, places and circumstances of her/his case, actually contributing actively to constructing it.

4.2.1. Laura's initiatives

The first case, that of Laura, is one that for the sake of simplicity I call a case of mobbing, since that is also how Laura herself describes it.

The plot analysis and in particular the passages analysed using the categories of naming, blaming and claiming illustrated how Laura gradually became aware of being a victim of a strategy practised by her employer. Once she has gained this awareness, she starts authoring a series of initiatives. The main initiative taken by the client is to 'provide information', for the purpose of illustrating not only her own professional career in detail, attesting to the professionalism she has acquired over the years and the type of position she has held in the firm, but also the condition of underutilisation and oppression she is obliged to suffer in the context of her firm. The documentation provided is very detailed, from a point of view both of the responsibilities she has executed and of the salaries and benefits she has received. An examination of Laura's file reveals an intense exchange of correspondence with her attorney, which the client herself defines from her vantage point as "mail bombing" (excerpt from an exchange of mail between the client and her attorney, March 2006). The other, equally recurrent, initiative is that of 'contesting', nearly always in relation to her colleagues and/or superiors and to the arrangements made that worsen her status, such as the proposed move to another city. Numerous initiatives can be classified as 'alleging':

> **[The firm's] persecutory intent is clear to me, not only because I had two consecutive legal medical visits in just four days of being off sick [. . .], not only because of the date and time when this message was sent, but also and above all because the mail does not say that I shall be a project manager**, but it only lists three tasks for a completely undefined role of 'responsible Project Officer' . . .
>
> **Their mail is clearly almost a tactical pre-emptive move [. . .]; it is obvious** that their line is and will always be more focused on demonstrating that absences for sickness have been and remain the causes of the professional problems they complain about and not, as is in fact the case, the consequence [. . .]; **the mail lies about a crucial point [. . .].**
>
> (Excerpts from Laura's correspondence with her attorney, November 2005–July 2006)

Similarly, the initiatives classifiable as 'expanding' are also considerable: "we have to exploit the opportunity to 'nail' the firm [. . .]." Laura takes another interesting initiative when she asks questions about her own condition ('questioning'): "**Is the firm** – irrespective of its evaluation of my work (whether that evaluation is right or wrong) – **allowed to behave like that? Is it allowed to act and react like that? Is it allowed to approve holidays and then launch accusations about them? Is this or is it not mobbing?**"

An analysis of the initiatives taken by Laura, which mostly take the form of questions of clarification and of interpretation of the facts, demonstrates that the client is neither a mere source of information, nor a passive recipient of information and decisions, but contributes actively to the knowledge and to framing the facts in the solution to her case. As already highlighted in the previous paragraphs, it was in fact thanks to Laura's collaboration that the attorney managed to unmask the employer company, which aimed to marginalise its employee and force her to resign.

4.2.2. Luciano's initiatives

Luciano's case is characterised by initiatives of 'expanding'. In addition to providing his attorney with a written note containing detailed information about the milestones in his career – so 'giving information' – Luciano also draws up a precise listing of the requests to be made to the court, so 'expanding': 1) laying claim to his status as an executive; 2) breach of contract with respect to his salary in the year 1998 in the absence of all personal calculations on his part; 3) laying claim to the productivity premium for January 1992 (50% of the year 1992) + seniority bonuses; 4) laying claim to reimbursement and personal damages.

Lastly, Luciano refers significantly to his emotional state as confirmation of how he 'names' his condition of professional and personal difficulty, starting from the interview. The complete ostracism he suffers in his relations with the company's top management generates a profound sense of personal frustration in reaction to his workplace, with the result that his doctor diagnoses: "a state of depressive anxiety with reactive disturbances" (medical diagnosis, November 2005).

Unlike Laura, who contributed to constructing the legal strategy by acting on the manifestations of the trouble and on its possible definition in juridical terms, Luciano's initiatives were taken after the trouble had become evident. Anyway, he shows evidence of being a client capable of participating in solving the case (Rubinson, 1999) when he takes initiatives that tend to suggest clear questions to be addressed to the company.

4.2.3. Franco's initiatives

As anticipated previously, Franco's case is analysed here only because it is particularly interesting from a point of view of his 'enlarging' initiatives, which are so strong as to influence how the dispute is subsequently structured and transformed.

4.2.3.1. FRANCO'S STORY. SUMMARY

Franco is a school principal with a formal employment contract whose actions are influenced by a moment of 'legislative chaos' that makes him lose all confidence that he will ever progress from the level of a formal contract to an effective one that really allows him to work as a principal. As a result, he tenders his resignation, so that he can at least benefit by receiving the golden handshake that is due to him by virtue of his status as a formally employed principal. When he realises that this precludes his being able to take part in a forthcoming competition to recruit a 'practising school principal', he decides to withdraw his resignation, but the school authority refuses to recognise the validity of his withdrawal, deciding that it was submitted beyond the admissible deadline, so Franco goes to a lawyer. The lawyer applies for an injunction in accordance with Art. 700 of the Italian Code of Civil Procedure, so as to enable Franco to enter the forthcoming recruitment competition. The application asks the judge to recognise that Franco's withdrawal of his resignation was valid, since he had tendered it at a time when the legislation was so uncertain as to induce his client to make an 'error'.[25] The judge accepts the application, declaring the illegitimacy of the Ministerial ruling – Art. 1 of Ministerial Decree dated 9 December 2004 – which sets "a (time) limit on the faculty of the interested parties as per the superior legislative authority, Law N° 417/89", with the effect that he strikes out its application *in parte qua*.

Franco is a client who is well informed about the legislation that governs his role. As such, for example, he provides a detailed analysis of the legislative framework that governs his current position as a 'school principal with a formal employment contract', who is awaiting the competition to recruit a 'practising school principal'.

The most important initiatives taken by Franco are those of 'explaining' what his current role consists of and what his current position is, of 'enlarging' the information available about the position of other colleagues in the rankings for jobs that become available and in some cases 'contesting' it; of 'giving information' about the evolution of the legislation and the consequences that, in his opinion, may derive from it (so 'alleging'), and of stating and asking (so 'expanding') for a specific type of ruling (a suspensive injunction). The following passages are taken from Franco's correspondence with his attorney:

Giving information: "**I am** a school principal with an annual employment contract."

Explaining: "There are generally very few positions available in senior schools".

Contesting: Indeed, for years **I received** no appointment, despite the fact that **I was** the first in the rankings . . . Even people who do not hold the necessary qualifications – three years acting as a principal – are 'slipped in' surreptitiously. They manage to complete the course for the competition and are inserted into a listing, albeit with a reservation. [. . .] By making an application to the Labour Tribunal in 2004, they also asserted that they were entitled to be given priority in 2004 in the assignment of principals' positions in the province, but the judge denied it to them, because the reservation needed to be clarified first.

25 The legislative norm cited by Franco's attorney in having recourse to Art. 700 of the Code of Civil Procedure for the purpose of obtaining recognition of validity of the withdrawal of her/his resignation is Law N° 417/89 (which converted Legislative Decree N° 357/89). This in fact provides for the possibility that the resignation could be withdrawn until 31 March (Franco withdrew his resignation on 26 March). The law classified as "Norms governing the recruitment of school staff" provides that "members of staff responsible for inspections, management, teaching, educating and non-teaching in the state's kindergarten, primary, secondary and art schools, who have tendered their resignation from their respective positions, may not withdraw said resignation after the subsequent 31 March".

Enlarging: At the end of December 2004, an amendment was passed to enable . . . the candidates admitted with the reservation . . . to be assigned to positions gradually, starting in 2005. . .

Alleging: Hence my sense of discouragement. Their assignment to positions, **in my opinion**, reduced my chance of getting a place for the next year . . . both would come before me in the rankings . . . There are only two places that are certainly available. **I risked** going back to the rank of teacher. So **I made** the difficult decision, by the [date], to tender my resignation . . . Then **I presented** an application to withdraw, justifying it with the change in the legislative framework and the fact that the pension provision has not come into force yet. . .

Expanding: Apart from the merits and the justification, **in my opinion** and **according to how I read** the judge's ruling, this is just a question of asking for the deadline of 31 March set by the law, and not the one set by the Ministry's decree, to be respected: THERE IS AN URGENT NEED FOR THE JUDGE TO ISSUE A SUSPENSIVE INJUNCTION TO ENABLE ME TO APPLY FOR THE POSITION OF PRINCIPAL BY 22 MAY NEXT. OTHERWISE IT IS ALL POINTLESS!![26]

An analysis of the initiatives taken by Franco – as in Laura's and Luciano' cases – illustrates the capacity of the client to participate in a range of ways that involve a variety of initiatives in solving his case. Evidence of this capacity can be found especially in expanding initiatives that are made even more visible, with respect to how the content is shaped, by the use of block capitals in the text, for example.

Moreover, in terms of the analysis of language, what stands out in the passages marked previously in bold is the frequency of the client's use of the first person: **I am / I received / I was / In my opinion / I risked / I made / I presented / In my opinion / According to how I read.**

According to Bruner's theories (2002), but also those of Charon (2006), this is an element that – as an expression of the client's ability to take initiatives – may be considered in psychological terms to be a sign of self-awareness on the part of the client. In socio-legal terms, it also confirms the hypothesis that I will further develop in Chapters 7 and 8, according to which there is a strong connection between knowledge and broader awareness of how the (legal and social) system works and a successful legal agentivity.

In this framework, narrative thus become the tool for self-affirmation in legal settings.

26 At this point, the text written by the client and delivered to his attorney is written both in block capitals and in bold.

4.3. *The third kind of analysis: conclusions*

What emerges at this third level of analysis is that the initiative most commonly taken by a client is certainly focused on providing 'explanations' about her/his own situation, which as a matter of fact tends in most cases to be compared with that of the other people who belong to the same group (such as the colleagues or the superiors).

The client's role is not limited to this, of course: in addition to 'providing information' and offering 'explanations', the client also 'contests', 'states', 'presumes' and 'asks questions', sometimes even 'suggesting strategies' to the attorney. The client contributes to 'constructing' the facts, not only by providing information on her/his own initiative or at the request of her/his lawyer (information that in any case goes over and above the mere data about the career, the salary and so on), but also by taking an active part in the investigations. As we saw previously, Franco provides his attorney with some extremely useful background information about the legislation governing schools.

The client also 'interprets' her/his own situation, for example by framing questions about the legal status of the case, as we saw in Laura's case, a casebook example of the 'construction of the fact', achieved as a result of a close partnership between the client and her attorney. Working in concert with her lawyer, Laura develops a strategy and puts it into practice in dealing with the firm, in such a way as to alter the original configuration of her case. After Laura is invited by her firm to tender her resignation, she avoids mentioning this request, instead complaining that she was underused in previous years. Her approach elicits a series of reactions from the firm that provide glimpses of discriminatory intentions on its part, culminating in the use of such decisions as the instruction to Laura to transfer to another city. These decisions stimulate Laura's attorney to make an application for an injunction under Art. 700 of the Code of Civil Procedure.

5. Conclusions

The plot analysis of Laura's and Luciano's stories demonstrates that a legal story is generally provoked when tensions arise between two interagents who are driven by contradictory purposes, e.g. Laura and the human resources manager, Luciano and the bank or Franco and the schools administration. The trouble that calls for reparatory action comes to light gradually, through initial actions and subsequent complications that are generally caused by the agency of an actor. To repair the breach in the order or create a new one, clients may then take steps to solve the situation (either acting in partnership with their attorneys or not). If we compare the two stories of Laura and Luciano, we can see that initiative actions and complication actions alternate in more or less the same way in both stories, but it is in only in Laura's story that we come across problem-solving strategies, at least in good time for orienting the solution of the case before it takes on the characteristics of a legal dispute.

My hypothesis, which I shall develop in greater detail in Chapter 7, is that efficient action taken by the client calls for a degree of awareness of the problem. In fact, as from the analysis of clients' perceptions (naming, blaming, claiming) illustrated, the client does not always succeed in attributing the trouble to somebody else at the first attempt, nor in understanding that it constitutes a breach of rights, partly because this insight/awareness would call for familiarity with the law and a legal awareness that laypeople do not always possess. As a consequence, Laura's and Luciano's cases call for the intervention of an attorney for the client to understand whether and to what extent her/his rights have been breached. It is in this phase that action strategies are agreed between the client and the attorney: from sending an e-mail to asking for a day off for sickness, as in Laura's case, or collecting information, as in those of Luciano and of Franco.

The cases illustrated here, together with their characteristic initiatives, certainly demonstrate the potential of the client playing an active role, in terms both of the intensity and of the quality of her/his participation in the 'construction of the facts', rather than the passive formal role of being no more than a party: the plaintiff or the defendant, in a civil law system (in these cases that of Italy).

It is quite clear that, when the attorney is in agreement and competent, the client's role is actually somehow 'indispensable' to managing the conflict, not only for the purpose of 'constructing' the proceedings in accordance with her/his expectations, but also, as we shall see in due course, for the purpose of achieving the desired result. To what extent the initiatives taken by the clients in the cases illustrated here contribute to constructing and transforming the conflict is something that will be further monitored when analysing the attorney's narration (Chapter 5). In Franco's case in particular, the attorney will be seen to adopt a substantial part of his client's narration, not only as it pertains to the facts, but also with regard to his legal arguments, complete with references to laws and decrees quoted by his client, although he of course adds the necessary technical insight and arguments. It is also already expected that the judge, in turn, will adopt the majority of the arguments advanced by the attorney, especially when they pertain to the law. To some extent, then, it is already now possible to draw the conclusion that, when it is well-documented in terms of what happened (dates), the indication of places and the sequence of the events, as well as from the standpoint of mastery of the legislative framework and of possible judicial rulings, the client's narration enables the attorney to keep attention focused effectively on the topics he has proposed.

From a more general standpoint of the articulation of client-attorney relations, there is certainly a trend towards change: the client is neither marginalised, nor dominant in the process, but partners with the attorney, as to some issues standing on the same level. The client contributes to structuring the conflict in terms of her/his expectations, so as to achieve the desired result.

I shall return to the issue of the client's agency introduced here and develop it further in Chapter 7, where the cases will not only be analysed from the standpoint of the structure of the stories and of the interactions between the actors, but also situated in the broader context of the social relations in which they are shaped and solved. The aim is to show how law and culture interact and how legal actors' awareness of the environments in which they live can channel them towards the solution to their case.

References

Alfieri, A. (1987–1988). The Antinomies of Poverty Law and a Theory of Dialogic Empowerment. *New York Review of Law & Social Change*. 16: 659–712.

Alfieri, A. (1990–1991). Reconstructive Poverty Law Practice: Learning Lessons of Client Narrative. *Yale Law Journal*. 100: 2107–2147.

Alfieri, A. (2016). Rebellious Pedagogy and Practice. *Clinical Law Review*. 23(5): 36.

Amsterdam, A.G. and Bruner, J.S. (2000). *Minding the Law*. Cambridge, MA: Harvard University Press.

Aronsson, K., Sätterlund Larsson, U. and Säljö, R. (1990). *Medical Diagnosis and the Micropolitics of Care*. Linköping: Linköping University.

Atkinson, J.M. and Drew, P. (1979). *Order in Court. The Organization of Verbal Behavior in Judicial Settings*. Princeton, NJ: Humanities Press.

Bandes, S. (1996). Empathy, Narrative, and Victim Impact Statements. *The University of Chicago Law Review*. 63(2): 361–412.

Brooks, P. and Geewirtz, P. (1998). *Law's Stories*. New Haven: Yale University Press.

Bruner, J.S. (2003). *Making Stories*. Cambridge, MA: Harvard University Press.

Charon, R. (2006). *Narrative Medicine*. New York: Oxford University Press.

Conley, J.M. and O'Barr, W.M. (1990). *Rules Versus Relationships: The Ethnography of Legal Discourse*. Chicago: University of Chicago Press.

Conley, J.M. and O'Barr, W.M. (1998). *Just Words: Law, Language and Power*. Chicago: University of Chicago Press.

Cummings, S.L. and Eagly, I.V. (2001). A Critical Reflection on Law and Organizing. *UCLA Law Review*. 48(443): 443–517.

Daiute, C. (2014). *Narrative Inquiry: A Dynamic Approach*. Thousand Oaks, CA: Sage Publications.

Daiute, C. et al. (2017). *Minority Teachers – Roma in Serbia – Narrated Education Reform*. Belgrade: Institute of Psychology, Faculty of Philosophy, University of Belgrade Association of Pedagogical Assistants of Serbia.

Danet, B. (1980). Obstacles to the Study of Lawyer-Client Interaction: The Biography of a Failure. *Law and Society Review*. 14(4): 905–922.

Davis, P.C. (1991). Contextual Legal Criticism: A Demonstration Exploring Hierarchy and "Feminine" Style. *New York University Law Review*. 66: 1635–1681.

Delgado, R. (1989). Storytelling for Oppositionists and Others: A Plea for Narrative. *Michigan Law Review*. 87(8): 2411–2441.

Di Donato, F. and Garros, E. (forthcoming). Agir avec le droit: récits et actions. In: Di Donato, F. et al. (Eds.). *La fabrique de l'intégration*.

Ellmann, S. et al. (2009). *Lawyers and Clients. Critical Issues in Interviewing and Counseling*. St. Paul, MN: Thomson Reuters, American Casebook Series.

Engeström, Y. (1996). The Tensions of Judging: Handling Cases of Driving Under the Influence of Alcohol in Finland and California. In: Engeström, Y. and Middleton, D. (Eds.). *Cognition and Communication at Work*. Cambridge, New York and Melbourne: Cambridge University Press. 1999–2032.

Felstiner, W.L.F., Abel, R.L. and Sarat, A. (1980–1981). The Emergence and Transformation of Disputes: Naming, Blaming, Claiming. . . . *Law and Society Review*. 15(3–4): 631–654.

Haavisto, V. (2002a). *Court Work in Transition. An Activity Theoretical Study of Changing Work Practices in a Finnish District Court*. Helsinki: Helsinki University Press.

Haavisto, V. (2002b). Breaking the Courtroom Code: Client Initiatives in Finnish Civil Hearings. *International Journal for the Semiotics of Law*. 399–409.

Hosticka, C.J. (1979). We Don't Care About What Happened, We Only Care About What Is Going to Happen: Lawyer-Client Negotiations of Reality. *Social Problems*. 26: 599–610.

Jönsson, L. and Linell, P. (1991). Story Generations: From Dialogical Interviews to Written Reports in Police Interrogation. *Text*. 11: 419–440. de Gruyter.

López, G.P. (1992). *Rebellious Lawyering: One Chicano's Vision of Progressive Law Practice*. San Francisco: Westview Press.

López, G.P. (1996). An Aversion to Clients: Loving Humanity and Hating Human Beings. *Harvard Civil Rights-Civil Liberties Law Review*. 31: 315–323.

López, G.P. (2004). Shaping Community Problem Solving Around Community Knowledge. *New York University Law Review*. 79(1): 59–114.

López, G.P. (2005). Living and Lawyering Rebelliously. *Fordham Law Review*. 73(5): 2041–2054. *Review*. 79: 59–114.

López, G.P. (2009). Changing Systems, Changing Ourselves. *Harvard Latino Law Review*. 12(15): 16–38.

López, G.P. (2017). Transform-Don't Just Tinker with-Legal Education. *Clinical Law Review*. 23: 471–576.

Marková, I. and Foppa, K. (Eds.). (1991). *Asymmetries in Dialogue*. Savage, MD: Barnes & Noble Books.

Marková, I., Graumann, C. and Foppa, K. (Eds.). (1995). *Mutualities in Dialogue*. Cambridge: Cambridge University Press.

Meyer, P. (2014). *Storytelling for Lawyers*. New York: Oxford University Press.

Miller, B. (1994). Give Them Back Their Lives: Recognizing Client Narrative in Case Theory. *Michigan Law Review*. 93(3): 485–576.

Perret-Clermont, A-N. (2001). Psychologie sociale de la construction de l'espace de pensée. In: Ducret, J-J. (Ed.). *Actes du colloque. Constructivisme: usages et perspectives en éducation*. Genève: Département de l'Instruction Publique. Service de la Recherche en Education. 65–82. Vol. I.

Piomelli, A. (2016). Rebellious Heroes. *Clinical Law Review*. 23: 283, 310.

Rubinson, R. (1999). Constructions of Client Competence and Theories of Practice. *Arizona State Law Journal*. 31: 1.

Säljö, R. et al. (1990). *Formulating the Past. Remembering in the Police Interrogation*. (The 2nd International Congress for Research on Activity Theory, Lahti).

Sarat, A.W. and Felstiner, W.L. (1986). Law and Strategy in the Divorce Laywer's Office. *Law & Society Review*. 20: 93–134.

Sarat, A.W. and Felstiner, W.L. (1995). *Divorce Lawyers and Their Clients. Power and Meaning in the Legal Process*. Oxford and London: Oxford University Press.

Scamardella, F. and Di Donato, F. (2012). Il silenzio "a più voci" nelle narrazioni di clienti e avvocati. *Sociologia del diritto*. 2: 127–150.

Shalleck, A. (2015). *Toward a Jurisprudence of Clinical Thought: Investigating the Contours, Urges and Trajectories*. Manuscript on file with the author.

Troutt, D.D. (1999). Screws, Koon and Routine Aberrations: The Use of Fictional Narratives in Federal Police Brutality Prosecutions. *New York University Law Review*. 74: 18.

White, L.E. (1987–1988). Mobilization on the Margins of the Lawsuit: Making Space for Clients to Speak. *New York University Review of Law & Social Change*. 16: 535–564.

White, L.E. (1994–1995). Collaborative Lawyering in the Field? On Mapping the Paths from Rhetoric to Practice. *Clinical Law Review*. 1: 157–171.

White, L.E. (1997). The Transformative Potential of Clinical Legal Education. *Osgoode Hall Law Journal*. 35(3–4): 603–611.

Zulack, M.M. (1994–1995). Rediscovering Client Decision-making: The Impact of Rome-Playing. *Clinical Law Review*. 1(593): 593–638.

5 The lawyer as translator

The stories analysed in Chapter 4 are expanded in this chapter to show how the narration of facts evolves from one stage to another of the case reconstruction, with a focus on the role played by the lawyer. In particular, the lawyer is depicted as a translator, whose function is to transform the human story into a legal one. The legal story involves rereading elements of events provided by the client – such as dates and places, the general organisation of the professional context, duties performed and responsibilities assigned – with the aim of defining 'who has done what, how, when, why and where?' For some of the cases analysed, the lawyer shows ability, sometimes as a result of collaborating with the client, in identifying the causal and temporal connections that contribute to giving the legal narrative contextual meanings. Lawyers' narratives may have a subversive impact on the pre-defined legal order.

1. The multiple roles of the lawyer in fact construction

> Throughout their relationships, lawyers and clients tell stories to each other. [. . .]. Clients usually come to lawyers for help [. . .]. They have stories to tell that express their reasons for, hesitation or excitement about, and fear of whatever prompted their need for legal help. [. . .]. In the course of clients' narratives, lawyers hear how particular experiences and choices relate to complicated and diverse aspects of clients' lives and the worlds they inhabit. [. . .]. Lawyers also tell stories to clients – about themselves; about lawyers, judges, legal institutions and other actors in the legal system; about the law and multiple interpretations of it [. . .]. In each interaction between lawyers and clients, the stories of both intersect, each penetrating and shaping the story of the other. [. . .]. As clients and lawyers engage through reciprocal and interconnected narratives, they create the lawyer-client relationship.
>
> (Ellmann et al., 2009, pp. 139–140)

Starting from this picture of the ongoing narration and re-narration process between lawyer and client, proposed by Ellmann et al., in this chapter I shall retell the stories of Laura, Luciano and Franco in the versions provided by their attorneys, both in the course of interviews and through the reconstruction of the official records of the legal proceedings. The aim of this analysis is to understand how the 'legal story' is constructed by the lawyer with the client, to what extent the attorney takes the version as narrated by her/his client into consideration, what kinds of causal and temporal nexus are used to reconstruct the factual elements that come into play, how evidence is used, what role is played by rhetoric in the discourse advanced by the attorney, how do the attorney and the client co-operate in solving the case and, ultimately, what kind of reasoning is adopted by the attorney in constructing the case.

While much has been written about how judges reason and their way of discussing a case, analysis of how attorneys reason has been rather neglected (Alpa, 2008). There is a widespread belief that the attorney's principal task is to 'persuade' the judge or the court to decide in favour of her/his client with regard to the factual or legal motives that are drawn up in the preliminaries and then expressed through the arguments (s)he presents. Twining ([1990, 1994], 2006, p. 296), for example, drawing on Llewellyn (1962) calls attention to the fact that, "in his statement of facts, the advocate has the first, best and most precious access to the court's attention".[1] The advocate's statement of facts is not simply part of the legal argument, but constitutes its very core. The court/the judge is informed about the facts when the advocate introduces an official document into the proceedings. In this sense, the attorney has privileged access to the facts and to the construction of the story.

The role played by attorneys, can actually be very complex, involving a plurality of other roles: actor, narrator, translator[2] etc. As I explained in Chapter 3, the attorney's role and narration tend to be considered as oriented towards defending the interests of the client (Taruffo, 2009; Trujillo, 2013). Nevertheless, the 'story' of a case does not end with its mere narration by the attorney, nor does it end up as no more than a mere exercise in rhetoric. In general, we will see that the first thing that the attorney does is to make the story that (s)he is constructing together with her/his client acceptable and 'conventionally' legal, as well as difficult for the other party to dispute. When identifying the essence of the case, of the question for litigation, the attorney starts from the client's point of view and 'translates' everyday events into 'legal stories', mediating between the world of the client and that of the administration of justice: "the world in which the legal issue arose (the facts) and the world into which the client's story has ventured for a solution (the governing law)" (Berger and Stanchi, 2018, p. 52). This operation of translation undertaken by the attorney with regard to the other party, the judge and society itself is conducted not only in co-operation with the client, but also starting from her/his requirements, giving due consideration, among other things, to the local culture, construed as a set of practices against whose background the events took place.

1 Cf. Llewellyn (1962, 341–342), quoted in Twining ([1990, 1994], 2006, p. 296)

2 Interest has recently started being shown in the role played by attorneys as storytellers. See Brooks and Gewirtz (1998); and the more recent work of Meyer (2014). In addition, it is traditionally a subject of interest for legal clinicians, as we saw in Chapter 4.

In this chapter, then, it will be interesting to explore how the attorney's thinking develops at a more complex level, on the basis of concrete examples. The chapter has this structure: it lists several typical uses of storytelling in legal disputes (par. 2); it furnishes reconstructions of the stories of Laura, Luciano and Franco, as narrated by their attorneys (and compared to the ones narrated by the clients in Chapter 4) (par. 3); it highlights the role of 'translator' typically played by the attorney (par. 4); it analyses the role played by evidence in constructing legal stories (par. 4.1); it dwells on certain typical aspects of the plot's construction in the three stories (causality, temporality and ambiguity in defining the facts) (par. 4.2); it focuses in particular on analysing the role played by the rhetorical dimension within the legal discourse (par. 5), and it offers suggestions about how the attorney thinks, starting from the cases under examination (par. 6).

2. Uses of storytelling in legal processes: questions of fact and questions of law

The assumption has been made here, from the third chapter onwards, that the stories told in court can be considered to be 'narrations'. Alper et al. (2005)[3] hold that litigators are inextricably immersed in the narrative, albeit subconsciously. They therefore propose something of an inventory of possible uses of narration in court proceedings, so that the parties can use storytelling as an integral part of their work, making the best of the opportunities offered by narrative to construct 'possible worlds' and legal meanings and to make strategic choices between potential alternatives. In this way, Alper et al. identify the possible practical uses that a litigator can make of a narrative that is in any case particular. The result is a profile of the underlying structure and of the narrative processes, a specification of the characteristics, of the conditions and of the elements of the narrative in the setting of court proceedings.[4] They propose, among others, eight possible uses of narration in court proceedings.

- *The use of narration to generate hypotheses that guide investigations and avoid their being closed to possibilities by premature judgments.*

The 'investigation of the facts' should be conducted by formulating hypotheses about what happened and why. These hypotheses are constructed in a narrative form, complete with a scene, characters, actions, instruments and motives. The plot of the stories is generally constructed on the basis of these elements, which guide the litigator's 'imagination'. In their turn, of course, these elements suggest others that may or may not coexist, providing a specific focus for the

3 The authors' inventory was conceived of for a trial by jury: reference to those applications that are suited exclusively to legal proceedings of that kind is omitted here.

4 On the uses of narration in court proceedings, cf. also Bennett and Feldmam (1981), Pennington and Hastie (1991), Feigenson (2000), Berger and Stanchi (2018).

investigation. The possibility of exploring multiple hypotheses to propose could be a guarantee of benefits for a litigator/attorney, and this function of 'exploring alternative possibilities' is typical of narration. I will highlight this aspect in the case of Luciano, for example (par. 4.1).

- *The use of narration may be functional to developing a representation of the case: questions of fact and questions of law.*

What makes narration in court proceedings effective in the construction of the case is its role of mediator between facts and norms, so that the entire theory about the case proposed by a litigator takes the shape of a narration that calls for a favourable decision, with the facts organised in such a way as to invoke the application of rules of law or rules of procedure, to prompt the consideration of equity, to reference elements of proof, and so on. As Meyer explains (2014, p. 3): "All arguments, at any level or in any type of practice, are built upon arrangements of the facts of a particular case. These facts are shaped into stories carefully fitted with legal rules and precedent. It is impossible to make any legal argument without telling some stories about the facts and about the law".

It is also generally agreed that storytelling as a crucial technique of advocacy tends to adopt various different characteristics, probably according to whether it is applied to questions of fact or of law. Questions of fact and questions of law constitute the key stage in the "transformation of ordinary stories into judicial stories": they are the procedures whereby judicial stories are analysed juridically and ultimately appraised by the judge (Bruner, 2003, p. 42). Who did what to whom and with what intentions? These are the questions of fact that need to be answered in compliance with the rules of evidence. But deciding whether a given action breaches a given law involves interpreting a legal rule. Midway between one and the other, we then find the decision about whether the action has actually damaged the party who brings the action. Bruner (1992) believes that this subtle separation does not always hold and that jurists have recently started realising that, in certain cases, the subtle separation is no more than a fiction.

In an orthodox perspective, a question of law is the object of contestation when there is disagreement about the meaning of a norm or when there is controversy about whether a particular set of facts matches its application. Conventionally speaking, an argument about a question of law is organised as though the facts are 'given'. On the other hand, an argument about a question of fact proceeds as though the applicable law is consolidated. In the theory of law, on the contrary, there is a recognisable problem of the distinction between questions of fact and questions of law, just as there tends to be recognition that in some cases this distinction is somewhat artificial in character or even of no relevance whatsoever, especially with respect to the application of norms and the appropriate classification of a given factual situation. Establishing whether "Tom is dishonest" or whether "this is a case of murder", for example, may be a question of fact, a question of law or a mixture of both. In addition, how questions of this kind are tackled and how the story is told (i.e. plot structure and other qualities) varies from one system to another and from one context to another (Twining [1990; 1994]; 2006, pp. 271–278). In Laura's case (par. 3.1., 4.2.), for example, the attorney had a rather difficult time establishing whether the case was one of mobbing or of dequalification, or whether the client's effectiveness at work had really been reduced. As a result, the attorney played the card of ambiguity of definition as a way of constructing a winning strategy.

In the framework of all legal proceedings, there are facts that are related to dates and to the conditions of the weather and of work that may be based on evidence in the stories told by both parties; yet there may be 'factors beyond the control' of the parties that are of significantly lesser import and also 'open' categories, such as the 'bona fide effort' based on circumstances or the general economic crisis, as in Luciano's case (Bruner, 2003, p. 43).

Lastly, it is important to remember that, while the process of ascertaining the facts in the course of legal proceedings is regulated by procedural rules and by the oath made by the witness to "tell the truth", the only way of judging whether and to what extent a juridical interpretation is correct is by applying the tradition embodied in precedent.[5] The party who proposes a given interpretation refers substantially to the similarity between his interpretation of the relevant facts and the facts contained in the relevant precedents.[6] According to Bruner (2003, p. 43), the underlying procedure for establishing these lines of precedent is similar to placing a story in a literary genre and advocates often show skill in choosing the precedents to illustrate, even though their choice is sometimes restricted to the precedents used in the past. While literature uses cunning plots to imitate conventional reality and create verisimilitude, the law does the same, citing the corpus juris and sticking to precedents. Dworkin in turn used the metaphor of the chain novel to call attention to the need for a form of narrative coherence between the judge's decision and the precedents (Gearey, 2005, p. 273). These analogies between law and literature, everyday narratives and judicial narratives confirm the theses illustrated in Chapters 1 and 2 that the principles governing how literary narrative and legal narrative are governed are similar.

Nevertheless, while nobody disputes that the scrutiny of questions of law is not covered by any complex of procedural and evidential restrictions comparable to the one that applies to the scrutiny of questions of fact, it cannot equally be taken for granted that such questions of fact can also be subject to interpretation. This is what I shall illustrate in Laura's case, for example, where Laura's attorney and her employer proposed different interpretations of the temporal meanings of events.

The transition from the fact under discussion to the question of law comes about by means of typical narrative procedures of interpretation and construction of a communicated, shared and legitimised meaning. The reasoning about the

5 Although all this may also apply to Civil Law systems, Bruner's reference is of course to Common Law systems.

6 Cf. also Bruner (2003, pp. 44–49).

questions of fact and the questions of law that are the issue in the judicial decision will be further analysed in Chapter 6.

- *The narrative is functional to probing or influencing how witnesses or other sources of information (members of the jury and others taking part in the court proceedings) are thinking.*

Litigators are constantly obliged to make strategic decisions as a function of how people think and of how they will react to the actions taken by the attorneys. Moreover, under normal circumstances, if the litigator makes use of categories typical of contemporary culture when constructing her/his case, (s)he will induce a more favourable reaction from decision makers if (s)he refers to factual elements (scenes, plots and characters) of typical stories accepted by contemporaries. This is what I shall demonstrate both in the case of Luciano (par. 4.1.), where I shall illustrate how the attorney makes detailed use of the evidence to demonstrate the version of the facts narrated by the client, and in those of Viviana and Carlo (Chapter 7). In cases where the familiar narratives are not favourable to the client, on the other hand, the attorney may imagine different (new or subversive) narratives to sustain her/his client's thesis. This is what we find, for example, in the cases of Kirin (Chapter 8) and of Amenze (Chapter 9).

- *Narration can be used to enable a judge/jury to familiarise himself/itself with lines of thinking that are functional to inducing the litigator's case to emerge or to push the counterpart's case into the background.*

Narrative is unquestionably a special way of thinking, of processing information and of proceeding from premises to conclusions, a method whose purpose is to enable members of the jury to piece the story together. The use of the distinct qualities of narration (see Chapter 1, par. 7) – the fact that it is context-laden, for example; the fact that it generates expectations through presumptions of 'relevance'; the fact that it translates time into a sequence of events and so on – enables a litigator to induce the judge or the members of the jury to 'process' what they are hearing and what they are seeing in the course of the proceedings, so as to make her/his own story prevail over that of the counterpart. This aspect recurs in all the cases under examination in this book.

- *Particular narrations can be used to credit or discredit elements of proof or of information, to configure them or to put them into code.*

Stories are functional to coding elements of proof and other parts of the case.[7] Narrative construction in fact implies a considerable amount of coding that helps

7 Coding is the process whereby words, images, objects and ideas are associated with others, so that the past brings the present to mind.

make good stories come across as plausible.[8] This can be seen in Luciano's case (par. 4.1.), for example, where the attorney employs the detailed evidence given by his client's colleagues to show that he was the victim of a plan on the part of the bank to expel him from his position.

Starting from the uses thus identified that are made of narration in court proceedings, it is worth remembering that, although stories have common characteristics, they differ with respect to the purposes for which they are told, their settings and the conventions and rules typical of the setting in question (for example, legal proceedings with or without a jury). As I explained in Chapter 3, legal proceedings are not given entities, but culturally laden contingent events that influence how the stories are told. In the specific context of adversarial proceedings, with which I deal specifically, each party opposes the other's story in its attempt to convince a decision maker of the truth of what happened, for the purpose of restoring her/his own initial status or of constructing another and restoring the social order by means of the judge's final decision. Every civil, criminal or other case takes the form of a 'contest', in which one party's story somehow reflects the truth of what happened, in such a way that establishing one party's truth means denying the truth of the adversary's story. The rule that everyone taking part in such proceedings shares is that only one of the litigants will be determined to be right about what happened. All the effort expended by the litigants is concentrated in this direction. The stories that litigators ask the judge to believe are the 'facts of the case', which have to appear to be 'true'. As a result, the litigator has to be capable of telling stories that are resistant to any potential challenges from the other party, which means that fragile or irrelevant elements of the story (Taruffo, 2009) must be gleaned out or minimised, so that the defence is not left in a vulnerable condition (Rubinson, 1999). These skills in using narration in professional legal circumstances can be made explicit by adopting a clinical approach to reflect about cases and to solve them.

Lastly, the story that a litigator tells the judge is a story whose last chapter has not yet been written, because it is the decision that still has to be made (this is the focus of Chapter 6). This last resolution of the story should of course be a verdict in favour of the attorney's client. Let's take a look at how this transition comes about in reality by analysing three stories: those of Laura, Luciano and Franco, which were already analysed in Chapter 3 according to the clients' perspectives about their cases.

3. Luciano and Laura's stories as narrated by their attorneys

For the purpose of analysing the role played by the attorney in constructing the 'legal story', I shall once again use the definition of 'story' proposed by

8 Points 6, 7 and 8 listed by Alper et al. (2005), which are more closely concerned with cases of trial by jury, are omitted.

Amsterdam and Bruner (2000) as well as Daiute (2014) – as proposed in Chapters 1 and 4 – to frame the stories of Luciano and Laura as narrated by their attorneys in the interviews. The aim is to identify the characteristics of how these two different attorneys go about their reasoning, through the identification of "core narrative themes that, in turn, determine the functional choices the storyteller makes in selecting, shaping, and sequencing the events into a story" (Meyer, 2014, p. 16). Does the plot of the attorney's story coincide with the plot of the client's story? Can the same events be reconstructed differently in order to have different meanings?

3.1. Laura's story: the causal and temporal connection between the factual elements

The following passages which are analysed here are taken from the interview with Laura's attorney in July 2006:

I. *An initial steady state grounded in the legitimate ordinariness of things;*

[. . .]

II. *That gets disrupted by a trouble – the initiating action that marks the break with the steady state – attributable to human agency or susceptible to change by human intervention:*

a. Initiating action:

[. . .] Laura came to me because the company had suggested she should resign, but we had to understand why it had made this suggestion. **It transpired that there were several reasons, because she had been off work, she had been ill and so in general had become less efficient at fulfilling her very generic function in the company**: although she was offered an incentive to accept redundancy, it was very limited.

[. . .] **This matter of an incentive to accept redundancy could be connected – I tried to connect it – to a retaliatory and persecutory intention** that had evolved in the course of time, **trying to establish a concatenation between a whole series of facts that were, in my opinion, objectively quite separate from each other, both logically and historically**.

III. *In turn evoking efforts at redress or transformation, which succeed or fail – under the form of complicating actions that rise to a high point (climax, conflict or turning point):*

b. Complicating action (of the stated trouble to connect disconnections):

I tried to put them together in a way that would show how everything first sprang from a message sent by this client to the

company, because she had to undergo treatment for infertility, and how this then led to retaliation from the company, which first stripped her of her working activity, then sent her a constant stream of medical control visits in an attempt to find a way to terminate her contract of employment, culminating in informing her that she was to be transferred to another of the company's locations.

c. High point/turning point:

The transfer order in itself could have proved to be useful, had it been connected, as in fact it later was, to a whole series of facts, so that it could be given a connotation of 'objectivity', as also of 'retaliation' . . . We suggested this latter interpretation to the judge, who held that the transfer was not legitimate.

IV. *So that the old steady state is restored or a new (transformed) steady state is created. This often takes several steps in naturalistic stories, so we refer to them as 'resolution strategies':*

The judge's order enabled us to focus more clearly on the aspects of retaliation on the part of the company. **All this gave our approach a more objective nature: the company started fearing that it might actually end up being harmed, so altered its redundancy offer, trebling it.**

V. *And the story concludes by drawing the then-and-there of the tale that has been told into the here-and-now of the telling through some coda – say, for example, Aesop's characteristic moral of the story.*

[. . .]

These are therefore the salient elements of the attorney's reasoning in reconstructing Laura's story, based on the interview.

a. Description of how the 'trouble' came about.

The attorney attributes the trouble partly to the agency of the client. Although he gave the behaviour of the company that employed Laura a connotation of retaliation, the attorney hypothesised that part of the reason why the trouble came about was the reduction, albeit generic, in her client's working responsibilities inside the firm. This is demonstrated by her request for sick leave and the time she took off work as a result. When qualifying the fact, the attorney thus added – within the story – an element that could in part be traced back to Laura's own agency. The narration of the fact was thus modified as a function of the role of the narrator – in this case, the narrator was the attorney – who qualified the events referring to a legal norm, while also taking the version furnished by the client into account.

b. The legal strategy: constructing the nexus between the events.

According to the attorney's story, the 'construction of the fact' was thus achieved by forging a causal and temporal linkage between facts that, if taken separately "could have a stand-alone significance", but that in an *ex post* reconstruction "indicated something more and different when taken together". Through the client's narration, the attorney captured the logical and legal connection between these facts, revealing the clear decision made by the company with the aim of isolating and excluding its employee, with an intent that was both discriminatory – with regard to Laura's request for sickness leave so that she could receive treatment for infertility – and retaliatory in terms of Laura's attempt to negotiate. The strategy proved to be a winner: the day before the complaint lodged by the actor was due to come before the court, the firm made a proposal for an out-of-court settlement that would give Laura three times the sum originally offered as an incentive to her to accept redundancy. In terms of narrative strategies and of problem-solving, the attorney's reading of the events as a concatenation presented Laura as the victim of the company's strategy, turning up the volume of the drama and the narrative pathos.

3.2. Luciano's story

The following passages, which reconstruct Luciano's story from a legal standpoint, are taken from the interview with his attorney in June 2006.

I. *An initial steady state grounded in the legitimate ordinariness of things:*

He had very rashly agreed to a proposal to transform his working relationship with the bank: this transformation involved transferring his employment contract to a small company belonging to the group, but with a quite different set of corporate aims and objectives, and this is what in fact happened. **The bank justified the transfer with the idea of giving this group company a fresh start, also by involving this person who occupied a quite high level, since he was an executive** [. . .].

He agreed to the proposal with enormous enthusiasm: from the documents he showed me and the studies he had conducted, he had also drawn up some very concrete working hypotheses, establishing how many employees he would need, what budget, what kind of services would have to be guaranteed, how to tackle relations with the business community etc. **In short, I realised that he had really believed in this idea.**

II. *That gets disrupted by a trouble – the initiating action that marks the break with the steady state – attributable to human agency or susceptible to change by human intervention:*

a. Initiating action:

So what happened? **He agreed to the transfer on condition that he would be promoted, so I'm not saying that he was lured into**

this affair . . . the promotion had some objective conditions in terms of his employment relationship and rather high-level functions he would be responsible for, so it did not look very suspicious. . .

He came to me some time after he had resigned, after he had got over a period of serious depression and also a crisis in his personal life (he had separated from his wife etc.), **asking me to re-read and take a fresh look at the whole recent business of his relationship with the bank . . . his idea, which however was not very feasible, was to challenge the legitimacy of his own resignation . . . I did not subscribe to that proposal because too much time had passed** . . . In addition, he had not even lodged an informal extra-judicial challenge to his resignation. . .

III. *In turn evoking efforts at redress or transformation, which succeed or fail – under the form of complicating actions that rise to a high point (climax, conflict or turning point):*

b. Complicating action/high point:

In actual fact, the entire programme, the plan that had been theorised, quickly melted into insignificance and the bank of course disregarded the programme according to which it had suggested that Luciano should resign and be re-employed with the other company. Remember that this company's status – I checked it immediately – was quite marginal: it was a company with no assets, no share capital, no employees, none of the safeguards provided for in Italy's Statute of Workers' Rights, especially with regard to dismissal. This is more or less how things stood. This situation, which was very distressing for him, then dragged on for about a year. **I believe that this distressing situation ended up having an impact on him, not only existentially, but also inducing him to tender his resignation as a last act of dignity, among other things, of taking back control of his life.**

c. Resolution strategies:

As I saw from his story that he had suffered some very serious infringements of quite important rights, **I considered that I could ask for the infringements thus suffered to be ascertained with a view to obtaining redress. So I then proceeded to do this, reconstructing the last stages of his working relationship.**

I went to court, explaining all the milestones in this business point by point and referring to the documentary records etc.; then we called the witnesses. We had a long evidential hearing, with witnesses whom I would describe as very well-informed and meticulous in piecing together the story of this person's unfortunate working relationship. We then drew up a statement of defence and I tried to simplify the reasoning further, considering that the judge appointed to hear the case is not notorious for his ability to apply himself to studying the documents.

IV. *So that the old steady state is restored or a new (transformed) steady state is created. This often takes several steps in naturalistic stories, so we refer to them as 'resolution strategies':*

Then the judge's decision was negative, stating reasons that were rather unconvincing and in some points maybe logically contradictory.

V. *And the story concludes by drawing the then-and-there of the tale that has been told into the here-and-now of the telling through some coda – say, for example, Aesop's characteristic moral of the story:*

The judge downscaled the impact deriving from the applicant being deprived of his level of professional qualification: **in my opinion, he did not actually understand the case properly. You also have to remember that the judge's reasons are always published some time after he has given his ruling.**

These are therefore the salient elements of the attorney's reasoning in reconstructing Luciano's story:

a. Evaluation of the initial state of legitimacy.

In interpreting Luciano's case, the attorney believes that, although his client acted "very rashly", he did nevertheless really "believe" in the firm so resolutely as to conduct a very detailed design study for the company being established. The attorney's thesis is therefore that the employee was 'lured' into this situation.

b. Evaluation of Luciano's personal and professional position.

The only uncertainty that the attorney hints at is that it would have been to his client's advantage to have given closer consideration to the new company's assets and share capital before accepting the proposal. That much said, though, he was not the only one to accept: at least four other bank employees also agreed to the project.

c. Evaluation of the bank's behaviour.

The conclusion reached by the attorney is that, regardless of the bank's intention (or lack thereof) to carry out the project in which Luciano had been involved, it was not entitled to deprive him of his qualification for reasons of downscaling the company's plans. In other words, it had the "legal duty to offer him the chance to return whence he came".

On the basis of these hypotheses, in his document instituting the proceedings, the attorney drew up a reconstruction of the recent events in his client's career, so as to ascertain whether the infringement of Luciano's rights could entitle him at the very least to obtain a suitable redress for the damage suffered. The attorney then introduced his petition, prudently concluding:

> **Despite the reasoning being based on circumstantial evidence, it is impossible to consider that there was no preordained intention to convince the employee to accept a transfer to employment in a small company in the same group that was destined to enjoy no development**, so as then to revoke his responsible functions and qualifications and to marginalise him once and for all from the company's environs, obliging him to accept a distressing deprival of his qualifications and thus drive him to tender his resignation. This overall illicit behaviour on the part of the employer [. . .] avoids the field of application of regulations designed to guarantee employees' rights and [sets out to] expel the employee from the firm painlessly.
>
> (Excerpt from the plea entered by Luciano's attorney, dated May 2000)

This passage is reminiscent of the first cases mentioned by Alper et al. (par. 2) of the use of narration to shape hypotheses to guide the factual reasoning. On the basis of circumstantial evidence, in fact, the attorney drew up the hypothesis of a "preordained intention" to expel its employee on the part of the bank. Note that Luciano's case, unlike Laura's, was constructed completely on the basis of evidence. The evidences given in support of Luciano seems to have confirmed the hypothesis that he was in practice deprived of his qualifications after the firm's plans had come to nothing. Nevertheless, the petition was not upheld. As in Laura's case, there is an increase in resolution strategies in the narration furnished by Luciano's attorney's compared to the complication actions characteristic of the clients' narrations – both Laura and Luciano.

4. Translating clients' stories

White (1990) compares the attorney to a translator, thus enabling me to argue that the attorney's role is that of translating what I could describe as 'everyday occurrences' (narration of events, emotions, characters and motives) into 'legal stories'. As White describes it, the translator is not a 'bureaucrat' who moves from one technical idiom to another, but the person who aspires to connect two worlds and two different ways of 'being' and 'seeing'. According to him, translation is the art of the impossible, of tackling the unbridgeable discontinuities between texts, languages and persons. A good translation proceeds not from one attempt to another to dominate or take control, but by practising respect. It is characterised by a set of practices that enable us to cohabit with difference, with the fluidity of a culture and the flexibility of the self. This not a simple mental operation, but a way of relating to others: the attorney translates the client's problem in relation to the other party, to the judge and to society itself, starting from the client's requirements and working in co-operation with her/him. (S)he fulfils this task by deciphering the rules, explaining to her/his client how they have to be applied to the situation in question and presenting the facts and the applicable rules sufficiently clearly for them to be guaranteed recognition in an institutional context. The facts, or objective constraints (e.g. the e-mail sent to the personnel manager, the letter of resignation, an unsigned contract etc.) are placed in a legal story, which gives them a form, while also fulfilling the function of using the narrative to restore the legitimate order that has been breached, either by repairing the previous status or by creating a new one.

Laura's and Luciano's cases confirm, in different ways, the thesis of the attorney-as-translator. In fact, the two cases show that the attorney's first fundamental activity in reconstructing the case is the identification of the essence of the controversy (Moro, 2004, p. 51), starting from the story as narrated by the client and giving due consideration to possible interpretations of the law as well as of practice.[9] When constructing the plot of Laura's story, for example, her attorney bears in mind that framing the facts narrated by the client as dequalification rather than as mobbing could produce a more effective result in terms of legal protection. The client and the attorney then construct a theory of the case (Miller, 1994) that tends towards dequalification, but using a language that somehow conjures up the category of mobbing, for example from the point of view of the emotional impact that the affair has had on the client.

Similarly, in Luciano's case, the attorney identified the essence of the case as his client's request for redress for the damages suffered, rather than for the revocation of his resignation, which is what the client had suggested. The following passage from the interview, defined previously as an initiating action, can be considered as an example:

> **He came to me some time after he had resigned,** after he had got over a period of serious depression and also a crisis in his personal life (he had separated from his wife etc.), **asking me to re-read and take a fresh look at the whole recent business of his relationship with the bank . . . his idea, which however was not very feasible, was to challenge the legitimacy of his own resignation . . . I did not subscribe to that proposal because too much time had passed** . . . In addition, he had not even lodged an informal extra-judicial challenge to his resignation. . .
>
> (Luciano's attorney, dated May 2000)

The first step that the attorney seems to have taken was thus his attempt to obtain the story from the client, in his own words, so that he could then translate it into a different form of language. As this operation unfolded, the clients – Laura and Luciano – learned something about legal language, while for his part

9 The intelligence of the case – as defined by Moro (2004) – takes the form of the identification of the question to be discussed in litigation. For the author (ibid., p. 51), this "constitutes the hinge on which the result of the case depends and represents the fundamental element that has to guide the approach adopted to consultancy or assistance in the individual concrete situation".

the attorney learned something about the language used by his clients to express themselves. In this way, the client and the attorney together constructed something 'new', a 'story' with the potential to acquire meaning and force in another genre: the genre of the law. This meant that the attorney – as theorised by White (1990) – fulfilled the function of a "mediator between different languages": (s)he had to be ready to speak the client's language, but also to address the court in terms that, at least in the beginning, would be alien to the client.

In Franco's case, for example, when describing the work of what we have described here as 'translation' done by his attorney in the course of his interview, Franco expressed himself in these precise terms. "The attorney knew how to give the force of the law to fragile thinking" (Franco, April 2006). Similarly, in a passage in her interview, Laura referred to part of her conversation with her attorney about whether it would be opportune to represent the facts in accordance with a given legal practice: "I may sound cynical, but the facts should be rephrased like this . . ." (Laura, July 2006). In this case, the attorney helped the client to understand what was happening in the context of the company and to attribute a meaning to the decisions made about her by the company. As Laura herself reported:

> I started thinking about this way of seeing things [. . .] **I took a fresh look at all the relationships I had had when working on various projects with various colleagues: I suppose I made a mistake here or there.** They must have decided to tell the personnel manager about everything that I had not been able to do . . . So that's the idea I had [. . .] As I was actually experiencing this conditioning, that's truly how I felt. . . **My attorney helped me understand that these complaints were not at all precise, but more like pretexts** [. . .]
>
> **I gradually came to put what they were telling me in a different light:** I got a clearer view of the reconstruction of the events, of everything I had been through in the previous years. . . **so it was obvious that everything I had suffered had actually been a strategy aimed at making me tender my resignation** . . . So, until that famous meeting with the personnel manager, they hoped that I would resign of my own free will, that I would not be able to stand it any more and would simply go away.
>
> (Laura, July 2006)

These examples show how the client gradually learns to give events a different meaning by seeing them through the lens of the law, primarily as a result of discussing them with the attorney.

They also support the original hypothesis that there is a process of negotiation at the root of the client-attorney interaction and that the attorney's work is not limited to merely representing the client: "What has happened" is not "fixed in objective reality", but is more of "a social construction".[10] The client and the

10 Cf. Hosticka (1979; cit. in Cunningham, 1989, p. 2472).

attorney co-operate with one another to 'construct' a new reality for which they apply for official legitimation.

4.1. *The role of evidence in constructing Luciano's case: the involvement of the lawyer and the position of the witness*

Once the objective constraints that contribute to the 'construction of the facts' brought about by the attorney and the client have been identified and negotiated, the next step is to ensure that the judge recognises them to be 'true', so that the narration can achieve its perlocutionary function. The crux of the problem, in fact, is: how to enable the judge to get to know the fact or, more precisely, how to convince the judge of the facts?

The role played by evidence is fundamental for this purpose. Before providing some examples of presentation of evidence, I would recall some ethnographic studies that illustrate some mechanisms of evidence acquisition, questioning whether it is possible to achieve an 'objective truth' in the framework of court proceedings. According to Brooks and Geewirtz (1998), witnesses are no more and no less than 'sponsored' storytellers. Yet in actual fact they only seldom have the chance to tell the story: in general, all they can do is answer a series of questions, which in turn are disciplined by rules. The attorney pieces the story together, step by step, by means of the sequence of questions and answers that make up the testimony. In addition, the knowledge furnished by a witness is obviously 'selective', just like that furnished by the client: there is no narration with a beginning, a middle and an end. The witness's story crosses paths with the story told by the other party and the other party's witnesses.

So the question is 'what makes a story or a storyteller credible?'. Of interest in this respect are the studies undertaken by Conley and O'Barr (1990) about the style in which evidence is given in court. According to these authors, the "style of presentation" of evidence plays a very significant role in determining whether the evidence will be accepted or not. Experiments in the ethnography of legal discourse confirm, for example, that apparently minor variations in the way a witness gives evidence produce major differences in how that evidence is evaluated with regard to such key factors as the witnesses' credibility, their competence for testifying, their intelligence etc. The purpose of all this being primarily to demonstrate the link between language and its strategic uses in the judicial arena.[11] The thesis advanced by the authors is that "the form is at least an important

11 Studies of law and language, a multidisciplinary field that first emerged around 1975, set out to break down the disciplinary barriers around the study of 'how language fulfils the functions of law in society'. These days, many psychologists and socio-linguists have devoted their attentions to studying language in its context (see Loftus, 1979; Danet; 1980, pp. 445–565). To speak, to interact verbally, means to build the world, not just to be reflected in it. The language used by a profession is a tool of power that creates dependence in the public. For example, the use in legal jargon of the modal verbs (to be able to, to want to, to have to), of mental verbs (I believe, I think, I imagine) and of qualifying adverbs (apparently,

element of the message as a whole and of its reception" (ibid.). Since the judicial examination is organised so that the attorney asks the questions and the witness answers them, the ultimate control of this exchange is left to the attorney. The studies conducted by these authors into the activities of the courts indicate that long, narrative answers are only possible when the attorney abandons all forms of control, giving the witness greater freedom to answer. Conley and O'Barr's (1990) ethnographic observations about judicial interactions also show considerable variations in the length of the answers compared to the questions asked by the attorneys: some witnesses tend to give relatively short answers, while others are habitually more loquacious. At the same time, they indicate that it is the examining attorney who wants the witness to speak longer and in greater depth. On other occasions, shorter, more incisive, unelaborated answers seemed to be desired. These are described conventionally as 'narrative' and 'fragmented' styles. In exchanges in open court, these observations demonstrate the tendency among witnesses to use one or the other of these styles. Every individual tends to use a personal style, somewhere along a continuum from a highly narrative style to a highly fragmented style. As for the contents of the answers, these are of course influenced to a great extent by the style of the questions. In fact, attorneys as narrators, even when questioning, have tools that enable them to exercise a greater or lesser degree of control of how the story is told by witnesses (depending upon the rules governing questioning, as well as their skill). Of course, witnesses are often not passive and can find ways to resist or subvert control by the lawyer.

In the case of Luciano, for example, an examination of the court proceedings confirms the real variability in the style used to testify, as a consequence of how the attorney conducts the examination, but also of the kind of witness. The longest evidence, for example, was given by the bank's deputy director: this was also the only one that suffered no interruptions and started with a very strong statement: "I am the deputy General Director of the bank and also held that position at the time of the facts. . . " (evidence entered on January 2000). It was on this evidence, together with that given by the General Director, that the judge came to base his decision.

If witnesses are sponsored storytellers, the position adopted by the attorney when presenting the evidence is typically that of involvement, since what interests her/him is to safeguard the client. This means that the attorney can only illustrate one side of the case, attempting to demonstrate that this is the more truthful and reliable version of the facts. As a result, the role played by the attorney is to act for one side of an adversarial context, where (s)he has to oppose the version advanced by the other side.[12] The attorney's story is only one of the possible

approximately, probably) may restrict or expand the range of possible interpretations in the representation of the facts. On the language of attorneys, cf. also Alpa (2003, pp. 15–39).

12 "He is not obliged to be coherent with the reality of the facts in issue: he must assert the case of his client, not the case of truth. His attitude cannot be independent und umpireal with reference to the dispute but partisan and adversary" (Taruffo 1994, p. 273).

stories about the facts of the case: it is a 'strategic' story whose purpose is to prepare the groundwork for a victory.[13] The facts to be sustained are chosen on the basis of their juridical relevance and according to whether they are suitable for achieving a favourable decision. For this reason, the attorney tends to present only those elements of proof that are likely to have a favourable impact on the final decision, to present only evidence that supports her/his version of the facts, or evidence that undermines the relevance or admissibility of the evidence fielded by the other party, or opposes the evidence fielded by the other party with the aim of counterbalancing it. In addition, (s)he chooses the sequence of the depositions that seems most advantageous to supporting her/his case for the purpose of defending it. In particular, the attorney extracts a mosaic of responses from the examination of the witnesses, responses that are of interest not so much to the truth of the facts of the case, but to the version of the facts that (s)he stated previously on the basis of her/his version of the case. What (s)he aims to achieve when (s)he examines the witnesses is therefore to piece together a story that corresponds to the story on which the position of the client is based.

The conclusion I can draw – which may appear to be obvious – is that the attorney's role is to act for one side in the process of constructing the facts: the ultimate aim is to use the evidence given by the witnesses to demonstrate that her/his client's story is more or less confirmed, that it is a reliable version of the facts and that the other stories told in the same context are not reliable. The ultimate aim, then, is to get back to the story as told in the beginning and to show the judge that it is on the basis of this story that the decision should be made. On the basis of elements extracted from the results of the evidence, the attorney again constructs a consistent and narratively coherent story that (s)he presents as 'true'. This is what happened in Luciano's case, for example.

On the basis of the evidence mentioned in the writ issued, the witnesses called by the attorney to testify in the hearing demonstrated the following circumstances characteristic of the configuration of the trouble in Luciano's case:

- Luciano's transfer from the bank to the group company pursuant to the agreements between him as an employee and the bank's management: "we had a meeting – the President, Luciano, the General Manager and myself – in which we offered the plaintiff the possibility to take care of the new company, which was to be charged with providing assistance to firms (real services to business)" (evidence given by the bank's Deputy Manager).
- The attribution of the General Manager's tasks: "the plaintiff had the task of organising the structural aspect of the new company, defining the roles and tasks of the staff assigned to it"; and also "Luciano was appointed Manager with the status of executive and the Board of Directors delegated powers to him" (evidence given by the bank's Deputy Manager).

13 Ibid.

- The revocation of these attributions and the alteration of the company's strategies. In particular, according to the witness Andrea:

> The provisions of the memorandum of understanding failed to be complied with almost from the start of my professional experience, both by the bank and by the company that had employed me [. . .]; **the projects to provide training and services for business did not take off, primarily because the structure was decapitated, in other words deprived of its most recurrent functions, by which I mean myself**.

And this is what the witness Bernardo had to say: "in any case the company's activity, as it had been mapped out with regard to providing consultancy to businesses, never started [. . .], the projects concerned with providing real services to business were not taken up by the bank any more".

In addition, the witness Ciriaco stated: "After the plaintiff's position as the company's General Manager had been revoked, he was left with nothing but residual tasks, i.e. giving formal approval for holidays and monitoring that the staff had signed in. In other words, Luciano had been left in a condition of enforced inactivity".

The witness Andrea added: "I remember that a situation of conflict arose and Luciano, I don't know whether he chose to or was forced, no longer had any significant responsibilities in the company". Lastly, his request to transfer back to the bank was also confirmed by Dario: "I know that Luciano asked to be transferred back to the bank several times. I know this because of my continuous contact with Luciano". And this is from another witness, Eligio: "I should point out that some employees who worked for the company later went back to the bank. I know that Luciano asked to be taken back on by the bank and the bank refused him".

All these are excerpts from the minutes of the court proceedings (November 2001–January 2002).

On the basis of the evidence given during the hearing and above all on the basis of how some of the elements thus testified were interpreted, the attorney, in his statement of defence, stressed the legal hypothesis he had already formulated in his introductory statement to the court, on which he also grounded his further development of the proceedings:

> **Considering the sequence of the facts, we almost inevitably presume that when the company's management formulated an attractive proposal to the other party to guide a new branch of the business to work in the field of training and services for business, promising a promotion that, as the counterpart's defence rightly points out, signified an important career advance for the plaintiff**, it was already aware that it could not or did not want to pursue the programmes as agreed. **It would be naïve to believe that a corporate strategy that had been pondered for months and elaborated in every tiny detail could be overturned completely in just a handful of weeks without there being any reasonable awareness of**

> **it. In any case, the bank's behaviour displays a clear breach of the rules of loyalty and fair play deriving from its general clauses.**
>
> (Excerpts from the notes drawn up in Luciano's defence by his attorney, dated 27 September 2004)

The counsel for the bank, for its part, appeared in court to "challenge, word for word, all the circumstances of fact deduced and the juridical evaluations expressed by the plaintiff, asking the court to reject the unfounded and reckless plea, with all the inherent consequences" (except from the authorised notes drawn up by the bank's attorney, dated 28 September 2004).

In particular, by adopting as its main argument the occurrence of a serious crisis in the bank by way of justifying the frustration of the company's projects and the downgrading of its employee, the defendant used the results of the evidence to illustrate this thus:

> **As has been acknowledged by all the witnesses examined, "the reasons why the business consultancy sector was not developed . . . were related to major difficulties concerning overdue payments. The bank was on the brink of substantial difficulty**. We had cuts to our salaries. I remember that, at that time, we had to subject all our projects to an executive, who had then bought a 20% share in the company".
>
> (ibid.)

All the witnesses are therefore said to have confirmed that the bank was objectively in a critical condition. The need to modify the company strategy was thus said to be justified by unfavourable economic and market conditions:

> **The witness Giulio honestly admitted that the employee's transfer was the consequence of a convergence between the interests of the company and of Luciano; the company "also had to have the task of providing assistance to businesses . . . Luciano was identified because he had a business training that had already seen him draw up specific projects"**, but then defined the strictly economic entrepreneurial reasons that put a brake on the initiative to expand the company and added: ". . . there were economic and market reasons unfavourable to credit intermediation that obliged us to make this decision. **To be precise, the company's strategy was altered in the year 1996 and the company developed more in the branch of financial mediation . . . the change in corporate strategy obliged the company to employ human and financial resources in its financial mediation activity, removing them from the activity that had been planned by Luciano".**[14]
>
> (ibid.)

14 Note that this evidence quoted by the defendant in support of his own thesis is longer than what is recorded in the minutes of the proceedings of the hearing between Luciano and the bank.

In the defendant's narration, then, "a period of major crisis", exploding in the course of a couple of months, was said to have obliged the bank to undertake a series of initiatives and decisions destined to impact on its corporate policy and on the destiny or actually on projects so "unrealistic" as to induce Luciano to "demand" the recognition of the title of General Manager and the exercise of the functions connected thereto, which were the reasons why he had agreed to being transferred to a company connected to the bank. This was the conclusion:

> **So Luciano has no cause to blame the employer or the top management at the Bank, except for having revoked (with a measure that was actually accepted, since it was never opposed) his formal title of General Manager and for not having been able (for the reasons listed above, albeit in the brief form necessary for this occasion) to pursue projects that were maybe too unrealistic**, or maybe only inserted in a temporally unfavourable context, or maybe, more probably, **STOKED BY THE EMPLOYEE'S PERSONAL AMBITIONS in an overly individualistic view of the company,** such as to lead to a belief that the employer's right to pursue his employees' working projects can be safeguarded.
>
> (ibid.)

On the basis of these reconstructions, the bank comes across as holding no responsibility for Luciano's destiny, which depends on an abstract agentivity attributable on the one hand to the general crisis and, on the other, to Luciano's personal ambitions.

4.2. *The legal construction of Laura's story: causality, temporality and ambiguity*

While Luciano's case was constructed entirely on evidence used to confirm the hypothesis of the facts argued by the attorney in his introductory statement, Laura's case was constructed primarily on a particular narrative articulation of the nexus of cause and time between the elements of fact. Laura's attorney in fact partnered with his client to identify a linkage of cause and time between events that only offered themselves to a logical connection and a causal concatenation in a reconstruction achieved with hindsight, as the attorney declared in the interview:

> **Trying to establish a concatenation between a whole series of facts that were, in my opinion, objectively quite separate from each other, both logically and historically. I tried to put them together in a way that would show how everything first sprang from a message sent by this client to the company, because she had to undergo treatment for infertility, and this led to retaliation from the company**, which first stripped her

> of her working activity, then sent her a constant stream of medical control visits, **culminating in informing her that she was to be transferred to a related company**.
>
> (Laura's attorney, May 2006)

With the result that the attorney partnered with the client, who started out by acting on her own behalf, shaping a strategy that induced the firm to make a series of mistakes that ended up revealing a substantial discrimination and the intention to isolate its employee, inducing her to tender her resignation. The first significant step came when Laura sent an e-mail to the company's human resources manager. Without referring to the suggestion made to her sometime earlier that she should tender voluntary resignation, Laura complained that, after an important project that she had run successfully had come to a close, she had been relegated to inferior tasks, with periods of inactivity caused by the fact that she had not been assigned to any more projects:

> **The persistent deprival of responsibility to which I was subjected generated both biological and existential harm to my person and prejudiced the progress in my career** for which I asked on several occasions and which had also been proposed to me several times. **This progress was in fact reserved to other colleagues of mine and to external staff who did not have my professional experience**.
>
> While reserving my right to take action in the competent courts for redress to the damage sustained, and also to avoid further impoverishing my existential and professional situation with all the legal consequences that derive therefrom, **I am asking you to arrange as soon as possible my assignment to a client located in Naples**, consistent with the professional qualification I have acquired.
>
> (Excerpt from the mail sent by Laura to the company, April 2006)

The human resources manager's answer contained some elements that recognised Laura's work and others that criticised behaviour described as negligent, although no official (or unofficial) complaint about this had ever been made until that moment, concluding with a declaration that:

> **Against our will and primarily because of your – absolutely justified – absences for curative therapies** (which obliged you to be absent from work for many days in the months of April, May, June and July)**, then for the holidays legitimately requested by you and granted by the company for almost an entire month** (4 August – 2 September) **and lastly another absence for personal reasons in the month of September, your presence at work on the project [. . .] was objectively much reduced.**
>
> (Excerpt from the mail of response sent to Laura by the company's human resources manager, April 2006)

Traces of the company's discriminatory attitude could also be found in a subsequent e-mail:

> I also repeat that Mr Rossi has always assigned you to projects. **Your reduced presence in projects in recent months does not in fact depend on any lack of assignment made by Mr Rossi, but on your numerous absences (absolutely legitimate, but that precluded any active and constant participation on your part in the projects assigned to you)** [. . .].
>
> (ibid.)

The next stage, following an attempt at reconciliation, was the introduction of a court plea (in accordance with Art 700 of the Italian Code of Civil Procedure) against a measure taken by the company to transfer its employee to another city. In the plea laid before the court in accordance with Art 700 of the Italian Code of Civil Procedure, which described the company's measure as "illegitimate", the attorney then linked the company's strategy to a clear "persecutory intention", describing the measure "as a retaliatory act in response to the legitimate claims moved by Laura for the rights pursuant to her working relationship with the defendant to be recognised" (excerpt from the plea entered on May 2006).

With regard to the 'moment in time' said to have marked the beginning of the affair, in her official plea, the attorney chose to identify the moment when the trouble first started with a message sent by Laura to her superior in 2005 about her need to take a leave of absence to undergo medical therapy. The different time frames practised by Laura and her attorney with respect to the beginning of the affair, dating back to 2003, give the impression of the 'narrative dimension' of time as well as of the 'temporal dimension' of the narration. The 'significant' organisation given to the events within the narration has nothing to do with either what is usually called 'objective' time (i.e. the time we count in hours, days and years), as argued by Taruffo (2009), or with the subjective perception of events, but with the decision to give the narration a beginning, a middle and an end, in tune with the functional requirements of storytelling. Laura's attorney wrote:

A reading of the facts of the case, in their temporal sequence, will demonstrate without a shadow of a doubt:

- **In May 2005, Laura informed her superior Mr Rossi that she needed to take a leave of absence from work to undergo medical therapy to counter infertility and, in the same month, she was replaced in the project** [. . .], without any explanation whatsoever, with another colleague, who was younger and had less experience, because he had been employed subsequently;
- **In the month of September 2005, the plaintiff formalised her evaluations about the under-usage being made of her services, reporting the deprival of responsibilities she had suffered and the lack of updating, whereupon she was called in by the human resources manager Mr Verdi, who invited her to end her employment by**

tendering 'voluntary' resignation and aired the possibility of a 'conflictual' relationship if she failed to accept his proposal;

- Laura did not accept the proposal and repeated her persistent deprival of responsibilities and the "progressive impoverishment" of her existential and professional situation, asking to be assigned to an activity in keeping with the professional qualification she had held for many years, and received a message from the Human Resources manager in which her professionalism was once again questioned. **The isolation she was forced to endure brought about a worsening in Laura's health that obliged her to take leave of absence for illness and the company sent medical control visits, many of them consecutive and on non-working days**;
- The plaintiff decided to apply to the competent judicial authorities, for the purpose of making a proposal of reconciliation in accordance with Art. 410 of the Italian Code of Civil Procedure, and the company informed her that it was transferring her to Milan.

(Excerpt from the plea entered on May 2006)

Using the nexus of causality and temporality enabled the attorney to forge a 'functional' link in the narration between two or more events, between which it would not necessarily have been possible to demonstrate any 'historical' connection: i.e. Laura's replacement in her position after her message to the firm about her leave of absence for medical treatment. In Laura's case, the attorney constructed a narration whose meaning was that of a process of deprival of professional qualification, combining cause and time consistently and with the support of documentary proof, objective constraints that would probably be of no juridical relevance if taken singly. The result was therefore a reconstruction suitable for giving 'objectivity' to a subjective perception of the fact, so as to be able to present them in court as a logical reconstruction of the events.

The re-narration by the attorney was that:

> **The retaliatory attitude was conveyed moreover by the obstinate intention to remove the plaintiff from her place of work and from the setting where she lived, perfectly aware that this would have caused her further harm. . .** [. . .] Ultimately, then, it is clear that the measure proposed to the plaintiff is null and void for the unlawfulness of the motive that determined it, since it was proposed in breach of the rules of fair play and good faith as specified in Art. 1375 of the Italian Civil Code, as well as of the obligations incumbent on the employer to safeguard its employee, in accordance with Art. 2087 of the said Civil Code.
>
> (ibid.)

And yet in some passages in his plea, her attorney did highlight that:

> **Laura's illness was in itself a direct consequence of the harm caused to her personal and professional sphere on behalf of the company.** [. . .]

> **The plaintiff had accurately attached documentary evidence to the effect that a transfer would have obliged her to interrupt the therapy to cure her sterility and a worsening of the state of anxiety and depression that afflicts her, a pathology that has a direct causal relationship with the harassment to which she had been subjected.**
>
> (ibid.)

From a standpoint of juridical qualification, the construction of Laura's case also rested on a certain degree of 'ambiguity of definition'. Ambiguity, also due to the interaction of narrative and logical (i.e. paradigmatic) constructs, seems to be an extremely effective technique in legal discourse. Since it is always possible to provide alternative modes of interpretation, attorneys tend to choose somewhat ambiguous formulae. As a result of this, the attorney in Laura's case never spoke about mobbing, as Laura herself said:

> **My attorney never actually spoke about mobbing; let's say that he gave me to understand that we were certainly dealing with a case of deprival of qualification** . . . especially of one that had in itself generated harm to my professional image . . . already the fact that I was unable to work for two years and was not able to keep up to date was in itself harmful of my professionalism.
>
> (Laura, July 2006)

While accepting without reservation that it is far from simple to draw a distinction between processes of deprival of qualification and of mobbing,[15] the question arises spontaneously as to whether it was not the attorney's knowledge of the practice, his expertise, that induced him to believe that there was a better chance that a question of deprival of qualification would be accepted, because it was considered to be more 'objective', than one of mobbing.

5. The multidimensional nature of the concrete case: rhetoric and persuasion in Franco's story

Rhetoric unquestionably plays a decisive role in the construction of the fact: all the efforts of the parties are focused on making the facts 'knowable', on persuading the judge of their version of what happened.

Amsterdam and Hertz (1992) observe that in any case, however simple the facts are and despite the restrictions imposed by the rules of evidence and by substantive and procedural law, attorneys can construct different stories about the same events. Every story is inseparable from how it is told: it is through the artifice of language that attorneys evoke their opposing visions for the judges.

15 For the definition of mobbing and dequalification, see Chapter 4.

The aim of legal storytelling is to persuade the judge that a story is 'true' (Brooks and Geewirtz, 1998). The 'rhetorical function' of narration, what Berger and Stanchi (2018, pp. 50–55) define more technically as "narrative persuasion", is achieved by attempting to adapt the story to the audience, by involving the audience also in emotional terms in listening to the story or reading it. It is as though a sort of intersubjective pact is pieced together with the audience: the story that tells what happened is not simply one possible version of the events, but 'the reality' about which all the discussants agree. In this regard, Amsterdam and Bruner talk about "interpretative frameworks" (Amsterdam and Bruner, 2000, p. 172), frames of reference that do not imply something ready-made, but something to be built, in part, on the spur of the moment, so as to give a meaning to the communication taking place in the process of interpretation.

All this is achieved by somehow moving and consolidating what is already in the expectations of the people to whom the narration is aimed, in compliance with shared cultural models. This does not mean that the judicial narrative is not yet anchored to legal procedures. The function of the legal narrative is to enable the absolute principles of the *corpus juris* to be connected to the current real and concrete cases about which those people are expected to judge, arbitrate or negotiate. And rhetoric is the linguistic tool that specialises in negotiating between controversies and ultimately in achieving the desired effect, by means of contestation: the advance of alternative visions and persuasion.

Unlike logical reasoning, which tends to exclude debate and comparison, admitting only one 'correct' solution, 'rhetorical narration' plays on the fact that events can be organised in terms of alternative perspectives. The debate takes the form of a reconstruction that is approached from multiple standpoints, supporting the greater credibility of one story as opposed to the others and thus enabling the concrete facts to be linked to a broader, more general category. "Contestation" is the rule of the game par excellence, a typical characteristic of the discourse in the courtroom. It is a typical trait of the methods used by attorneys to try to undermine the other party's perspectives by insinuating a different one (innocence/guilt), whereby the relevance of the facts is justified on the basis of values considered to be important and shared unanimously, so that it is worthwhile sacrificing others so as to safeguard them (*ubi major minor cessat*).[16] There are expectations with regard to the disputation, but the exact circumstances and real dimensions can seldom be foreseen precisely, because the adversaries choose the time, place and terms of the dispute strategically. Every party generally has more than one valid line of attack or defence at its disposal, which can be varied on the basis of what the other party does (Amsterdam and Bruner, p. 165 and ff.).

In the course of litigation, the task of the plaintiff's attorney is to narrate a story in which a 'trouble' has arisen that had a negative impact on the plaintiff and that can be attributed to an action on the part of the defendant, in a

16 In this respect, Moro (2004) talks about the attorney's spirit of antagonism and defensiveness and more generally about the method of confutation.

specific set of circumstances and for a precise purpose. The defendant, in her/his turn, has to construct a story in which it is demonstrated that nothing negative happened to the plaintiff (or that the definition of the 'trouble' suffered by the plaintiff does not coincide with the legal definition) or that, if there has been a legally recognisable problem, it cannot be attributed to the defendant, or that the problem or 'trouble' did take place, but can be attributed to the plaintiff (for example by applying for compensation for damages). In theory, both versions could be true, although clearly neither of them can be a priori: the fact that they are different and opposed to one another means that they represent the typical situation of the dispute, which is solved by making a choice about which story is more 'reliable' with regard to the facts of the case (Taruffo, 1994).

The following passages are excerpts from the plea lodged by Franco's attorney in accordance with Art. 700 of the Italian Code of Civil Procedure, which make a particularly characteristic use of rhetoric. Note the assertive and justifying tone adopted by the arguments supporting the client's position and the decision he had made to retire:

> In 1996, the plaintiff won the contest by public call for school principal, but did not accept the suggested assignment of Cossato, in the province of Turin, for family reasons. **For this reason, he is entitled to be included in the listing of seniority with rank A.**
>
> [. . .] **Ultimately, the plaintiff opted to take a retirement pension when faced with the imminent prospect of a serious penalisation of his career prospects. The only person now listed with seniority at rank "A" is thus Franco**, as no other teacher in the province of Bari has won the contest by public call for school principal.
>
> (Excerpt from the plea entered on May 2005)

The rhetorical function of the method of reasoning increases in the legal arguments used in the plea for the purpose of persuading the judge that serious economic and career disadvantages would accrue to the client if his plea were not to be approved:

> **It goes without saying that, for the reasons indicated in the introduction at points 2) and 3), as the plaintiff is the only person ranked "A" in the list of seniority** (teachers who have won the contest for principal), **this position is virtually certain** (there being two places available in the province) [. . .].
>
> [. . .] **In this case, if the position of principal is excluded, the plaintiff would find himself, for the period necessary for the court to hand down a favourable decision on the case, in the position of having to rely on nothing but a pension and thus 'condemned' to a distressing inactivity while awaiting the result of the court's deliberations. In addition, should the judge decide to approve the plea, the plaintiff, upon**

> **returning to work, would find himself without any position as a school principal and would therefore be obliged to return in the role of teacher while awaiting the result of the new competition.**
>
> **This situation would be seriously prejudicial to the plaintiff, for both economic and professional reasons.**
>
> [. . .] Ultimately, all the preconditions for an urgent precautionary relief to be granted are present.
>
> (ibid.)

The attorney's thinking is aimed at persuading the judge that the client risks suffering serious harm from the changes in the legislation if his request for his resignation to be revoked is not accepted, together with the possibility to have immediate access to the functions of principal for which he was previously qualified.

The narration of Franco's case gives due consideration to the multiple dimensions in which the case was articulated. In fact, when the attorney narrated his client's story, his reasoning took primarily the client's individual dimension into account, with a special focus, for example, on the "frustration of his career prospects" ("As there were no other places available in his province [see list of places vacant dated 1.9.04: attached doc. N° 17], Franco, as a person who had passed the necessary public examination, would be forced by the new law to go back to his job as a teacher" [excerpt from the plea entered on May 2005]) and on the "economic burdens" that would ensue if the situation that he was trying to avoid were indeed to come about:

> **The norm introduced in the text of the law of conversion would thus have completely frustrated the plaintiff's efforts to achieve progress in his career, obliging him to go back to his role as a teacher.** In addition, the consequences in terms of severance pay were set to be penalising, involving the clear loss of about €31,000 (that being the difference between the severance pay as calculated on the basis of a school principal's salary and that due to teaching staff).
>
> (ibid.)

In conclusion, in such a situation of normative uncertainty and personal difficulty caused by the serious career disadvantages he was suffering, the plaintiff acted in a "state of emotional turmoil": the choice made by the plaintiff was thus made of his own free will but under the influence of a defect:

> **There are therefore good reasons for presuming that, in the days leading up to the annual deadline for resignations to be tendered, Franco's intentions were noticeably influenced (and disturbed) by the situation that awaited him, stopping him from forming a genuine decision of his own free will.**
>
> (ibid.)

The attorney then also considered the client's 'family situation', in the broad sense of the term:

> **In 1996, the plaintiff won the contest by public call for school principal, but did not accept the suggested assignment of Cossato, in the province of Turin, for family reasons** [. . .]. **With this in mind, it should be highlighted that the plaintiff's family nucleus comprises his spouse and two adult children, neither of whom earns an income**, since both are engaged in university and/or postgraduate studies, with all the economic burdens that this entails, since they have no income other than what is received for working activities.
>
> (ibid.)

He then considered the comparable position of other colleagues:

> **In the light of the positions available for the 2005–2006 school year** (two: see attachment N° X), on the basis of the regulatory legislation described, since they had to be placed in the same ranking of seniority as Luca (rank 'A'), **the two designated principals, Nino and Guglielmo, appear to have 'overtaken' him and moved up before him in the ranking.** In fact, since they won public competitions, pending their definitive assignments at regional level, they would be entitled to take precedence in provincial listings of appointments.
>
> (ibid.)

The attorney tried to locate the possible consequences of a refusal on the part of the court to accept his client's requests in a broader "social and cultural context", imagining that "the impossibility of doing his work" would be "extremely mortifying", since it is considered to be "an inevitable moment of the manifestation of the personality in the framework of our social formation" (excerpt from the plea entered on May 2005). Last but not least, the attorney considered his client's 'emotional attitude' with respect to the prospect of going to court: "I had some difficulty to begin with, because I had to overcome his uncertainty . . . I saw that he was afraid of going to court" (Franco, April 2006).

From a linguistic standpoint, I note the attorney's tendency to use the third person when referring to his client, who tends to be represented using a passive verb, as a victim of others: "he would have been overtaken", "he would have been preceded", "he would have been forced", "he found himself obliged". When analysing Franco's case from his own point of view in Chapter 4, I noticed a difference: the use of the first person (par. 4.2.3.). These changes enable me to evaluate, on the one hand, the extent to which the attorney was aware that he was dealing with 'cases' that were all about human beings and also, on the other, the tendency to treat his client as a victim.

6. Conclusions

Some possible roles that a lawyer may play have been analysed in this chapter by considering the reasoning underpinning how the cases of Laura, Luciano and Franco were constructed. Considering that elements have emerged that could easily be described as 'typical', in the sense that they are shared in part by the reasoning adopted by both attorneys in the cases thus analysed, the one engaged by Luciano and by Franco and the one engaged by Laura, it is nevertheless evident that some variables are more preponderant than others, according to the case in question.

From the point of view of how the story is narrated, then, what emerges is the fact that the attorney's story is generally enriched by several additional elements compared to the one narrated by the client, especially with regard to the definition of what can be considered to have been the 'trouble' that generated the conflict: this means that the attorney relates the occurrence of the 'trouble' in part to the agency of the client. For example, as we see in Laura's case, the attorney links the company's invitation to her to tender her resignation to the generic reduction in Laura's working capacity caused by the sick leave she takes, so to a reduction in effectiveness of her function. In his interview, the attorney in Luciano's case also gives an indication of an appraisal of 'naiveté' on the part of his client, who had not considered the company's flimsy financial conditions. Another common element shared by all the cases examined, albeit to a varying extent, is the consideration of the multiple dimensions in which the cases are articulated: i e. the client's individual dimension and social position, the cultural context in which the story about fact is told and so on. The attorney also gives due consideration to the kind of judge who will deliberate about the case, taking his prospective audience into account in this way and adapting his narration to make it persuasive. We saw this in Franco's case, but also in Luciano's. In the latter, for example, the attorney tries to include an appraisal of the judge who was due to hear the case in the construction of his reasoning: "I tried to simplify the reasoning further, considering that the judge appointed to hear the case is not notorious for his ability to apply himself to studying the documents" (Luciano, May 2000).

Specifically, in the cases examined here, the following elements were taken into consideration by the attorney when constructing the official story:

- The client's individual dimension: in Laura's case, her conditions of physical and mental health, including such elements as claustrophobia, the fear of flying and the need not to move from her house so as to be able to take therapy for infertility; in the cases of Luciano and Franco, their economic impoverishment, lost professional status and emotional condition.
- The dimension of private human relations: in Luciano's case, the breakdown of his marriage as a consequence of his professional difficulties; in Laura's case, the need to safeguard her private life, which would suffer by being transferred to another city.

- The dimension of professional human relations: in the cases of Laura and Luciano, their sense of discomfort in the workplace context, brought about by being deprived of their functions and being inactive as a consequence, plus the frustration of their career prospects; in Franco's case, the sense of discomfort about the disadvantageous position in which he found himself in the school seniority ranking.
- The breach of professional relations suffered: in Luciano's case, deprivation of responsibilities and economic losses; in Laura's case, mobbing.
- The cultural context in which the facts were constructed: the thesis argued by Laura's attorney, that the company adopted a retaliatory attitude towards its employee after she had made a request for leave of absence so as to be able to undergo treatment for infertility, is evidently 'culturalist' in nature, giving due consideration to a right guaranteed in the Italian legal order by the Constitution: the freedom from discrimination on the grounds of gender. What was at stake here was not, in fact, the objectively biological consideration of being a woman, but the cultural consideration of the figure of a woman. It can therefore be imagined that the attorney chose this kind of defensive strategy because he consciously believed it to be a winning gambit, also in consideration of an awareness of the sociocultural context in which the case took place and how it relates to policies of equal opportunities. Comparably, it could be argued in Luciano's case that insufficient consideration was given to a thesis of discrimination when applying for damages for breach of contract on the part of the employer because of the employee's known trade union activities.

When constructing the story, attorneys generally use evidence and interpret its results in a way that supports their client's version of reality. They also draw on connections of cause and time, of which they make 'instrumental' use, so as to give a 'meaning' to the events. If we then also consider some of the elements specific to the cases of Luciano and Laura and the different ways that their two attorneys operated, it is notable that Luciano's attorney first made a very detailed analysis of the 'elements of reality' characteristic of the affair, then drew up a series of evaluations about his client's position inside the firm where he worked, the possible breaches of contract he had suffered and finally the potential consequences of the affair on his client's personal life. All this for the purpose not only of evaluating to what extent the client's 'everyday' story could be translated feasibly into a 'legal' story, but also so as to offer his client a key for interpreting the events that concerns such aspects of his everyday life as how the working world functions (e.g. corporate strategies typical of isolation, bureaucratic practices and so on). For example, in terms of resolution strategies, since the effect of the action taken by Luciano (his resignation) was produced sometime ago, the attorney made no attempt to reverse it, but to maintain the case for breach of other rights (such as a payment of damages, for example). He constructed the case by using 'objective elements' (dates, places etc.) and hypotheses about such things as the reasons why his client's functions were revoked. He also identified elements of evidence, which he used instrumentally to 'prove the reality' constructed in his interaction with his client.

In the second case examined, that of Laura, the attorney adopted a different approach.[17] Facts, circumstances and corporate decisions that, if taken one by one in isolation, might have had the connotation of a certain degree of 'objectivity', were brought together and used in a construction that ended up being capable of conferring a connection of cause and time on the various events, with the consequence that the retaliatory attitude adopted by the company that had practised it stood revealed.

Lastly, another feature that is found to be characteristic of the construction of a case is a certain degree of 'ambiguity of definitions', maybe because a case dealing with the deprivation of qualification can probably be connoted more substantially in terms of the efficacy of the norm in Laura's situation than one of mobbing, so that it constitutes a greater guarantee of success for the attorney.

Quite apart from the possibility that they may be generalised, the observations described so far with regard to the individual cases certainly underpin the conclusion that the legal construction of the case is the product of a process of negotiation between the client and her/his attorney: 'what happened' is not 'fixed in objective reality', but is more of a construction that is pieced together starting from the story told by the client and giving due consideration to normative and institutional limits of reference and to the cultural dimension, in the broad sense of the term, in which the case takes place. The client and the attorney work together to construct a 'new reality' for which they then apply for an 'official legitimation'.

References

Alpa, G. (2003). Il linguaggio dell'avvocato nell'evoluzione dei metodi interpretativi, delle prassi e delle tecnologie. In: Mariani Marini, A. e Paganelli, M. (Eds.). *L'avvocato e il processo. Le tecniche della difesa*. Milano: Giuffrè. 15–39.

Alpa, G. (2008). *L'avvocato. I nuovi volti della professione forense nell'età della globalizzazione*. Bologna: Il Mulino.

Alper, T. et al. (2005). Stories Told and Untold: Lawyering Theory Analyses of the First Rodney King Assault Trial. *Clinical Law Review*. 12: 1–202.

Amsterdam, A.G. and Bruner, J.S. (2000). *Minding the Law*. Cambridge, MA: Harvard University Press.

Amsterdam, A.G. and Hertz, R. (1992). An Analysis of Closing Arguments to a Jury. *New York University Law Review*. 37: 55–122.

Bennett, W.L. and Feldman, M. (1981). *Reconstructing Reality in the Courtroom. Justice and Judgment in American Culture*. New Brunswick: Rutgers University Press.

Berger, L. and Stanchi, K.M. (2018). *Legal Persuasion. A Rhetorical Approach to the Science*. London and New York: Routledge.

17 Remember that the attorney in Laura's case was not the same as in Luciano's case.

Brooks, P. and Geewirtz, P. (1998). *Law's Stories*. New Haven: Yale University Press.
Bruner, J.S. (1992). A Psychologist and the Law. *New York Law School Law Review*. 37(1–2): 173–183.
Bruner, J.S. (2003). *Making Stories*. Cambridge, MA: Harvard University Press.
Conley, J.M. and O' Barr, W.M. (1990). *Rules Versus Relationships: The Ethnography of Legal Discourse*. Chicago and London: University of Chicago Press.
Cunningham, C.D. (1989). A Tale of Two Clients: Thinking About Law as Language. *Michigan Law Review*. 87: 2459–2494.
Daiute, C. (2014). *Narrative Inquiry: A Dynamic Approach*. Thousand Oaks, CA: Sage Publications.
Danet, B. (1980). Language in the Legal Process. *Law and Society Review*. 15: 445–565.
Ellmann, S., Dinerstein, R., Cunning, I.R., Kruse, K. and Shalleck, A. (2009). *Lawyers and Clients. Critical Issues in Interviewing and Counseling*. St. Paul, MN: Thomson Reuters, American Casebook Series.
Feigenson, N. (2000). *Legal Blame: How Jurors Think and Talk About Accident*. Washington, DC: American Psychological Association.
Gaakeer, J. (2017). The Perplexity of Judges Becomes the Scholar's Opportunity. In: Olson, G. and Reimer, F. (Eds.). *German Law Journal. Special Issue Law's Pluralities*. 2: 233–440.
Gearey, A. (2005). Narrative, Philosophy and Jurisprudence. In: Herman, D., Jahn, M. and Ryan, M-L. (Eds.). *Routledge Encyclopedia of Narrative Theory*. London and New York: Routledge. 273–274.
Hosticka, (1979). We Don't Care About What Happened, We Only Care About What Is Going to Happen: Lawyer-Client Negotiations of Reality. *Social Probs*. 26: 599.
Llewellyn, K. (1962). *Jurisprudence: Realism in Theory and Practice*. Chicago: The University of Chicago Press.
Loftus, E. (1979). *Eyewitness Testimony*. Cambridge, MA: Harvard University Press.
Meyer, P.N. (2014). *Storytelling for Lawyers*. New York: Oxford University Press.
Miller, B. (1994). Give Them Back Their Lives: Recognizing Client Narrative in Case Theory. *Michigan Law Review*. 93(3): 485–576.
Moro, P. (2004). *Fondamenti di retorica forense. Teoria e metodo della scrittura difensiva*. Pordenone: Libreria al Segno Editrice.
Pennington, N. and Hastie, R. (1991). A Cognitive Theory of Juror Decision Making: The Story Model. *Cardozo Law Review*. 13: 519–557.
Rubinson, R. (1999). Constructions of Client Competence and Theories of Practice. *Arizona State Law Journal*. 31(1).
Taruffo, M. (1994). Involvement and Detachment in the Presentation of Evidence. In: Kevelson, R. (Ed.). *The Eyes of Justice*. New York: Peter Lang. 267–289.
Taruffo, M. (2009). *La semplice verità. Il giudice e la costruzione dei fatti*. Roma-Bari: Laterza.
Trujillo, I. (2013). *Etica delle professioni legali*. Bologna: Il Mulino.
Twining, W. ([1990, 1994,], 2006). *Rethinking Evidence. Exploratory Essays*. Cambridge: Cambridge University Press.
White, J.B. (1990). *Justice as Translation. An Essay in Cultural and Legal Criticism*. Chicago: The University of Chicago Press.

6 The judge as a creative decision maker

This chapter examines the role played by the judge in constructing the decision about a case. In a hermeneutic-constructivist perspective that considers the legal process as an interpretative community, the judge's decision is presented as the result of a complex activity that involves interpretative and narrative dimensions. An analysis of the cases illustrates how the judge's narration is decisive in sieving through the factual meanings proposed by the various different stakeholders (clients, lawyers and witnesses) in the phases prior to the decision being handed down, and in establishing links of cause and time between the events. It aims not only to restore the juridical order that has been breached or to create a new one, but also to preserve social order. In this sense, the judge's decision can be described as 'creative'.

1. The hermeneutic circularity of the relationship between fact, law and narration

An important role is played in the 'construction' of the judicial decision by the appraisal of the facts, in other words by the entire process that leads to establishing what the actual facts in question are, as a function of the legal rule that the actors intend to apply, and to ascertaining it by means of appraising the evidence and of weighing the results of the evidence. As I illustrated in part in Chapter 2, in recent years, legal scholars have developed the tendency to study the decisions made by judges as phenomena mediated by the context of cultural and social relations that produce them, by increasing the awareness that the meanings of law can only be interpreted in relation to the specifics of the concrete case and taking the cultural, political and social factors that influence its solution into account.[1]

1 In another sense, with regard to the study of the activities of the courts in context (practices, actors, rituals), I have already mentioned the works of ethnographers, in particular the research conducted by Conley and O'Barr (1990) and by Atkinson and Drew (1979). This is a strand of research, first launched in the United States, that has now also enjoyed considerable diffusion in various fields of the law in Europe. See Baer (2017).

The consideration of this relationship that may exist between contexts of cultural, social and institutional activities and a judicial decision is one of the ways that scholars tend to speak of the judge's creativity.[2] When referring to Civil Law systems, for example, some authors identify the judge's creativity in her/his scope for exercising discretion when identifying the *regula juris*, specifically when interpreting and/or applying a norm (Taruffo, 2002, pp. 195, 197). If, in fact, there is no disputing the consideration that the judge can exercise her/his discretion when choosing and interpreting the norm to apply to the case before him, the fact is often neglected that (s)he can also exercise extensive discretion at other crucial moments in the decision that are related to how the law is applied in the case in hand and so to how the *regula juris* is determined (Pariotti, 2000; Viola and Zaccaria, 2003).

One of these moments when the judge exercises discretion in the activity of interpreting the norm concerns the choice of the facts to judge, as stated among others by Taruffo: "facts play a central and decisive role in the framework of interpreting norms: norms are applied to facts and judges decide on the basis of the facts to which the norms have to be applied" (2010, p. 197).[3]

In a hermeneutic perspective (cited in Chapter 2), it has been stressed that the fact constitutes the first element of the so-called 'pre-understanding' that, in its turn, furnishes the starting point for the interpretation and aims at establishing which of the possible meanings of the norm is applicable to the fact.[4] The idea of the hermeneutic circle – which contributes to the ultimate questioning of the model of syllogistic reasoning – efficiently encapsulates how the raw facts acquire legal meanings only through reference to the abstract norm; the norm, in its turn, can be chosen to regulate the case only through the facts. The origin of the hermeneutic circle is thus constituted by the fact on which the decision, or actually the narration of the fact, rests. That is because the norm operates as a criterion for selecting the circumstances that "deserve to be included in the description of the fact, enabling what jurists call the 'main fact' to be defined, since it corresponds to the 'legal issue' defined by the norm in question" (Taruffo, 2018, p. 31). The identification of the elements of fact sometimes leads to the norm being applied as an effective decision-making criterion in the case.[5]

The judge is thus said to exercise her/his creativity in this activity of identification of the factual elements, as well as of identification of the meanings of the norm, using a dialectic or circular process that is creative to the extent to which

2 Ost points out that, rather than taking note of the creative potential of jurisprudence, there is a tendency in some cases to present this phenomenon as a "pathological deviation of the system, a threat to democracy, an unacceptable manifestation of government by the judiciary" (Our translation; Ost, 2002, p. 14).

3 Our translation.

4 Cf. Hruschka (1965), Hassemer (1968), Pastore (1996; 2013), Taruffo (1992; 2018, p. 29); Carlizzi (2012).

5 On the concept of the construction of the case, cf. Hruschka (1965); see also Ubertis (2018, pp. 57–59).

the configuration of the fact determines the identification of the new meanings of the norm (Taruffo, 2010, pp. 197, 205).[6]

The theories of hermeneutics have thus had the merit of considering the numerous implications arising from the relationship between fact and law and[7] its characteristic circular nature, highlighting how many are the variables that come into play in the complex process of decision-making, which have nothing to do with mechanisms of subsumption and, above all, are extensively discretional[8].

In addition, authors like Gaakeer have specified three of these variables, i.e. narrative rationality, emplotment and narrative glue, as elements that inform the hermeneutic movement that underlies the interpretative reasoning and ranges back and forth between facts and legal rules and between legal concepts and the judicial decision:

> They guide the way in which the judge develops her own 'perspectival narrative' that in turn allows her to engage in the decision-making process. Put differently, judicial emplotment and application when taken literally as *ad plicare* – the folding of the fact and the legal rule into a reciprocal union in order for a new meaning to unfold – requires a narratology. First of all, this process is guided by one's interpretive framework. Second, because of the similarity between narrative and legal interpretation, they do not constitute the application of the abstract rule to the story of the case, but involve a judgement about probability, verisimilitude and truth on the basis of one's whole knowledge of the world.
>
> (Gaakeer, 2017, pp. 351–352)

According to Gaakeer, since judges are human beings, they are also "narrative beings", who are equipped with a narrative intelligence as well as an aptitude for deliberating and adjudicating. Inspired by phronesis and reasonableness, their reasoning is structured in accordance with a narrative plot, which in its turn is modelled by procedural and formal constraints, as well as cultural scripts. Thus, being aware of the pervasive nature of the narrative dimension in law can help not only theorists, but also practitioners, understand how the use of narration may generate different results in solving cases. It is vital that the judges – as well

6 Taruffo suggests the example of the recently defined category of existential damage, which generates a form of extra-contractual responsibility. In a broader sense, he refers to a certain tendency in the doctrine to claim the specificity of concrete cases, going beyond general and abstract norms. Such is the case of problems related to race or gender, for example.

7 For a complete discussion of the fact in the judgement and for a reconstruction of the literature in the field of the relationship between the judgement of fact and of law, cf. Taruffo (1992, p. 48 ff). See also Aa.Vv. (1961) and Ivainer (1988). For a detailed historical and cultural reconstruction of the continental organisation of justice, cf. Damaška (1997).

8 On this topic, see the recent issue of the Italian journal *Ars Interpretandi* dedicated to "Ermeneutica e diritto processuale" (Hermeneutics and procedural law, 2018).

as lawyers – activate their imagination (White, 1973) to predict the potential results of their decision, which will be based on the selection of certain facts rather than others and will have an impact on the lives of the people to whom it is directed.

Starting out from these theoretical premises that further enrich the framework pieced together in Chapters 1–3, in the following paragraphs I shall show how the judge's decision has a narrative structure on a par with the legal acts or narrations of the client, as analysed in the previous chapters, regardless of the fact that it was produced in a civil law system – specifically that of Italy.[9] In addition, basing my argument on the cases of Laura, Luciano and Franco, I shall illustrate what it means to say that the judge has a 'power of creation', in terms not only of the meanings to attribute to legal rules, but also of selecting the elements of actions and evaluating the results of the evidence on which (s)he bases her/his decision. This operation leading to the construction of the judicial decision, taken as a whole, leads to the emergence of new legal meanings that take shape in a narrative structure and are culturally framed.

This chapter is structured as follows: it analyses the narrative structure of a judicial decision (par. 2); it discusses the relationship between the judge's narration and that of the attorney, as well as the role played by evidence in constructing the facts (par. 3); it focuses on the judge's discretionary powers (par. 4), and it then offers some concluding remarks ranging from theory to the practice of the cases examined (par. 5).

2. The judge's decision: between normative and narrative frameworks

In order to analyse the decisions handed down by judges in the cases of Laura, Luciano and Franco, I refer to the concept outlined originally in this book, which assumes how judicial decisions, like any other text – so no less than the narrations framed by the advocate and by the client – create the reality they speak of while they are in the very act of providing it with a structure. In this sense, they are 'narrative constructions'.

As we saw in Chapter 3, court proceedings may be considered as a place of conflict between opposing narrations that aim at achieving a judicial decision or some other provision, so as to define a juridically relevant fact. Since what emerges when the parties and/or the witnesses present their different stories in the hearings is not actually a single overall narration of the facts, the task of the

9 Gaakeer (2017) stresses that some distinctions between Civil Law and Common Law systems risk ending up as a commonplace. For example, the statement that, unlike the reasoning adopted by Common Law, Civil Law reasoning is merely syllogistic and deductive, or that Common Law reasoning is based on precedent. Since we know that Civil Law also bases its reasoning on precedent as a source of law, these situations are comparable, rather than different. The narrative dimension is certainly pregnant and common to both types of system.

judge is to choose between the two parties' conflicting narrations or to construct a narration of the facts of her/his own. As Gaakeer points out:

> 'To judge' is 'to choose': between events and human acts considered legally relevant facts or not (in civil law systems without juries, it is the judge who decides what the relevant facts and circumstances are); between stories plausible in a legal context and those that are not; between narratives to which a legal value can be attached, or not, and for what reason, because at the end of the day the judge as narrator tells the world how she interprets and evaluates what others have told her; and between the consequences of different choices. What weight should be attached to specific facts? What pieces of evidence should be valued as sufficient proof? The success of this evaluative and interpretive process depends on the quality of the judge's phronetic discernment.
> (Gaakeer, 2017, p. 356)

When making a decision, the judge chooses between facts on the basis of the degree of their perceived relevance to the law, between stories to which a legal meaning can be ascribed and others that have no relevance for the law and between evidence that serves to demonstrate the facts, pondering the consequences of these different choices. When deciding in accordance with what Gaakeer calls "phronetic discernment", the judge generates a new narration where the elements of reality identified previously by the parties will probably have a different location. This operation corresponds to what Charon (2006) and White (2008, p. 137) call "emplotment": "by emplotment, sets of events can be transformed into stories with beginnings, middles and ends and thereby provided with positive or negative moral or ideological valences".

When examining the role played by the attorney in constructing the case (Chapter 5), I highlighted how everyday events narrated by the client are translated into a legal framework on the basis of links in cause and time that are created *ex post* to suit the requirements of the narration. Similarly, in the context of the judicial decision, the emplotment "demands an understanding on the part of the judge of the temporal order of an action" (Gaakeer, 2017, p. 337) and "involves a judgement about probability, verisimilitude and truth on the basis of one's knowledge of the world" (ibid., p. 352).

To illustrate this in practice, I shall once again adopt Burke's Pentad structure, as reinterpreted by Amsterdam and Bruner (2000, p. 145, ff). The focus is on the plot's articulation, on the characters and on the temporal framework.

The following elements that characterise the judicial decision's structure can be identified in the stories of Laura, Luciano and Franco: 1) the outline of the plot; 2) the cast and the characters; 3) time frame; 4) destinies/human plights.

2.1. *The outline of the plot*

The first part of the decision contains a sort of orientation, or preamble: an abstract of the story that orients the reader's attention. It defines two fundamental elements in particular: the issue that needs to be solved, which I have called the 'trouble', and the condition for solving it. This excerpt is taken from the introduction to the decision that defined Luciano's case: "With the claim lodged on April 2000, Luciano applied to this bench, stipulating that he had been an employee of the bank from January 1980 and that he had been promoted until April 1996, when he was appointed to be an official of the first degree. He stated that [. . .]. He added that [. . .]. He highlighted that [. . .]. He concluded that [. . .]" (excerpt from the judge's decision, dated October 2004). In the decision on Luciano's case, the judge used a reconstruction of the reasons for the case introduced by the plaintiff, first in fact, then in law, going no further than to add, almost by way of an *obiter dictum*, a reference to the breaches of the contractual agreements he had suffered: "He added that he had reorganised his working relationship as a result of a series of negotiations, agreements and expectations that had been completely disregarded by the other party [. . .]. He demonstrated that [. . .]" (excerpt from the judge's decision, dated October 2004).

In this way, and with this explanation, the judge reduced the scope of the breaches denounced by Luciano in his case.

2.2. The cast and the characters

The first part of a judge's decision identifies the characters who inhabit the story, the subjects of the disagreement, who are described as the plaintiff and the defendant, these being the formal roles that are assigned to them institutionally (Ferrer, 2004, p. 81 ff). In the decision handed down in Luciano's case, we also read: "Once the discussion had been initiated according to the correct procedures, the bank established its presence though its legal representative, denying the counterpart's version and applying for the claim to be rejected and to be awarded costs" (excerpt from the judge's decision, dated October 2004).

2.3. Time frame

The story is organised in a time frame structure that features a starting point followed by the unfolding of the story and arrival at an epilogue. A story's starting point is particularly important, because its purpose is to establish the limits to the range of possible actions and to provide what happens next with a structure, so that simple events each acquire a particular significance and a "narrative necessity". In the field of human affairs, there are of course no natural beginnings and ends: the solution to problem number one generates problem number two and so on. Exactly what the problem is and what its solution will be are questions that are defined to a considerable extent by what the narrator chooses as the starting point (Amsterdam and Bruner, 2000, pp. 152–153). The problem that needs to be solved, like the imagined solution, is expressed from the outset as though there could be no other logical conclusion but the epilogue. Once the premises have been established with legal arguments, the case to be solved and the solution that will derive from it seem to be nothing but the logical consequence of those premises.

2.4. Destinies/human plights

Once the story has been concluded and the new arrangement (individual, professional, institutional and/or social) has been defined with an "integrative" procedure (restoring the previous order) or a "disintegrative" procedure (defining a new order), the story will convey a kind of message that strengthens the new arrangement and makes it the new norm, the new social order, so that it is recognised as legitimate and necessary.

By way of example, I propose to examine the different messages conveyed in the decisions handed down in the three cases discussed here. In Franco's story and in Luciano's story, all the human events are presented as happening independent of the individual's will, as natural and superhuman facts. In the first case, Franco was induced to make the mistake of tendering his voluntary resignation by the legislative chaos that existed in his sector, while in the second case it was a moment of economic crisis brought about by insolvency that determined the decisions unfavourable to Luciano made by the company that employed him. The management of such situations cannot be attributed to the actions of individuals, but can only depend on the strength of an institution that surpasses the limits of the human being: in the first case, that was a change in the relevant legislation, in the second the arrival on the scene of another company with more substantial assets. In particular, in the decision relative to Luciano's case, we read:

> **It has been ascertained that, starting from the second half of the year 1996, the bank was affected by a period of economic difficulty that caused it to cut its costs, to modify corporate strategies that had already been decided** and embarked upon and to seek investment from other enterprises for the purposes of solving the problems of insolvency. **The sole solution employed to remedy this situation was the intervention of the bank and the transfer of shareholdings to it.**
>
> (Excerpt from the judge's decision, dated April 2004)

According to this kind of reconstruction, which traces these events back to a superior and abstract agentivity, no other remedy was possible in Luciano's case, as the alteration of his position in the firm's hierarchy was caused by an irrefutable critical condition.

Unlike these two cases, the decision handed down in Laura's case conveyed the opposite message, i.e. that everything that happens to a human being is the consequence of her or his own efforts and responsibility: there is no such thing as chance or nature, but only human action. In this case, Laura's situation could only be solved if she made a clear individual commitment:

> **The damage to her health appears to concern the pathology of depression she is currently suffering, although at present this appears to be insufficiently serious to justify the Plaintiff's months of absences as demonstrated in the documents and that in any case has not enabled her**

> **to work in Naples either, so that a transfer to Milan, albeit temporary, would not appear to worsen the above-mentioned pathology consistently and irreparably as things stand at present.**
>
> (Excerpt from the judge's decision, dated May 2006)

Lastly, the conclusion reached by the judge in Franco's case conveyed a message about the need to recognise the defect in the legislation – as a consequence ruling that the Ministerial decree did not apply – so as to be able to solve the situation for Franco, whose *de jure* qualification as a school principal had not been translated *de facto*:

> **Art. 1 of the Ministerial Decree dated 9 December 2004 set 10 January 2005 as the final deadline** (not only for the presentation of the request for early retirement, but also for the same request to be withdrawn), **thus very significantly compressing the *spatium deliberandi* made available to school staff by the legislation.**
>
> (Excerpt from the judge's decision, dated June 2005)

In conclusion, judges' decisions tend to convey a message that is general, yet also capable of legitimising and building consensus around a specific view of the world, of human actions and of the events related to it.

3. Narrative interdependences between the judge's story and the attorney's story: the role played by evidence in constructing the decision

The judge's task to appraise reality seems to be exercised by choosing one of the numerous stories told during the hearings – a choice that can only be made on the basis of the results of the admissible and relevant evidence – or by constructing a new story. Taruffo holds that the judge's story generally corresponds to the story told by one of the two attorneys, because the judge finds it to be reliable and backed up by relevant evidence (Taruffo, 1994).

In the decisions examined, in the cases of Laura, Luciano and Franco, a certain discernible narrative interdependence can be identified between the story told by the judge and that of the attorney, which emerges when the narrations are compared. Although I do not intend to generalise, what comes across rather clearly in the cases described is that the judge tends to take up the narration of the side in whose favour he decides. Not only does he echo the attorney's narration as a whole, he also echoes the arguments in law and the interpretations of the results of the evidence presented.

In Franco's case, for example, the judge allowed the suspension, recognising the existence both of the *fumus boni juris* (the likelihood of a right) and of the *periculum in mora* (the risk of delay) with regard to the plaintiff's application for an urgent procedure. He took up both the arguments about the facts and the reasoning about the law, as expounded by the attorney, with regard to the confused condition of legislation that had induced the plaintiff to make a mistake, then concluded by recognising the validity of Franco's revocation of his resignation. It is quite clear that the judge used the same arguments as the ones advanced by the attorney to justify his decision. Here are some of the ones he used: "as the plaintiff was found to be the winner of the competition for school principal in the location Cossato, which he did not accept for personal reasons" (excerpts from the judge's decision, dated November 2005). And later on: "with the consequence that, he reverted to the position of a simple school teacher, losing his right to take early retirement with the severance pay calculated on the basis of the salary payable to a principal" (ibid.). He then concluded that:

> **The case in question thus has all the elements for the resignation tendered by Franco on 4 January 2005 to be considered the result of an essential error of law** (as per Arts. 1428 and 1429 N° 4 of the Civil Code) **and thus recognisable by the public-sector employer** (about this, compare the copies of the notes issued by the trade unions CISL, CGIL School division and ANDIS; att. N°s 7, 8 and 10 of the documentation presented by the plaintiff).
>
> (ibid.)

The thesis that decisions can be interpreted as 'stories' does not in fact indicate that they should be in any way detached from their references to norms or to procedural or institutional restrictions. Instead, the narration is considered to be an active element that lends structure to the process of legalisation within which the elements in question acquire their position and meaning. The reasoning about the questions of fact that are the issue in the decision is structured and guided in accordance with rules drawn from substantial and procedural law, from logic and from the law of evidence.[10]

Twining ([1990; 1994]; 2006, p. 226) specifies that the questions of fact are concerned with such questions as: "what facts can be considered or presented as evidence? Who should present them? About which proposals is there no need to present any evidence"? Gaakeer (2017, p. 356) in turn, underlines the following questions: "what weight should be attached to specific facts"? What pieces of evidence should be valued as sufficient proof"?

This of course is neither the time nor the place to discuss the question of the interpretation of the law, nor to develop a full-fledged theory of evidence.[11] At

10 The doctrine discusses whether it is really the function of the judge to seek the truth and whether any truth can be found in the proceedings. About this, cf. Taruffo (2018, pp. 37 ff); Ubertis (2018, p. 58).

11 On this, it is worth consulting the work of several eminent scholars whose writings pertain to different types of legal systems: Ferrer Beltrán (2007), Damaška (1997), Taruffo (1992), Twining ([1990, 1994], 2006). Cf. also Giuliani's entry (1987), which identifies two basic models of evidence. According to the first, the function of evidence is demonstrative, aimed at obtaining a scientific knowledge of the facts. According to the second, the function of

the same time, however, we cannot avoid making some reference to evidence as a tool used by the parties for the purpose, among other things, of enabling the judge to learn about the fact as it is constructed in the plea. In every modern legal system, the parties have the possibility to introduce evidence in favour of the reconstruction of the facts that they argue before the bench. The context of the court proceedings naturally sets limits and bounds to the evidence, such as the fact that the presentation of the evidence must be encompassed within a certain time frame and that, once it has been completed, the judge must use the law to decide about the facts of the conflict (Ferrer Beltrán, 2007)

What, then, is the function of evidence? To answer this, I refer – albeit by way of example – to certain authoritative positions found in academic literature.

For Twining, for example, proof consists in establishing the existence or non-existence of a certain fact for the purpose of satisfying a court (a judge) that has been charged with the responsibility for determining the fact in question. The degree of satisfaction required is prescribed by the applicable standard of proof (e.g. by "the balance of probabilities" or "beyond all reasonable doubt"). Evidence,[12] on the other hand, is one of the meanings of proof, which has been defined as the effect, the tendency or the design to produce in the mind a persuasion to confirm or disprove the existence of some other question of fact. This means that the logic of proof is concerned with the validity, the obligatory nature and the appropriateness of arguments considered to be the rational foundation for persuasion in creating or justifying a decision or a conclusion about a question of fact (ibid., p. 193).

Taruffo (2002, p. 293), in his turn, considers evidence to be a tool (which he construes as any method, person, thing or circumstance) capable of furnishing information of use for solving the uncertainty about the 'truth' or 'falsity' of the parties' narrations. The parties use evidence to demonstrate the veracity of their statements and the judge uses it to decide whether the factual elements are true or false. According to this approach, the truth of the facts is the result of rational operations based on knowledge that is certain, because it has been verified using evidence acquired in an intersubjective context, and whose results are evaluated using operations of logical probability.[13] Evidence is thus said to have a dual

---

evidence is to persuade the judge to accept a given version of the facts. For Giuliani, these two models are characteristic respectively of the Civil Law system and the Common Law system.

12 The study of evidence and of inference has roots that go deep into the long history of rhetoric and of probability, but interest in reasoning about questions of fact has been rather more intermittent. Within the scope of studies about evidence, a distinction can be drawn between the literature that investigates the logic of evidence and the more extensive corpus of empirical literature about the role played by narration and stories in determining the fact. About the phases of evolution of the study concerning evidence, cf. Twining ([1990; 1994]; 2006, pp. 332–334).

13 As already mentioned in Chapter 3, Taruffo considers the truth to be a reasonable purpose of legal processes typical of modern democratic legal orders and so sees evidence as a tool that the judge can use to achieve this result. The conception of the truth as the purpose of the proceedings and of the presentation of the evidence takes priority over the traditional conception that

function: both that of persuasion and that of fact-finding.[14] While it is true that attorneys use evidence to persuade the judge that the fact is true as they narrate it, it is also true that the judge finds out about the fact by experimenting with the evidence (Taruffo, 2002, pp. 292–304).

As I shall illustrate when I return to analysing Luciano's case, it is hard to maintain this distinction in practice, because when interpreting the evidence, the judge gives it a meaning and a place that may not coincide with the ones identified by the parties, coherently justifying his choice in the text of his decision. Within certain limits, this justification adopts persuasive tones. The realisation of what actually happens in practice obviously does not authorise us to say that rhetoric must be part of the judge's reasoning, as Taruffo has clarified on several occasions (2002; 2013).[15]

The next question then concerns how we establish whether the fact is proven: when hypothesis X receives a certain degree of confirmation, how does the judge establish whether this hypothesis can be considered to be true? According to Taruffo, what the judge establishes is whether it has a sufficient degree of logical probability to be accepted as a reliable description of the fact: if the degree of confirmation is considered to be sufficient, the hypothesis is reliable and can be accepted as a basis for the decision; if on the other hand the degree is considered to be insufficient, then the hypothesis is unreliable and the decision cannot be based on it. In other words, this is a question of the judge's discretional evaluation, which escapes all attempts at strict quantitative determination. It is the moment when what is known as the judge's prudent evaluation comes into play, albeit by making use of rational criteria of decision-making.

One of the hypotheses to be considered is the case in which one of the parties maintains that a fact exists, while the other denies its existence, or argues that the way in which it took place was different from that presented by the first party, and both of these hypotheses furnish elements that confirm them to a certain extent. In this case, Taruffo refers to the criterion of the 'preponderance of evidence': the winning hypothesis is the one that receives the greater degree of

states that a proposition is proven if it is true and if there are sufficient elements of evaluation in its favour (cf. Bentham, 1823, vol. I). A substantial part of the doctrine about legal proceedings has thus abandoned the conceptual relationship between evidence and truth.

14 On the distinction between the rhetorical form and persuasive function of evidence, see the latest work by Taruffo (2018, pp. 31–32). The author also specifies that evidence has an epistemic function, since it has to contribute to knowledge of the facts.

15 Taruffo clarifies that the attorney and the judge employ rhetoric differently: the attorney employs rhetoric to persuade the judge, while the judge does not have to persuade anyone, but does have to justify her/his decision on the basis of the evidence, demonstrating that her/his judgement is supported by good reasons (Taruffo, 1994). In actual fact, as Ferrari (1987, pp. 191–195) has observed, the judge also speaks to an audience, whether internal (the parties, or the judges of the superior instance) or also external (his colleagues, legal journals, the media and the public), who (s)he expects will agree with and legitimise her/his actions. In more technical meanings, using argumentation rationally means trying to avoid arbitrium by the judge (Abignente, 2017).

logical confirmation. In conclusion, Taruffo holds that the criterion of the 'preponderance of logical probability' is the one that best reflects the relationships that comes about between different hypotheses, in the real-world case, about the fact and the available elements of evidence. Alongside the possibility of rational models of evaluation, there are also of course vague spaces of discretion that are inevitably left to the judge to evaluate, in the real-world case, yet are nevertheless guided by rational criteria, above all when two hypotheses have only slightly different degrees of probability or when their values are different, but both are rather improbable.

The model proposed by Taruffo for determining the value of evidence and of the degrees of confirmation of the hypotheses about the fact concerns an abstract typical situation, which takes into account neither the procedural conditionings and peculiarities about how the judge formulates her/his decision about the fact, nor how the evidence is formulated during the court proceedings.

The epistemologist Susan Haack (2012) adopts a different stance when she discusses the suitability of entrusting the evaluation of the admissibility of the evidence to be accepted in legal proceedings (above all criminal trials) to nothing but scientific instruments, as well as the extent to which the nexus of causality between facts and consequences can be demonstrated, considering that an epistemological approach to the proceedings must be capable of combining the objective elements of evidence – including in terms of their scientific value – with a subjective activity of perspective deriving from the reconstruction of the facts, from the context, and from all the subjective evaluation elements (how the judge and the attorneys go about their reasoning, but also what the parties believe and how they behave).

3.1. Uses of evidence in Luciano's ruling

On the basis of these theoretical premises and in order to move from theory to practice, let's now take a fresh look at one of the cases analysed earlier, that of Luciano, trying to throw light on how the evidence was evaluated by the judge in this real-world case.

To start with, the judge referred to the results of the witness evidence to support his interpretation of the case. For example, we read in his decision: "The witness evidence (which took the form of the examination of the ***General Manager of the Bank***, of his ***Deputy*** and of an ***employee*** of the same level who was appointed to the office of ***General Manager***" (excerpt from the judge's decision dated October 2004).

The witnesses were mentioned in the decision in a different sequence from that in which they were examined. In fact, according to the minutes of the proceedings, the witnesses called ranged from Pippo (an employee of the bank), who was called by Luciano's attorney, to the General Manager, who was called by counsel for the counterpart. Yet the order in which they are mentioned in the description of the motivation for the judge's decision was reversed, seeming to be more in line with their perceived importance, from the General Manager to his deputy and so on to other employees. In the description of the motivation, the judge also mentioned the longer testimonies, which moreover coincide with those given by the witnesses who occupied more important professional positions in the context of the bank.

Above all, the judge referred to the 'thesis of the company's economic difficulties' argued by the defendant to justify the revocation of Luciano's appointment and the bank's failure to fulfil its contractual agreements, concluding that "the company's decisions were incontestable":

> **As Silvio stated,** after Luciano had passed to the bank's marketing division, the decision was made to expand the sphere of ZERMAT[16] operations by adding the activity of assistance and consultancy for client firms, in particular in the area of Atripalda. **It was then established, however, that the bank was hit by a period of crisis, starting in the second half of the year 1996, which induced it to cut its costs, to modify corporate strategies that had already been decided and embarked upon and to seek investment from other banking concerns to solve its problems of insolvency**.
>
> (ibid.)

The judge also made general use of the time element, allowing circumstances to pass unobserved that had been clearly highlighted in the application, i.e. that the nature of the bank's business projects changed in a very short time frame, from April to July, months in which Luciano received two letters from the bank: first the letter that employed him and then the one that revoked his managerial position.[17] As the decision reads: "it has been ascertained that the bank X, with effect from the second half of the year 1996 – Luciano had been employed in May – was hit by a period of financial difficulties" (ibid.). What happened ultimately with the judicial decision is a sort of comparative evaluation of the circumstances described in the evidence:

> The preliminaries led to the conclusion that, **after the plaintiff's position of General Manager had been rescinded, the responsibilities attributed to Luciano in the framework of the company really were subjected to a contraction and reduction (the natural consequence of the revocation of the powers delegated to him after he had been appointed to office), but he was not put in a position of enforced inactivity**. In fact, it transpires that the plaintiff was offered the opportunity to deal with the training activity, i.e. to be responsible for all the aspects of organisation of training courses

16 This is a pseudonym.

17 This is discussed in an important excerpt from the interview with Luciano's attorney (in May 2006), who mentioned the issue of the bank's economic difficulties: "As for the issue of defending itself against its economic difficulties, I do not believe it was so crucial, except for admitting that it fell on the management one day like a bolt out of the blue . . . even if we assume that any direct causal relationship could be proven".

> **(testimony of the General Manager)**, and to co-ordinate the company's activities and staff operations **(testimony of the Deputy Manager)**, albeit in a company structure whose range of action and resources would have been limited compared to the original forecast. [. . .] **The testimony of the witness Pippo is therefore found to be unconvincing,** according to which the projects for training and for services for business had not taken off primarily "because the structure had been decapitated, in other words the plaintiff had been deprived of his functions". **The situation that emerges does not enable us to agree with the plaintiff's argument that the reduction in scale of ZERMAT depended on the intention to isolate Luciano, but rather to hold that the contraction in the company's activities depended on the contingent situation.**
>
> (ibid.)

The interpretation of the evidence made by the judge confirms the hypothesis maintained by the bank that it was suffering a financial crisis and throws light immediately on the importance attributed to the individual testimonies, as a function of their social and institutional roles (testimony of the General Manager, testimony of the Deputy Manager). It also highlights the judge's 'choice' to attribute no value to one of the testimonies (Pippo's) that was particularly favourable to Luciano, with the – unmotivated – reasoning that it was "found to be unconvincing" (ibid.).

Despite the large discretion that the judge shows in this specific decision, judicial decisions must be motivated in the Italian legal system, as we shall see in the next paragraph.

3.2. *The obligation to furnish a motivation in the Italian system: Laura's ruling*

The judicial story is unquestionably a story that must be 'justified' and based on arguments that support it.[18] The obligation to specify a motivation corresponds in the Italian legal order to a constitutional guarantee, marking the changeover from an absolutist conception of power to a liberal-constitutionalist conception that requires the justification of the exercise of power.

18 Ferrer Beltrán (2004, p. 117) suggests drawing a distinction between the judge's decision as an act and the judge's decision as a norm. In the latter sense, the decision is justified when the conclusion derives from the premises of fact and law adopted in the reasoning. It also calls for the premises of fact to be true. The judge's decision as an act is justified if its execution is allowed or obligatory in terms of the laws that govern the execution: in that case, the act whereby a decision is made may also be justified, while the content (i.e. the individual norm) is not. For Taruffo, the decision is justified when the arguments start from premises represented by the evidence and are structured in inferences drawn from them with respect to the final judgement about the fact.

The motivation for the decision in the judgement is the premise for the disccurse of justification, which consists in advancing such good reasons that the decision in question comes across as justified on the basis of arguments.[19] Good reasons need to be well argued and based on inferential passages that are acceptable regardless of the subject, thus also enabling the decision to be subject to external control. The formulation of hypotheses, their comparison, confirmation and falsification, are said to be characteristic traits of the kind of reasoning that enables the decision to be reached, from the verification of the statements to the final choice.

This control is extra-judicial in nature. The reference is not only to checks conducted during the proceedings, to the appeal judge, for example, but also to how the exercise of power is justified vis-à-vis society and public opinion: the people in whose name the decision is justified. The judge has to justify all the choices (s)he makes, explain why each witness is or is not credible, clarify why a given statement is not considered valid and so on.

Also in the case of the motivation, as with regard to the decision as a whole, the elements of the normative determination of the decision were few and far between at the time when the decision in Laura's case was handed down (in 2006): Art. 111 of the Italian Constitution merely provided that there should be a motivation; Art. 132, s. 4, of the Code of Civil Procedure provided primarily for its contents: "the concise exposition of the motives for the fact and of the law in the decision"; Art. 118 of the rules implementing the Code of Civil Procedure reiterated that "[t]he motivation of the decision as per Art. 132, s. 4, of the Code consists in the exposition of the relevant facts of the case and of the legal reasons for the decision". What emerged from the combination of the provision of Arts. 118 and 132 of the Code of Civil Procedure can be summarised as the need for the:

- expression of the facts and the reasons at law;
- conciseness of the motives of both facts and law.

Lastly, Art. 360 of the Code of Civil Procedure, which defined the defects that can be identified in the Court of Cassation, hints at the need that the motivation should be sufficient and not contradictory.

Art. 132 of the Code of Civil Procedure has now been simplified, specifying the need for a brief motivation or one described as *per relationem*.[20] The effort

19 Of course, it cannot be ruled out that the way in which the decision was formed may be employed in the course of the motivation. There may be links between the two types of reasoning between the context of discovery and the context of justification. The doctrine takes the consideration for granted of the consequences that the distance in time between the moment of the decision and the subsequent moment when it is written down and recorded generate for the purposes of constructing the final motivation of the decision. The judge sometimes writes her/his formal decision not until several months after it has been given in court. In addition, the work (s)he does is not unlike that of the attorney in seeking out the arguments to back up her/his decision.

20 About this, see the decision N° 17403 dated 3/7/2018 of the Italian Court of Cassation, which states: "With regard to judicial decisions, a motivation *per relationem* to a

required of the judge is that of combining the obligation of a motivation, as a requirement at the level of the Constitution and an expression of the requirement for transparency, with the equally important requirement for incisiveness.

Since a motivation is obligatory, it is interesting at this stage to take a look at how this obligation was interpreted in one of the cases under examination, that of Laura, in an attempt to throw light on how the motivation was conceived by the judge in this real-world case.

One of the arguments employed by the judge in Laura's case – in the intermediate phase when the preliminary judgement had been unfavourable to Laura (before the parties decided to reach an agreement)[21] – was an evident reliance on his evaluation (to a certain extent a 'pseudo-justification' or 'apparent motivation'):

> **With regard to the risk of delay, the irreparable damage cannot consist in the general injury to her family life consequent upon any move of a few hundred kilometres from her home, because it is necessary to illustrate and prove a *quid pluris* that shows evidence of such irreparability and gravity of the injury as to justify the use of the preliminary proceedings, which in this specific case did not take place.**
>
> (Excerpt from the judge's decision, dated May 2006)

The judge, as the attorney later pointed out in the application, did not take into account the circumstance that Laura and her husband were undergoing cycles of therapy to treat infertility. In addition, with regard to the pathology of depression said to be suffered by Laura, the judge did not refer to any expert evidence, but expressed himself in the following terms:

> **The damage to her health appears to concern the pathology of depression she is currently suffering, although at present this appears to be insufficiently serious to justify the Plaintiff's months of absences as demonstrated in the documents and that in any case has not enabled her to work in Naples either, so that a transfer to Milan, albeit temporary, would not appear to worsen the above-mentioned pathology consistently and irreparably as things stand at present.**[22]
>
> (ibid.)

---

legal precedent absolves the judge from the need to develop her/his own legal reasoning, although the path to that reasoning must in any case enable the actual matter in hand to be understood, the process of deliberation undertaken to remain autonomous and the facts examined to be relevant to the principle of law cited, since a lack of these minimum requirements must lead to the conclusion of the complete absence of motivation and the consequent nullity of the decision".

21 Indeed, Laura's case was not settled by a judicial decision, as we have seen, but by an out-of-court agreement reached between the firm and Laura's attorney.

22 This passage already features in par. 2 (provided previously) for different reasons.

Unfortunately, in the specific case of Laura, the examples illustrated are clearly simple evaluations (maybe based on gender stereotypes) made by the judge (which moreover differ from expert opinions) that are only partly reminiscent of logical arguments, based on evidence and produced by inferential reasoning, as a substantial part of the doctrine of legal proceedings would expect. This means that we are nowhere near the fulfilment of the obligation to motivate as defined by the norms in the Italian Code.

4. The judge's discretion

According to the model of procedural legality proposed by Taruffo (2009) and others, the judge evaluates the evidence for the purposes of reaching her/his final decision. This is the exercise of the judge's discretion, which is used to establish the value of the individual pieces of evidence and the value of the whole body of evidence that refers to the elements of fact contained in the parties' narrations.

In the Italian legal system, which is based on the principle of "freely convincing the judge", the kind of terminology used includes the concept of "prudent appreciation", which is construed to mean not that the judge is obliged to use rules of evaluation of the evidence, but that her/his practice of a sort of discretion is backed up by motives (except in the case of a defective statement of reasons). The question is therefore: on the basis of what supposedly rational criteria is it established whether or not a fact has been proven in civil proceedings?

According to the analytical model espoused by Taruffo, the criterion to be applied in a decision at civil law is that of the preponderance of evidence; in other words, it is a question of determining which of the hypotheses about the individual case gets the highest degree of confirmation compared to the others. This is a logical probability that is determined by inference. Certain elements of reality, or "factual statements", as Taruffo calls them, get higher degrees of confirmation. At least three possibilities can be identified:

- A statement of fact can be true or false: it is more probable that a statement will be true rather than false (for example, the probability that it will be true is 80%).
- The same fact can be told in different ways: each of the statements can be true or false, so the judge must evaluate every one of them for the 'relative probability' of the statement, in either a positive or a negative sense. If all the statements have received a certain degree of confirmation, the criterion of the preponderance of evidence obliges the judge to choose the one that has the highest degree of probability.
- All three statements have rather low degrees of confirmation: none of the three passes the test of proof. A weak evidential confirmation is the equivalent of no confirmation. In this case, the judge must decide on the basis of the onus of proof: the party that has failed to prove the fact and that has the onus to do so is destined to succumb. For example, a questionably reliable testimony is not sufficient to establish which statement of the fact has been

> proven. The rule of the onus of proof does not say what level of proof must be attained, but what happens if that level of proof is not attained. If none of all the possible versions of the same fact achieves the necessary degree of probability, the result is that the proof of the fact has not been achieved.

In the end, the judge has to evaluate each individual statement and establish which of the ones that have achieved a sufficient degree of confirmation remain in circulation and which ones have not achieved a sufficient degree of confirmation, so are to be discarded.

What does the judge do with the statements in circulation? Once again, there are various possibilities:

- All the statements are more or less confirmed, the judge has good reason to believe that the narration of one of the parties is proven.
- It may be that the party has demonstrated only some of the statements: if the judge does not succeed in constructing a meaningful narration of a factual affair, this means that the party has failed in its claim.
- It may be that the judge constructs a narration that is different from the one proposed by the party. This is the case when the judge constructs her/his own narration.

The other possibility is that the elements of reality proven may be employed to construct different narrations with different designs. In the case of multiple narrations that are equivalent from a narrative standpoint because they are all proven in the same way, since they all rely on the same statements of fact that are individually proven, if different narrations are possible, it makes sense to choose the one with the greatest narrative consistency. This will be the one that narrates a more credible story than the other stories (in which the categories are used correctly and the ideal types of persons, behaviours and situations are employed correctly). It is on the basis of these criteria that the judge must choose one narration that is more consistent than the others. In any case, the criterion of narrative consistency is only applied to statements that are true, because they are proven. Since an absence of proof cannot be replaced by narrative consistency, these are analytically true statements. The narration does thus come into play, but only in very reduced conditions, according to Taruffo.

The judge also has to evaluate whether or not a legal norm is applicable to the situation of fact that emerges from this construction and whether the norm thus applied should be the one first proposed, or a different one. The question then is no longer one of the construction of the fact, but one of the power wielded by the judge with regard to the legal qualification of the particular case as a consequence of the principle of *jura novit curia.*

In the cases examined here, in particular in the case of Luciano, the judge declared that the plea was unfounded and motivated his declaration, reinterpreting the plaintiff's requests and identifying the legal question to be tackled as just the "deduced illegitimacy of the revocation of his appointment as General

Manager, which took place to his detriment on the date [. . .] and the envisaged breach of contract" (excerpt from the judge's decision, dated October 2004).

He then made a new reconstruction of the facts, starting from the question of law, as he had identified it, reaching the conclusion that Luciano:

> **Was never formally appointed as an executive, but always as a first-level functionary to whom the position of General Manager of the company had been attributed, together with a series of powers related to this office.** And no provision was made in the company ZERMAT for the qualification of executive (or, rather, the files contain no proof that rebuts this circumstance), as objected by the defendant.
>
> (ibid.)

In other words, the judge believed that there was no question to discuss about the position of general manager, as it was a matter of delegated functions and not of a formal appointment. In this passage, instead of choosing between the different narrations offered by the parties, the judge constructed a new narration, of his own. Lastly, the judge employed the following arguments in his decision to evaluate the results of the evidence, interpreting them in favour of the thesis advanced by the bank:

> **From this standpoint, then, there is no evidence of a breach on the part of the employer of the fundamental duties of fair play and good faith in conducting the working relationship. Moreover, it has not been established, nor does it constitute the object of specific deduction, that the plaintiff was assigned, after the revocation of his executive appointment, to new responsibilities of a lesser nature than those suited to his functional qualification, which was that of a first-level functionary. In addition, in no written document has Luciano made a formal request to return to the bank, for the very reason that none of the hypotheses agreed had come about.** [. . .] The verbal requests made to the company's top management, to return to the bank, which have also been confirmed by the witnesses, are of no relevance for the purposes of the claimed breach of contract.
>
> (ibid.)

In this passage, the judge once again adopted different reasoning from those proposed by the parties to contradict the argument proposed by Luciano's attorney, who aimed to demonstrate the breach of fair play and good faith in the professional relationship and his client's dequalification. In the light of nothing but the evidential proof, the judge thus decided that the plaintiff's assignment to lesser responsibilities had not been proven; he ruled that the conditions necessary for him to be re-employed by the bank had not taken place, and he ruled that Luciano had not even made a formal request to be re-employed by the bank. In the case under examination, then, the criterion of prudent appreciation appears to have ended up as the judge's decision to adopt the thesis of 'corporate economic difficulty' on the part of the bank, as advanced by the defence, and to attribute pre-eminent significance to the testimony given by the General Manager and his Deputy, without even checking the bank's financial statements for the purpose of ascertaining the substance of the company's assets and verifying that the economic difficulty had really come about so suddenly after Luciano had been transferred to the service company, a crisis so severe as to trigger the immediate paralysis of the company that Luciano had been intended to manage.

To some extent, these examples – especially Luciano's case – show that the results of the evidence are subject to interpretation and that this interpretation is constructed in accordance with legal rules, principles and investigation, but also in compliance with a consolidated social order. In other words, although the judge's decision uses logical arguments inspired by the laws of probability and the likelihood of being true (in accordance with the model defended by Taruffo and other authors), it also responds to a certain extent to the expectations of the social and cultural context where the facts and the actors are situated. I therefore tend to conclude that there is a kind of irreducible though prolific tension between the analytical as well as the hermeneutical models that I have discussed in this chapter and the culturalist ones that drove my investigation.

5. Conclusions

Although the aim of these analyses, as I already mentioned in the previous chapters, is not to propose results that can be used for generalisation, the examples described highlight some critical elements in judges' reasoning. They also help us understand whether the judge's role can be interpreted as a creative one and, if so, with what meanings.

In the first place, the analysis of the complex operation of constructing the judicial decision has enabled a kind of reciprocal dependence between the judge's story and that of the attorneys to be detected. When the judge adopts the attorney's narration as a whole, the judge's story also tends to reproduce its arguments at law, together with its interpretation of the results of the evidence. The judge seems to decide on the case by choosing one of the two stories told during the proceedings and adopting its narration. These characteristics seem to be shared, especially in Laura's and Franco's cases. In Luciano's case, the judge tends to provide new arguments to justify his decision to support the bank's thesis, although he does not construct a different story with a different plot, so as to present causation in a different way and without evidentiary support or, at least, with serious evidentiary lapses.

There are further critical elements that concern the use of the results of the evidence, such as the tendency to base the decision on the most important and longer items of evidence (Luciano's case), thus confirming the thesis advanced by Conley and O'Barr (illustrated in Chapter 4) that longer items of evidence are more credible than shorter and fragmentary ones. Maybe because the context they tend to provide is more or more salient.

The judge uses his discretion (moreover without always motivating it) to interpret the results of the testimonies, for example choosing not to attribute any value to a testimony that is particularly favourable to the plaintiff with the motivation (or pseudo-motivation) that it "was found to be unconvincing" (excerpt from the judge's decision in Luciano's case, dated October 2004). In addition, the judge seems to practise a form of simplification of reality, or at least does not seem to give due consideration to the fact that there are multiple dimensions in the way that the case's construction is articulated by the attorney in the official documents. In Luciano's case, for example, the arguments employed by the judge with regard to the results of the evidence went no further than to consider the working role occupied by Luciano in the framework of the company where he had agreed to be transferred and the context of economic difficulty in which the bank made its choices to the detriment of its employee. Maybe the judge, by providing his own context for facts, intends to create a reality that coincides with the story he is telling.

An analysis of these cases, situated in specific times and places, leads to the conclusion that, while the clients and lawyers seem to play an effective 'creative' role in the construction of facts – in providing new or alternative visions for reading the facts – the judge shows a tendency to explain facts in general and familiar terms. His decision tends to refer to abstract situations, attributing them to a kind of abstract agency, in order to justify his choice. In two of the cases analysed, for example, the decision of the Bank to dismiss its employees on the basis of such generic metaphors as "the economic crisis" or the employee's purported reduced working efficiency, we see the judge resorting to abstract situations.

In more general terms, the judge seems to look for a kind of social and cultural plausibility for his decision, what Berger and Stanchi (2018, p. 25) also call "sensemaking" or "constructing plausible stories or frameworks that make sense of what they (decision makers) have been told".

In this sense, it would therefore seem that the creative function of the judge, in the cases examined, is expressed not so much and not solely as the interpretation of the norms and the facts, which tend to be the same as the ones cited by the parties, but more as the process of coherently including the decision about the case in a broader framework of social and cultural elements. The judge's function thus plays a more extensive role that combines law and culture and that in this sense can be defined as creative and aimed at achieving cultural juridification (Mittica, 2006).

References

Aa.Vv. (1961). *Le fait et le droit. Travaux du Centre National de Recherches de Logique*. Bruxelles: Etablissements Emile Bruylant.

Abignente, A. (2017). *L'argomentazione giuridica nell'età dell'incertezza*. Napoli: Editoriale Scientifica.

Amsterdam, A.G. and Bruner, J.S. (2000). *Minding the Law*. Cambridge, MA: Harvard University Press.

Atkinson, J.M. and Drew, P. (1979). *Order in Court. The Organization of Verbal Behavior in Judicial Settings.* Atlantic Highlands, NJ: Humanities Press.

Baer, S. (2017). Speaking Law: Towards a Nuanced Analysis of "Cases". In: Olson, G. and Reimer, F. (Eds.). *German Law Journal. Special Issue Law's Pluralities.* 2: 271–292.

Bentham, J. (1823). *Treatise on Judicial Evidence.* Paris: Dumont. Vol. I.

Berger, L. and Stanchi, K.M. (2018). *Legal Persuasion. A Rhetorical Approach to the Science.* London and New York: Routledge.

Carlizzi, G. (2012). *Contributi alla storia dell'Ermeneutica Giuridica Contemporanea.* Napoli: La Scuola di Pitagora.

Charon, R. (2006). *Narrative Medicine.* New York: Oxford University Press.

Conley, J.M. and O'Barr, W.M. (1990). *Rules Versus Relationships: The Ethnography of Legal Discourse.* Chicago: University of Chicago Press.

Damaška, M.R. (1997). *Evidence Law Adrift.* New Haven: Yale University Press.

Ferrari, V. (1987). *Funzioni del diritto. Saggio critico-ricostruttivo.* Roma-Bari: Laterza.

Ferrer Beltrán, J. (2004). *Prova e verità nel diritto.* Bologna: Il Mulino.

Ferrer Beltrán, J. (2007). *La valoracíon racional de la prueba.* Madrid, Barcelona and Buenos Aires: Marcial Pons.

Gaakeer, J. (2017). The Perplexity of Judges Becomes the Scholar's Opportunity. In: Olson, G. and Reimer, F. (Eds.). *German Law Journal. Special Issue Law's Pluralities.* 2: 233–440.

Giuliani, A. (1987). Prova. In: *Enciclopedia del diritto.* Milano: Giuffrè. XXVII.

Haack, S. (2012). The Embedded Epistemologist. Dispatches from the Legal Front. *Ratio Iuris.* 25: 206–235.

Hassemer, W. (1968). *Tatbestand und Typus. Untersuchungen zur strafrechtlichen Hermeneutik.* Köln, Berlin, Bonn and Münch: Carl Heymanns Verlag.

Hruschka, J. (1965). *Die Konstitution des Rechtsfalles. Studien zum Verhältnis von Tatsachenfeststellung und Rechtsanwendung.* Berlin: Duncker & Humblot.

Ivainer, T. (1988). *L'interprétation des faits en droit. Essai de mise en perspective cybernétique des "lumières du magistrat".* Paris: LJDJ. T. 30.

Mittica, M.P. (2006). *Raccontando il possible. Eschilo e le narrazioni giuridiche.* Milano: Giuffré.

Ost, F. and van de Kerchove, M. (2002). *De la pyramide au réseau. Pour une théorie dialectique du droit.* Bruxelles: Publications des Facultés Universitaires Saint-Louis.

Pariotti, E. (2000). *La comunità interpretativa.* Torino: Giappichelli.

Pastore, B. (1996). *Giudizio, prova, ragion pratica. Un approccio ermeneutico.* Milano: Giuffré.

Pastore, B. (2013). Costruzioni e ricostruzioni. I fatti nel ragionamento giuridico. *Ars Interpretandi.* 1: 73–81.

Taruffo, M. (1992). *La prova dei fatti giuridici.* Milano: Giuffrè.

Taruffo, M. (1994). Involvement and Detachment in the Presentation of Evidence. In: Kevelson, R. (Ed.). *The Eyes of Justice.* New York: Peter Lang.

Taruffo, M. (2002). *Sui confini. Scritti sulla giustizia civile.* Bologna: Il Mulino.

Taruffo, M. (2009). *La semplice verità. Il giudice e la costruzione dei fatti.* Roma-Bari: Laterza.

Taruffo, M. (2010). Il fatto e l'interpretazione. *Rev. Fac. Dir. Sul de Minas,* Pouso Alegre. 26 (2): 195–208.

Taruffo, M. (2018). Ermeneutica, prova e decisione. Ars Interpretandi. *Special Issue on Ermeneutica e diritto processuale.* 23(1): 29–42.

Twining, W. ([1990, 1994,], 2006). *Rethinking Evidence. Exploratory Essays*. Cambridge: Cambridge University Press.
Ubertis, G. (2018). Dialettica probatoria e terzietà del giudice. *Ars Interpretandi. Special Issue on Ermeneutica e diritto processuale*. 23(1): 57–70.
Viola, F. and Zaccaria, G. (2003). *Le ragioni del diritto*. Bologna: Il Mulino.
White, H. (2008). Emplotment. In: Herman, D., Jahn, M. and Ryan, M-L. (Eds.). *Routledge Encyclopedia of Narrative Theory*. London and New York: Routledge. 137.
White, J.B. (1973). *The Legal Imagination: Studies in the Nature of Legal Thought and Expression*. Boston: Little, Brown and Company.

Section II – Narratives in cultural contexts

7 Laypeople in action I

Natives' stories[1]

In this section of the volume, I aim to analyse cases that took place in two different cultural and legal contexts: the south of Italy and north-western Switzerland. The culturalist hypothesis which I test here is that a certain degree of 'cultural consciousness' on the part of ordinary people – whether natives or foreigners – makes a decisive difference in whether or not their legal actions are successful. In this specific chapter, cases of people living in southern Italy are analysed for the purpose of highlighting clients' ability to deal with local legal culture and to solve their cases. A second group of cases, which took place in north-western Switzerland, follows in Chapter 8, where I shall analyse cases involving foreigners tackling procedures of naturalisation, illustrating how their gradual command of the rules of custom and of local practices, as well as of the country's legal culture, enables the clients to develop a successful legal agentivity.

1. Culture in law: explicit and implicit dimensions

In the course of recent decades, pluralistic and culturally oriented approaches to law – which may be framed within broader movements such as Law and Society, Law and the Humanities, Law and Visual Culture and Law and Popular Culture, with a consequent proliferation of journals and professional societies[2] – have contributed to highlighting that legal processes cannot be separated from human and historically contingent settings, and that law can only be understood in living contexts. Starting out from the culturalist approaches that were partly explored in the first part of this volume, this paragraph now launches a discussion about such concepts as 'legal culture' and 'legal consciousness' introduced by legal sociologists in recent decades, recognising their usefulness for a culturally

1 An early version of this chapter was discussed at the Clinical Law Review Writers' Workshop (NYU) on September 2013 and at the Workshop on Law as Mode of Existence (SciencesPO) organised by Bruno Latour on April 2014. Further parts of it were discussed at the Conference on Issues of Facts in Rotterdam on September 2015, and it was then published in https://ssrn.com/abstract=2469436 or http://dx.doi.org/10.2139/ssrn.2469436 (consulted on 9 August 2018). See Di Donato (2014).

2 See, for example, the Law and Society Review, Law Culture and Humanities, and others.

oriented analysis, but also the need to expand them through the creation of new socio-legal categories, such as the one that I call 'legal agentivity', to describe the ways in which laypeople act with regard to the law.

In sharing Cotterell's (2004) claim that the influence of culture on law has not been sufficiently analysed by legal theorists, I would like to attempt to identify some of the possible reasons for this lacuna of analysis by legal theorists. A first reason may be found in the domain of positive law as an exclusive source of legality during the twentieth century. As explained in Chapter 2, the formalistic and legalistic tradition in adopting a 'law-first' paradigm to analyse legal phenomena did not take the contextual and human factors of the influence of the law into account (at least, not seriously).[3] A second reason, related to the first, is of a methodological order: legal theorists tend to use categories that are internal to the legal discourse and cannot be extended to the analysis of the relationship between law and society, law and culture etc. A third reason may be linked to the difficulty of capturing culture in the law, because of the vagueness of such a notion.

Since 'culture' is a highly complex concept to define, with cultural meanings being both explicit and implicit, conscious or unconscious and arising in everyday practices as well as in institutional discourses, it may be very difficult to trace the influence of culture on law. I agree with Cotterell and others[4] that the first thing to do in outlining the 'law and culture' binomial is to define the meaning of the term 'culture' for a culturally oriented analysis of the law. It is well known that there are more than 160 definitions of this term in literature.[5]

The concept of culture, how it structures the mind and how individuals come into contact with it was already discussed in Chapter 1. We have seen that, in a Geertzian sense, culture can be construed basically as 'webs of significance' shaped by human beings in sharing a common language, symbolic resources (i.e. religion, cooking, storytelling and other daily activities; 1973). If we adopt Geertz's definition of culture, we accept that 'cultural meanings' are not 'given', but shaped by human beings in specific (social, institutional and material) contexts (Geertz, 1983). To queue at the post office, give up our seat on the bus to a pregnant woman or apply for a certificate from the town hall are practices that do not exist in nature, but are modelled within specific frameworks of action.

To some extent, then, the interpretation of Geertz's notion of culture – as a basis for a network-building process – deals with the implicit relational dimension of the law that has been described by legal philosophers and sociologists. In the early 1960s, in fact, the American philosopher Fuller (1968; 1969) emphasised a kind of continuity between formal and informal law, alleging that the life of formal law, its effectiveness, is conditioned by informal law, being dependent on

3 According to Silbey (2005), law and society were treated as if they were two empirically and conceptually distinct spheres.
4 See also Mezey (2001).
5 See the classic Kroeber and Kluckhohn (1952).

a network of meanings and tacit unwritten conventions rooted in social interactions.[6] Fuller's conception of implicit law or customary law does not seem to be so far from that of Bourdieu, who used the concept of practice to explain the functioning of some specific context of activity, which he called "fields". According to Bourdieu (1986–1987), the law, like every other social field, is organised around a body of internal protocols and assumptions, typical behaviours and self-referential values.[7]

Contemporary legal sociologists and anthropologists in turn introduced the notions of 'legal culture' to describe "patterns of legally related attitudes and behaviour"[8] and of 'legal consciousness' "to analytically name the understandings and meanings of law circulating in social relations" (Silbey, 2008; 2010). As Febbrajo explained in a recent essay: "the concept of legal culture is closely interwoven with different theoretical perspectives. This explains why sociologists of law often prefer to use it implicitly" (2018, p. 28). Two dimensions of legal culture are usually identified: internal and external. As interpreted by Friedman (1969), they refer to the contrast between popular culture and insiders' perception of law. This distinction thus encapsulates the reciprocal relationship between law and society, between customary rules and formal law.

The sociological concepts of 'legal culture' and 'legal consciousness' mentioned here have contributed to the cultural turn in the humanities and social sciences, in re-orienting human and socio-legal research from a legalistic perspective towards "the unofficial, non-professional actors' participation – citizens, legal laymen".[9] Specifically, sociologists of law – Merry (2012), Ewick and Silbey (1998), Silbey (2001; 2005) – discuss the concept of 'legal consciousness', referring to the individual's perception of how the legal system functions: visions and perceptions about law that become part of a collective process of creation of legal meanings, in the broad sense of the term, and that influence how law itself functions (Ewick and Silbey, 1998).[10] Legal meanings take shape in a narrative structure and contribute to create new socio-legal orders or to consolidate the pre-existing ones.

In depicting how "the law and its agents were understood and interpreted by American citizens", Ewick and Silbey (1998) classified three kinds of narratives about law and courts circulating among ordinary people in everyday life. A first one was defined by the two socio-legal scholars as "before the law", meaning

6 See also Postema (1994). For the distinction between law, norm and customs, see also Bohannan (1965).

7 According to Bourdieu, the function of the law consists in the transformation of "regularity into rule".

8 On the definition of legal culture, see primarily Nelken (2012b). See also Friedman (1997) and Merry (2012).

9 See the new legal realism project: www.newlegalrealism.org/about/bottomup.html.

10 In a different sense, Cominelli emphasises the personal legal cognition of legal actors "understood as the complex of activities by which we each perceive and analyse the law and make decisions in connection with it" (2018, p. 2).

that the law was described "as a formally ordered, rational and hierarchical system of rules and procedures operating in carefully delimited times and spaces" (Silbey, 2014, p. 148). In this kind of account, "[r]espondents conceived legality as something relatively impervious to individual action, a separate, discontinuous, distinctive yet authoritative sphere" (ibid.). Law is represented as apart from the routines of daily life: there is a lack of connection between law and ordinary life. In a second account, which Ewick and Silbey call "with the law", legality is understood by ordinary people as an "arena for strategic interactions, sometimes engaged playfully and sometimes seriously, but always simultaneously alongside and within everyday life". This second account emphasises "the room for personal agency and intervention in the system" (Ewick and Silbey, 1998, p. 150). Finally, "against the law" is the account of citizens describing "the law as an arbitrary power against which they feel impotent. [. . .] People reveal[ed] their sense of being up against the law, and unable to play by its rules" (ibid., p. 151).

As has been pointed out on several occasions, the introduction of the concept of legal consciousness has brought about a shift in this attention from an objective dimension, from law as we generally understand it – in the form of statutes, codes, rules and procedures – to a subjective dimension, to how it is perceived and represented by the people in the street. In this kind of investigation, law operates not apart from or 'on' social life, but within and through the very cognitive experiences and intersubjective relations of routine social practice. Legal knowledge forms part of each citizen's 'consciousness', which develops and changes over time through practical experience with legal conventions.

Yet despite having the merit of shifting attention from a conventional way of perceiving law, from an objective dimension that concerns legal texts and decisions, to how the law is experienced, this kind of research tells us little about "how the law is acted on by ordinary people".[11] Bearing legal consciousness research in mind, my intention is thus to attempt to bridge the gap by investigating the relationship between formal law, social customs and personal preferences, particularly emphasising the role played by individuals (clients) in acting on the law and potentially influencing the solution of their case. By situating this concept in the context of my work, I propose first to expand it to the collaboration between clients and lawyers and the other socio-legal actors involved in the solution of a case. Secondly, I propose to shift the focus of socio-legal investigation from the plane of perceptions and representation of the law to that of actions, analysing the stories told by powerless people, such as certain categories of foreigners. These are stories that are otherwise 'unheard' or 'silenced', since those who tell them do not necessarily have the power in society to show what impact the law has on their lives (Kruse, 2011–2012, p. 9). In terms of sociological analysis, I adopt the concept of 'legal agentivity' (see the following paragraph), starting from the proposals made as long ago as the early 1970s, first by sociologists and then by linguists to demonstrate how human action can model and influence the

11 See He et al. (2013).

formation of social and political structures (Ahearn, 2001).[12] Situating the concept of agentivity within a legal discourse I aim to frame individuals' capacity to act in administrative and legal frameworks, mostly emphasising shared collective or collaborative actions.

I will also show to what extent case analysis is a useful pathway to trace the possible connections between law, culture and individual preferences, despite the difficulties explained previously that are entailed in managing a law and culture investigation.

2. Defining legal agentivity

In the previous chapters, especially in Chapter 4, by adopting a clinical law approach, I drew attention to the attitude of the client – as a layperson – towards co-operating with the lawyer and playing a role in solving her/his case. I also described which kinds of 'initiatives' the client is capable of taking to solve the case, in collaboration with the lawyer. I now propose to shift the focus of the investigation from the plane of the interactions inside the legal dispute to that of the relationship between legal actors and the wider sociocultural context.

The question I would like to ask is: how can a dimension of the representation of the law ('legal culture' and 'legal consciousness') be reconciled with 'law in action'?

In terms of sociological analysis, as I mentioned earlier, the concept of agentivity was first elaborated by sociologists and linguists, for the purpose of illustrating how human actions can have an impact on the institutions. It was then further developed by researchers belonging to the school of pragmatism, whose aim was to study language, so as to highlight the performative dimension of language in context (Duranti, 2007). More generally, it can be framed in a socio-constructivist perspective of the study of reality (Berger and Luckmann, 1966), which considers laypeople's ability to define the paths taken by their lives and actions, within the bounds of specific limits, both legal and cultural. In fact, agentivity is forged directly into the cultural context where people live and act and is oriented to

12 For a general definition of the concept of agency, see Ahearn (2001) or also Eteläpelto et al. (2013). Proposing a selected bibliography about "Agency and Anthropology", High (2010) makes the following distinction between the concept of 'agency' (as developed in anthropology) and 'agentivity' (as developed in linguistics): "Whereas anthropological discussions often implicitly rely on a notion of agency as an individual or collective capacity for action in terms of self-consciousness and resistance to power structures (particularly in subaltern studies and early feminist anthropologies), linguists tends to understand agentivity in terms of an agent/patient construction in language based on a subject/object relation. While ethnography provides new ways of construing human and non-human agency, studies of linguists' features such as ergativity have inspired linguists to consider closely the ways in which 'culture' is encoded in grammar. Recent work in ethnosyntax thus holds considerable potential for bridging anthropological and linguistic understanding of agency". For a recent conceptualisation of agency (at work), see Eteläpelto et al. (2013). See also Zittoun and Gillespie (2016), for a consideration of the links between agentivity and imagination.

search out appropriate strategic solutions – as in the case of a legal disagreement. In this sense, the concept of agentivity is also related to that of 'context', throwing light on the active role played by individuals who interact in social contexts with the aim of producing results that can be shared in a community, as well as by creating new tensions and subsequent accommodations.[13] Context – construed to include educational practices (Daiute et al., 2017) – acts reflexively on the case, by giving it origin and influencing its solution, as values, beliefs and representations converge in the proceedings through the legal actors' initiatives.[14]

In order to adapt the concept of agentivity to a legal discourse, I consider certain specifications as suggested by Bruner, for example, so as to focus certain social characteristics of this category of analysis. Bruner provides a list of what he calls "identity indicators". In the first place, he defines agency as one of the "indicators of the ability to act": these are "acts of free choice", "voluntary actions" and "initiatives taken freely in view of a purpose" (Bruner, 1997, p. 3). To clarify, in terms of "dynamic narrating" (Daiute, 2014), these characteristics (which basically pertain to individuals) should be construed to be socially connoted by how individuals act in a social world.

The indicators considered by Bruner include "indicators of commitment": "these concern an agent's consistency with a line of action planned or taken, a consistency that transcends the moment and the impulse. Indicators of commitment tell us about tenaciousness, the postponement of gratification, sacrifice, volubility and inconstancy" (Bruner, 1997, p. 3). Then there are "indicators of resources": "these tell us about the powers, privileges and goods that the agent has at her/his disposal to put her/his commitments into practice. They include "internal resources", such as patience, perspicacity and the ability to forgive and persuade and so on" (ibid., p. 4). There are also "social reference indicators" that "tell us where and to whom an agent looks when in search of legitimation and evaluation of her/his aims and commitments and the distribution of her/his resources. These may refer to real groups, such as schoolmates or cognitively constructed reference groups, such as trade unions or co-workers",[15] or to "the set of those who take care of law and order" (ibid.). Some of the factors listed – Bruner mentions many more – contribute to making individual agentivity socially constructed or shared between individuals in society.

The notion of 'agentivity', as outlined previously, may be expanded on by also considering the definition of agency as proposed by Latour (2005), who interprets this word as "modes of existence". In fact, Latour holds that the actor

13 For the analysis of the relationship between culture, context and the law, see Bruner et al. (2013).

14 Consider, for example, a divorce case in a small suburb of a city in southern Italy, where the sociocultural context has specific characteristic values, such as honour, the role of the family, origin and so on. It comes as no surprise that the litigation may concern the dowry, as a way for the woman to reclaim her violated honour and reputation. See Di Donato, 2012 (Chapter 3).

15 My addition.

cannot be reduced to her/his social dimension and a canonical script of action, without surprises on the stage. That is to claim that the actor also has a dimension autonomous of society; the actor is never alone on the stage, since (s)he is part of a network of interacting actors and the network is part of her/him (ibid., pp. 169–170).

In this oscillation between the individual and social dimensions of action, the psychologist Zittoun (2012) in turn emphasises the uniqueness of the subject. She argues that there is something in each person that escapes social determinations and deals with its uniqueness as a subject, thereby describing a kind of tension between the individual and social dimensions of what she calls the "life course".

My aim in adopting the concept of 'legal agentivity', which underlies all the theoretical approaches reconstructed previously, is therefore to highlight how clients behave when searching for a solution to legal problems, how they construct a defensive strategy, with the help of the lawyer and in co-operation with the institutions, and how their knowledge of the social context orients their perception of the facts and their agency in the course of the administrative or judicial proceedings. How the facts are narrated and re-narrated by clients and their attorneys is of course part of this agentivity. Specifying how the individual's story is reconstructed depends, of course, on how the researcher examines it, as well as on how the individual tells the story in the first place.

I shall then test the use of this concept first to analyse a group of cases that took place in southern Italy – the cases of Carlo, Viviana and Michele –illustrating the different consequences deriving from the legal proceedings, according to how familiar the client was or was not with the context of relations and with local practices and to what extent they benefitted from support in the form of legal or other aid in the context.

3. Three cases from the South of Italy

The three stories that I am going to narrate here are symbolic of the intricate tangle of components with a cultural-relational matrix and others with a legal matrix that together give rise to legal disputes in a given context. The reconstruction of the stories, based on analytical categories borrowed from the narrativist theories mentioned in the first part of this book (Chapters 1–2), as well as the methodology sketched in Chapter 3, will illustrate how the client can act dynamically to find solutions to her/his own legal issues, drawing them both from cultural norms and from her/his own legal knowledge.

For the reconstruction of the plot of the issue, I use a dynamic approach designed to shed light on the articulation of the relations that furnish a story with its structure (Alper et al., 2005, p. 148 ff; Amsterdam and Bruner, 2000; Daiute, 2014, p. 114 ff), by focusing in particular on the following elements: the context, the characters, i.e. those who are the lead actors in the story, the functions they fulfil in the story, their inter-actions, the type or types of agentivity applied by the lead actor and that dominate the story and, finally, the emotional fabric.

3.1. *Carlo's story*

The first story is Carlo's, which takes place in the area of Labour Law and is midway between a case of dequalification and one of mobbing. As we saw in the cases of Laura and Luciano in Chapter 3, mobbing and dequalification correspond respectively to horizontal or vertical forms of psychological subjugation in working relations and to the failure to acknowledge higher qualifications. Both of these phenomena are found in Carlo's case.

The setting of the case is the inland area known as Irpinia in Italy's south-central region of Campania. This context has very marked political connotations, featuring the domination of the political, economic and social scene – at the time of the facts, in the 1980s and 1990s – of an important Italian political party, the Christian Democrats. The protagonist, Carlo, was director of a service management consortium in Irpinia (a publicly owned company), which he successfully put through a recovery programme in a period of financial disarray. After the consortium had undergone a reorganisation whose reasons were political in nature, a longstanding political rival of Carlo's was elected to serve as its President. The day after his appointment, this rival, Paolo, embarked on a gradual dequalification of Carlo. Carlo's managerial post was progressively deprived of its functions and of all positions of any import (in both internal and external relations), until one Davide was eventually appointed to replace Carlo, becoming his opponent. The revocation of the functions fulfilled by Carlo until this point was followed by administrative orders that attributed different professional qualifications to him every time. In practice, Carlo was gradually reduced to a state of complete inactivity, ending up as the victim of dismissal for disciplinary reasons (justified, apparently, by a breach of administrative orders), which were subsequently to be described by the judge as "spurious". The entire affair took on the semblance of what Carlo describes as something straight out of a novel by Franz Kafka, because of the surreal nature of the objections raised.

3.1.1. *The context and its protagonists*

That Carlo was a successful manager was reported in the local press of the day in December 1999. In a newspaper published in Irpinia, the city where Carlo lived, we read: "The consortium was on the verge of collapse in '96. It is now growing, as a result of quality investments". The following excerpt was taken from an interview with Carlo conducted by the newspaper's journalist: "**I have no hesitation in agreeing with those who describe the Consortium in terms of a veritable 'miracle', brought about by the joint effort of everyone,** with a focus on the blue-collar workers, to overhaul a service company that seemed to be irretrievably bankrupt". As the journalist states in the article reproduced here, Carlo got the firm up and running again: "**this was stated by employees and by Carlo, the company's managing director**, 46 years of age, with past experience of managing an employers' association and a present that features a strenuous commitment to relaunching the leading company in which the consortium ISA based in Irpinia holds an interest" (excerpts from *Mondo Impresa*, dated August 2000). And yet the day after the new president, Paolo, had been elected, Carlo was assigned to other functions and a new manager, Davide, was appointed. In the letter reproduced here, Davide cautioned Carlo not to use the title of General Manager:

> **You are hereby invited to abstain from signing any correspondence of external relevance, making use of any general terminology, such as "the Management", which may cause third parties to understand things that do not correspond to the truth, considering equally that this is the exclusive remit of our President**, [. . .] or of such person as he may designate for the purpose.
>
> (Notification from the President, Paolo, to Carlo, dated November 2001)

In the framework of these complicated interactions in the context of his employment, Carlo paid a visit to the office of the manager, Davide, so as to contest the spurious nature of the accusations levelled against him, which were tailored to give the impression of non-compliant behaviour on his part. The meeting degenerated into an argument and Carlo left his workplace without leave. What follows is an excerpt from a message sent by his opponent, the new general manager, Davide:

> In compliance with Art. 7 of Law N° 300, dated 20 May 1970, and of the contractual rules currently in force, **you stand accused of the following cases of misfeasance**. To wit, **on 25 July 2008, at approximately 9.30 a.m., our General Manager, Davide, issued an administrative order addressed to you in which he requested a report about how leaves of absence are managed**, including such leaves as are pertinent to attendance at trade union assemblies. **A few minutes after having received it, you did pay an unexpected visit to Davide's office and launch a verbal attack on him, using the following kind of wording: 'you are a real pain in the [. . .];**[16] **'go to xxx' and others in a similar tone,** while at the same time, stating that you were under no circumstances obliged to carry out the activity thus requested, you did tear the said administrative order into pieces in a spectacular manner, as a sign of your further disregard for the general manager. [. . .] **Lastly, as was subsequently found, you did abandon your workplace at 11.15 a.m. without having received any authorisation to do so.**
>
> (Notification from Davide to Carlo, dated July 2008)

After this episode, Carlo received notification of his dismissal during his summer holidays.

16 Using the informal form of the second person singular, a sign of familiarity in Italian, trans.

3.1.2. How did Carlo defend himself in this affair – as an employee and a citizen? An example of shared agentivity

Carlo is to a certain extent an expert in the mechanisms of qualification in law, having been called to the bar to practise as an attorney. In his relations within the company, so with his superiors in the hierarchy, he retold the narration of the events, tracing them back to their true underlying logic, which is in fact 'spurious' as well as 'political', because it is concerned with attempts to expel him from the consortium. As Carlo's attorney comments: "There is a 'disconcerting' identification between fact and law: each dynamic of the facts is matched by an immediate corresponding qualification in law, by means of a pattern of actions and reactions partly provoked by Carlo and that Carlo uses as a defence strategy in his relationships within the company" (excerpt from the interview with Carlo's attorney, dated September 2010). Here are some narrative passages in which Carlo comments on the case of his dismissal for disciplinary reasons mentioned previously, addressing his remarks to the general manager Davide, his nemesis:

> **It was with surprise that I discovered your umpteenth unjustifiable act of harassment which – as I wrote to you just recently – could actually be described as 'persecution' (as it must in any case be assigned to an investigating magistrate), moreover carried out in a holiday period and without allowing me even the slightest psychological break, thus perpetuating the stress that you also caused in the period around Ferragosto.**[17] [. . .] With regard to your undeserved objections, I therefore emphasise the following points: **I am not in the habit of using vulgar language of the kind you quote in the objection bearing the register number 18/08, since seldom in my life do I make use of such exclamations and, when I do, I use rather different language, such as 'I have had enough' and 'just get lost'. In any case, as anyone can testify, I did not address those insults to you, nor did I speak in those terms. What I do confirm, on the contrary, as I wrote to you in my note N° 735/08, is that your behaviour may, in my opinion, be criminally relevant, as it can easily be classified under the heading of mobbing,** as I in fact stated to you in that circumstance in consideration of the absurd requests you expressed, of which the objection in question is merely a consistent aftermath. [. . .] **Your objection, then, reverses the reality of what actually happened and contributes even more to degrading my professional dignity.** In this sense, nobody can fail to perceive that the only appraisals possible with regard to what I have been accused of are those that I have used myself, **when referring to discussions whose tenor is so unreal that they might have been recorded in nursing homes or in the surreal stories told by Kafka.**
>
> (Notification addressed by Carlo to Davide, dated August 2008)

17 This is the holiday period in mid-August when Italian business traditionally closes down completely (trans).

How did Carlo tackle what he defines as a surprise, as well as a surreal situation? In the first place, Carlo officially commissioned an attorney to impugn the disciplinary measure. On the basis of the documentation provided by Carlo, the lawyer confirmed the interpretation of the events as proposed by the client, stating that the "just cause" specified by Italian law as a prerequisite for dismissal did not stand up to examination and indicating the spuriousness of the employer's behaviour, translating the case in accordance with elements of the context and in compliance with local legal and judicial practice. The lawyer nevertheless refrained from attributing any political connotations to Carlo's case:

> **As it is motivated, the measure in question is devoid of the prerequisites specified for completing the just cause of dismissal in accordance with Art. 2119 of the Italian Civil Code**, i.e. the justified subjective motive, and follows upon persecutory and completely spurious behaviour carried out by Davide. **In particular, the hypothesis that Carlo behaved as described in the measure dated 18 August is contested, since he did no more than object, in firm but civil tones, to abnormal requests *contra legem* expressed by the consortium's general manager.**
>
> (Plea entered by the attorney, dated September 2008)

Secondly, Carlo turned to the social partners, the trade unions: since they had had the opportunity to appreciate his work at the time when he was managing and restoring the consortium, they mobilised the local press and public opinion in support of his reinstatement. Carlo's dismissal became a veritable *cause célèbre*, generating much discussion in the press and reactions from the trade unions. Here are some of the more important headlines that were published in August 2008, after Carlo had received the letter communicating the disciplinary measure:

> *Corriere:*
>
> **Unions on the warpath after the Carlo case**
>
> *Otto Pagine:*
>
> Consortium: Carlo sacked. Unions: **unmotivated act**
>
> *Il Mattino:*
>
> Consortium, **unions against Carlo's dismissal.**
>
> *Buongiorno Irpinia:*
>
> Unions: **No to manager Carlo's dismissal.**

The local press stressed that there was no justice in the dismissal in the light of the Consortium's virtuous management when it was run by Carlo, before he was replaced by Davide. This is an excerpt from a note published by the union representatives, in the same period, in another local newspaper, *Otto Pagine*:

> The Consortium's union representatives, certain in their minds that they are interpreting a feeling of human solidarity that is shared by all the consortium's employees, express their indignation at the unmotivated dismissal of Carlo by the top management of a company that, on the contrary, ought to have been particularly grateful to him. Despite the fact that a resolution had been passed to disband it, the Consortium actually recovered and revived miraculously under his management, as a result of an unprecedented professional and human involvement of all of us as employees, who were motivated and involved by the management's decisions, making us feel like a band of brothers. This same company was then sold for a song and asset-stripped by the rapacious, incompetent managers who took possession of it. Certain that this cheap attempt at back-stabbing will be revoked by the judiciary and intending to decide forms of protest that may be controversial in the course of an especially-convened workers' assembly, the union representatives nevertheless want the following to be made known to public opinion and to the politicians:
>
> [. . .] during the period of management entrusted to the Managing Director Carlo, we experienced an exemplary, inimitable case of good management, which many of us who had been laid off have to thank for having been able to go back to nourishing certainty for our families. [. . .] Every one of us, even those of us who had occasion to be reminded severely of our responsibilities, therefore has a grateful memory of Carlo, for his transparency, dedication and human sensitivity. Every one of us, on the other hand, has recently had the opportunity to experience the most cynical insensitivity to workers' problems, combined with forms of proprietary arrogance worthy of days long gone by.

The trade union representatives expressed their solidarity with Carlo as they stressed his human and management qualities, stating that they considered there to be no grounds for his dismissal and underlining the miracle he had achieved in managing the company, which had now been sold off cheap to individuals they described as cynical and rapacious.

This first phase of the conflict between Carlo and the consortium ended with the management's decision to reinstate him, without following up on the disciplinary dismissal. Subsequently, Carlo initiated legal proceedings to achieve a full reinstatement with the level of management, complete with the related salary differences, and to ascertain that he had been a victim of mobbing.

Thirdly, there is also another kind of 'agentivity' – in addition to that practised by Carlo himself and by the social partner organisations – which could be described as 'abstract' in nature to be taken in account (Amsterdam and Bruner, 2000). In fact, to be precise, when the term 'agentivity' is used in defining a case, it refers to the forces at work that bring the story about and influence how it develops – maybe a person or an institution (a bank, a ministry, the Court of Cassation), an abstraction (the market, the legal system), a supernatural force (God, lady luck), or to a complicated tangle of all of these and how the protagonists act socially.

Here it is concerned with the geopolitical context where the affair originated: the consortium's activity was constantly permeated by the political influence of the Christian Democratic Party. Paolo's appointment as President of the Consortium thus constituted an act of political investiture, According to Carlo:

> **Rather than a legal significance, all these affairs have a political significance:** [. . .] **This is the underlying truth: there was a prejudice at work against me, there was the intention to use the consortium for purposes of political nepotism, for personal and partisan purposes, regardless of efficiency and the company's balance sheets**. The consequence is that the company **is now in a critical condition,** it will take years to revive it: **Paolo achieved the personal result he wanted, because he was elected. And he has achieved the use of the service structures for purposes of nepotism.** [. . .] **I achieved results and they pushed me to one side, using me as a doorman, even though they kept on asking me things, because they didn't know how to do anything.**
>
> (Carlo, July 2010)

3.1.3. How was Carlo's case closed?

After many years of internal negotiations within the consortium, several instances of legal proceedings and considerable damage to the professional's life, the case was solved with a legal settlement between the parties that recognised the qualification of executive of which the protagonist had been deprived, together with a payment of damages. What now follows is the content of the agreement between Carlo and the consortium's legal representatives:

> *Terms and Conditions*
>
> While reiterating the most sweeping objection to every request formulated by Carlo in his action before the Court of Avellino sitting as a labour tribunal, deposited on 30 June 2009 and registered at N° X as embedded in the statement of defence entered by the company, a company representative, in the office as indicated, offered the following to the employee, also in the office as indicated, for the purpose of settling the issue, but also of making

the best interpretation of his professional status, so as to optimise the benefit to be obtained from his activities:

- **Promotion to executive, with effect from today, with an increase in salary** of €xxx per month net and express provision that the employer may only terminate for "just cause" [. . .].
- **The application to the executive employment status thus established of the national labour contract currently in force for executives in the industrial sector**, with the conferment of the executive functions of General Manager of the company's Administrative Area as specified hereunder, which may only be revoked in the case specified at point A) above or in case of the conferment of another responsibility agreed and approved by the parties.

  Functions of the General Manager for the Administrative Area:

  - **Responsible for the company's administrative management, in co-ordination with the President of the Board of Directors**, through the organisation of the operative procedures of accounting and of the company's financial statements.
  - **Responsible for administering and managing the company's human resources, in co-ordination with the President of the Board of Directors**, also by means of establishing working standards for the purpose of optimising individuals' professional performance; [. . .].

- **the payment to Carlo of the sum of € XX,000.00, by way of compensation for the biological injury suffered**. This sum will be paid in monthly instalments together with his monthly salary, from January 2012 up to and including November 2012.

(Out-of-court settlement, dated October 2011)

Carlo ultimately achieved recognition of his management functions, together with an improvement in his salary and compensatory damages. Although the case was solved and the 'agent forces' seem to have found some form of equilibrium because the political forces were counterbalanced, one way or another, by social, judicial and other forces, the divergence between the two protagonists, Carlo and Paolo, remained on an unequal footing. In the meantime, the consortium's President Paolo, Carlo's rival, moved on to occupy an important position in the regional government, with the support of his political party.

Carlo's case is typical of the inseparability of human and legal dimensions in legal proceedings. In fact, the strong pressures to which Carlo was subjected in the context of the consortium had an impact on his personal and family equilibrium.

The day after he was dismissed, Carlo paid a visit to the Department of Mental Health, where he was certified to suffer from a "depressive state of anxiety with somatoform notes of a reactive, situational nature" (certificate dated September 2008). In the same period, Carlo also received notification of a request for separation from his wife. This excerpt from the act of legal separation confirms Carlo's state of alienation and 'estrangement' within his family:

> **The marital relationship that originally featured reciprocal respect and true sentiment had been deteriorating for several years because of misunderstandings between the spouses and in particular on account of irresponsible, uninterested behaviour on the part of Carlo**, who had objected on several occasions to the family environment, **detaching himself from it and creating an independent status for himself in the framework of the family**, without leaving any possibility for dialogue or real discussion.

Finally, it is also interesting to peruse Carlo's own direct evidence about his personal affairs: in the course of his interview, he talked about experiencing this story "as though it were a novel" and feeling that he moved around in society "like a ghost" (Carlo, July 2010).

3.1.4. Conclusions about Carlo's case

Despite the legalistic form used in its telling, it would not be possible to understand Carlo's story outside the social context in which it took place and in the light of nothing but the legal proceedings that frame it: first as the story of a dismissal, then as one of dequalification and mobbing. Carlo had in fact tendered his resignation not of his own free will, but because he was subjected to psychological pressures in the working context (in the form of mobbing and of the failure to acknowledge the higher qualifications he had achieved). Carlo's decision to resort to legal proceedings was only apparently motivated by the breach of legal rules, but actually by political thinking and by the breach of customary rules, such as standards of upright behaviour and good faith in working and hierarchic relationships.

By attempting to make an objective appraisal of the facts, the dispute that the attorney decided to conduct according to legal ritual ended up leaving the 'truth' of the case in the background, since it was only apparently legal in nature and more properly a 'political truth'. Thus, although it was apparently channelled in the forms of ritual justice and was solved through a form of legal settlement, a fair proportion of the case was also solved as a result of the 'culturally aware' action of the protagonist, Carlo, and of the support of the community that enabled it to be said that 'justice had been done', not only by removing Davide (Carlo's rival), who was dismissed as a scapegoat for the entire affair, but also by Carlo's reinstatement in the executive functions of which he had been deprived.

In conclusion, the client succeeded in keeping pace with the events in his professional context – although this effort was not without consequences for his personal life – because of his familiarity both with local practices and with formal laws. While the legal proceedings were unfolding, he skilfully combined personal abilities (intelligence, consistency in his actions, patience and sacrifice) with social abilities. As a result of his good reputation as the company's manager, he could count on the support of the trade unions and of public opinion, which legitimated his work socially and contributed indirectly to strengthening his position in the legal proceedings. Carlo's case can therefore be defined as a perfect combination of legal consciousness and legal agentivity, since both dimensions are shared collectively in this case.

3.2. *Viviana's story*

Developing in ways that share some similarities with the events that concerned Carlo, Viviana's story took place against a backdrop of individual actions and one shared socially, culminating in her winning a battle whose significance is legal, but also social and with gender implications.

Viviana is a theatre actress who was invited to work as a promoter in a theatre company in the province of Naples. The co-operative adopted illegal internal working practices, such as salaries that did not comply with current legislative parameters, camouflaged by the use of false pay packets.[18] Viviana's activity – together with that of the other employees – ended up clashing with the co-operative's 'bad management', which was also facilitated by the lack of controls on the part of the local funding authorities. In the particular case of Viviana, obstacles were put in the path of her ability to achieve professional targets by key characters in the theatre co-operative, who tended to frustrate her work by adopting attitudes designed to achieve her psychological and physical submission, culminating in fully fledged attempts at mobbing and expulsion from her work that made it necessary for her to go to court. Viviana's story is interesting, both because of the context where it took place and because of the methods she adopted to 'manage' her case, calling on assistance from her colleagues and from a broader territorial network.

Another factor that makes this case interesting is that, unlike Carlo, Viviana had no legal skills in the strict sense of the term, yet managed to solve her case nonetheless.

The story is based on the record of the court proceedings made available by Viviana's attorney, in its turn based on a memorandum drawn up by Viviana to aid in reconstructing the facts and an interview given by her.

3.2.1. *The context and the protagonists*

The scenario where Viviana's story took place was a theatre co-operative entrusted with the management of a civic auditorium in a geographical location in the province of Naples that does not enjoy a very high level of economic, social

18 Meaning that the amount declared did not correspond to what the employees actually received.

and cultural development. The intention of the local institutions and funding authorities (most of them public) was that this theatre was to fulfil a function of promoting cultural activities in its surrounding territory, generating a broader form of bond with social and institutional networks. Many of these activities were intended for school groups.

Viviana, the story's central character, is an actress by training. She was hired by the co-operative with the key role of promoting and organising the theatre activities in the territorial network. This was a great challenge for Viviana, who was well aware of the difficulties involved in operating in a context that was disadvantaged, although rich in human and social resources. The first time that Viviana worked with the co-operative was when it organised a performance of the classical Greek tragedy *Antigone*, a play in which she worked as assistant director. Drawing on the play's success, one of the structure's manager, Zero – a lighting technician who was also joint manager of the co-operative – asked Viviana to illustrate the play's didactic function, promoting it to one of the most prestigious schools in the area. Viviana succeeded in recruiting support from this school, which had the reputation for being highly selective, and this excellent result led Zero to invite Viviana to work with the theatre structure on a permanent basis. Viviana was initially uncertain about accepting the position, since it only corresponded to part of her training and to her aspirations as an actress. This is how she tells the story herself:

> **I had absolutely no intention of working there with the responsibility of promoter, seeing that I had completely different plans.** I answered that I'd think about it. Several more telephone calls followed, but I prevaricated.
>
> **[. . .] I started working with the co-operative in September, making it clear that I fully intended to continue to grow artistically, maybe inside the co-operative.**
>
> **I was provided with the annual plan for all the schools, from the kindergartens to the high schools, and I was asked to disseminate it, organising the audience, taking care of transport and the performances in question. [. . .]**
>
> **For every play, the company contacted me, giving me instructions about its technical requirements, the type of audience and the maximum number required for the performance. [. . .]**
>
> **I managed to get organised, contacting all sorts of different people related in one way or another to the state education system: school inspectors, culture councillors in neighbouring towns and villages [. . .], school district managers, school principals (I have stayed in contact with several of these). I was often on the road with my car, without ever receiving any expenses: [. . .].**
>
> **People were happy to come to the theatre, sometimes to satisfy their curiosity about the condition of a structure that had previously been left abandoned for ten years and for the numerous activities that the co-operative promised would be organised in the years to come.**
>
> (Excerpt from Viviana's memories)

According to this telling, overcoming her initial uncertainty, Viviana had no hesitation in plunging passionately into the new professional challenge, building synergies with local institutions and promoting the co-operative's image to the outside world. Despite the hard work put in by Viviana and some of her colleagues, the management of the theatre activities seems to have been extremely improvised and to have had no planning whatsoever. Viviana reported that some of the activities were only organised on paper, without ever being communicated to their intended target, i.e. the public, nor ever actually being performed. She referred to the existence of advertising materials created for the sole purpose of "simulating" the completed organisation of performances but that in practice had never been disseminated to audiences. Nevertheless, as Viviana reported, the employees tried to make up for this poor management:

> **With a constant, tenacious commitment aimed at plugging the gaps of service malfunctions created by the poor management witnessed by the season ticket holders** [whose opinion was of particular significance to the employees]. The employees were also prepared to do overtime, which was not paid, and to do tasks of all kinds [. . .]. **The co-operative's projects multiplied without incurring any additional costs, because of the employees' commitment and the sacrifices they made.**
>
> (Memorandum of staff employed in the auditorium)

The initiatives developed by Viviana and her colleagues (cycles of film projections, premières, concerts etc.) and the results achieved enabled the co-operative to continue receiving public funding, although this did not seem to be used for everybody's benefit: the sacrifices made by the employees seemed to benefit nobody but the president, Maria, and the lighting technician, Maria's lover, Zero.

3.2.2. The troubles

As Viviana reported, this situation continued until the first peculiarities became obvious: employees were dismissed for reasons that had nothing to do with their work and conflicts, some of them physical, took place between Zero and some of the theatre's workers. This led to a period of formal complaints being registered and of manifest discontent, as we can also read in a memorandum written by Viviana:

> **On 6 June, after Zero attacked a male colleague of mine, we all took the precaution to lodge formal complaints against Zero: for my part, I only made a formal complaint about his verbal harassment of me.**
>
> Nevertheless, no disciplinary measures were taken by the management to protect us: **Zero continued spending his time provocatively in the offices on the upper floor, despite the fact that his workplace was the stage**; in fact, Maria (the director and president) herself told me that the judge had

> ordered Zero to stay away from the workplace . . . The level of stress suffered by the staff was extremely high.
>
> (Memorandum of staff employed in the auditorium)

In this context of general discontent, Viviana reported that she was subjected to sexual harassment by the theatre technician, Zero as follows:

> **It was at this time that I started being molested by Zero, who was the theatre technician, as well as the lover of Maria, the director of the co-operative. At the same time, Zero also molested another member of staff, a cleaner, who was later dismissed by Maria. The dismissal was opposed and the employee won the case before the Labour Tribunal.**
>
> **It was gradually made more difficult for me to work in tranquillity. I continued working with commitment, but I found the presence of Zero very disturbing. He often called me into his office, so I asked the bookkeeper to be kind enough to accompany me. On some mornings, when I suffered an anxiety attack, I asked my friend Giuseppe to accompany me from Naples to Carnevale, so that he would give me some moral support**. Zero even persecuted me on my mobile phone! One day, I received a call from him while I was in the offices and I had a panic attack that affected everybody on the floor where I was located.
>
> (Excerpt from Viviana's memories)

Viviana decided to report Zero to the police for sexual harassment. Here is the text of the complaint dated January 2002:

> *To the Carabinieri Station in Carnevale*
>
> The undersigned Viviana, born in Avellino [. . .], by profession employee responsible for promotions of the co-operative [. . .] working in the structure [. . .] managed by the co-operative [. . .], married, lodges a formal
>
> **COMPLAINT**
>
> Against Zero resident in [. . .], a technician with the co-operative [. . .] for the following reasons:
>
> **Zero a stage technician who is also responsible for safety in the workplace in the structure** [. . .] (a theatre managed by the co-operative [. . .]) **has on repeated occasions given expression to violent, aggressive behaviour towards me. Addressing me with psychological threats** (on several occasions he has behaved in an aggressive, violent manner for no reason, slamming doors, shouting, distracting me from my work and instilling a sense of anxiety in me) **and verbal threats** (whore, go and get f*****d, slut etc.). For the reasons listed above, **I hereby request (since I am afraid for**

my personal safety) that Zero be punished and prosecuted in accordance with the law.

Zero did not restrict his actions to physical molestation: Viviana's refusals of him were followed by attempts to discredit her with the co-operative's president, his lover. Viviana was gradually deprived of responsibilities until she ended up being on the receiving end of at least two attempts of dismissal.

One day in March 2002, when Viviana was supposed to stage an important theatrical performance, she received a first attempt to dismiss her, signed by the co-operative's president, Maria, which tried to explain away the professional problems that had arisen as being part of the dynamic of more complex personal relationships with Viviana. As we can read in this letter addressed to Viviana, the president Maria's complaints focused on a presumption of "absenteeism" from the workplace on the part of Viviana and the reduction of her role to an activity of "merely selling" the performances for schools, with the consequence of frustrating the original plan to build synergies between the theatre and the schools:

> **I am embittered to have to take due note, once and for all and in a mandatory manner, that it is impossible to pursue a working relationship any further that is mortifying for both sides in terms of human dignity and seriously detrimental to the co-operative** [. . .].
>
> **The situation is equally complex with regard to your professionalism: no passion, no interest in the specifics required of your role, a devastating reduction in the field of application restricted to the brutal 'selling' of events for schools, practically a commercial representative of the lowest order, obviously without even any commercial success.**

The conclusion reached by the president was that of replacing Viviana:

> **The only thing that remains is to affirm the need for a change of personnel so as to create the 'school office'** – at Carnevale Art – **as a benchmark location and cultural enrichment at the service of schools, that I have long been suggesting in my proposals, so as to qualify the co-operative further and achieve a positive development**, in economic and corporate image terms, in the quality of our structure of services for the territory.
>
> **I therefore consider the working relationship between you and the company [. . .] to be terminated with effect from next April 2002**, obviously leaving open, on a level of private relations, the same affection that has been a mark of this time spent together.
>
> (Notification addressed to Viviana by the Director, Maria, dated March 2002)

This letter made it clear to Viviana that there was a need for a more decisive reaction on her part and that of her colleagues.

3.2.3. *Attempts to solve the 'troubles' between individual and collective agentivity*

Conscious of the illegal dynamics that come about in the workplace, Viviana also involved the other employees, drawing on their sense of solidarity in an attempt to restore legality in their working context. Here is an excerpt from the interview in which Viviana describes how she went about convincing her colleagues to co-operate, inviting them to join a union and to elect her as their union representative:

> **I think I did the right thing to use the argument of the false pay packets, so I convinced my colleagues that they could actually get some money by using this fact, making a documentary record of the situation etc.; because they [the co-operative] took the contributions from the ministry on the basis of the amount recorded on the pay packets, but in reality what we received was half of what was on the pay packet, so I motivated them about this.** So I got them all to join the union [. . .]. **Then they elected me as their representative, not even then did I believe in this thing.** [. . .] **And I have to say that I found this solidarity instead. I was very gratified by my colleagues, in any case.**
>
> (Viviana, February 2010)

As a result of some of the initiatives taken by Viviana and her colleagues, the co-operative was paid a visit by the labour inspectorate, leading to the revelation of a series of irregularities that came to light from a check run on the company books and the actual presence of the employees in the workplace.

Another initiative was tailored to denounce the co-operative's failure to apply the national collective labour contract correctly and its misuse of the pay packets, addressing the local authorities, in particular the mayor of the town where the co-operative was located. The municipality – which was one of the co-operative's funding authorities – called a meeting to push for the employees' pay packets to be treated correctly by the co-operative's management:

> *Municipality of Carnevale*[19]
>
> A meeting is convened for 9.30 a.m. on X/02/2003 in the town hall to discuss the problems related to the application of the national collective labour contract to the workers employed in the structure of the auditorium entrusted to theatre cooperative
>
> (Excerpts from the convocation of the meeting of the Town Council, dated February 2003)

19 Carnevale is an imaginary name.

Although, during the course of the meeting with the Municipality, the president of the co-operative, Maria, denied everything stated by the employees and at the same time sent Viviana another letter of dismissal, the co-operative lost its contract to manage the auditorium theatre for the following years.

3.2.4. Viviana goes to court

Despite the collective measures that she and her colleagues initiated, in terms of her personal position, it was necessary for Viviana to call in an attorney to oppose the second dismissal.

The attorney applied for an injunction as per Art. 700 of the Code of Civil Procedure, as is the practice in the Italian legal order, asking for the employee to be reinstated in the context of her job and arguing that this was a case of "a discriminatory and retaliatory dismissal" in reaction to Viviana's trade union activity in the co-operative.[20] The attorney also contested the existence of the "justified objective cause" for the dismissal, which the co-operative had motivated with the apparent abolition of the specific tasks carried out by Viviana,[21] demonstrating that these tasks had meanwhile been carried out by others.

From the precautionary phase onwards, the judge recognised "the existence of serious, unequivocal and concurring prima facie elements that lead this court to tend towards a ruling of validity of the thesis presented by the applicant" (excerpt from the judge's ruling dated July 2003), i.e. the retaliatory nature of the dismissal. The court also recognised that the measure of dismissal was influenced by the trade union activity of the applicant "capable of calling attention to a notoriously thorny problem (the correspondence between the wages received and the wages indicated on the pay packets), of involving the institutions and of creating conditions that might also lead to the loss of the theatre's management by the respondent in this case" (ibid.). Similarly, on the basis of the witness

20 Italian Law N° 300, dated 20 May 1970, better known as the Workers' Statute, provides strict regulation of any hypothesis of anti-union activities by the employer, including a special procedure for the repression of anti-union behaviour that is enshrined in Art. 28. With the passage of time, the constant intervention of the courts has extended the interpretation of Art. 28, construing "anti-union behaviour" on the part of the employer to mean any behaviour that, though it may not be established specifically by legal or contractual norms, tends in any case to harm the image of the trade unions or to restrict or harm the worker who also carries out union activities, punishing such behaviour through the special proceedings instituted by Art. 28.

21 Art. 3 of Law N° 604 dated 15 July 1966 provides for two reasons for dismissal: for "subjective justified cause" and for "objective justified cause". In the first case, there must be "a notable failure to comply with contractual obligations" on the part of the worker; in the latter case, there must be "reasons inherent to the productive activity, to the organisation of the work and to its regular functioning". While dismissal in the former case is thus justified by behaviour on the part of the worker that is contrary to her/his contractual obligations, in the latter case it is justified by the development of events, irrespective of the worker's behaviour, but that equally make it impossible to pursue the working relationship any further.

evidence presented, the judge ruled the thesis of the abolition of the tasks carried out by Viviana in the co-operative to be unfounded or "not corresponding to the truth", since it had been proven that these tasks were being carried out by others. As the judge stipulated:

> **The informer Zero, the respondent's technical manager** (and certainly not well-disposed towards the applicant, having been the object of several formal complaints lodged by her), **declared that 'the activity previously carried out by the applicant was then carried out by Pietro, who was employed on a three-month fixed-term contract from November 2002**. Pietro continued working with us as an actor.' It therefore does not correspond to the truth that the activity previously carried out by the applicant has been abolished, at least not in full.
>
> (ibid.)

The preventive conclusion reached by the judge was as follows: "the dismissal in question appears to be motivated spuriously and this cannot fail to constitute a further grave indication of the substantially retaliatory nature of the dismissal in question, considering that the employer executed the dismissal approximately one month after the trade union meeting to which reference was made previously" (ibid.).

The preventive ruling was confirmed by the judge of first instance, who recognised that the applicant had proven the "discriminatory nature of the dismissal" (excerpt from the judge's ruling, dated June 2008), thanks to the numerous witnesses who gave evidence to the hearing.

Viviana thus achieved her reinstatement in the co-operative, which however stopped its working activities, and the recognition of her right to the differences in back pay.

3.2.5. The solution to Viviana's story, between legal and cultural matrices: "a show within the show"

How did human, legal and cultural factors interact in the development and solution of Viviana's affair?

Viviana developed and used personal resources (her intelligence, patience, courage and perseverance) and social resources (her ability to involve her colleagues and the local institutions) to interpret what happened in her working context and try to find solutions, picking her way between cultural behaviour and formal law. Several different kinds of 'agentivity' can be sketched out in the solution to this story. The first kind of agentivity concerns the individual initiatives taken by Viviana, who acted in partnership with the other theatre workers. In fact, Viviana played the part of the 'director', but not without collaboration from her colleagues, who played the parts of the 'actors on the stage'. Their purpose was not only to support Viviana in her personal battle against the theatre management, but also to restore their own damaged rights, such as adequate payment and just treatment in the context of their work. As Viviana reported:

> **I have been quite good at turning things to my advantage and using all the cards that have been dealt against me, in short, the director [. . .], so I'm not afraid of anything any more [. . .]. My colleagues backed me up [. . .]; I had their full support: I can't complain.**
>
> [. . .] **in personal terms, I was gratified by my colleagues, despite my uncertainty. I was strong because – as you said – I was . . . I was the 'director'. And they [my colleagues] were good at playing on two fronts [. . .] we organised 'a show within the show', you see.**
>
> (Viviana, February 2010)

The second kind of agentivity concerns the highly incisive role played by the political, social and cultural elements of the affair: social partners – the trade unions, the mayor of Carnevale and the Labour Inspectorate – took steps to 'tidy up' the theatre's management. The third kind of agentivity concerns the decision to go to court. In this affair, the court seems to have acted as a 'balancing force', in harmony with certain social partners and political forces rather than against them (as is sometimes the case). The judge focused on the internal equilibria in the workplace, evaluating both the soundness of the requests made by Viviana (about the discriminatory nature of her dismissal and the possibility of receiving the differences in pay), and the interpersonal dynamics at work between Viviana and Zero for example. These dynamics were not considered to be sufficiently serious to recognise them as indicative of mobbing, but more as a kind of interpersonal incompatibility typical of the way in which Zero related to other people.

In summary, in the case of Viviana, her decision to go to court constituted the ultimate expression of a conflictual relationship that was managed and in part solved independently by the actors in the affair (Viviana and her colleagues), starting from the levels of their awareness of implicit 'local' or 'cultural' rules. The main actors in this story, in the first place Viviana, based their calculations on these rules, partly so as to restore the legal and social order that had been breached and partly to achieve recognition of their damaged individual rights.

In this interplay of social and cultural regulation, the judge's ruling also played a role in terms of restoring balance to the positions in the professional context, only going so far as to influence the 'improvement' of the social fabric whose 'management' actually seems to have been entrusted primarily to the 'cultural participants' in question

3.3. Michele's story: "Ignorantia culturae non excusat"

Michele's case differs from the first two analysed in that the client acted in a socio-cultural context in which he was an outsider. In fact, the case originated in a complicated mass of 'apparent' breaches of legal norms and cultural norms, whose function is to regulate the dynamics of human and professional relationships, in a work and life context into which Michele was plunged when he moved from a city in northern Italy to one in the south for his job. Michele is an engineer who was employed in an executive position in a well-known Italian metallurgy concern located in northern Italy. At a certain stage in his career, he received a job offer from an Italian multinational that was trying to establish production activities in the south of the country, in the area of Avellino. The firm did everything in its power to convince Michele and his family to move from the northern Italian city of Turin, where they lived and worked, down to Avellino, where the production unit that Michele was to manage was located. The company also promised to provide a job for his wife. As a result, although Michele and his family were originally not quite certain of such a move, they ended up accepting the offer of the new company in the south. Michele received an enthusiastic reception from his new colleagues to start with, but sometime after he and his family had moved south, he ran up against the difficulty both of getting a team to function on the basis of his own parameters and of starting out from his own professional experience and confronting a more generalised difference of visions inside the working context. The difficulties that he encountered in fitting into his new professional setting were joined and complicated by the ones he experienced in adjusting to and fitting into the everyday local life where he and his family now lived. They proceeded to buy a house to renovate and entrusted the project to a local building concern. Nevertheless, Michele also decided to ask two of his company's employees to provide him with advice about how the work was executed. This circumstance provided his executives with the pretext for organising Michele's disciplinary dismissal for just cause, accusing him of having breached the obligation of 'fair play and good faith', deriving from his contract of employment. The judge decided that the reasons for the dismissal "do not fall within any of the hypotheses provided for in the national collective labour contract" and noted "the evident disproportion of the sanction of dismissal with regard to the facts as contested" (excerpt from the judge's ruling, dated January 2011), ordering Michele's reinstatement and return to the company. Even so, when Michele returned to the company, his superiors did not even allow him to access his office, but took him to one side and, in the presence of seven other employees, notified him of the reasons for a renewed dismissal. The notification of this renewed dismissal was based on the same facts, with the addition of new "vague and spurious accusations". This second dismissal was also revoked by the judge, who ordered Michele's reinstatement. Yet this reinstatement never took place: the affair was closed by a settlement between Michele and the company, which agreed to pay him damages.

3.3.1. The background to the story

Michele's debut in the new company was preceded by a series of enthusiastic e-mail exchanges between him and his new colleagues, which are reproduced here:

> Sent: Friday 29 February 2008 at 16.33
> Re: Early arrival

Let's leave the date at 5 May 2008 at 9.00 a.m. as specified in the letter of intent.
We – the undersigned and the company X – have brought things back to common sense so that nobody loses out.
See you soon, I can't wait to start.
M

Sent: 29/02/2008 at 18.26
Re: R: Early arrival

I am happy for you
Don't hesitate to call me for any doubts.
See you soon
S

And here is the letter written by the company before Michele was employed to confirm the purpose and conditions of his employment:

This is to confirm that it is our company's intention to proceed to employ you no later than 5 May 2008, on the following conditions:

Position: Avellino Plant Production Unit Manager
Rating: category 7 as per the national collective labour contract for the metallurgy industry, with contractual qualification of manager and company qualification of expert.
Gross annual salary: €X0,000.00 gross.
In addition, this is to confirm that, for a period of 24 months with effect from the date of your employment, you will be paid a gross monthly lodging allowance of €X00.00.
In addition to this, we hereby confirm our intention to provide an integrative economic plan structured as follows:

* On the date of your employment = gross annual salary of €X0,000.00.
* On the date of your employment = one-off payment of €X,000.00
* within 6 months of your employment = one-off payment of €X,000.00
* within 12 months of your employment = gross annual salary of €X0,000.00
* outplacement service via Adecco for your wife for a period of 12 months, renewable for a further 12 months in case of non-allocation.

Best wishes

Torino, February 2008

This exchange confirms the positive premises on which Michele based his working relationship with his new colleagues. About one year after he had been hired, Michele's salary was increased by the company and he received a bonus, in recognition of the good results he had achieved.

3.3.2. The trouble: what happened about two years after Michele had been hired?

Despite starting work happily and the apparently positive human impact, less than two years after being hired, Michele received a notification of a disciplinary breach. The company accused him of having used several of its employees in renovation work in his apartment, free of charge and during their working hours. Here is the content of the notification of the disciplinary breach:

> Re: Notification of Disciplinary Breach as per Arts. 8 and 10, s. B), ss 4, heading VII of the national collective labour contract and Art. 7, Law N° 300/70.
>
> **In compliance with and by virtue of the stipulations as above, this is to contest your behaviour as described hereinafter:**
>
> **In the course of the month of April 2010, you did ask Messrs [. . .],** employees of this company employed in the condenser workshop for which at the time of the facts herein contested you were responsible, so that they were hierarchically subordinate to you, **to execute work to your benefit in the framework of the building renovation of a property belonging to you located in Avellino. To this end, you did contact Messrs** [. . .] personally and Alberto via the team leader, another member of the condenser area staff. **You did then conduct the above-named to your property in Avellino, at different times and on different days, to illustrate to each of them the work to be done and subsequently did entrust respectively to Antonio the work of painting the apartment and to Giulio that of tiling, while Andrea, despite being convened by you to the building site, did not execute any work on your behalf.**
>
> **The activities commissioned by you were actually carried out by Antonio on the days 10, 15 and 22** April, while he was absent from work. On the first two days because he was using his annual paid leave and on the third because he was benefitting from temporary lay-off support.
>
> **As for Andrea, on the other hand, he went to the building site shortly after the end of his work shift on April 2010, working for the entire day until about 6.00 p.m., before going back to work with this company** at about 10.00 p.m. of the same day and until 6.00 a.m. of the following day. As a consequence of the work done on your behalf, then, as you know, **Giulio remained awake and did not benefit from a period of adequate rest before returning to his work in this company, thus compromising the level of attention that he could pay to executing his responsibilities and thus of safety for himself and for his colleagues.**

Your requests did generate in the employees the conviction that it was necessary or at the very least opportune to indulge you, because of your superior position in the hierarchy.

(Notification of disciplinary breach, dated May 2010)

In a nutshell, Michele was accused of having made use of the firm's staff, to whom he was a superior in the company's hierarchy, to carry out renovation work in his own home. This was said to distract them from their work and to be in breach of the code of ethics. Michele tried to justify himself:

Re: Verbal justification for disciplinary notification against Michele

As requested in the registered letter dated 12 June 2010 received by us on 14 June 2010, Michele furnished his verbal justification in the presence of Domenico:

I am here to ascertain that the justifications furnished by letter are clear: the work in my home was carried out by firms and craftsmen who have nothing to do with this firm and I did nothing to force our workers to give me advice or suggestions, in other words to breach the code of ethics. The persons mentioned in the notification offered their services to give me said advice in the framework of our friendly relations and to refuse them, in this area, would be considered a slight.

I am astonished: my only mistake is to have chatted too much at the coffee machine about the work I was doing in my home. I can demonstrate who did the actual work, with witnesses and receipts. I may have done the occasional stupid thing (by which I mean talking too much about the work done by the firms and craftsmen), but I have done nothing wrong.

If this were the case, then the same approach should also be adopted for the time when I accompanied my boss to the restaurant, using my own car.

I have never used my superiority in the hierarchy to obtain favours or benefits; moreover, I am not the direct superior in the hierarchy of the workers named in the notification, since at the time of the events the heads of the Technical Office answered to me directly and the workers in question answered to them, and not even all of them, since Giovanni answered to Technologies and not, at that time, to the Condensers and Modules Product Operating Unit of which I was the manager. In addition, with effect from the first week in May, I was flanked by Domenico in taking responsibility for the Radiators and Masses Product Unit.

For everything else, I refer in full to what has already been communicated in writing and stress that everything took place in the framework of purely friendly relations, when your team becomes a family.

> ***I reiterate, moreover, that these suggestions were furnished during breaks or outside the company context, for example on Sunday.***
>
> I trust that this addition may serve to re-establish a reciprocal serenity with the company as would be the case in a family.
>
> (Letter of justification, dated June 2010)

In the version of the facts as told by Michele, these people – the firm's workers – had offered to help him on a friendly basis. He had accepted their offer, believing that a refusal would have been offensive in that kind of context. Although Michele justified his decision to involve colleague employees in renovating his apartment, he received the disciplinary sanction of dismissal "for just cause", since the company held the facts of which he stood accused to be "completely unjustified". The company reiterated that it was unlawful to involve people who were employed directly by the company. Here is the content of the letter of dismissal:

> Re: Disciplinary dismissal
>
> Pursuant to our letter dated 08/06/2010 [. . .], these justifications cannot be accepted. **The facts described in our notification thus remain completely unjustified and in fact, contrary to what you assert about the fact that the work done in your house was carried out by individuals who "have nothing to do with the firm", the circumstance that we have ascertained is substantially confirmed, viz. that you did entrust our employees with responsibilities for carrying out activities outside the firm and its exclusive interest.**
>
> **[. . .]** We therefore regret to have to inform you by means of this letter that we have taken the disciplinary step of dismissing you for just cause, as per Art. 2119 of the Civil Code, Art. 7 of Law N° 300/70 and Art. 10, letter B, section IV, subsection VII of the national collective labour contract governing your working relationship. **Your employment papers will be made available to you in our offices with effect from the day subsequent to the termination of this relationship**. Sums due for the severance indemnity will be made available to you in accordance with the methods prescribed in the contract.
>
> Yours sincerely
>
> XTS
>
> Sender:
>
> XTS
>
> Industrial Estate
>
> 83100 Avellino
>
> (Excerpts from the letter of disciplinary dismissal, dated June 2010)

3.3.3. *How Michele's legal affairs developed: twice the victim of dismissal*

How did Michele react to the dynamics generated in his working context?

Let's analyse the various stages in this development. In the first place, Michele decided to consult with an attorney. After receiving the notification of disciplinary dismissal, he decided to consult a law office in the city where his new work and life interests were focused, the city of Avellino. The attorney requested an injunction, as per Art. 700 of the Italian Code of Civil Procedure, asking for Michele's immediate reinstatement in his position "for lack of the just cause" for dismissal. The judge also noted the existence of what is known as *periculum in mora*, identified as the need for Michele to return to work, because his income constituted his family's sole form of support.[22] The judge accepted the petition as per Art. 700 of the Code of Civil Procedure, ordering Michele's immediate reinstatement in his position, recognising both the existence of the *periculum in mora* and the "disproportion" between the facts as contested and the measure of dismissal. The judge ruled that the facts that had been used to justify the dismissal were "not proven", also after discussion before a collective bench that heard evidence from several of the company's employees who had been accused of working for Michele, to the detriment of the company. Here is the judge's ruling:

> **The conduct attributed to Michele, including in the reconstruction thereof proposed by the complaining party, does not feature extremes of such gravity as to warrant dismissal,** not even in the form of dismissal with advance notice. [. . .]
>
> **Even should the bench wish to attribute a negative value to the fact in disciplinary terms, it would not be sufficient to justify the maximum reaction possible on the part of the employer, i.e. dismissal, not even in the form of dismissal with advance notice, since this is objectively unsuitable and harms the relationship of trust between the parties, and thus also for considering the quality of Michele and his role within the company.**
>
> **However the results of the investigation conducted are construed, the fact remains that the two employees were involved in the work at Michele's home outside their working hours and without this in any way interfering with the ordinary execution on their part of their duties to their employer.**
>
> (Excerpt from the judge's ruling, dated November 2010)

The judge thus held the sanction of dismissal to be out of proportion: the facts were not serious enough to justify it. Michele then returned to work and was

22 'Just cause' is one of the reasons for dismissal in the Italian legal system.

dismissed once again. Following upon the first ruling handed down by the court, the company invited Michele to come back to work. Nevertheless, no sooner had Michele set foot in the building once again than he was once again notified of the facts and informed of another dismissal, on the basis of similar arguments to those used previously. The company's objections concerned a generic responsibility on the part of Michele for not having asked the competent authorities for the necessary administrative authorisation to start work on the building site in his home and for a failure to comply with the law governing safety in the workplace. According to the company, these circumstances put the safety of the workers at risk. In addition, it asserted that there were presumed irregularities in the labour relations with the workers employed on the site, including the company's employees – in terms of income tax, insurance and wages. Lastly, Michele was accused of a generic breach of the company's code of ethics. Here is Michele's version of the facts once again:

> **The first time the judge reinstated me, they did not even allow me to enter the factory, but took me from the entrance to a small room and, in the presence of six or seven people, repeated the same accusations, the same facts, and then sent me away with a second dismissal. I then obtained a second reinstatement**: the judge ruled that this second dismissal was highly damaging to the "principles of loyalty and good faith in the employer's conduct".
>
> (Michele, June 2010)

Michele once again applied to the court through his attorney. Here are some of the arguments used in his defence to highlight the instrumental and persecutory attitude adopted by the company:

> **The decision to stop Michele from entering the company's plant openly demonstrates, once again, the gravely harassing, persecuting attitude that harms the applicant and reveals the entire instrumental construction of the illicit action undertaken by the company for the purpose of 'remodelling'** (!) the use of its disciplinary power to the detriment of Michele.
>
> (Excerpt from the plea entered by the attorney as per Art. 700 of the Code of Civil Procedure on December 2010)

The judge in turn once again accepted Michele's reasons, ruling that the company's objections were generic and unfounded:

> **It appears to be significant that the facts cited in the second notification are absolutely generic, so much so that the employer itself is incapable of defining the precise nature of the breaches, whether criminal and/or administrative, that are supposed to derive from any irregularity involved in the work itself.**

As things stand, then, and within the limits and for the purposes of proceedings for an injunction, the dismissal cited in this application appears to be unfounded in law. There are therefore grounds for ruling *fumus boni iuris*. There are also grounds for ruling the *periculum in mora*.

(Excerpt from the judge's ruling, dated January 2011)

3.3.4. What kind of agentivity did Michele bring into play to contribute to solving his case? His partnership with his attorney

It is interesting to analyse the kind of agentivity brought into play by Michele in solving his legal and personal affairs. On an individual scale, Michele tried to straighten out his internal relations with the company, using the letter dated 15 June 2010 sent to his superiors in response to the threat of a disciplinary dismissal to explain his good faith in involving colleagues in the renovation of his property. He explained this decision not only with his own lack of free time and the difficulty this entailed for him in keeping contact with expert workers in an area with which he was still very unfamiliar, but also with the implicit wish to consolidate the esteem and affection of the people around him. Transferring his action from an individual dimension to one of institutional relations, in his relations with his attorney, including the process of constructing a legal strategy, Michele admitted his 'ignorance' of the company's ethical or deontological code, when he involved employees in the work in his apartment. He summarised his description of the events here, reconstructing the events in chronological order:

Dear Professor,

As per our agreement, I am sending you the detailed chronology of the maintenance work carried out in the property mentioned in the letter of notification and I repeat that this work was carried out by persons and firms who are all external to the firm and for which I shall produce documents and witnesses.

I must however admit that the contestation derives from an underlying ignorance and superficial approach on my part with regard to my belief that it was not a problem to stimulate and/or receive, outside working hours and the context of the company, opinions, advice, suggestions, recommendations and minor adjustments, in support of the work I was having done, from colleagues and members of staff, also because it is an everyday practice of everyone. In addition, as I also mentioned in my verbal justification, **since I only recently arrived in the area and because of the kind of work I do, which is so intensely demanding as to leave me very little free time at the right times of day, this seemed to me to be the most effective and efficient way to solve the question of the work being done.**

All the workers whom I shall cite later did nothing in the context of the company and/or in their working hours; moreover, they are not

under my direct responsibility, so neither in the workplace nor even less so outside can I oblige them directly to do anything at all.

All the persons involved in this contestation have therefore had no kind of contact with me since May 2010.

The persons I asked and/or who offered their services to help me defining, executing and checking the work are:

Gerardo, Giovanni, Carmine, Gino, Valerio and Antonio.

The details of the activity of each of these are as follows [. . .]

In the attempt to assist his attorney in reconstructing the facts, Michele drew up a matrix for each individual involved in the affair, explaining how he came into contact with him, the kind of activity he did, the exchanges that took place between the people involved and the company's executives. Here is an example:

Gerardo, who is a childhood friend of my brother-in-law, was not contacted by me, but by my brother-in-law, who is the person who painted the apartment. Gerardo carried out this activity using his free time: during those weeks, he was laid off and was bored with staying at home. To begin with, I knew nothing of their agreements: I only became aware of them directly at a later stage, having accompanied them to paint on Friday 30 April 2010, when I joined them and procured the necessary equipment for them. Gerardo subsequently came to help Giovanni on other occasions, occasionally and during his free time, to finish the following activities April 2010:

- painting the ceilings white;
- painting the walls yellow.

I first spoke to Gerardo by telephone; after the hearing, he contacted me to inform me and subsequently, last week, when I was in the company of my brother-in-law, who is a carabiniere, and his brother-in-law, an attorney. He confirmed to me that he had been contacted for the hearing on 8 June 2010 in the morning. He arrived on his own, let's say at around 12.00, and was heard about the work, received the notification now in his hands and subsequently, subject to an intercession on the part of the union delegate Carmine, a 'verbal warning' measure. **He repeated to me that the intention of the questions was to find and push towards answers that would be useful to the process of 'ascertaining my responsibilities'**, as Domenico had given him to understand. In particular, they asked him:

Question: **How I had contacted him.**

Answer: **Michele did not contact me, but his brother-in-law: we are friends and ex-colleagues.**

Question: What did I ask of him.
Answer: **Nothing, but my brother-in-law asked him to lend a hand painting a house that he later learned belonged to Michele.**

Question: **When had he done the work.**
Answer: on 30 April, and a couple of times again later, after the end of his shift and/or at the weekend.

Question: **If I had brought any pressure to bear on him to obtain the work he did.**
Answer: No, no pressure.

Question: If I had paid him or asked for any favours.
Answer: No, it was an exchange of favours with the brother-in-law.

(Matrix drawn up by Michele)

As the following passage extrapolated from the plea entered by the attorney shows, Michele's attorney made extensive use of Michele's reconstruction during his court application:

- **As emerged during the course of the injunction hearing, Gerardo was contacted by the applicant's brother-in-law, actually without the prior knowledge of Michele: Gerardo was carrying out the work of painting the apartment and, on his own initiative, he asked Giovanni for help, Giovanni being a friend of his and hailing from the same village, as well as an ex-working colleague** (they worked together as painters in their youth). The applicant only learned of this circumstance subsequently;
- **as far as the applicant is aware, Giovanni only turned up at the applicant's home once, remaining there for no more than a couple of hours and, in any case, outside his working hours.**
- in the hearing for the summary judgement, Gerardo declared that he had been to Michele's home two or three times for a few hours, deciding freely if and when to go.

(Excerpt from the plea entered by the attorney as per Art. 700 of the Code of Civil Procedure, dated December 2010)

3.3.5. The judge's contextual evaluation of Michele's case

The interesting thing about the decision in Michele's case is the contextualised evaluation of the facts and the witness evidence made by the judge, who did not attribute any illicit behaviour of significance, in terms of Michele's working relationship with the company, to events that he classified more in terms of practices of human relations, in exchanges internal to the firm and that seem to have caused no damage to the company that proceeded to dismiss Michele. As we have seen, from the very first phases of his appraisal, the judge declared the sanction of dismissal to be "disproportionate" to the behaviour contested by the company. Here is an excerpt from the ruling covering the evidentiary findings:

> **Furthermore, the findings demonstrate that the work in question was carried out for a limited period of time, in parallel with the work carried out by other workers (taken on by Carlo and extraneous to the firm) and in any case outside the company's working hours** (cf. declaration made by the workers examined, by the informer Gino and contested in the course of the disciplinary proceedings by the same defendant).
>
> (Excerpt from the judge's ruling, dated November 2010)

The judicial affair ended with a reconciliation procedure before the Labour Tribunal, reaching an economic settlement in which the parties – Michele and the company – agreed that:

> **With this document, the company undertakes [. . .] to pay to Michele, purely by way of a general transaction, the above-indicated sum of € XX,000,00.**
>
> - **Michele on the one hand and the company, acknowledging the non-existence of any reciprocal claim, thus agree mutually that they have no further claims to make upon one another with regard to the working relationship *de quo* and to any other obligatory relationship or heading**, having agreed to use this general transaction of settlement to define each and every reciprocal pending suit in compliance with Arts. 2113 of the Civil Code and 410 and 411 of the Code of Civil Procedure.
> - **The court's costs and fees, together with those of this settlement agreement, with the exception of the subject matter described at point 5 above, shall be construed as entirely paid**: between the parties and their respective procurators who, by signing this document, hereby waive the obligation of professional solidarity as per Art. 68, l. p.
>
> (Excerpt from the settlement, dated June 2010)

3.3.6. The breach of cultural rules in Michele's case: "either you are part of the system, or you shoot yourself: 'it's the end of morality'!!!"

During the research interview, I asked Michele to tell me his story:

Flora: What's the story? What's your story?
Michele: [. . .] **Joining the company was a very, very turbulent experience . . . It was as though the firm immediately, or at least after a very short**

time, realised that I was not 'compatible' with the organisation: in terms not so much of training and competence as of behaviour. The basic problem for them was that I should adapt to their way of doing things. And that was a fundamental problem.

The way I saw it was this: **'if you have bought this competence from the market, you then have to use it, otherwise there was no point in hiring me and making me change to become like you'. It's a basic logical mistake that led to absurd problems right from the start. The firm then started using a 'mobbing' strategy . . . trying to intimidate me, to delegitimise me, holding meetings when I was away, discrediting me with my staff . . . Strategies to which I never attributed any importance, because that's how I am made: I was hurt, but I told myself 'it will all come out right in the end'.** [. . .] **They spied on me first internally, then externally, using a private investigation company whose services led to my dismissal.** [. . .] They discovered that one of my two staff members, an indirect subordinate of mine, had come to supervise some floor tiling work when I was renovating my apartment. . . **They spied on the building site, maybe that worker was their mole.**

They accused me of having profited from being a superior in the hierarchy and told me they would dismiss me for just cause.

(Michele, June 2010)

What emerges from Michele's narrative is a form of incompatibility between his professional visions and more general approaches to life and the company's visions. Michele was originally employed on the strength of his specific skills, but his differences of vision and behaviour seem not to have met with approval, being perceived as not complying with the system of values and of representations that held sway in the working context. This led his employers to organise a series of behaviours as a means of expelling him from the firm.

The fact that, in Michele's case, the implicit ethical rules in the professional, as well as the relational and cultural, context – rules that cover how professional relationships and friendships overlap – were underestimated ended up acquiring the same degree of gravity as the breach of a legal rule, with 'devastating' effects in the applicant's life. Michele had to find a new job and meanwhile had to pay the instalments on the mortgage he had taken out to pay for the house. This is the story as told by Michele, which can in part be taken as the 'moral to the story'.

Michele: **It makes me suffer anxiety to talk about it. . .** I am almost in the grip of a panic attack: I have been getting these moments of anxiety and of panic ever since I lost my job . . . I am trying to manage it because I have become something of an expert by now. .

What we have here is the determination to annihilate another person . . . You don't expect it from a multinational.

It's a question of knowing or not knowing how to work: the firm is not something abstract, it is made up of a group of people who work more or less well or more or less badly if the people are badly assorted . . . I see a problem of professional approach. . .

Either you are part of the system, or you shoot yourself: 'it's the end of morality'!!!

[. . .] **It doesn't take much: they put someone on your trail . . . If they accuse you of making an undue profit, they then have to show that there is an undue profit**: if I call you and I ask you if you went of your own free will, were you paid? Yes! Then there's no undue profit!

Flora: Did your colleagues speak spontaneously?

Michele: Yes, some of them were laid off, others were threatened.

It makes me anxious: remember that they proposed a transaction to make me 'mobile'.[23]

I repeat: it's like the question of continuous improvement. To improve people, you have to talk with them, not threaten them, deprive them of their jobs, which are the most important things after life itself. Depriving someone of his job illegitimately is like killing him. These people and their lawyers are real killers, except that they don't kill you by depriving you of your life, although they may induce you to do it yourself.

Flora: And then there's the family to consider?

Michele: **My children see their father at home who cries, or their mother who cries. . .**

(Michele, June 2010)

Michele's case – that of a client who was ignorant of the mechanisms that seem to have been typical of certain working contexts, as the cases of Carlo and Viviana also illustrate – concluded with him unexpectedly having to learn a lesson in life's harsh realities, not without consequences for himself and his family.

4. Conclusions

The aim of this chapter was to highlight some of the links between law and culture, illustrating how the application of the law and the solution of cases do not take place in a vacuum, but are closely connected to social practices and to the network of relations that provide the backdrops for the stories examined.

My use of the category of 'legal agentivity' – shifting the focus away from a dimension of mere representation or psychological dimension (legal consciousness) and towards one of collective action, also understood as collaborative lawyering (specifically referred in these terms to the lawyer-client relationships in

23 This is the first step towards losing his job (trans.).

the three cases) – has enabled me to achieve progress in the study of 'law in context', showing how an understanding of the law on the part of the client and the possibility to orient the solution of her or his own case are the result of an intersubjective process. In at least two cases out of the three, the fact that legal actors – clients, but also attorney and judges – are aware of the implicit or explicit 'meanings' characteristic of everyday practices enables the conflicts to be solved, making use not only of formal law, but also of local resources. This can be seen especially clearly in Carlo's case: since he was aware of the mechanisms of legal qualification, he was capable of re-narrating what happened, shedding light on its retaliatory significance and tracing it back to its original matrix, which was political rather than legal. Moreover, in the cases of both Carlo and Viviana, the solution to the case was supported effectively by a form of collective legal agentivity: the two clients mobilised public opinion, social and institutional organisations, their working colleagues and their friends to shed light on illicit practices and restore order to their working contexts. Several factors contributed to solving these cases: personal resources, skills acquired in the framework of their professional careers, experience and social competence in the broad sense of the term.

Legal agentivity is thus a blend of all these components (individual as well as social) that are not to be taken for granted, are commensurate to the individual's understanding of the system, broadly speaking, and contribute to strengthening how the law functions and even its shortcomings. Comparably, how the client-attorney relationship takes shape has an impact on clients' agentivity, as I already highlighted in Chapters 4 and 5.

From a methodological standpoint, the adoption of an approach that is holistic for analysing the stories of Carlo, Michele and Viviana enabled their cases to be reconstructed in their entirety, from the moment when the complication, or trouble, that gave rise to narration first arose to their attempts to solve it using different kinds of individual or collective action. By studying documents pertaining to the legal proceedings, including unofficial ones, an analysis of the exchanges and interactions between the stories' actors enabled me to demonstrate that the root cause of the conflicts tackled here was the breach of norms of behaviour, such as fair play and good faith in working relationships, even before the breach of formal law.

In these cases, the law's function is to furnish a juridical channel for a conflict that comes about as a consequence of bad local practices: the imposition of a political priority in the functioning of a partly publicly funded company, as in Carlo's case; attempts to subject colleagues who were placed lower down in the company hierarchy to psychological and physical mobbing, in all the three cases that I have analysed; irregular payments and the fictitious organisation of shows, in the case of Viviana, and so on. It is also significant that in all three cases, but in Viviana's in particular, the judge was capable of reading between the lines of what happened, identifying the attitudes typical of the working context (gender relations, for example), as well as legal mindsets.

In the next chapter, I shall show how clients' 'legal agentivity' takes different forms if they act in a cultural and legal system that identifies them as foreigners.

Nevertheless, it will be surprising to discover that, even in a context like that of Switzerland, which is apparently stricter in terms of forms and rituals, the application of the law is strongly conditioned by local interpretations and practices.

References

Ahearn, L.M. (2001). Agency. In: Duranti, A. (Ed.). *Key Terms in Language and Culture*. Malden, MA: Wiley-Blackwell. 7–10.

Alper, T. et al. (2005). Stories Told and Untold: Lawyering Theory Analyses of the First Rodney King Assault Trial. *Clinical Law Review*. 12: 1–202.

Amsterdam, A.G. and Bruner, J.S. (2000). *Minding the Law*. Cambridge, MA: Harvard University Press.

Berger, P. and Luckmann, T. (1966). *The Social Construction of Reality: A Treatise in the Sociology of Knowledge*. London: Penguin.

Bohannan, P. (1965). The Differing Realms of the Law. *American Anthropologist*. 67(6): 33–42.

Bourdieu, P. (1986–1987). The Force of Law: Toward a Sociology of the Juridical Field. *Hastings Law Journal*. 38: 805–853.

Bruner, J.S. (1997). A Narrative Model of Self-Construction. In: Snodgrass, J.G. and Thompson, R.L. (Eds.). *The Self Across Psychology: Self-Recognition, Self-Awareness and Self-Concept*. New York: New York Academy of Sciences. 145–161.

Bruner, J.S., Di Donato, F. and Smorti, A. (Eds.). (2013). Contesto, Cultura e Diritto. *Special Issue of Psicologia Culturale*. 3: 1–134.

Cominelli, L. (2018). *Cognition of Law*. Dordrecht: Springer.

Cotterell, R. (2004). Law in Culture. *Ratio Iuris*. 17(1): 1–14.

Daiute, C. (2014). *Narrative Inquiry: A Dynamic Approach*. Thousand Oaks, CA: Sage Publications.

Daiute, C. et al. (2017). *Minority Teachers – Roma in Serbia – Narrate Education Reform*. Belgrade, Serbia: Institute of Psychology, Faculty of Philosophy at the University of Belgrade and the Association of Pedagogical Assistants.

Di Donato, F. (2012). *La realtà delle storie. Tracce di una cultura*. Napoli: Guida.

Di Donato, F. (2014). *Narratives in Cultural Contexts: The Legal Agentivity of the Protagonists*. SSRN: https://ssrn.com/abstract=2469436 or http://dx.doi.org/10.2139/ssrn.2469436 (website consulted on 9.08.2018).

Duranti, A. (2007). *Etnopragmatica. La forza nel parlare*. Roma: Carocci.

Eteläpelto, A., Vahäsäntanen, K., Hökkä, P. and Palonienni, S. (2013). What Is Agency? Conceptualizing Agency at Work. *Educational Research Review*. 10: 45–65.

Ewick, P. and Silbey, S. (1998). *The Common Place of Law. Stories from Everyday Life*. Chicago and London: The University of Chicago Press.

Febbrajo, A. (2018). A Typology of Legal Cultures. In. Febbrajo, A. (Ed.). *Law, Legal Culture and Society*. London and New York: Routledge. 28–43.

Friedman, L.M. (1969). Legal Culture and Social Development. *Law and Society Review*. 4: 29–44.

Friedman, L.M. (1997). The Concept of Legal Culture: A Reply. In: Nelken, D. (Ed.). *Comparing Legal Cultures*. Brookfield, VT: Darmouth Publishing. 33–39.

Fuller, L.L. (1968). *The Anatomy of Law*. Westport, CT: Greenwood Press.

Fuller, L.L. (1969). Human Interaction and the Law. *American Journal of Jurisprudence*. 14: 1.

Geertz, C. (1973). *The Interpretation of Cultures. Selected Essays.* New York: Basic Books.

Geertz, C. (1983). *Local Knowledge.* New York: Basic Books.

He, X., Wang, L. and Su, Y. (2013). Above the Roof, Beneath the Law: Perceived Justice Behind Disruptive Tactics of Migrant Wage Claimants in China. *Law and Society Review.* 47(4): 703–738.

High, C. (2010). Agency and Anthropology: Selected Bibliography. *Ateliers d'antrhopologie.* 34: https://journals.openedition.org/ateliers/8516 (website consulted on 9.08.2018).

Kroeber, A.L. and Kluckhohn, C. (1952). *Culture: A Critical Review of Concepts and Definitions.* New York: Vintage Books.

Kruse, K.R. (2011–2012). Getting Real About Legal Realism, New Legal Realism, and Clinical Legal Education. *New York Law School Law Review.* 56 659–681.

Latour, B. (2005). *Reassembling the Social: An Introduction to Actor-Network-Theory.* Oxford: Oxford University Press.

Merry, S.E. (2012). What Is Legal Culture? An Anthropological Perspective. In: Nelken, D. (Ed.). *Using Legal Culture.* London: Wildy, Simmonds & Hill Publishing. 52–75.

Mezey, N. (2001). Law as Culture. *Yale Journal of Law & the Humanities.* 13: 35–67.

Nelken, D. (Ed.). (2012a). *Using Legal Culture.* London: Wildy, Simmonds & Hill Publishing.

Nelken, D. (2012b). Introduction. In: Nelken, D. (Ed.). *Using Legal Culture.* London: Wildy, Simmonds & Hill Publishing.

Postema, G.J. (1994). Implicit Law. *Law and Philosophy.* 13(3): 361–387.

Silbey, S. (2001). Legal Culture and Consciousness. In: *International Encyclopedia of the Social and Behavioral Sciences.* Amsterdam: Elsevier Science. 8623–8629.

Silbey, S. (2005). After Legal Consciousness. *Annual Review of Law and Social Science.* 1: 323–368.

Silbey, S. (2008). Legal Consciousness. In: Cane, P. and Conaghan, J. (Eds.). *New Oxford Companion to Law.* Oxford: Oxford University Press.

Silbey, S. (2010). Legal Culture and Cultures of Legality. In: Hall, J.R., Grindstaff, L. and Lo, M.C. (Eds.). *Handbook of Cultural Sociology.* London and New York: Routledge.

Silbey, S. (2014). The Courts in American Public Culture. *Daedalus: The Journal of the American Academy of Arts & Sciences.* 140–156.

Zittoun, T. (2012). On the Emergence of the Subject. *Integrative Psychological and Behavioral Science.* 46(3): 259–273.

Zittoun, T. and Gillespie, A. (2016). *Imagination in Human and Cultural Development.* London and New York: Routledge.

8 Laypeople in action II

Foreigners' stories

The aim of this chapter is to situate case analyses in a different legal context – in north-western Switzerland. It proposes four stories of naturalisation in the Canton of Neuchâtel, so as to illustrate how the protagonists act within the administrative and legal paths in their country of adoption. It starts presenting some results of the Swiss interdisciplinary research project entitled "Immigrants' trajectories of integration, between indeterminate (legislative) criteria and uncertain life courses: Analysis of legal cases", from which the data are extracted. With this aim, it first describes the Swiss legislative framework governing the procedure of naturalisation, giving an account of the current political and legislative debate in Swiss society; secondly, it analyses the stories by focusing on the clients' legal agentivity with the aim of showing their' attitude to dealing with a foreign cultural and legal environment. Finally, it compares the results of the different clients' administrative legal paths, trying to explain whether and how they were successful or unsuccessful in obtaining Swiss citizenship.

1. Introduction

The aim of the research project "Immigrants' trajectories of integration, between indeterminate (legislative) criteria and uncertain life courses: Analysis of legal cases",[1] from which the stories I am going to present are extracted, was twofold: on the one hand, it was to reconstruct and analyse the concept of integration as it is found in Switzerland's body of law in the course of the twentieth century, and as it is currently applied in practice by certain administrative and judicial authorities; on the other hand, it also set out to examine the impact of the concept on the life histories of applicants for naturalisation, as well as on the people who work in the cantonal and municipal administrations and apply the legislation in question. Based on an in-depth empirical analysis of concrete cases in Canton

1 This research project was conducted at the University of Neuchâtel (Faculty of Law and Faculty of Arts) between 2013 and 2017. For further information, see the following link: http://p3.snf.ch/Project-147287. The full results of the project are forthcoming: see Di Donato et al. (forthcoming).

Neuchâtel, it aimed to give voice to the people involved in these administrative and legal procedures of naturalisation, retracing the complexity and the effects of the process of integration from their point of view.

In order to illustrate some of the results of the analyses that I conducted specifically in the framework of the broader project, in the following paragraphs I shall first give an account of the Swiss debate about naturalisation and reconstruct the current legislative framework (1.1.); second, I shall present some cases of naturalisation by highlighting the administrative legal paths of some of the clients that I met, with my colleagues, during the development of the research project: Line, Charles, Kirin and Johan (par. 1.2.; 2. and ff). On the basis of the reconstruction of these various stories, I shall then discuss some proposals about the issue of client agentivity, furnishing comparisons between the cases analysed in this chapter and the previous one (par. 3).

1.1. A brief account of the historical-political evolution of the procedure of naturalisation in Switzerland: the legal meanings of integration

Since its origins – between the end of the 1800s and the early 1900s – Switzerland's naturalisation procedure has been conceived of as a political act, linked to the power of the local bourgeoisie of the Swiss cantons and municipalities. Subsequently, at the time of the creation of the nation states, around the 1920s, the procedure was considered to be a tool for dealing with the increasing presence of immigrants in Switzerland: due to the large number of foreigners in the territory, a form of 'forced naturalisation' linked to the principle of *ius soli* was proposed by the Federal Council. In due course, the 1952 Federal Act on the Acquisition and Loss of Swiss Citizenship (the Citizenship Act, SCA) was amended in the second half of the last century. Art. 14 of this Act provided that the competent authority had to check the 'attitude' of the applicant before granting permission for a foreigner to be naturalised. Further amendments to Art. 14 (passed in 1990) explained the concept of 'attitude', requiring that the applicant: a) be "integrated" into the Swiss community, b) have become "accustomed" to the Swiss lifestyle and customs, c) comply with Swiss law and d) does not affect Switzerland's internal or external security.[2] While in a first phase of the debate (under the 1952 SCA), emphasis was placed on the subjective qualities of the applicant (her/his 'attitude' to becoming Swiss), in a second phase (under the 1990 amendments), the applicant's 'integration' (comprising both formal and

2 On the meaning of "being" or "becoming" Swiss, see Centlivres (1990). Several accounts about Swiss culture, including the 1970 film *Les faiseurs de Suisse* by Rolf Lissy, have highlighted the degree of discretion of the authorities in interpreting the notion of 'integration'. See also Di Donato and Mahon (2009). On the right to be Swiss, see the work of Studer et al. (2013). For a complete reconstruction of the Swiss legislation governing foreigners and naturalisation and the historical evolution of the concept of integration in the Swiss legal system, see Di Donato (2016) and Di Donato and Mahon (forthcoming, a, b).

subjective conditions) in the local Swiss community was required.[3] Being integrated is thus considered to be a consequence of the adoption of a Swiss way of life and traditions by foreigners.

Furthermore, since the beginning of this century, 'integration' has gone beyond the right of citizenship, becoming a 'duty' in the daily life of 'ordinary' foreigners, those who simply want to live in Switzerland, without necessarily applying for citizenship. According to the 2008 Foreign Nationals Act (FNA), "degrees of integration" are thus required not only of people who wish to be naturalised, but also of those who wish to be granted residence permits. New reforms recently amended the criteria for naturalisation: 'successful' integration is now considered to be a preliminary condition for naturalisation, rather than naturalisation being treated as a precondition for integration, as it used to be in the 1920s, for example.[4] Although its profile remains vague and its interpretation discretional, making due provision for this criterion sheds greater light on the distinction that exists between the integration expected of applicants for citizenship and other foreigners, who may hope to receive a residence permit or pass from one form of permit to another.[5]

In addition to the rigid nature of the legislative criteria, the difficulty that applicants have in responding to the expectations of the administrative authorities is also due to the complexity of the procedure of naturalisation. In fact, the naturalisation procedure is articulated in three steps in the Swiss Federal system: the federal level, the cantonal level and the municipal level.[6] At the federal level, the authority linked to the Federal Office of Justice (SEM)[7] checks the prior conditions for granting naturalisation, as established by Arts. 14 and 15, SCA.[8] Although federal authorisation is a prior condition to naturalisation being granted by cantons and municipalities and the general requirements are established at the federal level, the naturalisation procedure may differ from one canton to another. As a consequence of the broader power of appreciation of the local authorities, in addition to having raised many legal and political debates, applications of the SCA have also provoked disparate practices by the cantonal authorities in the course of time.[9] A role of objectification is normally absolved

3 Integration today is basically meant as a mutual process of rapprochement between foreigners and Swiss. See the Messages of the Federal Council: FF 2011 2639 and the FF 1987 III 285.

4 The 1952 Federal Act on the Acquisition and Loss of Swiss Citizenship (the Citizenship Act, SCA) remained in force until 31 December 2017 and was replaced on 1 January 2018 by the new law on nationality dated 20 June 2014.

5 For a diachronic and synchronic reconstruction of the meanings of integration in the two bodies of legislation (SCA and FNA), see Di Donato and Mahon (forthcoming, a, b).

6 For a schematic rendering of the procedure at the various stages, see Lavanchy and Mahon (forthcoming).

7 The SEM is the Federal Office competent for the harmonisation of cantonal and federal policies about naturalisation and integration: www.sem.admin.ch/sem/en/home.html (website consulted on the 14.02.2018).

8 In the cases examined in this chapter, this refers to the previous law, which was in force until the end of 2017.

9 See Wichmann et al. (2011).

by the Federal Supreme Court in evaluating administrative refusals of naturalisation. In fact, although there is no 'right to naturalisation' that can be enforced in the courts, the Federal Court has repeatedly been called upon to act on these non-uniform interpretations and applications, especially in light of Art. 8 (s. 2) of the Swiss Constitution, which prohibits discrimination.[10] As a result, a "duty of motivation" for the refusal of naturalisation was introduced in 2012 (Art. 15b, SCA) and a consequent "right to appeal against arbitrary and discriminatory decisions" was recognised.[11]

1.2. Fieldwork: analysing concrete cases and people's life histories

On the basis of this legal framework and working in partnership with four other researchers (one professor of public law, two social psychologists and an anthropologist) in the "Immigrants' trajectories of integration, between indeterminate (legislative) criteria and uncertain life courses: Analysis of legal cases"[12] project, we reconstructed the experiences with administrative law of a certain number of individuals who had taken the step of applying for naturalisation in Switzerland's Canton Neuchâtel. These different real-world cases were subjected to a variety of in-depth analyses, in accordance with the various different disciplinary methods used by the researchers involved in the project.

Concerning my own analysis of the cases, based on an examination of the administrative dossiers and on in-depth interviews with the applicants, applying the methodology described in Chapter 3 shed light primarily on the obstacles encountered by the applicants in complying with the criteria of integration established by the law and responding to the expectations of the administrations. The results of the research – which led primarily to cases that could be described as atypical, because they are not necessarily representative of the reality of Canton Neuchâtel, which is rather well known for a high rate of granting nationality – enabled us to determine that the leading obstacles facing applicants for naturalisation are related to several factors, some of which can be classified as personal or subjective, others as contextual. The first kind of obstacles was related to the specific nature of certain individuals' life histories. One example of this is the difficulty involved in finding a job, caused by the fact that the education system in

10 A resounding ruling of the Swiss Federal Court dated 9 July 2003 (ATF 129 I 217, Einwohnergemeinde Emmen– Municipality of Emmen) recognised that applicants have a right to appeal and, on this matter, upheld their appeal, considering the popular decision that rejected their naturalisation as discriminatory. Similar cases include the ruling of the Federal Court (ATF 134 I 49, Gemeinde/Municipality of Buchs), concerning the rejection of a Muslim woman's application for naturalisation on the grounds that wearing an Islamic headscarf at the time of the naturalisation examination was discriminatory on the basis of Arts. 8 and 15 of the Constitution. In this case, the judges considered that wearing the veil was not a sign of non-integration.

11 See the ruling ATF 138 I 305.

12 See footnote 1.

the country of origin is out of step with the needs of the labour market in the host country, as we shall see in the cases of Charles and Kirin. Another was the wish to preserve the applicant's own customs in issues such as clothing when dealing with the naturalisation commission, as we shall see in the case of Line. But there is also the difficulty of understanding, interpreting and accepting the law and the practice of the administration with regard to expectations about integration, as we shall see in the cases of Line, Charles and Kirin. This last difficulty, which could also be classified among the contextual factors, is also related to certain structural characteristics of the procedure of naturalisation, which were partly described previously (par. 1.1.): since the procedure is articulated on three levels (municipal, cantonal and federal), it is not always easy to understand the different stages in the procedure and which steps to take, so as to know what stage the dossier has or had reached.

The factors of the second type (contextual) also include economic crisis, for example, which often prevents the individuals in question from finding a job in the canton and also from being able to cater for their own needs, from being financially independent and, when applicable, settling their debts, particularly with the taxation authorities, while also catering for the requirements of the law or, at least, of how it is interpreted in practice.

Of the cases analysed in the framework of this research project, I am reconstructing only four here, focusing on the stances adopted by the applicants for naturalisation vis-à-vis the law and the institutions. The following is the question I set out to answer here specifically: how do clients become legal actors in the procedure? To do this, I use the concept of legal agentivity – which I explained in the previous chapter – to illustrate how each applicant for naturalisation articulates the legal and administrative path (s)he chooses for obtaining citizenship in a different manner. I shall show that people are not merely subjected to the hazards of the administrative procedure but, on the contrary, can take action with regard to the law or to the developments of administrative law, making use of different competences and resources.

By also recalling the sociological concept of legal consciousness (defined in Chapter 7, par. 2.), we can observe how applicants for naturalisation start from their understanding, their expectations, their experiences and the positions they adopt with regard to laws and the institutions and gradually become experts in the legal system, mobilising their skills to act in accordance with the law and the institutions, building strategies for action and getting to grips with the meaning of certain notions (such as that of integration), so as to further their request for citizenship. Although all of these paths share common features inherent to the priorities of administrative procedures, such as filling in the application form for naturalisation, each one is an original and unique model. The relationship with procedure seems to be conditioned by each individual's personal legal and social path, which also ends up having an impact on how the individuals behave in administrative situations: using handwritten or typed notes for addressing their specific requests to the administration, with a view to obtaining explanations, or again asking for assistance, whether from attorneys, cultural associations, social workers or friends.

On the basis of this framework, I shall reconstruct the cases of Line, Charles, Kirin and Johan (par. 2 and ff), for the purpose of identifying the links between the legal consciousness, the experience of the law and the legal agentivity (individual or collective) developed by these clients. In order to highlight how these links are articulated and how they evolve, I decided not to present the complete stories, but to focus specifically on the stages that I have singled out as key moments for these individuals in the procedure of naturalisation.

2. Analysing the cases: the case of Line[13]

Line's case is exemplary, since it encompasses the majority of the elements that enable me to retrace the concept of legal agentivity as defined in Chapter 7. Some of those elements also put in an appearance in the other cases, those of Charles and Kirin, albeit in a simplified form or with certain variants.

2.1. Summary of the story

Line arrived in Switzerland with her parents from Cambodia in 1979 at the age of 11 as asylum seekers. In 1989, she married a doctor from Pakistan and converted to Islam. They have two children. In 1999, Line applied for naturalisation for herself and her children. The opinion of the municipal committee was negative, since it judged that Line did not show signs of integration to Swiss uses and customs, as she wore Pakistani clothes to the naturalisation test and showed signs of affection for Islam, while the children were found not to be attending the public schools. In 2006, Line filed a new naturalisation application, but new obstacles arose: irregularities in tax payments were allegedly found by the cantonal Department of Justice, which suspended the procedure. In 2009, the Council of State refused naturalisation and Line was invited to restart the procedure once she had fulfilled all the conditions for naturalisation (including tax payments). Line then appealed against the decision of the Council of State, claiming that the financial situation had been incorrectly evaluated by the cantonal authorities. Finally, after several administrative and judicial steps (administrative appeal to the Council of State, subsidiary Constitutional appeal to the Cantonal Tribunal), the Federal Court recognised shortcomings in the fact-finding procedure conducted by the naturalisation committee. The Federal Court sent the case back to the lower court as well as to the Council State, instructing them to re-examine the case in the light of constitutional principles, as well as Swiss law, and to establish the correct personal and financial situation of Line and her family, in order to give them the opportunity to accomplish the procedure for naturalisation. Some twenty years after starting the process and after further negotiations with the

13 Some of these cases are taken from Chapter 7 of Di Donato and Garros (forthcoming). I thank Elodie Garros for having permitted the reproduction of part of the original text.

administration, Line obtained her citizenship as a result of coming to a financial agreement with the local authorities in 2016.

2.1.1. Being "with the law"

In a first phase of the research, the story was narrated by Line's husband, Paul. He presented the story as that of his wife and his wife's family, finally defining it as "their story":

> My wife and I have been in Switzerland for 27 and a half years, since 1979. She was ten years old when she came with her parents. **So, there's my wife's story, my story, and then her family's story, as well as those of other foreigners who live here, so I have a lot of experience.**
>
> (Paul, June 2013)

Paul continued the narration with the description of the citizenship law in Switzerland, which he described as largely discriminatory in its formulation, since it draws distinctions between "facilitated" naturalisation (for people married with nationals or for children born from a Swiss parent) and "ordinary" naturalisation for everyone else.[14]

Paul: [. . .] **Laws in general, when you say laws that means equality for everyone**: regardless of whether they are Swiss or foreign it ought to be the same, OK? **If you look at the law governing [. . .] naturalisation** – as this is typically the issue there – **the law of naturalisation, there are already steps and conditions at the very start: first there is simple naturalisation, then there is facilitated naturalisation. There is already a contradiction there.**

Flora: Yes, why?

Paul: **because when you say the law is equal, equality for everyone, there's no equality any more. You have already made two sections: you have introduced facilitation for people who are married with a Swiss citizen** [. . .] for those who are married or who live here and have a Swiss partner.

(Paul, June 2013)

During a second interview with Paul and Line, Paul also described his experience in relation to the law, in particular with reference to appeals about applications for asylum:

Paul: **I studied a lot of procedures.**

Flora: Here in Switzerland?

14 The distinction between ordinary and facilitated naturalisation (for those who are married to a Swiss person) was introduced with the SCA of 1952.

Paul: Yes, **here in Switzerland. So I had a lot to do with legal issues.** So that's how it is.

(Line and Paul, March 2014)

From the very beginning of the story, Paul found no recognisable rationality or impartiality in the law. He did not find himself 'before the law' – to cite the distinction proposed in Chapter 7 – but sought to understand how it functions and to play by its rules. In this sense, he acted 'with the law' and, together with his wife, took part in a pattern of actions and reactions vis-à-vis the authorities for the purpose of contesting decisions that appeared to them to be incorrect, even unjust, during the procedure of naturalisation.

Going into greater detail about the administrative procedure followed by his wife during his first interview and showing me the related documents, from the first meeting Paul helped me to reconstruct his wife's first attempt to be granted naturalisation for herself and her children under the 1992 SCA:

> In 1998, she applied for ordinary naturalisation, and at that time the municipal authorities said: **'Listen, you wear Islamic clothes because you are influenced by your husband and you dress like a Muslim'** – she converted to Islam, it's normal – [says Paul] **'so we believe that you are not integrated into society'.**
>
> (Paul, June 2013)

He also described the obstacles encountered during the first (municipal) level of the naturalisation procedure, showing me the document containing the answer of the naturalisation committee, which was negative based on the following arguments:

> Line only attended the compulsory school and worked in a factory when she was young [Swiss factory]. **On marriage, she converted to the Muslim religion – the same religion as her husband – and she appeared before the commission wearing traditional Muslim garb, stating that she prefers to dress in this way.** [. . .] Her motivation for the application for naturalisation are generic. She is worried about the future of her children. She refuses the idea that the uncertainty faced by her children could derive from the Muslim tradition and from the paternity of her husband. [. . .] **Her children are not integrated at school.**
>
> (Excerpts from a letter from the Naturalisation and Aggregation Committee, dated September 1998)

Also, consider the following conclusions:

> [T]he Naturalisation and Aggregation Commission finds that **the applicant does not give the impression of being integrated or assimilated to our uses and customs and has decided unanimously to give a negative**

> **answer to her application**. [. . .] She may reapply when Paul will also be entitled to do so. In the meantime, time will allow the family to demonstrate its integration, through the integration of the children at school.
>
> (ibid.)

The committee's negative prior notice was thus motivated by Line's failure to assimilate to Swiss habits and customs and by her children's failure to integrate at school. Her husband's situation was also presented as problematic, since he had not accumulated the necessary number of years of residence. This first answer marked the beginning of a long series of actions undertaken by Line and Paul and of those of other actors involved in the application. I shall analyse these various different actions and the different roles played by all of them.

2.1.2. Kinds of agentivity performed by Line and her husband to prove "the fact of their integration"

In 2000, Line asked for advice from an attorney, who suggested that the family show the authorities the children's school certificates and the family's tax payments, since some of the conclusions of the local committee of naturalisation were not true. At a later stage, Paul and Line felt there was no point in being assisted by an attorney, because of the high cost involved and because the action he took had no effect:

Flora: **So was there anyone who helped you in this procedure?** You spoke about an attorney. Did he point you in the right direction. . .

Line: **Not for me! [laughing] Not for me!**

Paul: **For the first thing, when we had the refusal, we asked this attorney to step in, but he didn't do anything.**

Ann:* What do you mean?

Paul: **It was just a question of giving him money. . .**

Line: **Just one of paying**, and then. . .

Paul: **So the second time that's why I did not engage an attorney: I had had a bad experience (he laughs), it's better, I can do it myself! In any case, you go to see the attorney and he asks what you have to write. And that's what happened to me several times.** I was with friends, in several cases, and I said 'but if I'm the one who has to explain everything we have to do, then in that case I'll do it myself!'

(Line and Paul, March 2014)

While Paul described the attorney as someone who was rather inactive, in the case of Line, on the contrary, he comes across as having savoir-faire and being mobilised and operating actively to achieve a favourable outcome for her

* Ann is a member of the research team.

application. Like Laura, Luciano and Franco (cases analysed in Chapter 4) and Carlo, Michele and Viviana (cases analysed in Chapter 7), Paul is classifiable under the heading of clients who can be described as 'active' (Di Donato, 2012).

Paul and Line stimulated other actors. According to Paul's testimony, they asked for advice from the Justice Service which, as they report, suggested they should wait for a while before filing a new application:

> **After I spoke with the Head of the Naturalisation Service, Zed – this is at the cantonal level – she told me: 'Listen, you can wait a while and then appeal'**. She didn't tell me to re-apply, no, no, no. **So I waited until 2004 and I wanted to** appeal and this time I phoned Zed who said 'no, you need to make a new application'.
>
> (Line and Paul, March 2014)

Then, Line presented a new application in 2006. This time there was a new obstacle in the naturalisation process: irregularities in tax payments were presumably found by the Cantonal Justice Service that threatened to interrupt Line's procedure if she did not pay the entire amount required. The following is a passage from the document issued by the Justice Service:

> Madam,
>
> **We hereby inform you that the committee appointed by the Council of State to examine naturalisation applications has decided, upon studying your naturalisation request, to suspend your application because you have tax payments outstanding. One of the federal requirements for issuing Swiss citizenship is to respect the law in Switzerland which includes the obligations of public law. Tax payment is the civic duty of all citizens**. The Council of State thus requires candidates to be fully up to date with their tax payments in order to grant naturalisation. [. . .].
>
> (Excerpt from the Justice Service letter, dated August 2009)

Payment of taxes is presented in this letter as one of the "federal conditions for granting Swiss nationality", together with "respect for the Swiss legal order", in compliance with Art. 14, section c, of the 1990 Law on Nationality. In reaction to the Justice Service's decision to suspend her application for naturalisation, Line wrote a letter to the service to explain that she had made an arrangement with the tax collection office that authorised her to pay in instalments:

> Thank you for your letter dated August 2009, which was deeply disappointing, especially to my children, although we thank you for it nonetheless. **After checking my tax account, I have established that the figures you mention are not exact** (evidence attached). For the year 2007, I was behind with my payments to the sum of CHF [. . .] and, since I was not in a position to pay

> this large sum, **I asked to come to an arrangement with the Neuchâtel tax collection office, which granted my request**. At the moment, I am up to date with my payments (evidence attached). My 2008 taxes have been paid in full (evidence attached).
>
> (Excerpt from Line's letter, dated September 2009)

In this first letter, Line wrote in the first person, first expressing her disappointment, and that of her children, then challenging the exactness of the figures quoted in the letter she had received. She attached several documents to prove that her financial situation had been evaluated incorrectly by the authorities and to show that she had taken the necessary steps to pay her taxes. Pursuant to this arrangement, she stated that she was up to date with her payments.

Despite the initiative taken by the client, the Council of State informed her that her application for naturalisation had been rejected "because of the delay in the payment of [your] public contributions" (excerpt from a letter from the Council of State, dated December 2009). Once she had complied with this criterion, she would be able to file a new application. No mention was made of Line's own arguments in the answer she received from the Council of State.

Considering the lack of results from their exchanges with the Justice Service, Line and Paul changed strategy and decided to appeal to the courts. In 2010, Line lodged a petition against the decision of the Council of State with the Cantonal Administrative Court. In a response to this appeal entered in January 2010, the Council of State wrote a letter to justify its negative decision, sending its response to the Cantonal Administrative Court in March 2010. Line was judged to have failed to have settled her tax bills.

In that letter, the Council of State underlined the "discretionary power" it has at its disposal in reaching decisions about naturalisation and the "strong political component" of the act of naturalisation. Although unfortunate shortcomings in the preparation of the dossier were acknowledged, the appeal filed by Line was rejected by the Cantonal Administrative Court on April 2011. Non-payment of her taxes was presented as indicative of a "condition of fitness" required at cantonal level for the applicant to obtain naturalisation:

> **Despite these unfortunate gaps in education and record-keeping, it is, however, worth recalling that the appellant did not fulfil the attitude conditions for ordinary naturalisation required by the cantonal government**, since the payment of taxes for the year 2007 has not being recognised to date. It is therefore appropriate to assume that the contested decision, which led to the rejection of the appeal, must be confirmed.
>
> (Excerpt from the Cantonal Administrative Court's decision, dated April 2011)

Following this decision, Line appealed to a higher court, the Federal Court of Justice, in May 2011, introducing a subsidiary constitutional petition against the "arbitrary decision" of the Cantonal Court and claiming a breach of her constitutional rights.[15] As the foundation for her appeal, Line stated that the decision was flawed in its motivation and that the facts were not underpinned by the evidence. Line used two main lines of argument:

- *The decision was incomplete:*

> **In its decision of 14 April 2011, the court broke the law by making an incomplete decision, it also noted relevant facts inaccurately and incompletely. The Court's decision ignored a relevant part of my life, considering the year of my marriage as the starting point of my integration in Swiss society. I arrived in Switzerland at a young age (1979) and my compulsory education (primary and secondary) seems, in my opinion, to be essential to understand the path of my integration in Swiss society and gives me the right to naturalisation within the meaning of Art. 34 of the Convention governing the status of refugees,** above all since I belong to the second generation settled in Switzerland and my friends of the era are Swiss women.
>
> (Excerpt from the subsidiary constitutional petition filed with the Federal Court, dated May 2011)

- *The facts were not proven:*

> **No evidence established the facts. In its decision, the court recognised [. . .] that 'no evidence in the file establishes the allegation** that all the taxes in 2009 were billed in arrears at the time of the contested decision' [. . .]. *Evidence:* [. . .]. Although the Court's decision recognised [. . .] having noted the "unfortunate gaps in education and record keeping" by the cantonal authorities, it was guided to uphold the contested decision by ambiguous motives. **For this reason, I consider its decision on the basis of these findings to be shocking and arbitrary and therefore it should be annulled.**
>
> (ibid.)

Line's appeal was supported not only by relevant legal arguments, but also by strong emotional and identity arguments. Her sense of confidence in the authorities and of feeling at home had been impaired. Her children were wondering about their future and their identity:

> **The principle of good faith in its simplified requirement is a sense of trust in the authorities and institutions, a trust affecting declarations and behaviours.** Thus, it is a sense of security given by the citizen

15 Even if there is no real right to file an appeal against the refusal to grant naturalisation, is it possible to appeal against a breach of constitutional rights. See Sow and Mahon (2014).

> to the administration. **My children and I have always upheld the image of the Swiss as being welcoming, open to each other and appreciative of newcomers who offered their best for the well-being of Swiss and Neuchâtel society. This commitment is not strange for me, nor for my children, because I was 11 when I arrived in Switzerland** (I am a second-generation immigrant in Switzerland), **and my children were born here** (third generation). **This sense of security, of feeling at home, has regrettably been affected in this case. We have applied for naturalisation for the second time** (the first in 1998). **This situation has marked the lives of my children over the years**: **my children felt disappointed for a period and have raised the question of their identity, citizenship and future.** This is true on the one hand: **even without naturalisation, Switzerland provides good living conditions and social security; but the issue is deeper, because it touches a feeling of belonging that is consolidated by naturalisation.** *Evidence*: [. . .]. *Conclusions*: Violating my constitutional rights, the contested decision cannot, therefore, only be annulled.
>
> (ibid.)

Line's legal agentivity had some positive effects: on September 2011, the Federal Court recognised Line's reasons, holding that "it is not possible to refuse naturalisation on the basis of such an incomplete truth-acquiring procedure", sending the appeal back to the lower court, the Cantonal Court, for a new decision. The Cantonal Court recognised problems in the fact-finding procedure used by the naturalisation committee, which did not acquire the correct information about Line's case, and directed the Council State to re-examine the case.

Nevertheless, when, after admitting the appeal, the authorities asked for a re-examination, Line received no news. She wrote a letter to the Justice Service about this on May 2013, asking for information about the status of her application and citing her right to take steps to denounce the denial of justice. In response to this letter, the Department of Justice warned her to pay the amount due if she wanted to obtain naturalisation: "We can only confirm that your application will be considered at the end of May 2014 and that if, during the examination, you do not fulfil the naturalisation conditions described in the letter dated 23 January, the Council of State will certainly refuse your naturalisation" (excerpt from a letter from the Department Justice, dated March 2014).

Line again appealed to the Cantonal Court against the Council of State's decision, whose annulment she requested. In a decision dated November 2015, the court admitted her appeal and sent it back to the lower instance for a new decision. The following items can be found among the motivations provided by the court: "the lack of precision in the presentation of the appellant's financial situation" and "the contested decision does not contain the decisive elements of fact, nor does it satisfy the requirements of motivation" (excerpt from the decision of the Cantonal Court, dated November 2015). As before, the procedure of the Justice Service was considered to be tainted: "for the reasons mentioned above, there are grounds for considering that the decision made once again ensues from a procedure that is tainted for several reasons. The case should be annulled and sent back to the Council of State for complementary instruction" (ibid.).

Line obtained Swiss nationality in August 2016, following the decision of the Justice Service to draw a distinction between her obligations and those of her husband. She proudly showed me her passport with a photo in which she wears the veil. In conclusion, after nearly twenty years of what Line calls a fight with the administration, she obtained citizenship without having to renounce her cultural and religious identity in the process.

2.1.3. Reviewing Line's legal agentivity

The reconstruction of Line's case enables me to identify at least three modes of action in the trajectory of administrative law shaped by Line: 1) playing an active part in communicating with the administrative authorities (procuring information from the authorities for the purpose of establishing a dialogue, actively searching for information relevant to solving her case); 2) engaging an attorney and then deciding to do without the assistance of the attorney, whose services had been judged to be of little practical use and too expensive; 3) filing an appeal with the system of justice (activating the system of justice as a way of calling for the recognition of her rights vis-à-vis the administration).

One particular feature about Line's agentivity is the fact that she shared it with her husband. Although she was the applicant for the procedure of naturalisation, her husband was a participant in the steps she took. Quite apart from his involvement, the evaluation of Line's application was also linked to her husband's financial situation, since they were jointly responsible for certain financial obligations. Their agentivity was also shared in the close circle of their friends, in particular with a lawyer friend who helped them on the occasion of several appeals.

Coming together in the course of time, these different modes of action – oscillating between an individual dimension and one that is shared socially – enabled Line to obtain Swiss nationality nearly twenty years after she embarked on the first procedure.

As a 'foreign actor', Line has clearly shown a growing level of agentivity. In a first phase of the naturalisation process (1999), we were confronted with a kind of conflict between the Swiss authorities, who expected her to be integrated (with Swiss uses and customs), and Line, who wore Pakistani clothes to the naturalisation interview, stating that she shared her husband's religion (Islam). As Line confirmed during the second research interview (March 2014): "the first time I applied, it is true that they refused me because I wore a veil and they told me that I was not very suitable, despite the many years I had been in Switzerland".

In a second phase of Line's naturalisation process (2006), the authorities did not express any doubts about the cultural integration shown by the applicant (languages, uses and customs). This time, they merely cited financial issues (tax payments) – according to Art. 14c, SCA – to refuse naturalisation. Thus, while in a first phase of the naturalisation procedure, Line employed generic or everyday life arguments (feelings of uncertainty for her future and her children's future and so on) to convince the naturalisation committee to grant her citizenship, in a second phase, she demonstrated that she was capable of dealing with the legal and judicial system, using appropriate legal, cultural and emotional arguments to sustain her petition.

A positive solution to the case thus became possible as a result of the client's growing awareness of how the Swiss cultural and legal system functions, combined positively with appropriate legal action (the kind of authorities to access, whether or not to consult a lawyer, which kinds of arguments to use).

To complete the picture of Line's experience, it should be mentioned that the Federal Court's decision also had a degree of impact on local naturalisation procedures. Basing its decision on the acknowledgement that there had been shortcomings and defects in the fact-finding in Line's case, the Department of Justice amended the procedure used to construct the applicant's dossier, which from that moment onwards had to contain all the information about the applicant. In order to have a feedback on this point, I interviewed one of the employees at the Department of Justice naturalisation service:

Flora: **Why, anyway, does the decision of the Federal Court have a small impact on the process?**

Justine: **Yes, at the level of the composition of the file because, before, if you like, a folder like this is the record of our service, and then as soon as it is submitted to the commission, there are the views and reports made by the commission, which were not necessarily attached to the file**. They are in the reports of the decision that are sent to the Council of State. But they were not attached when Line's file was sent to the Cantonal Court: **what we should do is take it and put everything in the same file, before sending it.** And then it is not done.

Justine: **It's a small detail that changes our application**. Yes absolutely. [. . .] It changes the application in the construction of our file.

(Justine, December 2014)

In conclusion, Line – as a foreigner client – learned how to act within the Swiss legal system by increasing her knowledge and awareness about how the broader cultural environment functions. More generally speaking, in the course of her dealings with the authorities, she learned how to make the best use of her resources (her own, those of her husband, those of her friends etc.) and of her various different learning processes by adapting her behaviour to suit the changing situation. It was this agentivity that enabled her to take the right steps to obtain Swiss citizenship.

2.2. *Different stories, different modes of actions: the cases of Charles, Kirin and Johan*

In this section I shall furnish a somewhat shorter presentation of the other cases studied, those of Charles, Kirin and Johan, so as to analyse how the three levels of agentivity discussed in Line's case developed in their experience, i.e. 1) engaging in exchanges with the administrative authorities; 2) engaging an attorney; 3) appealing to the system of justice.

These three levels are always analysed in relation to how the client positioned himself with regard to the law and to the procedure (in the face of the law, with the law, against the law).

2.2.1. The case of Charles: summary of the story

Like Line, Charles arrived in Switzerland as an asylum seeker, at the age of seventeen, coming from Kurdistan. Ten years later, in 2003, he applied for Swiss citizenship, meeting with obstacles in the preliminary phase of the naturalisation procedure, at the municipal level, as the authorities judged that he was not "integrated". In fact, the police had been assigned to carry out an enquiry, consulting his former employers and writing a report, in which Charles appeared as having friends, being involved in local associations and mastering the language, while having had a few job changes and a period of unemployment. The report concluded that Charles seemed to be "integrated but has a degree of professional instability" (May 2005). This statement was then read by the municipal committee that recommended a negative preliminary notice: "Professional instability and doubt regarding his integration motivate our position" (December 2005). This opinion went to the Canton, which sent a negative recommendation to the Confederation. Charles finally received a letter from the SEM (State Secretariat for Migration)[16] saying that "the Cantonal authorities gave a negative reply. In particular, they doubted his integration in this Country [. . .]. Naturalisation seems hypothetical" (May 2006). Upon Charles' request, a second round of the enquiry came back to him with a second negative reply, after an administration employee identified some unpaid taxes. Then, ten years later and after having settled the debt, Charles asked the authorities to go "ahead with the current naturalisation application and take steps to accelerate the process" (November 2011). In a letter of reply, he learned that his application had been archived in the meantime and the only option he had was to start the procedure all over again.

Charles' case is interesting to analyse not only because his legal agentivity is different from Line's, but also because it is possible to see the transformative effect of the narrative, as an analysis of the various different documents illustrated. The representations made about his degree of integration evolved in the various stories told by the institutions and in the reconstruction made by Charles himself, to the point of being transformed into value judgements about him as a person, rather than about his experience.

16 The SEM is an institution of Switzerland's Federal Parliament, whose purpose is "to protect and defend the rights of migrants and refugees in their regions of origin and transit". For further information, see the following website: www.sem.admin.ch/sem/en/home.html (website consulted on 28 February 2018).

2.2.2. Charles' administrative-legal trajectory

Like Line, Charles motivated his application (dated November 2003), responding to the criteria of integration stipulated by the law and listed in Art. 14, sections a to d, of the 1990 Nationality Act, focusing in particular on his mastery of French and on the profession he had learned, as well as on his participation in the social and cultural life of the country.

The procedure followed its course: the police officer in charge of preparing a document summarising various aspects of Charles' institutional life (education and training, age) seems to have consulted with each of Charles' past employers, as witnesses of his process of integration. In addition, he stated that Charles "expresses himself passably well in French" and that he "plays football in the [regional] FC and practises several other sports":

> *Notes*
>
> At X, based on information obtained from the company, **he was a well-behaved person who had good relations with employees and the company's boss**. He went to Manufacture Y.
> At Y, based on information obtained from human resources, **the applicant resigned on 31 July 2001 without reason**.
> Y presents the applicant as a well-behaved person. He resigned on **31 May 2003 for salary reasons**.
> At Z, **the applicant had relationship problems with other colleagues. The management asked him to leave the company.**
> At W, **he had been working there for two months when he resigned**.
>
> *Integration*
>
> **Language**: he expresses himself fairly well in French.
> **Hobbies**: The applicant plays football and plays various other sports.
> Notes: During the various discussions with the applicant's employers, it **seemed that his career was not stable.** In fact, it is regularly interspersed with periods of unemployment.
>
> (Excerpt from Police Report, dated May 2005)

The police note focused on: a) Charles' conduct at work, b) his language and c) his hobbies, with a final negative note about his integration. These evaluations made Charles look as though he was "not integrated" well enough to be granted citizenship, so that on the basis of the police report, the reply from the local council (*commune*, or municipality) was negative: "this is to inform you that the Council has formulated **a negative prior notice in response to this application. Professional instability and uncertainties about his integration justify our position**" (dated December 2005).

On this basis, a letter was first sent from the Canton to the Confederation "Prior notice: NEGATIVE – we doubt this person's integration" (transmission of the dossier to the Secretariat of State for Migration from the Department of Justice,

Security and Culture, dated December 2005). Secondly, the Confederation sent a letter to Charles, telling him that the preliminary authorisation had not been given as naturalisation on the cantonal plan seems to be "hypothetical" (excerpt from the letter from the Secretary of State for Migration, dated May 2006).

Reading through the passages provided, we can observe some narrative transformations about the fact that "it seemed that his career was not stable", according to the first Police Report (dated May 2005) and his **"Professional instability"**, according to the opinion of the local council. On this basis the local council sends a negative preliminary notice to the Confederation, which in its turn finally states that naturalisation seems to be "hypothetical". It is also interesting to observe Charles' interpretation of "professional instability" as defined by the local council:

Ann:* And why did they refuse, what was the reason?
Charles: **Well, what was their reason, they had doubts, this is what they said, they had doubts about my integration. And also, I was unstable in my professional work. I was unstable.**

(Charles, June 2014)

Thus, professional instability is perceived by the client as his own instability, as a judgement of his person.[17] During a second phase of the integration inquiry (*enquête d'intégration*), when Charles requested reconsideration of his position, the police naturalisation report was positive (on August 2008). He was judged to be a "stable person and well-established with the Neuchâtel community". It is interesting to consider the whole report as well:

Reasons for the application

Charles was already the subject of a naturalisation report dated 3 May 2005, in which he confided to the officer of the local police of X that he felt well integrated in Neuchâtel. Charles was married to Miss X, also a citizen of Turkey. The latter had children from a previous marriage, with a Turkish national.

He had reported having a great deal of personal relationships with Swiss people and a sense of social well-being in the canton of Neuchâtel. During our last meeting with Charles, he once again confirmed his commitment to the city of X.

Personal information

Since his first application, Charles has evolved in his professional life. **On 3 January 2006, he signed an indefinite contract with Y, with the position of polisher. At present, he is still employed by this company.** The human

* Ann is a member of the research team.

17 For an analysis of the impact of the administrative law trajectory on Charles' personal relationships, see Zittoun (forthcoming).

resources manager of the company declared that he is a nice and accommodating person. **In the position he holds, he has the approval of his superiors. He regularly works overtime on Saturday mornings.**

In August 2007, Charles also opened the restaurant "Pizzeria X" at X. According to his statement, it works moderately, but he works every night and on Saturdays. It employs 2 people and to open it, he used private savings, as well as private credit.

Public services

Charles has dealt repeatedly with the police, in particular for breach of duty following a traffic accident. **Moreover, the applicant was the subject of a police report for insults and threats.** These both date back to 2008. In the settlement of his tax arrears for the period 2007, Charles has recently settled his account. No payment has yet to be made for 2007.

From the prosecution office of Montagnes and Val-de-Ruz, we learned that he has two lawsuits to his credit for a total amount of CHF 8,303.45.

Integration

Due to his professional commitments, as well as his family, **Charles does not have much time to indulge in leisure activities or hobbies**. After playing football for six to seven years, he goes weight-training in a gym from time to time and sporadically attends Krav Magal lessons, in a club in X.

Conclusion

Charles seems to be a balanced person and well-established in the Neuchâtel community. Despite opening the umpteenth pizzeria/kebab, he has concerns about his professional future.

(Excerpt from the Cantonal Police Naturalisation Report, dated August 2008)

According to this last report, there was an evolution in Charles' social and professional life, even though "the applicant was the subject of a police report for insults and threats". The conclusion drawn about his degree of integration was thus the following: "Charles seems to be a balanced person and well-established in the Neuchâtel community. Despite opening the umpteenth pizzeria/kebab, he has concerns about his professional future" (Police naturalisation report, dated August 2008).

Despite this second positive evaluation, the prior notice of the municipal committee was once again negative, this time because of "non-payment of public contributions". "Objective facts" now seemed to be taken into consideration by the authorities (at the local level): Charles had failed to pay public taxes (breaching Art. 14 LN). Moreover, he had had dealings with the police:

> Dear Sir/Madam,
>
> We acknowledge receipt of your letter of 11 September last concerning the application for federal naturalisation presented by Charles, born on October 1977, a [. . .] national, residing in Rue de XXX. After reading the reports of the relevant services, **we hereby inform you that our Council has given a negative reply to the application. Non-payment of public contributions on the part of the individual, pending proceedings and the fact that he is known to the police justify our position** [. . .].
>
> (Negative notification from the Municipal Council, dated September 2008)

On the basis of this municipal decision, the Justice Department (at cantonal level) recommended that Charles withdraw his application and restart the procedure by inviting him to give his opinion on this issue:

> Upon your request to the Federal Office for Migration, we have reviewed our negative notice. We have therefore carried out further investigations and must let you know that the town of X issued a second negative notice. [. . .].
>
> **It appears from the investigation report relating to your naturalisation file that you are known to the police and a criminal investigation against you is currently open. Moreover, you are not up to date in paying your taxes and have lawsuits in course.**
>
> **Considering these conditions, naturalisation cannot be granted and we recommend that you withdraw your application. You will have the opportunity to file a new application following this investigation, if you are not convicted, six months after the expiry of the probationary period and provided that your financial obligations are resolved.**
>
> Before making a final decision, we give you another opportunity to reply in writing about the above. If no response is received from you within 30 days, your request will be archived.
>
> (Letter sent by the Justice Department to Charles' lawyer, dated October 2008)

Considering that Charles failed to comply with one of the conditions stipulated in Art. 14 of the Swiss Citizenship Act (compliance with the Swiss legal system), this legitimised the recommendation by the Justice Department that he withdraw the application and then apply again when the financial and legal situation was settled. He was also invited to reply within thirty days.

2.2.3. Charles' legal agentivity

How did Charles react to the negative answers he received from the authorities?

The first time, he declared he was surprised at receiving a negative answer. He found the behaviour of the authorities to be "exceedingly unfair", since they cast doubt on his professional integration simply because he had been unemployed for a limited period of time in a period of general economic crisis. The following letter is Charles' reaction to the first negative reply from the cantonal committee:

> **Dear Sir/Madam,**
> **I was very surprised to read your letter** telling me that the cantonal authorities issued a negative response to my naturalisation application with the reason they doubt my integration in Switzerland. [. . .] **Therefore, I consider the unfavourable reply to my application for naturalisation from the cantonal authorities to be exceedingly unfair. I think, in fact, that it is unfair to characterise a person's professional integration as questionable because he found himself unemployed for reasons beyond his control and for a short period due to changing economic conditions.** I sincerely believe that the cantonal and communal authorities, who have given us examples of great openness toward their fellow citizens, will review the application in question.
> (Charles' letter to State Office, dated June 2006)

After the second negative reply, Charles then asked for advice from a lawyer, who contacted the Department of Justice in order to obtain information about Charles's position. This is the full advice given to Charles by his attorney on the basis of the negative reply received from the Department of Justice:

> Dear Sir,
> Please find attached copies of the correspondence I received from the Justice Department, with the accompanying appendices, i.e. the negative response from the City of X.
> **As you can see, the negative response is related to the non-payment of taxes, the existence of legal actions and the fact that you are known to the police.**
> [. . .]. I leave you to read the appendices.
> **Regarding the charges and the existence of tax arrears, it would be appropriate to activate the file, since the proceedings have been written off, and find an arrangement with the Inland Revenue. With regard to this, I believe it is necessary to engage in talks with the above service and your creditors. I am, of course, willing to take such steps for you.**
> **However, given the fact that you told me that you want to reduce the scope of my mandate as far as possible, so as to contain costs, I leave it up to you to tell me what to do in this regard.**
> **If I do not hear from you by 31 May 2009, I will deduce that you want to look after these aspects yourself and shall inform the Department of Justice that my mandate has been terminated.**
> If you wish to continue with me, I would appreciate if you would send me an additional sum of CHF 1,000 using the attached payment slip.
> Yours sincerely [. . .].
> (Excerpt from the attorney's letter, dated May 2009)

The attorney explained that the refusal was caused by two factors: "the existence of legal actions" and the fact that Charles was "known to the police" (excerpt from the attorney's letter dated 15 May 2009).

At this stage, the question was how to continue to act in compliance with the law and with the system. Charles had the option of taking care of the subsequent steps himself or of giving a further mandate to his attorney by paying him an additional sum of money.

As he was not satisfied with his attorney's performance and felt that the cost stipulated was too high, Charles dispensed with his attorney's services, as he testified in the research interview:

> **For the second application, I got a lawyer. I started, I opened a file, I was followed by a lawyer for some time: he was too expensive. And worse, I saw that he was not doing too much for me, because he just wrote a letter to get certain documents and, once he had them, I don't think he used them, I stopped using the lawyer, I said "well I'm my own file".** And after that, some time after, I received that. And without knowing, since I didn't have a lawyer, later after I received it, how my file was classified!
>
> (Charles, June 2014)

In June 2011, Charles wrote a letter directly to the authorities, reiterating the points suggested by the attorney in their last exchange, so as to convince the authorities that he complied with the criteria of integration. Charles declared that he "made it a point of honour to integrate as much as possible" in the social and professional life of the region (and to "comply with the rules of the highway code"):

> Dear Sir/Madam,
>
> As you know, I initiated a naturalisation application some time ago. I **would like to inform you of developments in my personal and family situation. [. . .]**
>
> **First, I would like to inform you that I have remarried.** [. . .] **My financial situation is quite healthy. [. . .] I have made it a point to integrate myself as much as possible in the social and professional life of our region.** As you know, I have been a member of the Security Commission of the City of Neuchâtel; after some years and until the end of the late summer 2009, **I also joined the General Council of the City X.** [. . .] In relation to the naturalisation report drawn up by the Cantonal police [of the municipality] on 13 August 2008, **I should like to clarify that the episode related to a traffic accident has been settled once and for all. It was an isolated incident**. Please note that this affair was resolved in a settlement dated 18 May 2008 (a fine of CHF 250.-). **As mentioned, this affair has been settled and I make it a point of honour to comply with the rules of the highway code.** [. . .]

> **I would be grateful if you would go ahead with the current naturalisation application and take steps to accelerate the process.**
>
> (Charles, letter to the Justice Department, dated June 2011)

In the reply from the Department of Justice, Charles learned that his application had meanwhile been archived: he could only start the procedure all over again.

2.2.4. Reviewing Charles' legal agentivity: coda

Throughout Charles' trajectory in administrative law, three types of action can be identified: 1) facing up to the law: taking steps to achieve naturalisation and engaging in proving his integration to the authorities; 2) being with the law: engaging an attorney and then deciding to do without the assistance of the attorney, whose services he had judged to be of little practical use and too expensive;[18] 3) being against the law, or even deciding to do without the law, when he no longer managed to understand the administration's logic. Some elements in the interview with Charles tell us what he thought about his case and about naturalisation policy in Switzerland. In particular, he stressed the gap between being integrated in everyday life in practice and what the authorities meant by integration:

> The more time you spend here, the more you're annoyed with the law, because **instead of it being "the more time you spend, the more you are integrated", it is "the more time you spend, the more you become de-integrated", why? If the economy in the canton of Neuchâtel is bad, and the person who made the request loses his job, being unemployed, what happens? Your file has already be rejected! So that's why I say: if for the Canton of Neuchâtel it is not good, if I re-apply for naturalisation, all these aspects go with integration today. For me, the current law does not apply to naturalisation** [. . .].
>
> (Charles, June 2014)

Despite the difficulties he encountered in fulfilling the requirements of the law and their interpretation by the authorities, Charles wants to continue living in Switzerland:

> **But I know that my future is here. But there are many things that discourage me, many aspects: inequality, politics is becoming increasingly**

18 It is also true that the decision to look for a lawyer in a naturalisation procedure generally turns out to be inappropriate, since it is known – from practice – that the role of a lawyer is not very effective. In fact, since naturalisation is a political act, there are not many openings for legal intervention in such cases, apart from maybe making communications easier between the applicant and the administration.

harsh against immigration, against foreigners, with referendums and the political system [. . .].

(ibid.)

2.3. Planned agentivity: the case of Kirin

Like Line and Charles, Kirin had arrived in Switzerland as an asylum seeker. Twenty-four years after arriving in Switzerland, he applied for naturalisation, because he felt "well integrated and well assimilated". He thought he also had a "duty to serve this country" that had welcomed him and had "enabled (him) to live in safety" (excerpts from his application for naturalisation, June 2005).

From the beginning of the procedure for naturalisation, Kirin asked several different people for help in obtaining information. During the research interview, he explained that he had asked his municipality for help: "I **first passed at the town hall one time, to see if they had any news.** They gave me a form. A form that asked me a fair amount of things. **They asked me a lot, for example, about the . . . what do you call it? . . . my criminal record . . . They asked me about taxes, they asked me . . . That's how I got information"** (Kirin, June 2015).

In October 2004, Kirin engaged an attorney, in view of the steps to be taken. The attorney filed the application for naturalisation with the Justice Service on 14 June 2005. In February 2006, just about eight months after his dossier had been created, an exchange of several letters started between Kirin's attorney and the Justice Service. The attorney wrote to the Justice Service on five occasions. In the fourth of these letters, dated in January 2008, the attorney asked for the procedure to be accelerated, because the minimum time for a procedure of naturalisation had been passed. In addition, the attorney justified her request for the procedure to be accelerated with the fact that her client had concrete requirements, such as the need to obtain an identity document so that he could travel abroad. The attorney also used an argument of a kind that we would describe as cultural to convince the authorities that Kirin complied with the criteria required for obtaining naturalisation:

> **As he is totally assimilated in our country, where he has been living for more than 25 years, he now aspires to be able to take its nationality. One is entitled to consider that this case deserves to be treated rapidly, since it has nothing to do with the case of persons who, on taking out dual nationality, can maintain relations with their country of origin: this is not the case of my client, who applied for political asylum.** I should like to thank you in advance for doing everything to enable the necessary authorisation to be sent to my client as soon as possible.
>
> (Excerpt from the attorney's letter to the Justice Service, dated January 2008)

She did not restrict herself to talking about integration – the term used in the law – but also spoke about assimilation in her letters to the Justice

Service, mentioning a criterion however outmoded in terms of how the legislation is formulated. In fact, the 1990 version of the Swiss Nationality Act no longer requires applicants to be assimilated, but familiar with Swiss customs and usages as a stage in the process of integration (see par. 1.1.). The attorney also stressed that, unlike other foreigners, her client did not keep dual nationality and relations with his country of origin. This made it urgent for him to get citizenship. The attorney sent a last request to the Justice Service in April 2008. Her letter crossed in the post with one from the Justice Service that was sent on the same day. The Justice Service "present(ed) its apologies" and "regret(ted) the situation", explaining however that a delay of 18 months was still necessary to deal with the dossier (excerpts from the latter from the Justice Service, dated April 2008).

At the end of April 2008, more than four years after having engaged an attorney and more than three years after his application had been filed, Kirin took the matter into his own hands again and wrote directly to the head of the Department of Justice to ask for information about the progress of his dossier:

> <u>Re.: my application for naturalisation.</u>
>
> Dear Sir,
>
> **I am writing to your office to tell you how shocked I am at the extreme length of the procedure of my naturalisation.**
>
> **My application for naturalisation dates back to 2005. In 2007, through the good offices of my attorney, Maître X, I received an answer from your department, asking me to be patient** (see copy).
>
> After that, I waited until 2008 to address your department again, and once again I received an answer that asked me first to make a payment of CHF 350 for the decree issued on 1 February 2006, after which I would once again have to wait patiently for a further delay of about 18 months, or one and a half years.
>
> I paid the invoice for CHF 350 (see receipted copy) and once again I wonder why I should have to wait such a long time (18 months) for an application that was made in 2005???
>
> **In writing to you, I am also asking you to make a statement, i.e. to pay just attention to this application for naturalisation.** ***I feel that I have become a victim of a long drawn-out wait whose sole justification is your department's staff shortages, I find that this is a little too simple as a reason.***
>
> ***About this, I would have hoped to have had an interview with you, so as to be able to clarify my situation.***
>
> Yours sincerely,
>
> (Kirin)
>
> (Transcription of the hand-written letter sent by Kirin to the Head of the Department of Justice, dated April 2008)

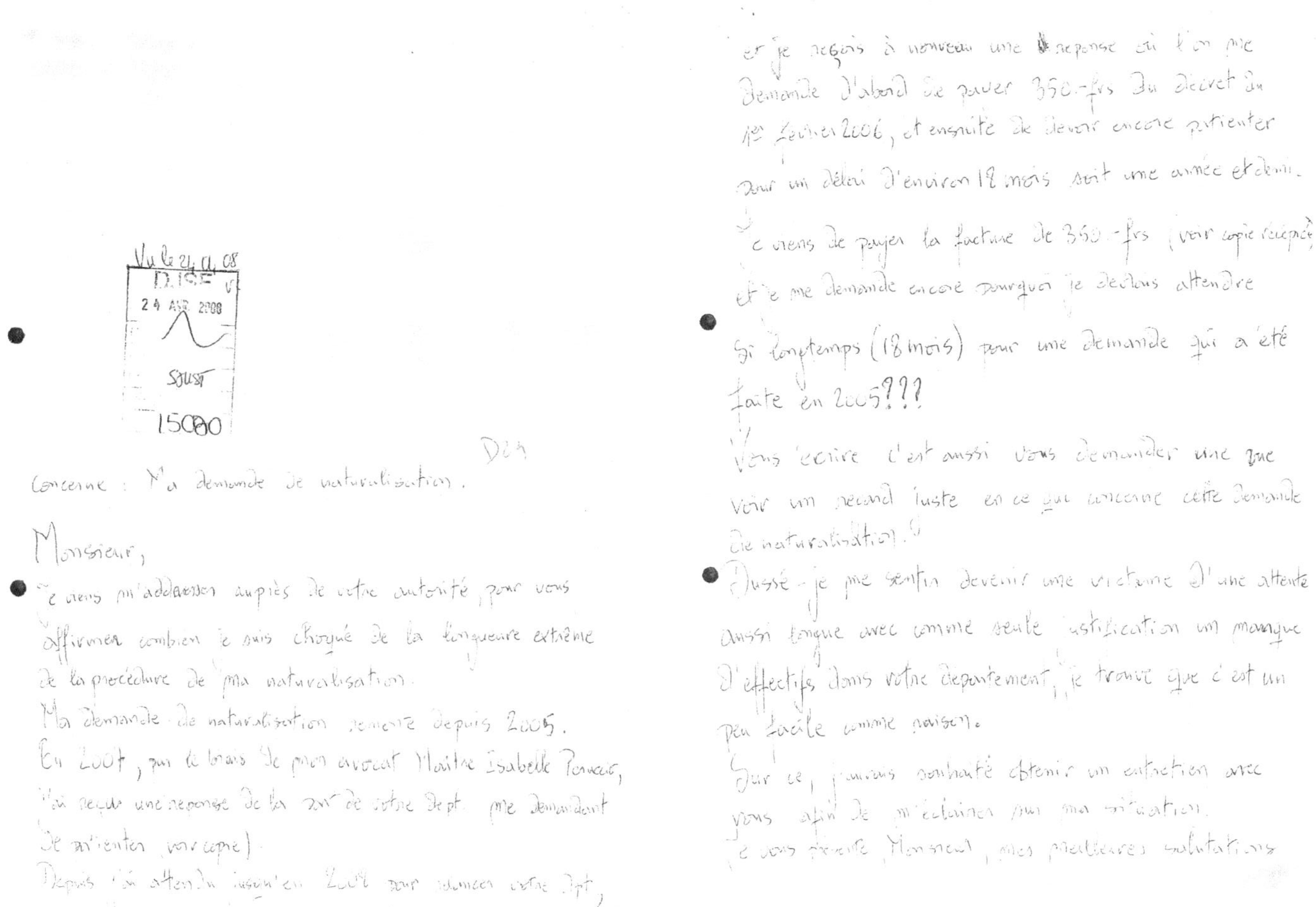
Vu le 24.4.08

D.I.S.E

24 AVR. 2008

SJUST

15080

Dén

Concerne : Ma demande de naturalisation.

Monsieur,

Je viens m'addresser auprès de votre autorité, pour vous affirmer combien je suis choqué de la longueure extrême de la procédure de ma naturalisation.

Ma demande de naturalisation remonte depuis 2005.

En 2007, par le biais de mon avocat Maître Isabelle Ponceau, j'ai reçu une reponse de la part de votre Dept. me demandant de patienter (voir copie).

Depuis j'ai attendu jusqu'en 2008 pour relancer votre Dpt, et je reçois à nouveau une reponse où l'on me demande d'abord de payer 350.-frs du décret du 1er février 2006, et ensuite de devoir encore patienter pour un délai d'environ 18 mois soit une année et demi.

Je viens de payer la facture de 350.-frs (voir copie récépissé) et je me demande encore pourquoi je devrais attendre si longtemps (18 mois) pour une demande qui a été faite en 2005???

Vous écrire c'est aussi vous demander une que voir un second juste en ce qui concerne cette demande de naturalisation.

Aussi je me sentir devenir une victime d'une attente aussi longue avec comme seule justification un manque d'effectifs dans votre departement, je trouve que c'est un peu facile comme raison.

Sur ce, j'aurais souhaité obtenir un entretien avec vous afin de m'éclairer sur ma situation.

Je vous prie Monsieur, mes meilleures salutations

Figure 8.1 Handwritten letter sent by Kirin to the Head of the Department of Justice (28 April 2008)

Kirin used abbreviations (dépt.) and multiple question marks (???) in this handwritten, rather informal, letter. Much like Charles and Line, he stated that he was "shocked at the extreme length of the procedure", which was apparently due to the shortage of administrative staff. He found this reason to be "a little too simple" and had no hesitation in asking for an interview. He asked for "just attention" to be paid to his application (excerpts from Kirin's letter, dated April 2008).

In May 2008, the Head of the Department of Justice answered Kirin personally, putting his attorney in copy. He stated that the "delay is certainly due to a shortage of staff at the Justice Service, but also to the complexity of dealing with the applications for naturalisation". In conclusion, if Kirin wanted to obtain Swiss nationality, "he must once again have a little patience".

In September 2008, Kirin received information about his application from the Justice Service: the notice given by his municipality was negative. As in the cases of Line and of Charles, unpaid sums were blocking his application. The letter stated that "it is clear" from the report of the enquiry that he had "not fulfilled his obligations with regard to the payment of his taxes". He was also advised to "withdraw his application" in "view of his situation". However, if the payment of his taxes could be settled within six months, the Justice Service clarified that it was "prepared to pursue the procedure". Kirin was to inform the office of his decision within a deadline of thirty days. Kirin answered, writing directly to the person responsible for the Justice Service to inform him that he had embarked on "a process of consolidation", already as long ago as 2002. He asked the Justice Service to pursue the procedure, guaranteeing that he would do everything in his power "to be a citizen and an honest taxpayer" (excerpt from the letter sent by Kirin to the Head of the Department of Justice, dated September 2008).

The form used for this second letter, which was typewritten, differed from the first handwritten one that Kirin had sent to the Head of the Department of Justice on 28 April 2008. The presentation and the style are meticulous and he used formal turns of phrase. This confirms what I announced earlier (Chapters 2, 3), that the specific forms of the documents furnished by the clients are used – more or less consciously – as elements for constructing the story and tools for performing legal agentivity.

In February 2009, the person responsible for the Justice Service sent an answer to Kirin's attorney, although the letter had been sent by Kirin himself. Despite the information about the consolidation arrangement, the negative notice remained in force. Nevertheless, the dossier was transmitted to the Secretariat of State for Migration (SEM) with a view to obtaining federal authorisation for naturalisation. The letter from the Justice Service specified that "even if the authorisation for naturalisation is forthcoming, this does not necessarily imply a favourable municipal and cantonal decision" (excerpt from the letter from the Department of Justice to Kirin's attorney, dated February 2009). The attorney answered the Justice Service in the course of the next two months, without addressing any specific recipient and asking to receive the negative notice which she had never received until then. She received Kirin's dossier in May 2009.

Three modes of action can be identified throughout Kirin's procedure:

- 'Being face-to-face with the law': at the beginning of the procedure, Kirin, like Charles, believed in the law and its rationality. He invested his efforts in understanding the procedure of naturalisation.
- 'Being with the law': faced with the complexity of the administration's application, Kirin engaged an attorney for the purpose of succeeding in his procedure. His attorney turned out to be more active than the other attorneys we have met so far (see the cases of Line and of Charles): she tried to plead in her client's favour, making a point of describing his assimilation in the country. Above all, she pushed the administration repeatedly to clarify her client's situation and enable Kirin to obtain citizenship.
- 'Being against the law or going beyond the law': frustrated by the answers received from the administration, by the lengthiness of the procedures that he felt to be unjustified and above all by the surprise of encountering an important obstacle, an unpaid debt that dated back to the time when he was a student, Kirin no longer acted with the law. Although he had engaged an attorney, he nevertheless undertook actions without consulting her. On several occasions, he took up his pen and wrote letters expressing his disagreement and his disappointment with the administration's actions. He called on those responsible for the institutions to give him a meeting.

Despite the personal resources he invested (tenaciousness, sacrifices and perseverance) and his various different modes of agentivity, Kirin unhappily did not win his case. Nevertheless, he did not give up on his desire to become a naturalised citizen. He stated that he had "a plan" to "reach a conclusion with this affair":

> **Of course I have my plan. Because I already had a plan to reach a conclusion with this affair**. But unemployment knocked me down [. . .] **I had a plan to conclude it all at the end of December here [. . .] I had my plans.** For example, in the month of April, **I had already planned to catch up with everything by the end of December**. ***But then unemployment hit me again. So unemployment hits me and every time its stops me just in time from putting an end to this delay. When I had already paid it. That created a hole for me. Once you are in that hole, it's hard to get back out of it, you know.*** But it's not so bad. **I'll try to do my best.** If I don't manage, then I don't. **I don't care, you know! I am not going to force the issue, you know. I have a delay with regard to the Bern agreement.** It's a delay considering that it's a delay of three years. That's how it went. From 2013 until 2016.
>
> (Kirin, June 2015)

2.4. *An "easy process of naturalisation": the case of Johan*

Johan's case is described here by way of offering a contrast with the three cases analysed previously, so as to show that no particular form of agentivity is required of the client if his life and administrative experiences have been typical. In fact, Johan was born in Switzerland to foreign parents and is considered a 'second generation' foreigner. As Johan wrote in his application for naturalisation as a Swiss and Neuchâtel citizen: "The main reasons are that my life is in Switzerland, I have no intention of leaving to live elsewhere, I been here for almost 25 years and I like it here. I've built my life here, I want my daughter, who is 3 years old, to make her life in Switzerland" (excerpt from the Application for naturalisation as a Swiss and Neuchâtel citizen, dated March 2013).

In terms of time, the whole procedure was accomplished in less than two years. Johan's daughter was also associated in her father's process of naturalisation. The procedure took the form of three main phases, between 2013 and 2015. The first steps were taken in 2013: the applications of Johan and his daughter were presented to the Department of Justice in Neuchâtel and the procedure was opened by the service of naturalisation, when it commissioned the naturalisation inquiry from the Service for multicultural cohesion (COSM).[19] In 2014, the naturalisation inquiry established that the applicant fulfilled the requirements of Swiss federal law (Art. 14 LN) and of cantonal law (Act governing the law of the City of Neuchâtel, 1955): respect for public order, integration into the Swiss community and the ability to speak French. The naturalisation inquiry was conducted by consulting the cantonal police department and the tax office, and by acquiring some evidence from Johan's friends about his social integration in Switzerland. In particular, these witnesses were asked to answer the followings questions:

Witness 1:

Q.1. How long have you known the applicant and in what circumstances did you meet?
R.1. I have known Johan since he was born. His parents and my parents were friends.

Q.2. How frequently are you in contact?
R.2. I meet him every couple of weeks.

Q.3. How would you describe his integration?
R.3. I think it's impossible to be more integrated than him. Johan works hard and is someone who likes to laugh, be open and who makes friends easily. He's a football fan and has many friends in his former club. His partner is a self-employed hairdresser and he has a lot of support when they had a child. They are a solid couple. In addition, he is someone who has gone through times that were not easy, but has still remained a nice guy.

19 The Neuchâtel COSM's mission is to encourage harmonious relations between Swiss people and foreigners.

Witness 2:

Q.1. How long have you known the applicant and in what circumstances did you meet?
R.1. I have known Johan since I was 16. So we have been friends for 19 years. I met him through mutual friends.

Q.2. How frequently are you in contact?
R.2. I meet him 2–3 times a month.

Q.3. How would you describe his integration?
R.3. Since Johan was born in Switzerland, he didn't have to be integrated as a foreigner and has been fully integrated since birth. He's Swiss with Italian papers. Everything he does every day, all this for me is proof of integration: he has started a family and also wants to naturalise his daughter.

The following is a summary of Johan's 'state of integration' according to the person responsible for this procedure in the framework of the COSM (Multicultural Cohesion Service):

7. Integration into Swiss society

7.1. Respect for security and public order [. . .].

Comment (see point 4) **the applicant has a criminal record** (register checked December 2014 attached) **but has no criminal police history** (according to the excerpt dated January 2014 attached).

7.2. Respect for fundamental principles of the Constitution

Incentives provided by the applicant during the processing of his application for naturalisation: Yes No *Comment:* **The file shows that the applicant has justified his naturalisation application and filed all necessary documents attached**.

7.3. Ability to communicate in a national language

Sufficient proficiency in French: Yes Knowledge of another national language: Yes
Comment: The candidate completed his entire compulsory education in Peseux and Neuchâtel. He also speaks Italian and Spanish, his native language.

7.4. Willingness to participate in economic life or acquire training

Training of the candidate: Yes
Professional status of candidate: employee Yes

Summary of integration:

Integration consolidated (full criteria 7.1; 7.2; 7.3; 7.4): Yes

(Excerpt from the Naturalisation Report issued by the Multicultural Cohesion Service, dated February 2014)

According to the conclusion of the inquirer, all the criteria for naturalisation were fulfilled. On the basis of this inquiry, the Department of Justice directed the local municipal council (of Hautlac[20]) to serve a preliminary notice of the grant of naturalisation to the applicants. The local council then served a positive preliminary notice, which was followed by the Federal authorisation for naturalisation. This Federal authorisation entitled Johan to apply to the Canton's Office of Population for citizenship of Neuchâtel. Finally, the local council declared that he and his daughters were citizens of the municipality of Hautlac, in accordance with the Act governing to the law of the City of Neuchâtel (1955). In 2015, the Department of Justice informed Johan that the Council of State had granted naturalisation to him and his daughter, that he had been included in the electoral register and that his right to exercise full citizenship by using his vote had been granted. The Canton Neuchâtel Council of State then sent certificates of citizenship to Johan and his daughter and, finally, the Department of Justice directed the municipality of Hautlac to enter their naturalisation in the civil registers.

2.4.1. Reviewing Johan's legal agentivity

Unlike the complicated administrative and legal processes involving Line, Charles and Kirin, Johan's case is a very easy one. In fact, Johan took no specific steps to respond to the requirements of the authorities. He provided a practical reason when he explained the motivation for his application in the course of the research interview (in June 2015):

> **I started this naturalisation because, well, I had a little girl in particular, especially that. She was born here so I wanted to do two things at once**: I'm not married, so we could not make a family application, so I applied for myself and my daughter, and then here. That's mostly why I want to be Swiss.
>
> (Johan, June 2015)

Johan described becoming Swiss as a kind of self-deliberation or appropriation, saying "I'm turning Swiss" (ibid.). In fact, he was aware of his multicultural roots and declared that he was not offended when the Swiss discriminated against him when he was a child:

Johan: **Yes, I went to the Italian school anyway, in parallel with the Swiss school, the Italian school.**

20 Hautlac is an imaginary name.

Ann:* **Did you feel like your classmates who had Swiss passports were different? Did you ever ask yourself this question?**
Johan: No, I didn't ask myself no, and then I had a great relationship with my friends, never no.
Ann:* Are you not playing a role. . . ?
Johan: It had to happen, but rather the adults who said, "dirty foreigner". Yes. Rather. Yes, rather. . .
Ann:* So rather negative remarks?
Johan: Yes. Not from children. So no, it was at all, not at all. . .
Ann:* And that made you felt treated as foreign, finally, a foreigner. . . ?
Johan: It was not, it was not often, but it must have happened, but it was nothing. It's me, it made me neither hot nor cold, it went in one ear and came out of the other, that's it.
Ann:* Yes. But, didn't you feel like a foreigner because of. . .?
Johan: No, no, no. But there were also a lot of foreigners. So I . . . No, but between the Swiss and the foreigners there were not too many. . .
Ann:* Too many differences?
Johan: No.

(ibid.)

Finally, for Johan, getting a Swiss passport was not going to change his own identity, but might make his everyday life easier, as well as making its simpler to pass from one country to another:

Ann:* **And do you now feel that a Swiss passport will change anything? How do you feel?**
Johan: **Maybe for them, when passing customs yes. Yes there, perhaps, at the airport or, what is more, more fluid, we'll spend less time here.**
Ann:* For example, to return to Switzerland after a trip or like this?
Johan: Exactly. Otherwise, if not, nothing has changed. . .
Ann:* You had a C permit before?
Johan: Yes. A C permit, yes.

(ibid.)

3. Conclusions

Starting out from a perspective of law and culture, I highlighted, in the previous chapter, illustrating how cases originate and are solved in the framework of social practices and in the network of relationships that provide the backdrop for each story. I hypothesised that a certain degree of understanding of the law (formal rules and customary rules) corresponds to a parallel degree of winning strategies on the part of the client.

In this chapter, I described a comparable experience, for the purpose of illustrating how the link between 'legal consciousness' and 'legal agentivity' is articulated

* Ann is a member of the research team.

when the client acts in a cultural and legal system in which (s)he is a foreigner. To this end, I reconstructed the experiences of four applicants for naturalisation in the Swiss Canton of Neuchâtel, illustrating their ability to become actors in the course of the procedure. This was also done with the aim of counteracting a passive vision of the foreigner as an individual to be assimilated, acclimatised and/or integrated, which is the one often conveyed in the legal texts and the messages emanated by the Swiss legislator.

I now present some concluding remarks about the specific experiences that I have analysed here: those of Line, Charles and Kirin, which are particularly complex and problematic, and that of Johan, which reached its conclusion without encountering any particular obstacles. The first question I have attempted to answer in reconstructing these cases and focusing on the articulation of the relationship between legal agentivity and legal consciousness is the following: what positions do these people adopt with regard to the law and to society in their host society?

The results of the analysis demonstrate that, at the beginning of the procedure, these people were 'with the law', or even 'before the law': they felt that they were in harmony with the law and entitled to apply for citizenship. Nevertheless, the responses they received from the institutions and the obstacles they encountered brought about a change in their attitudes: according to their particular cases, these clients adopted a collaborative stance (Johan), a subversive one (Line and Kirin) or a disputatious one (Charles). That is how Line and Kirin continued to fight and tried to work 'with the law', Charles announced his great disappointment and his anger with the obstacles he had encountered and gave up the struggle. For Johan, the experience generated no difficulties: his living conditions and his legal status (as a second-generation foreigner) enabled him to act in compliance with the administration's expectations.

The question that seems to arise in all these cases – apart from Johan's, since he encountered no problems – is this: how should an applicant react and overcome the obstacles for the purpose of achieving citizenship?

Confronted by unexpected issues, these people's first sensation was one of not understanding what they meant: during the research interview, Charles told us that, one week after filing his application, he was informed about the existence of a debt about which he had known nothing until that moment, while Kirin discovered that he had to pay a debt that he had taken on when he was a student. As for Line, she had to deal with her husband's debt, which had to be settled for her to be able to achieve naturalisation. Despite the attitude adopted by these clients of complying with the administration's expectations, these obstacles seem to be intrinsic to the procedure of naturalisation, which features a degree of opacity and fragmentation.

What did the applicants (the clients) do to tackle these unexpected complications?

First of all, they tried to understand the reasons for the refusal and/or suspension of their procedure of naturalisation: they sought information and they addressed questions to the administration. Subsequently, they tried to organise solutions, either alone or with the help of experts, for example an attorney, or again with the help of friends. While Charles acted in a rather individual manner, Line opted for different strategies, sometimes combining several different modes of action: asking her friends for help, engaging an attorney and engaging in a direct dialogue with the people responsible in the administrative offices. These are forms of agentivity that oscillate between an individual dimension and a socially shared dimension, complying with the theoretical premises of our discourse (Chapter 7).

Despite these applicants' more or less developed degrees of agentivity, the results were not always positive: with the exception of Johan, whose experience was characterised by a certain linearity, only Line obtained citizenship nearly twenty years after starting the procedure.

What happened to Charles and Kirin? For similar reasons, these two applicants went off track in the procedure in one way or another, although their reactions were different: since they were unemployed, they were not in a position to comply with the criteria of financial independence required by the law. Nevertheless, while Kirin was prepared to take the bull by the horns with his "plan", going out and looking for a job and settling his tax debt, Charles resisted the idea of having to "comply" with the administration. He did not share the same vision of integration, as he had a chance to explain during his research interview: "you can't play with the law", "I don't like it like this". At this stage, it wasn't the authorities any more who were refusing to recognise his integration: it was his own choice.

What form did the actors' legal agentivity take in practice?

In the various different cases examined, the characters assimilated the rules of the system step by step, either by playing with them (Line and Kirin) or by distancing themselves from them, for example by producing a dissenting discourse (Charles and Kirin). Their legal agentivity translated into a knowledge of the laws (both explicit and implicit) and a gradual mastery of a more formal style of communications with the institutions, passing from handwritten, personal letters to typed letters (Kirin) and from a subjective, emotional vocabulary to an appropriate and technical legal terminology, corresponding more to what might be formal expectations. This type of language evolves from the moment when the story is channelled into a legal path and transformed in compliance with the requirements of procedure. As their procedures progressed, the clients learned to use more formal style and language, without necessarily supressing the expression of values or emotions and more in general their identities.

Despite this progressive expertise, however, only in one case – that of Line – did the client's agentivity, founded from time to time on pertinent legal arguments and on cultural and emotional arguments – especially in the framework of her appeal to the Federal Court – prove to be a winning strategy. It also had a more general impact on the procedure of naturalisation, specifically in the framework of the construction of the administration's dossier, which from that point onwards had to contain all the information concerning the applicant. The mixture of human and legal arguments – in the letters sent by Line to the administration – constituted an element of novelty compared to the other cases, included the ones that I have already studied.

In fact, in Chapters 4 and 5, I described how in the first phase of the conflict the clients had perceived breaches of their rights in the form of traumas and tended to use an emotional language to represent the facts, while in a subsequent phase, with the characteristic of the formalisation of the appeal before the judicial authority, this kind of language tended to become more abstract and be translated into the technical terms of the law and of legal and judicial practice. This was also due to the specific kind of interaction between lawyer and client. The lawyer-client relationship was not formalised in the same way in Line's case, in fact, nor in part in those of Kirin and Charles. In cases of naturalisation, the role played by the attorney is almost exclusively that of consultant rather than that of a legal actor in the strict sense of the term.

So how can these clients' difficulties in obtaining citizenship be explained despite the evolution of their legal agentivity?

The difficulty involved in reaching the end of the procedure may be attributable to a variety of factors. One not incidental issue is the fact that the procedure for naturalisation is very hard for applicants to understand. In addition, naturalisation is not a right, and this is a circumstance that leaves the administration a margin for manoeuvre. In fact, although there are constitutionally guaranteed rights in the Swiss legal order – such as the right to be heard (Art. 29 of the Constitution) and the right associated with it of asking for one's own dossier (Arts. 26 and 28 PA), as well as the prohibition of the denial of justice – Switzerland's administrative procedures offer a certain latitude in their application, a factor that may also contribute to making them opaque. The existence of evident shortcomings in the investigation of facts gave Line (but only to her) the possibility to seek redress in the system of justice by appealing to the courts, specifying the breach of several constitutionally guaranteed rights. In the cases of Charles and of Kirin, on the other hand, there were no such apparent breaches to specify. These two individuals were merely the victims of the slow, opaque nature of administrative action: while awaiting the various administrative passages and decisions, these two clients passed from being employed to being unemployed, with the result that they were incapable of complying with the requirement of financial independence that is a stipulation of the law.

In conclusion, despite all the clients' efforts to achieve results, the procedure of naturalisation seems to have been an obstacle course to these applicants, because of the combination of personal factors (the applicants had to be up to date with the payment of their taxes, know the local language and demonstrate a certain degree of integration or assimilation) and of contextual factors. These latter include the difficulty they encountered in understanding the procedure and in responding in good time to the administration's implicit expectations.

Although the procedures in question were administrative and not legal proceedings like the ones analysed in Chapters 4–7, it comes spontaneously to imagine that, if clients were to play a more active role in the procedure, for example making use of methods of accompaniment in the construction of their dossiers, as well as guaranteeing a greater understanding of the practices used, an acceleration of the procedures and a reduction in the costs entailed, this could doubtless contribute to an increase in confidence among foreign clients and more in general among citizens vis-à-vis the state and its institutions.

Lastly, when it comes to drawing a comparison between how initiatives are taken by clients who act in their own context (Chapter 7) and in a foreign context (this chapter), it would seem that the mechanisms for raising awareness about how the law functions, with its specific characteristics, its opaqueness and its local practices, are in fact the same. Of course, when a client acts in a context that is foreign to her/him, there are more obstacles to be overcome, for reasons that are intrinsic to her/his civic status and to the duties and expectations that come with it, making all the related proceedings more onerous in terms both of time and of the resources that have to be invested.

References

Centlivres, P. (Eds.). (1990). *Devenir suisse: adhésion et diversité culturelle des étrangers en Suisse*. Genève: Georg.

Di Donato, F. (2012). *La realtà delle storie. Tracce di una cultura*. Napoli: Guida.

Di Donato, F. (2016). *L'integrazione degli stranieri in Svizzera. Genesi ed evoluzione dei significati giuridici*. Milano: Mimesis.

Di Donato, F. and Garros, E. (forthcoming). Agir avec le droit: récits et actions. In: Di Donato, F. et al. (Eds.). *La fabrique de l'intégration*.

Di Donato, F. and Mahon, P. (2009). Federalism and "Cultural" Identities: Some Remarks on the Naturalization Procedure in Switzerland. *Ratio Iuris*. 22(2): 281–294.

Di Donato, F. and Mahon, P. (forthcoming, a). Retracer la notion d'intégration: histoire du droit. In: Di Donato, F. et al. (Eds.). *La fabrique de l'intégration*.

Di Donato, F. and Mahon, P. (forthcoming, b). Définir l'intégration: significations légales actuelles. In: Di Donato, F. et al. (Eds.). *La fabrique de l'intégration*.

Di Donato, F. et al. (forthcoming). *La fabrique de l'intégration*.

Lavanchy, A. and Mahon, P. (forthcoming). Démêler l'écheveau: la procédure en schéma. In: Di Donato, F. et al. (Eds.). *La fabrique de l'intégration*.

Sow, D. and Mahon, P. (2014). ad art. 14 LN. In: Amarelle, C. and Nguyen, M.S. (Eds.). *Code annoté de droit des migrations, Volume V: Loi sur la nationalité (LN)*. Berne: Stämpfli Editions SA. 45–60.

Studer, B., Arlettaz, G. and Argast, R. (Eds.). (2013). *Le droit d'être suisse. Acquisition, perte et retrait de la nationalité de 1848 à nos jours*. Lausanne: Antipodes.

Wichmann, N., Hermann, M., D'Amato, G., Efionayi-Mäder, D., Fibbi, R., Menet, J. and Ruedin, R. (2011). *Les marges de manoeuvre au sein du fédéralisme: la politique de migration dans les cantons*. Neuchâtel: Swiss Forum for Migration.

Zittoun, T. (forthcoming). Faire l'expérience des procédures: trajectoires de vie. In: Di Donato, F., et al. (Eds.). (forthcoming). *La fabrique de l'intégration*.

Section III – Improving justice for vulnerable people

9 Collaborative lawyering with vulnerable clients

Asylum seekers' stories

In this last chapter, I shall focus my thinking on two cases of clients in situations of vulnerability: Amenze and Margaret, who came to Italy from Nigeria, the first to escape from a forced marriage and the second to break free of forms of sexual exploitation. The attempt is to illustrate what vulnerability consists of in these specific cases, that of clients coming from a cultural context that is very far from guaranteeing human rights and gender identity. The more general aim of the analysis is to understand the extent to which these clients' condition of vulnerability – due to their personal stories, their contexts of origin and their level of education – can be countered by enabling them to be 'legal actresses' on a par with other clients who, as 'natives' (Chapter 7) or 'foreigners' with a less fragile status than those of asylum seekers (Chapter 8), are already initiated to the mainstream culture and the institutions of their host countries.

1. Introduction

In Chapter 7, I highlighted the gap between the legal agentivity of clients like Viviana and Carlo – actors who were well entrenched in the social and cultural fabric and capable of finding solutions to their cases – and clients like Michele, who ended up paying the price of a disciplinary dismissal for his lack of familiarity with the context of his work and life. I then showed how the gap between the spontaneous story and the legal story increased when the protagonist is a foreigner, like Line (Chapter 8), for example, who took some twenty years to obtain recognition of her status as a citizen in her host country (Switzerland), despite having grown gradually more familiar with the local institutions and culture. The experiences of the other foreign clients were not very different: although Charles and Kirin exhibited methods of "legal agentivity" that were not very distant from those used by Line in seeking to understand and comply with the expectations of public administration, they nevertheless displayed less propensity for accepting the compromises and adaptations that, rightly or wrongly, the system expected of them. These are results that, taken as a whole, throw light on the hiatus that can exist between the culture of the institutions and the culture of individuals and between public narrations and private narrations (Daiute, 2018; Linde, 2001), in particular the narrations of people coming from unfavourable social and cultural contexts.

Starting from the premise that narrative practices and familiarity with the (both social and legal) norms evolve and develop together, I intend to show what happens when credibility is not given to the voice of asylum seekers or they are incapable of expressing their experiences adequately when faced with the committees and other organs deputed to assess their cases, either because they have no narrative skills or for other reasons. From the standpoint of the issue of access to justice, I shall argue the thesis that the possible development of a socio-clinical model of research and action, based on a narrative approach, may furnish more vulnerable clients with parity of opportunity with others in familiarising themselves with the norms, procedures and expectations of the institutions of their host countries, providing them with tools – such as narrative devices – for mediating their positions with regard to society.

In order to provide a tangible example of what might happen in practice, I shall furnish a brief version of the stories of Amenze and Margaret. One of the elements in common to these two stories is the fact that responsibility for protecting the clients legally and socially was taken on by a lawyer who is active in defending the rights of foreigners and by social workers committed to the anti-trafficking programme in Campania (the Dedalus social co-operative, based in Naples).[1] These are forms of legal, human and social protection that mark an important stage in the process of lawyering – what López (2017) has been describing as "collaborative lawyering" since the 1990s but which existed in related forms with different labels at earlier periods – in which clients, lawyers and voluntary associations work together to identify vulnerable people and their needs and to defend them (Galowitz, 2012). These forms of collaborative lawyering suggest ways for a more generalised appraisal of the possibility of developing methodological tools to help people (lay/vulnerable) to engage in problem-solving, supporting their participation in legal settings.

The chapter has the following structure. It first describes the normative framework that governs international protection in Italy (par. 2 and 2.1). On this basis, it reconstructs the administrative and legal route taken by Amenze, who was only recognised as deserving international protection after going through three levels of the courts (par. 2.2). It also proposes a brief fragment of the story of Margaret, a victim of trafficking and of prostitution, and of the administrative route on which she embarked with the support of Dedalus (par. 3). The chapter ends with a proposal to make more conscious use of storytelling as a tool for supporting vulnerable clients, in a socio-clinical space shared between researchers, professionals (attorneys, judges, voluntary associations) and clinical students (par. 4).

1 The Dedalus social co-operative, established in Naples in 1981 to give a voice to those who have none because they are emarginated, fragile or different, in a word, vulnerable, deals in particular with issues concerned with flows of migration and the rights and duties of migrants as they make their way towards emancipation and citizenship.

2. The institution of international protection: towards new forms of collaborative lawyering

As I already mentioned previously, the two cases of Amenze and Margaret that I shall describe here come under the heading of international protection. Both at international level and in the Italian legal system, the identification and recognition of the status of refugee are particularly arduous. In order to be credible, the applicant's story has to comply with two sets of parameters: it must be consistent in itself and it must correspond to what is known as COI (country of origin information). As I indicated in Chapter 3, this latter may be compiled by expert fact-finders belonging to specialised units created ad hoc by individual countries or be information that is commonly available from the official sites of such organisations as the United Nations High Commission for Refugees (UNHCR). The function of COI is to answer the following question: do the place, the event and the traditions that the asylum seeker mentions truly exist and do they fit the given description? As Damian Rosset has explained (2017):[2]

> The RSD process thus requires two types of knowledge: highly specific, ad hoc information to deal with the specificities of the individual case on the one hand and, on the other hand, general accounts about the situation in the countries of origin. COI units provide both types of knowledge (Gibb and Good, 2013; Engelmann, 2015). However, the legal assessment of this knowledge (deciding whether, according to the general information, risk-groups exist and whether, according to the specific information, the applicant belongs to one such group) relies on caseworkers in asylum administrations and judges in asylum appeal courts. Contrarily to the ad hoc knowledge generated by each asylum application, the general assessment of a country's situation is often a more stable knowledge. In several countries, the highest courts in the asylum system produce decisions including specific interpretations of the situation in countries of origin.

With respect to this dual process for ascertaining the facts, in Italy as in other countries, the trend is toward a predominance of the general information of the COI over the individual case. In other words, should the versions of the facts as narrated by the client fail to coincide with the country of origin information, the COI is likely to take precedence over the story told by applicants, who are not always in a position to prove the truth of what they tell. In practice, this gap may

2 Damian Rosset, Manuscript on file with the author. The author considers the case of Syrians seeking asylum in Switzerland. The procedures that apply to this kind of people envisage that the status of refugee is attributed on the basis of reports provided by fact-finders about the real situation of the asylum seekers in their country of origin: the applicants' credibility and the justifiability of their applications are appraised in the light of analyses conducted by fact-finders, which may contradict the information furnished by the applicant and that are difficult to disprove, despite the possibility of lodging an appeal, because their value is binding.

often be bridged by the obligation to verify the information, a burden of proof that in Italy is not borne by the asylum seeker alone, but also by the examiner. This means that not only the interested party, but also the person conducting the investigation (at the level of the territorial committee or of the judicial authority, in the case of judicial proceedings) may take steps to prove the facts in a different way. This may well lead to the COI being discredited or relegated to an inferior status compared to the story told by the asylum seeker and to the particular case in question.

The efforts made by social workers and/or attorneys who work to protect the rights of foreigners, who mobilise forms of expertise commensurate to this kind of clients' vulnerability, can be classified under the heading of this complex method for describing the paths followed by asylum seekers. This could be described as forms of collaborative lawyering (López, 1992, 2017), triggered by the circumstances that European law governing the field of asylum provides for a series of measures aimed at accommodating vulnerable migrants, such as the victims of human trafficking or of other serious forms of psychological, physical or sexual violence. Hence the need to adapt humanitarian, social and legal devices to some of the peculiarities of this category of clients: guaranteeing conditions of accommodation suitable for specific situations (e.g. gender or disability), providing pertinent legal advice, providing an interpreter capable of acting as cultural mediator in the broad sense and providing medical or psychological assistance (D'Halluin, 2016).

What makes the presence of these intermediaries in this kind of procedure priceless is thus the type of client. Given that these people come from countries where the protection of human rights is hardly ever guaranteed and customary law takes precedence over formal law, and considering the traumatic nature of the events they have experienced, relationships with these clients may be particularly fraught with difficulty if they are not always aware of the fact that they are victims, nor even of their rights. The primary task of non-lawyers is therefore to act as cultural mediators in the broad sense, aiming on the one hand to instil a minimum of legal awareness in their clients about how norms and procedures function in their host country and, on the other, to build a relationship of trust with social and legal workers. The purpose here is to enable them to identify as victims and help them build a plausible, credible version of their story, so that it will be worthy of legal recognition.

A variety of intermediaries has thus ended up taking on these roles in the field of international protection. They may be volunteers who are not lawyers or also fully-qualified attorneys committed to defending those who are most vulnerable. In this latter case, we also talk in terms of "cause lawyering" (Lejeune, 2011), since these practitioners' specialised knowledge in defending the cause of certain social groups benefits from their legal competence, but also from their political commitment, making as effective as possible an action possible (Israël, 2009; Miaz, 2018).

I shall show how these forms of collaborative lawyering can be articulated in practice by illustrating the cases of Amenze and Margaret, describing what the attorney's role comprises in acquiring the information that makes the client's story specific and plausible, the role played by voluntary associations in contributing to the asylum seekers' processes of integration and socialisation, and how these diverse people contribute or may contribute to empowering the performance of (vulnerable) clients in the procedures that involve them.

2.1. International and domestic legislation

The foremost international norm governing applications for international protection is the Refugee Convention, approved in Geneva on 28 July 1951, relating to the status of refugees. In Article 1, section A subsection 2, the Convention states that the term "refugee" shall apply to any person who:[3]

> Owing to well-founded fear of being persecuted for reasons of race, religion, nationality, membership of a particular social group or political opinion, is outside the country of her/his nationality and is unable or, owing to such fear, is unwilling to avail her/himself of the protection of that country; or who, not having a nationality and being outside the country of her/his former habitual residence as a result of such events, is unable or, owing to such fear, is unwilling to return to it.

The definition of the procedure for identifying the status of refugee is then left up to the contracting states. In Italy's domestic legislation, Art. 2, s. 1, of Legislative Decree N° 25 dated 28 January 2008 provides the following definition of "refugee":[4]

> Citizen of a non-European Union Member State who, for a fear of being persecuted for reasons of race, religion, nationality, membership of a particular social group or political opinion, is outside the territory of the country whose citizenship (s)he holds and is unable or, owing to such fear, unwilling to avail her/himself of the protection of that country, or who, having no nationality, is outside the territory where (s)he formerly had her/his habitual residence and, by reason of the same fear as that specified above, is unable or, owing to such fear, unwilling to return to it.

In Italy, an application for international protection should normally be presented to the office of the border police or to the *questura*, or main police station, with competence for the place where the applicant resides and should be

3 As amended by the Protocol approved in New York on 31 January 1967 and ratified in Italy with Law N° 95 dated 14 February 1970.

4 Italian Legislative Decree N° 25, dated 28 January 2008, transposes European Directive N° 2005/85/EC containing minimum standards for the procedures applied in Member States for the purpose of recognising and revoking the status of refugee.

addressed to the Territorial Committee for the district where the asylum seeker is located (Articles 3, 4 and 26 of Legislative Decree N° 25 dated 28 January 2008). According to the Art. 8, it is then examined:

> In the light of precise and up-to-date information about the general situation pertaining to the asylum seeker's country of origin and, where necessary, of the countries through which (s)he transited, drawn up by the National Committee on the basis of data furnished by the UNHCR (United Nations High Commission for Refugees), by the EASO (European Asylum Support Office) and by the Ministry of Foreign Affairs, also with the assistance of other human rights protection agencies and organisms operating internationally, or in any case acquired by the Committee itself.

A crucial stage in ascertaining the status of refugee or, as an alternative, the status of subsidiary protection,[5] is the "personal interview" (Art. 12 Legislative Decree N° 25, 2008), which takes place in the presence of a member of the Committee "paying due attention to the personal or general context in which the application arises, including the applicant's cultural origin or vulnerability" (Art. 15 Legislative Decree N° 25, 2008). According to Art. 13 of Legislative Decree N° 25, 2008, during the interview, "the applicant is guaranteed the possibility to express in an exhaustive manner the elements employed as a foundation for the application", as provided for in Art. 3 of Legislative Decree N° 251, 2007. Described as "Examination of the facts and circumstances", this article specifies in section 1 that:

> Together with the application for international protection or in any case as soon as they become available, the applicant shall present all the elements and the documentation necessary for justifying said application. The examination shall take place in co-operation with the applicant and shall concern all the significant elements of the application.

In section 5, in addition, the article specifies that[6]:

> Should any of the elements or aspects of the declarations made by the applicant for international protection fail to be supported by evidence, they shall be considered truthful if the authority competent for deciding on the application

5 Art. 2, section 1, subsection g) of Legislative Decree N° 25, 2008, defines the "status of subsidiary protection" as "recognition on the part of the state of a foreign citizen as a person admitted to subsidiary protection, pursuant to the acceptance of the application for international protection, in accordance with the procedures defined by this decree".

6 Italian Legislative Decree N° 251, dated 19 November 2007, transposes European Directive 2004/83/EC containing minimum standards for attributing the qualification of refugee or of person otherwise in need of international protection to a citizen of a third country or a stateless person, together with minimum standards governing the content of the protection thus recognised.

> believes that: a) the applicant has made every reasonable effort to describe the application in detail; b) all the relevant elements in her/his possession have been produced and a suitable reason for the absence of any other significant elements has been furnished; c) the declarations made by the applicant are considered consistent and plausible and do not contradict the general and specific information relevant to her/his case as available; [. . .]; e) from the checks pursued, the applicant has been found to be generally reliable.[7]

Considering the particular nature of the situation, caused by the geographical and cultural distance between the place where the facts presumed are said to have taken place and the country where the application is examined, and faced with the possible lack of documentary and other types of evidence to confirm or support the applicant's statements, there is a general lessening both of the burden of proof and of the examiner's duty to take steps to ascertain the information provided. In the absence of evidence in the strict sense of the term, the applicant's statements are thus considered to be truthful if they are found to be "consistent and plausible" and do not contradict both the general information – i.e. the COI – and the specific information about his case.

Research entitled *Beyond Proof: Credibility Assessment in EU Asylum Systems*[8] conducted by the UNHCR identifies the following credibility indicators used for the purpose of reducing the margin of subjectivity in assessing the credibility of the facts described by asylum seekers:

a) sufficiency of detail and specificity;
b) internal consistency of the oral and/or written material facts asserted by the applicant (including the consistency of the applicant's statements with supporting documentary or other evidence submitted by the applicant);
c) consistency of the applicant's statements with the information provided by family members and/or witnesses;
d) consistency of the applicant's statements with available specific and general information, including consistency with country of origin information (COI) relevant to the applicant's case;
e) plausibility and
f) the applicant's demeanour.

In addition, the UNHCR has specified that the COI must be used to support the objective, impartial individual examination of the application. It must be

7 Article 3 of Legislative Decree N° 251, 2007 is in line with the Handbook on Procedures and Criteria for Determining Refugee Status, published in Geneva by the United Nations High Commission for Refugees in September 1979. The Handbook (p. 32, par. 196) states that "while the burden of proof in principle rests on the applicant, the duty to ascertain and evaluate all the relevant facts is shared between the applicant and the examiner".

8 www.unhcr.org/51a8a08a9.html (website consulted on 5 April 2018).

independent, reliable, objective, precise and up to date and must come from diversified sources.

Meanwhile, the system used in Italy to verify the prerequisites for recognising the status of refugee, including the stipulation of the value and the role of international law as superior to domestic law, was clarified by a decision handed down by the Court of Cassation in 2008 (N° 27310). Among other things, the Court established on that occasion that Art. 3 of Legislative Decree N° 251 dated 19 November 2007, transposing the European Directive (as mentioned previously), reinforces and enhances the powers of investigation vested in the judge, recognising that:

> The examining authority plays an active and complementary role in investigating the application, separate from the principle of party disposition inherent in the ordinary judge at civil law and free of preclusions or procedural obstacles, with the possibility to acquire information and obtain all the documentation available for the purpose of verifying the existence of the conditions for international protection. [. . .] As a result, this outlines a marked enhancement of the unofficial investigative powers first of the competent committee and then of the judge, who is responsible for co-operating in ascertaining the conditions that entitle a foreigner to benefit from international protection, while also on her/his own initiative obtaining the information necessary for learning about the legal order and the political situation in the country of origin. In this respect, the diligence and good faith of the applicant are substantiated as elements that complement the insufficient framework of evidence, with clear reference to the ordinary rules governing the burden of proof established by the legal codes in force in Italy.

Lastly, the Court recognised that the scope of the unofficial powers attributed to the judge is reiterated in Legislative Decree N° 25, dated 28 January 2008, transposing European Directive N° 2005/85/EC (containing minimum rules for the procedures applied in Member States for the purposes of recognising and revoking the status of refugee and later amended by the Legislative Decree dated 3 October 2008), which also vests responsibility in the committee for ensuring that constantly updated country of origin information is provided to the judicial organs tasked with pronouncing on appeals against negative decisions.

In view of the plurality of the sources and the people who are called into account to define the credibility of the asylum seeker's story, we can state that we are dealing with forms of collective problem-solving and of collaborative narrative.

2.2. *The case of Amenze*

The first case I shall analyse here is that of Amenze, which comes within the scope of international protection as a result of gender-related persecution. The case is interesting because it offers an opportunity to illustrate the gap that may develop between information about the country of origin that circulates with the strength of authority and the specific story of the applicant, showing on the one hand the tendency among assessing organs to prioritise the former over the latter and, on the other, how an asylum seeker, assisted by an attorney, can take steps to prove that the facts are different.

2.2.1. The story in summary

Amenze is the pseudonym adopted by this attorney to keep the case anonymous during his presentation. In Benin dialect, Amenze means "stream water". In fact, if we observe the story as described in the minutes of the hearing, Amenze made no attempt to make her story coincide with the typical stories concerning her country of origin. For this reason, her story can be described as 'transparent', just like the stream water of her pseudonym.

Amenze fled her country (Nigeria), not for political or racial reasons, nor to escape from armed conflict or anything of that kind, but for questions related to her gender, since her father had promised her hand in marriage to an old man, against her will. Amenze fled her home first and then left her country to get away from the arranged marriage and her father's death threats. When she reached Italy, the territorial committee that gave her a hearing found her story to be incongruous and expressed doubts about "the plausibility and general reliability of the statements made", holding that her fear of persecution was not well-grounded as intended by Art. 1 of the 1951 Refugee Convention. It therefore rejected her application for international and humanitarian protection under Legislative Decree N° 286/98. Amenze, assisted by a lawyer, appealed the decision of the committee, first before the civil court, then before the Court of Appeal, asking for the status of political asylum to be recognised or, on a lesser level, that of subsidiary protection. At both instances, her appeal was rejected, so that Amenze decided to engage a different lawyer to lodge a further appeal with the Court of Cassation, where it was admitted. It was this second lawyer, whose chambers are in Naples, who provided me with information about the case, in the course of a lecture held during the latest edition of my course on "Clinical-legal training" (spring 2018), devoted to safeguarding foreigners.

2.2.2. The administrative and legal path

My intention now is to describe Amenze's administrative and legal path in the light of this normative framework. The first step – the hearing before the territorial committee – produced a negative result. The reasons given by Amenze for escaping can be found in a passage from the minutes of the territorial committee:

> **My father wanted to oblige me to marry a friend of his who was a member of the same fraternity, called Ogboni**. I went to stay with my aunt. **After I escaped, my father drove my mother out of the house,** saying that he wold not allow her to come back if she failed to convince me to marry

> his friend. **My mother went to stay with her family, but my father [. . .] sent people there on two occasions to check whether I was also there. These people turned the whole house upside down [. . .] then, as I was not there, they shot my mother in the arm** [. . .] some neighbours came running and took my mother to the hospital, but my mother did not have the money to pay for her care [. . .]. **After this episode, my aunt [. . .] started saying we should save the money to leave for Libya, as my father persecuted me and would not leave me alone** [. . .].
>
> (Excerpt from the minutes of the Committee, dated March 2014)

Amenze gave no other reasons by way of justifying her application for international protection, except that of having avoided an attempt at forced marriage, with the consequence that she was obliged to run away, so as escape persecution by her father. Yet the territorial committee felt that this justification was not enough for it to consider that Amenze's story deserved recognition. Here are some of the arguments advanced by the committee:

> CONSIDERING that the **general nature of the story as told and in some aspects its incongruence** raised some **doubts about the plausibility and the general reliability of the statements made**, in particular:
>
> - **the question concerning the forced marriage comes across as not very credible, as the applicant has stated that she continued living in her father's house for two years** – despite his having threatened her and wanting to oblige her to marry – even though she continued to refuse to marry the man of her father's choice;
> - **the fact that her father [. . .] did not think of searching for her at her maternal aunt's house is also not very credible.**
>
> HOLDING, for the reasons described above, **that substantial doubt has emerged in relation to the credibility of the story as told and that no elements are believed to exist for considering as well-founded the fear of persecution** as per Art. 1 (A) of the 1951 Refugee Convention [. . .], decides not to recognise international protection and rejects the above application.
>
> (Excerpt from the minutes of the Committee, dated March 2014)

Amenze appealed against this decision to the court, with the assistance of a lawyer. The court rejected her appeal, justifying its decision with a certain orientation in jurisprudence and reiterating that the premises for detecting the status of refugee are:

> **The socio-political and normative condition of the country of origin and the correlation between said condition and the specific position of the applicant** [. . .] detecting the situation of persecution of those who (for reasons of race, membership of a particular social group, political opinion or

religious belief, or for reason of their own tendencies or lifestyle) probably risk sanctions against their physical integrity or personal freedom (cf. Cass. 20.12.2007, N° 26822).

(Excerpt from the decision of the court of first instance, dated October 2014)

In this case, the court therefore felt that, by correlating the applicant's specific situation with the political, social and normative conditions of Nigeria, no elements emerged on which the recognition of the status of refugee could be based. The substance of its ruling was that "the affair [. . .] concerns private questions (the applicant fled Nigeria because she did not want to marry a friend of her father's) and not in fact any violence or degrading treatment for religious, political or racial reasons" (ibid.).

Moreover, the court also held that it did not find the conditions for subsidiary protection, in particular the 'serious damage' defined by Art. 14 of Legislative Decree N° 251, 2007, related to: a) a death penalty or a sentence decreeing its execution; b) torture or any other form or sentence of inhuman or degrading treatment detrimental to the applicant in his/her country of origin; c) a serious and individual threat to life from indiscriminate violence in a situation of internal or international armed conflict.

The court's decision was then confirmed by the Court of Appeal with largely similar reasons, since it shared the motives stated by the judge of first instance, who had decided that the premises for recognising the status of political refugee in accordance with Art. 13, s. 5 of the Legislative Decree did not exist. In this case, the Court of Appeal considered that the reasons for Amenze's escape related to

> **Private violence that cannot be related to violence or degrading treatment for religious, political or racial reasons.** [. . .] **There are therefore no concrete elements for holding that, were the applicant to return to her country of origin, she would be subjected**, by the authority of the state or by any other exercising control over the territory, **to persecution for political, religious or racial motives.**
>
> (Excerpt from the decision of the Court of Appeal, dated September 2015)

Since she had had no success in the first two instances, Amenze decided to play the last card in her hand, lodging an appeal with the Court of Cassation, although for this purpose she engaged a different attorney, who is well known in the field of defending the rights of foreigners. The first element that this new attorney highlighted in the appeal was the inadequacy of the investigation, which was based on the rule of subjective credibility, without putting what happened to the asylum seeker into the context of the situation in the country (as per Art. 8 of Legislative Decree N° 25, 2008). In his introduction to the appeal to the Cassation, the attorney mentioned that the committee's decision had already been subject to an appeal lodged with the Court of Catanzaro and that a further appeal had been lodged against that court's decision to reject the application, with the motivation that the judge had not co-operated in ascertaining the facts in question in the case and had merely expressed a belief about the supposedly 'private' nature of what had happened. In addition, the application for subsidiary protection had been rejected on the basis of arguments that were not grounded on the results of the investigation, but only on the rule of subjective credibility.

The attorney therefore asked for the appealed decision to be thrown out both for error in the decision-making process (*error in iudicando*) and for procedural errors (*error in procedendo*). With regard to the first kind of error, the attorney complained about the lack of co-operation on the part of the Court of Appeal in ascertaining the conditions that would have enabled it to recognise the existence of the premises for according the status of refugee and, as an alternative, subsidiary protection. The court had in fact argued that the events narrated before the committee did not concern the political, social and normative conditions of Nigeria, but episodes of private violence that could not be related to violence or degrading treatment for religious, political or racial reasons. According to the attorney, this reasoning was faulty because the Court had confused the premises for according the status of refugee with the ones of relevance for recognising subsidiary protection, reducing the motives of persecution (race, religion, nationality, membership of a particular social group or political opinion) to the sole motives of race, religion and political opinion. In actual fact, however, Art. 8 of Legislative Decree N° 251/07 provides for the motives of persecution to include also membership of a "particular social group". This group comprises "members who share an innate characteristic or a common history that cannot be changed". In addition, "as a function of the situation in the country of origin [. . .] due account is given to considerations of gender, including gender identity". When calling attention to the error at law (*error in iudicando*), the attorney underpinned his arguments with the Istanbul Convention, 2011, which came into force on 8 August 2014, adopting legislative measures to guarantee that gender-based violence against women can be recognised as a form of persecution under Art. 1, A (2) of the 1951 Convention relating to the status of refugees. Thus, the attorney argued that Amenze had escaped from Nigeria because of her:

> **Well-founded fear of being a victim of gender violence**, this being the reason why her status of refugee should be recognised [. . .]. **This kind of persecution was not the subject of any investigation on the part of the Court of Appeal, which, by reducing the motives of persecution to religion, race and political opinion, failed to assess the danger of persecution related to gender identity in a context (that of Nigeria) of endemic violence against women** (even featuring predatory behaviour on the part of state officials and the police: Amnesty International, Nigeria Annual Reports 2011, 2012, 2013, 2014–2015 and 2015–2016).
>
> (Excerpt from the appeal to the Court of Cassation, dated March 2016)

The second error pointed out by the attorney (*error in procedendo*) concerned the court's failure to pronounce on the application for recognition of the right to subsidiary protection as a consequence of serious harm, as defined by Art. 2, section g) and Art. 14, section b) of Legislative Decree N° 251, 2007. According to the attorney, the court neither examined nor pronounced on the specific issue of the risk of serious harm caused by inhuman and degrading treatment (Art. 14, section b) deriving from Amenze being obliged to contract a forced marriage in a context of absolute absence of safeguards on the part of the authorities, such as to justify the recognition of subsidiary protection as per section b) of Article 14. In this way, the court failed to comply with the duty to co-operate in the investigation vested in the international protection judge.

On the basis of these arguments, the Court of Cassation accepted the appeal for both errors, stating that the previous instances had unjustifiably restricted the scope of the motives of persecution of relevance for the purposes of recognising the status of refugee, "excluding the relevance of the persecutory behaviour attributable to membership of a particular social group and in the case in hand excluding the relevance of behaviour attributable to gender identity" (excerpt from the decision of the Court of Cassation, dated March 2016). The court thus held to be well-founded the application for recognition of humanitarian protection, about which the previous judge had not expressed her/himself, thus committing an *error in procedendo.* In conclusion, according to the Court:

> **The appeal is well-founded, as the Court of Appeal decision did not assess whether the practice of forced marriage constitutes an accepted social practice in the applicant's country of origin, nor did it consider that, for the purposes of subsidiary protection, the obligation to contract an unwanted marriage constitutes a serious breach of dignity and thus degrading treatment that integrates a serious harm** whose threat, for the purposes of recognising this measure, may also originate in subjects other than the state when the public authorities or the organisations that control the state or a substantial part thereof either cannot or do not want to furnish adequate protection (decision of the Civil section VI-1 of the Court of Cassation, N° 25873, dated 18 November 2013). **Nor, lastly, did it consider the jurisprudence of legitimacy, which states that the right to subsidiary protection cannot be excluded by the circumstance that the agents of the serious harm to the foreigner are private subjects if there is no state authority in the country of origin capable of furnishing her with adequate and effective safeguards**, with the consequence that it is incumbent upon the judge to conduct an unofficial check of the current situation in said country and thus of the potential pointlessness of lodging an application for protection with the local authorities (decision of the Civil section of the Cassation N° 15192, dated 20 July 2015).
>
> (Excerpt from the decision of the Court of Cassation, dated December 2016)

The case of Amenze, which had a positive conclusion thanks to the attorney's consolidated experience in this field of the law and to the adequate investigation he conducted personally into the political and social situation of her client's country of origin, is a typical example of how the story told by a (vulnerable) client risks being overwhelmed by routine decisions where general country of origin information (COI) is given precedence over the voice of a client like Amenze. According to the description tendered in its minutes by the territorial committee, we can confirm that Amenze's story was "pure and simple", just like the meaning of her pseudonym.

In addition to highlighting the dynamics whereby the COI tends to overlap and overwhelm the individual's story, an analysis of this case also raises a number of further issues that range from the problem of the gap between the strength of the person's story and its credibility compared to that of the judging authority, to the true ability of vulnerable clients to represent themselves and to be heard in the procedure of the hearing.

These are issues to which I shall return in the general conclusions to this chapter, where I shall discuss the possibility of making use of storytelling as an effective tool of client empowerment. In terms of judicial protection, Amenze's experience also offers a glimpse of the serious gap in gender identity protection in the application of legislation governing international protection as exercised by the judging authorities involved in the case. Ever since the eighties, it has actually been a well-established fact, both in academic literature and in international debate about asylum procedures, that breaches of human rights have a different impact on men and on women. This has led to amendments in the legislation of many countries, which have started taking gender-based persecution into account as coming under the heading of membership of a given social group (Miaz, 2014).

3. Sexual trafficking and exploitation: the problem of identifying the victims

In the framework of the asylum procedure, the Italian legal order furnishes special protection to victims of trafficking as vulnerable individuals in the procedure for recognising international protection (Art. 2, sections h-b, Legislative Decree N° 25/2008). For this category of people, Italian law provides that priority be given to the examination of their application for international protection, with the possibility to access the emergence, assistance and social integration programme as stipulated in Art. 18 of Legislative Decree N° 286/98. In the framework of this procedure, a significant role is played by voluntary associations like Dedalus, mentioned previously, which works officially in Italy on an anti-trafficking programme. In addition to contributing to identifying the victims, Dedalus accompanies them in the process of social integration that is also functional to the acceptance of their applications for international protection.

Trafficking is construed as forced and involuntary prostitution and is defined by Art. 3 of the United Nations Protocol to Prevent, Suppress and Punish Trafficking, adopted in 2000, as:

> The recruitment, transportation, transfer, harbouring or receipt of persons, by means of the threat or use of force or other forms of coercion, of abduction, of fraud, of deception, of the abuse of power or of a position of vulnerability or of the giving or receiving of payments or benefits to achieve the consent of a person having control over another person, for the purpose of exploitation. Exploitation shall include, at a minimum, the exploitation of the prostitution of others or other forms of sexual exploitation, forced labour or services, slavery or practices similar to slavery, servitude or the removal of organs.

For the purposes of protecting victims of trafficking, identification is the first delicate step towards organising adequate protection and assistance.[9] In Italy, the procedure takes place in two phases: a preliminary phase comprises a first analysis of the circumstances that could contribute to considering that the person in question is a victim of trafficking. Conducting this preliminary identification is the task of the forces of law enforcement, the border police, health personnel and the territorial committees. After conducting the preliminary identification, the territorial committee sends details about the possible victims of trafficking to organisations like Dedalus, which are responsible for protecting them. This is because, according to Art. 18, section 3b, of Legislative Decree N° 286/98, the interviews have to be conducted by qualified and especially trained personnel (belonging to social organisations, which may be public or private and which carry out programmes of emergence, assistance and social integration). These interviews are held in the presence of a cultural mediator and serve the purpose of formal identification. When the hearing has been completed, a report is written, which is then sent to the territorial committee, which treats it as an official opinion. The purpose of the report is to enable the committee to pursue the proceedings for recognising protection. In the proceedings for formal identification, the staff involved must collect information of various kinds that comes under the heading of anti-trafficking indicators: personal data (name, gender, nationality, country of origin); physical appearance (checking for the presence of wounds or signs of torture or of fear); living and working conditions and so on. For example, in the case of women from Nigeria – since 2015 one of the countries with the highest number of immigrants landing in Italy – anti-trafficking indicators include the young age of people coming from Nigeria (Edo State or Lagos), a low level of education, extremely precarious economic conditions and

9 See the European Union Strategy towards the Eradication of Trafficking in Human Beings, which provides specific, concrete measures for putting Directive N° 2011/36/EU into practice.

membership of a large family, a story of forced marriage with a man who is often older than the applicant, personal information that does not match with the contents provided in form C3[10] and a story that is not very clear or rather inaccurate about the places visited on the journey. In general, these reports mention the names of the people to whom the victim was entrusted during the journey or who obliged them to undertake it. Waiting for them at the other end of the journey there is nearly always a *Madame* who promises them a job or some form of reception, just as a mandatory staging post is the 'connection house' in Libya, from which they have managed to escape or been rescued by a benefactor.

3.1. *The case of Margaret: "Shall we go on a little part of this journey?"*

Since for a series of reasons it is not easy to identify a victim of trafficking (the person may be controlled by the traffickers, be afraid of reprisals, have little faith in the authorities or be unaware of being a victim), the work done by social organisations like Dedalus is crucial, also for the purpose of preparing these people to be examined by the territorial committee that has to decide their fate. Their work focuses on helping these clients understand the meaning of the administrative path they have to take: what parts of their story can be relevant for the purposes of the hearing and how their narrative should be put into the more general political, social and legal context of their country of origin.

In these procedures of identification, Dedalus is usually delegated by the territorial committee, from which it receives a dossier containing the information recorded during the first hearing and the form for processing sensitive data (C3). As already mentioned before, the interview is conducted in the presence of a cultural mediator who speaks the same language as the asylum seeker and of a lawyer. The aim is to piece together a consistent, detailed narrative that will be provided to the territorial committee responsible for assessing the application for international protection. Margaret's story – of which I only describe here the part that concerns the process of identification conducted by Dedalus – is a typical one.

In general, victims of trafficking are young Nigerian women who are often recruited by criminal networks for the purpose of introducing them to the market for prostitution, with the false promise that they will be able to build themselves a new life in Europe, with a safe, honest job, while encumbering them with the burden of repaying a sum of money. This commitment is sealed with a magical ritual (voodoo or juju) and, if they resist, with threats to harm them or the members of their family who have stayed behind in their country of origin.

The process of identifying Margaret undertaken by Dedalus took the form of a series of interviews that I was able to attend, held in the co-operative's offices

10 This is the form provided by the Italian police authorities for the purpose of making an application for international protection: https://portaleimmigrazione.eu/modulo-c3-protezione-internazionale/.

between February and April 2018. What now follows is my own brief description of some of the phases of these interviews, based on the notes I took during the meetings and subsequently edited.

The first meeting I attended took place at the beginning of February. Margaret arrived at the co-operative accompanied by a psychologist from the centre where she was a guest, of the kind known in Italy by the acronym of SPRAR.[11] Before the interview started, the psychologist informed the interviewers – the mediator, Barbara, and the lawyer, Evelyne – that Margaret had already started a traineeship and that she would start working with a company in the following week. The lawyer, who had prepared the setting for the interview and given me permission to attend, explained to Margaret how it would proceed, emphasising the function and significance of the path they were about to embark on together, that of piecing her story together and orienting it for the purposes of the interview she would have with the committee, which was due to meet Margaret several months later. Evelyne also underlined the importance of building a story that would give her a better chance of obtaining the status of refugee, explaining that recognition of asylum is based on the premise that that there are good reasons for believing that the applicant would be running a serious risk if she were to return to her country of origin: "We have to be very accurate in reconstructing your story from when you were still in Nigeria. We shan't get it all done today: it's a complicated job. If we make a good job of it, we have a better chance of constructing a story that will lead to a happy ending".

The lawyer, Evelyne, then asked Barbara to explain to Margaret that "we are here for her: she can ask us anything she wants if she has any doubts". Barbara, speaking partly in English and partly in her own language, added: "you must convince them about the risks you are going to face, you must show solid reasons. It's not a problem if you don't remember: feel free and relax".

Both asked Margaret to confirm her identity, although they also mentioned that the information could still be corrected during the hearing with the committee. Margaret confirmed that the information was correct. The lawyer then asked her for information about her family in Nigeria, which seemed to be made up of nine siblings (two boys and seven girls). Her father had died after a period of illness. Margaret grew up on the outskirts of Benin City and did not go to school. Her mother entrusted her to a woman who had promised to see her through her studies, but who sent her to work on the land instead. Margaret told how this woman would wake up in the morning and go out of the house to work, while she and the other children worked on the land. This story was confirmed by the state of her hands, which were not those of a person of her age (about twenty), but were deformed by hard labour.

11 SPRAR stands for *Sistema di protezione per richiedenti asilo e rifugiati* (System of protection for asylum seekers and refugees), which comprises the network of local authorities that guarantee systems of 'integrated hospitality'. These are not restricted to providing food and lodging, but also furnish information, accompaniment, assistance and orientation, by building individual paths towards socio-economic inclusion (www.sprar.it/lo-sprar).

Evelyne, asked her for how many years she had been fostered out in this way. The answer was for five years: she was eighteen years old when she left the woman. Evelyne also asked her whether anyone had come to visit her during this period. The answer was no, although at one point the foster mother had told Margaret that her real mother was unwell, whereupon she left to go and visit her in her own village. After her natural mother died, Margaret went to live with one of her sisters. This sister's husband put her in touch with a person who was supposed to bring her to Italy and then to Belgium, where she would be met by a madam who would give her a job. Evelyne asked her what proposal this person had made to her. Barbara translated this question as "what was the promise when you reached the woman?" Margaret answered: prostitution. In other words, she was aware of the fate that awaited her, but had nevertheless decided to undertake the journey that constituted the only chance she had to escape from a situation of poverty and difficulty. In the meantime, Margaret had become the mother of three children and was having difficulty taking care of them. Margaret also told how she had been subjected to a ritual that lasted seven days before leaving for her journey: they made her go through an examination by a local doctor, they made her take a shower, they took a sample of her hair and put it all in a pit underground. They made her swear that she would pay €30,000 once she reached her destination, threatening her that there would be repercussions for the members of her family if she failed. Evelyne asked her more questions about this ritual, which in her experience does not generally last seven days, and she asked whether Margaret had been afraid. Margaret answered that she had had no choice: she had to leave and had done what they asked of her. At this point, Margaret broke down in tears. Evelyne suggested they interrupt the interview at this stage and continue the next time, but Margaret asked to continue immediately. Her story progressed with the description of several stages on her journey, once she had left the starting point of Benin City in the company of three other girls. They travelled in a bus driven by armed men: when they reached their destination, Margaret and the other girls were beaten up and raped. Evelyne asked for more details about the various stages of the journey: "Shall we go on a little part of this journey? Let's say we are leaving Benin City." Margaret took up her story again, specifying that, after several hours of travelling, the person who was responsible for them had left them somewhere, giving each of them a number: they were to stay in this unidentified place until they were called for on the basis of this number. She and another person then travelled by bus for another two days and reached another destination. Since there were some gaps in the story, after about two hours of interviewing, Evelyne suggested stopping and taking it up again another time, commenting like this: "The journey is a very important stage for piecing the story together. So we'll stop now and continue next time." Margaret showed signs of impatience and asked how long she would have to wait before the committee would summon her for the hearing: she had lodged her application in November of the previous year and three months had already gone by. The lawyer answered that the waiting time was generally up to one year from the beginning of the procedure and that the aim was not to rush things, but to do a good job. She then observed that Margaret was wearing a gold ring on her left hand and asked if she was married.

After the interview was over, in a discussion with the psychologist who had accompanied Margaret, Evelyne expressed her fears about her interpretation of this element. The psychologist explained that Margaret often absented herself for three or four days to go and visit someone, a Nigerian man with whom she seemed to have a relationship and who lived in another city. Both of them (Evelyne and the psychologist) interpreted this situation with concern, as it might mean that Margaret was once again running the risk of becoming a victim of trafficking.

At the end of the interview, I asked the lawyer why she had asked certain questions, such as the ones about certain details of the journey, the better to understand which elements would be of interest to the committee. Evelyne gave me some examples of indicators of trafficking, in which the journey is crucial: the individual's transfer, her passiveness, the false promises given and the trickery are all such indicators. She also added that the fact that Margaret had consented was an element that made her case exceptional and problematic. For this reason, this element might be omitted from the report to be sent to the committee or at least furnished with a circumstantial explanation. To help me get a clearer understanding of what the committee expected, the lawyer gave me the URL of the website containing guidelines and country of origin information.[12]

During the next meeting, which took place two weeks later, Evelyne suggested that the mediator continue the process of reconstructing the story on her own with Margaret, in the hope that this would enable Margaret to open up more easily. Barbara and Margaret once again discussed her identity documents; in addition, Barbara set the agenda for the meeting by specifying that its aim was to clarify a series of elements in the story that did not correspond to or match with the more general narrative. Barbara encouraged her by telling her that there were gaps ("points we miss"): "They are direct; you must be specific." "From Nigeria to Libya, how many days did it take? How long you did stay in Libya? Where? How did you survive? Did they give you clothes?"

Considering Margaret's reticence, the mediator tried to encourage her further, suggesting she think seriously about the consequences of being sent back home, asking "What happens if you go back?" Margaret answered: "My life would be worse, nobody could care for my children." Barbara explained to her that the questions she would be asked during the committee hearing would be something like "Why did you leave your country?", reminding her that the committee would have to decide whether she would be allowed to stay in Italy: "They will ask you whether you were capable of defending yourself in Nigeria by going to the police. The committee has information about Nigeria, they combine information. You should be more aware about your country. You must be able to give an account. There are a lot of gaps we need to fill".

12 www.ecoi.net (website consulted on 8 September 2018).

In the third meeting, which took place after another two weeks, Barbara once again pointed out the need to achieve greater clarity about some of the stages of the journey, explaining the meaning of the questions better and asking her to be more precise and concise in her answers. Barbara started showing signs of impatience, because she and the lawyer had not compiled enough material to piece the story together: "I am not understanding anything, so what do we do? You don't forget the truth because it is your truth, truth is inside you, so you answer quickly." Barbara then burst out impatiently in Italian, asking "*ma che stiamo facendo*?" (What are we doing here?), then also in English "We are doing everything we can. I am not responsible because I tried. It is time! Who was that man? I want the name! What happened between the two of you? Is he the father of your baby? How long did you stay at that house? Who was he?"

Margaret now started talking in her own language, without stopping, but alternating her story with bursts of tears. Barbara added the occasional comment in Italian that enabled me to understand the gist of the story: "She [*the Madame*] brings in seven men every day and takes money for just three weeks." Since the reconstruction of Margaret's story has not yet been written up as an official opinion by Dedalus and the interview with the committee has not yet taken place, my account stops here at this preliminary phase of the identification procedure.

A retrospective look at these meetings, which constitute good examples of collaborative lawyering, enables us to examine the guide role played by Evelyne and above all by Barbara in reconstructing the path followed by Margaret and focusing on elements in her story that are significant for identifying her as a victim of trafficking: her poverty and enslavement, both during her earlier life in Nigeria and again later, during her journey and after arriving in Europe; the opportunity that Margaret turned to her/them and told them the truth that she did not want to run the risk of being sent back to her own country, and the need to focus clearly on the various stages in her journey, their dates and the people she met, and to formulate the most incisive responses to questions.

The short excerpts from these conversations also show how the kind of questions evolved from one meeting to the next, becoming more pressing and direct as the meetings grew ever more intense. In addition, this verbal behaviour was accompanied by Barbara's increasing impatience, as she tried to encourage Margaret to tell her story, saying that she had done everything possible to help and support her in the path she would tread towards the hearing before the committee. The steps taken by Evelyne, the lawyer, who was only present in the first of these meetings, were more incisive and restricted to defining the operative and legal framework.

4. Conclusions

The stories told by Amenze and Margaret enable us to understand certain aspects and critical points that may be found in the course of fact investigation during procedures for achieving the recognition of international protection. The reconstruction of Amenze's case, in particular, highlights the premise stated at the beginning of this chapter, i.e. the tendency for the territorial committee and the assessing organs to rely in their decision-making on general information about the asylum seeker's country of origin, to the detriment of the individual's story. Nevertheless, it does also make us aware of the possibility that the gap and the asymmetry between the story told by the institution, in the broad sense, and that of the client are bridged and solved by attorneys who specialise in the field of foreigners' rights and are capable of taking steps to unearth the correct legislative sources and adequate information about the country of origin, despite the general nature of the information available to the assessing organs in Italy, which, unlike those in other countries, do not have access to ad hoc analyses. The other shortcoming highlighted by Amenze's case concerns the failure of the assessing organs to pay attention to gender identity when applying the legislation governing asylum.

The vulnerability of this kind of client thus seems to be due to a series of factors: the type of procedure that attributes greater priority a priori to COI evidence than to the applicant's own narration, the difficulty involved in the client understanding and accepting the path that will lead her to the hearing before the territorial committee, language and cultural barriers, and the asymmetries that may characterise this kind of interaction in official procedures. Nevertheless, these are elements that cannot be investigated here in their entirety.

Where I would prefer to focus my attention here is on the vital nature of the asylum seeker's story and the role it plays in the proceedings of the hearing before the territorial committee. In the absence of documents and of other forms of evidence capable of confirming the truth and authenticity of the applicant's identity and origins, the cases of Amenze and Margaret illustrate how applicants base the possibility of obtaining recognition of their status as refugees on their performance, i.e. on their ability to tell a story that is consistent, plausible and probable (D'Halluin-Mabillot, 2012, pp. 44–46). Amenze's case, for its part, demonstrates that the fact that a story is spontaneous and transparent is not enough on its own to make it worthy of recognition and protection, because it is considered to be generic, incongruous and ultimately not very plausible or reliable. Hence the practice developed by Dedalus of accompanying clients like Margaret, for example, in the process of identification and in the hearing before the committee responsible for deciding their status. Although it is based on the competence and experience respectively of a lawyer and a cultural mediator, this practice could well be completed by other professionals and specific clinical techniques that hinge on the use of legal narrative.

This, in fact, is the question that I go back to asking here: How can laypeople – those who are silenced, marginalised or excluded – act successfully within the law and be heard in legal discourse?

Drawing on the cases of Amenze and Margaret, but also considering the others examined in previous chapters – such as that of Line, its duration and the resources employed to solve it – and channelling this thinking back into a more general debate about how legal clinics "might be consciously designed" to be "powerful agents of the progressive transformation of the social world" (Kruse,

2011–2012), making the inclusion of the powerless in public discourse possible (White, 1997, p. 607), my aim is to propose designing new socio-legal tools to achieve substantive justice (Block, 2011). Specifically, as I shall describe in greater detail in the conclusions to this book, I would propose conceiving of legal clinics as socio-legal spaces to raise different voices "democratically" (Daiute et al., 2017; Daiute, 2018) and realise effective forms of collaborative lawyering, with the active participation of lay and expert actors (lawyers, volunteer associations), in order to address the multidimensional problems faced by the client and to elaborate a common understanding of socio-legal problems, thereby increasing laypeople's consciousness and agency in legal settings. Such a space would allow clients to understand how the legal system works, what the formal and informal rules are and the practices with which they are expected to deal. In fact, as lawyering generally demands specific knowledge regarding the relevant audiences, stories and storytelling practices, my proposal is to train laypeople to adapt their specific problem-solving knowledge to 'unfamiliar audiences'. This could be the case of immigrants living in a foreign cultural and legal system – Line, Charles and Kirin (Chapter 8) – as well as the case of natives who are not able to deal with the specificity of the law and the broader system (Chapter 7). Last but not least, this could also be the case of particularly vulnerable clients, such as Amenze and Margaret.

References

Block, F.S. (Ed.). (2011). *The Global Clinical Movement*. Oxford: Oxford University Press.

Daiute, C. (2014). *Narrative Inquiry: A Dynamic Approach*. Thousand Oaks, CA: Sage Publications.

Daiute, C. (2018). *Narrative Inquiry Integrating Public and Personal Perspectives toward Social Justice*. (Lecture Given at the University of Naples, Federico II, 15.06.2018).

Daiute, C. et al. (2017). *Minority Teachers – Roma in Serbia – Narrated Education Reform*. Belgrade: Institute of Psychology, Faculty of Philosophy, University of Belgrade Association of Pedagogical Assistants of Serbia.

D'Halluin, E. (2016). Le nouveau paradigme des "populations vulnérables" dans les politiques européennes d'asile. *Savoir/Agir*. 2(36): 21–26.

D'Halluin-Mabillot, E. (2012). *Les épreuves de l'asile. Associations et réfugiés face aux politiques du soupçon*. Paris: EHESS, coll. "En temps & lieux".

Engelmann, C. (2015). *Common Standards Via the Backdoor: The Domestic Impact of Asylum Policy Coordination in the European Union*. Dissertation. Maastricht: Universitaire Pers Maastricht.

Galowitz, P. (2012). The Opportunities and Challenges of an Interdisciplinary Clinic. *International Journal of Clinical Legal Education*. 18: 163–178.

Gibb, R. and Good, A. (2013). Do the Facts Speak for Themselves? Country of Origin Information in French and British Refugee Status Determination Procedures. *International Journal of Refugee Law*. 25(2): 291–322.

Israël, L. (2009). Cause Lawyering. In: Fillieule, O., Matthieu, L. and Pechu, C. (Eds.). *Dictionnaire des mouvements sociaux*. Paris: Presses de Sciences Po. 94, 100.

Kruse, K.R. (2011–2012). Getting Real About Legal Realism, New Legal Realism, and Clinical Legal Education. *New York Law School Law Review*. 56: 659–681.

Lejeune, A. (2011). Le professionels du droit comme acteurs du politique: revue critique de la literature americaine et enjeux pour une importation en Europe continentale. *Sociologie du travail*. 53: 216–233.

Linde, C. (2001). Narrative in Institutions. In: Shiffrin, D., Tannen, D. and Hamilton, H. (Eds.). *The Handbook of Discourse Analysis*. Oxford: Blackwell Publishers. 518–535.

López, G.P. (1992). *Rebellious Lawyering: One Chicano's Vision of Progressive Law Practice*. San Francisco: Westview Press.

López, G.P. (2017). Transform-Don't Just Tinker with-Legal Education. *Clinical Law Review*. 23: 471–576.

Miaz, J. (2014). Les "persécutions liées au genre" en Suisse: les frontières du droit d'asile en question. *Cahiers du Genre*. 2(57): 55–75.

Miaz, J. (2018). *Politique d'asile et sophistication du droit. Pratique administrative et defense juridique des migrants en Suisse (1981–2015)*. Thése de doctorat soutenue le 2 juin 2017 à l'Université de Lausanne, Faculté de Sciences Politiques.

Rosset, D. (2017). *The Legal Frames of Social Representations: Negotiating Eritrea's Reality Through the Lenses of Refugee Status Determination in Switzerland*. Manuscript on file with the author. (Paper Presented at the International Meeting on Law and Society, Mexico City, 21.06.2017).

White, L.E. (1997). The Transformative Potential of Clinical Legal Education. *Osgoode Hall Law Journal*. 35(3–4): 603–611.

Conclusions

Moving towards new directions of narrative theory and clinical legal research

Now that I have reached the end of this process of theoretical thinking, methodological exploration and case analyses, the time has come to draw some conclusions.

Presenting itself as typical of a certain postmodernist trend, the law and narrative approach has used methodological rigour to achieve success, riding the wave of the cultural and narrative turn of the seventies and eighties in such a way as to define the study of legal narrativity as a useful enterprise and imagine that narration constitutes a legal category in its own right.

Intended as a contribution to this debate, my research offers a 'narrative legal analysis', highlighting on the one hand a theoretical and methodological path and, on the other, the basis for a research action that gives due consideration to voices that are otherwise not heard in legal discourse.

1. Theoretical and methodological paths

In the earlier part of this book, I explained my decision to adopt a narrativist approach to explore how facts come about within the legal process and how narrations of everyday problems are transformed into legal narrations, so as to be suitable for shaping a critical path aimed at shedding light on the polyphony of the voices and the multiple human and social dimensions that animate a case. In the middle part of this book, the adoption of this approach enabled me to illustrate the wealth of social and cultural implications of cases by situating clients' legal activities in different contexts. At the end of this process, I then imagined expanding the narrative framework to include the voices of vulnerable clients in research action projects based on collaborative lawyering.

In particular, my adoption of the paradigm of the "narrative construction of reality" (Amsterdam and Bruner, 2000; Bruner, 1991, 2002; Sherwin, 1994) as a lens through which to conduct my investigations enabled me to show how the construction of legal reality is context-dependent and culturally contingent and based on the negotiation of meanings within human relations (Daute, 2014). These relations take shape through communicative exchanges organised in narrative form, following most of the time typical plots or scripts. Since a narration depends on culture, it tends to adopt a conventional view, whereby it acquires a degree of normativity. Conflicting visions and objectives are often at the origin of breaches of social or legal norms that legal narration can induce to return to an ordinary situation or towards the creation of new possibilities (Chapters 4–8). In this tension between what is already established (by legal institutions) and what can be achieved (by human interventions), there is unlikely to be any space for unconventional, unassimilated or excluded voices (Chapters 7, 8, 9). Hence the usefulness of using the narrative lens to take a closer, deeper look, capturing the implicit and contextual meanings that furnish the backdrop to the story, and retrieving narrative elements that were omitted from the official storyline. As the analysis of the interaction between clients and lawyers has shown (Chapters 4–5), the client's narrative and the lawyer's narrative and their co-constructed narratives contain materials that never appear in the official story or appear in a new form.

Once the distinction between ontology and epistemology (Ferraris, 2012) has been clarified and it has been established that only the latter is relevant to the legal proceedings which create a communicative context including linguistic codes, procedural rules, rhetorical artifices and interpretative dimensions, narrative comes across as a constitutive process that operates in different ways to reorient our understanding of traditionally conceived dualities: facts and norms; theory and practice; individuals and institutions. Thus, if in Frank's day narration was generally associated with the linguistic distortions and manipulations practised by attorneys and witnesses (Frank, 1949), it later came to be analysed in terms of the consistency and plausibility of the stories told for the purpose of persuading a jury (Bennett and Feldman, 1981) and, more recently, as a tool for practising clinical lawyering (Shalleck, 2015) and a parameter for judging. In terms of clinical lawyering, narrative is on, one hand, the substrate to shape the lawyer-client relationship through iterative, reciprocal storytelling' process; on the other hand, it is the framework and the "glue" (Gaakeer, 2017) to putting facts and law together through the elaboration of a case theory between clients and attorneys.

The result is that we can now attribute additional values to narrations:

- a lens for conducting a contextualised analysis of the law, construed as a cultural and human product;
- a method for analysing court proceedings and legal conflicts, construed as social constructs and dynamic and interactive places, where meanings are negotiated among legal actors: clients, attorneys, judges, administrators etc.;
- a framework to understand and shape the activities that constitute the client-lawyer relationship;
- a tool to analyse and shape judicial decision by giving contextualised meaning to the results of evidences;
- a place for including and socialising excluded voices, where the various different narrations (official and unofficial, public and private) can serve as ways to communicate, to make comparisons and to engage in conflict with each other as they constitute a social patchwork.

2. Results of case analyses

Proceeding with an analysis of the plots of the stories told by clients and then retold by the attorneys themselves and judges (Chapters 4–6), the aim of the case analyses was primarily to understand whether any typical elements emerge in the various different narrations, how they evolve from one phase of the proceedings to another, what implicit (relational or political) meanings are concealed behind the stories (in terms of causes or consequences of the legal conflicts) and how the configuration of facts construct time and causation, thereby creating those meanings.

The use of a plot analysis enabled me to understand that clients' stories generally revolve around a central core comprising an original action, caused by an initiative taken by someone (a colleague, an employer, a request made by a public office), which is more or less complicated by subsequent actions that intrude into the objectives that the parties to the case set out to achieve, generating the trouble at the root of the conflict. This 'trouble' is first represented in emotional terms, gradually becoming more objective as the client becomes aware of being a victim of a breach of a right and of the legal significance that can be attributed to the affair. The initiatives taken by the client – in co-operation with an attorney – tend towards providing solutions to the conflict (by furnishing useful information or adopting strategies based on relations), which may also be alternative or transformative with respect to the ones suggested by the attorney and subsequently confirmed or refuted by the judge. In this sense, the spotlight falls on the role played by the client as a possible vehicle for social change, or at least for introducing unconventional views. In its turn, the attorney's narration translates the client's representations in the terms expected by the legal system or, on the contrary, tries to convey 'rebellious' visions of facts and law, thereby trying to change the contours of law. This happens through the contextualisation of the cases, by referring to foreign legal systems, for example, as in Amenze's case (see Chapter 9). The client-attorney's story is then seen to be oriented towards transformation, challenging the fixed and canonical nature that is otherwise typical of legal narrations. On the contrary, although it may be creative in terms of the interpretation and contextualisation of facts and law, the judge's narration is more oriented towards maintaining the consolidated order and preserving the status quo than towards creating a new order (Chapter 6).

3. Case analysis in context: the role of clients' legal agentivity

The examination of the role played by the actors and of the plot becomes dynamic when we pass from a perspective internal to the legal proceedings to an external one that gives due consideration to the relationships between law and culture, illustrating how solving cases is closely linked not only to applying formal law, but also to achieving an understanding of local mindsets (Chapters 7–9). The focus on the actions taken by attorneys' clients – by means of legal agentivity – has shown what personal and social resources may be involved in reaching a solution to a conflict: from the tenacity of participants to their ability to benefit from social support from trade unions, the institutions and skilled professionals. The ability to narrate events and a collaborative client-attorney relationship are constituent parts of a successful legal agentivity.

Using the broader lens of law and culture to analyse legal phenomena, even the role played by the judge, comes across as dynamic when he succeeds in penetrating beyond merely interpreting the versions provided by the parties, using their different narrations to deduce the dynamics that are concealed within working contexts and the political or corporate mindsets that give rise to labour conflicts (Chapter 7).

In transferring the analysis away from the south of Italy to another context, that of north-western Switzerland, I found that the results are not so very different, illustrating how the close correlation that exists between an understanding of the rules (both formal and informal) and the clients' ability to act – by means of an appropriate legal narration of the events – produces a successful agentivity: by addressing pertinent questions and answers and above all gradually penetrating the logic of how the system works. The obstacles naturally become greater when the client is a foreigner in the context where the action takes place, because of the limits intrinsic to her or his civic status and of what institutions expect from the client (Chapter 8). The degree of difficulty also increases when the client is not only a foreigner, but also in conditions of particular vulnerability, as in the case of asylum seekers or of women who are victims of trafficking. These clients are powerless, because they are uneducated and are not initiated to the culture and practices of their host country, as well as being exposed to prejudice and to political pressures (Chapter 9). So the question is this: how can this gap be bridged? How can these people be helped to deal with the expectations of the institutions, in such a way as to enable them to overcome the barriers that the power of law imposes on them, thereby also achieving new visions of substantive justice?

4. Educating lawyers to take clients' narratives seriously

The list of questions framed would not be complete without a complementary one concerning clinical legal education: how can lawyers be educated to adopt narrative methods and perspectives, increasing the client's capacity to act as an agent and participant in solving the case?

The best way to answer this question is to step back and peruse the typology of the attorneys encountered in the course of the analyses and how they shaped their relationships with their clients. The examples of attorney-client collaboration found in Chapters 4–5, 7 and 9 are positive: these are attorneys who tend in different ways to allow space for their clients' narrations, which are then used implicitly as a tool in the co-construction of the case. In Chapters 4–5, for example, the attorney representing Luciano and Franco – the same attorney who is also found working with Carlo, Michele and Viviana in Chapter 7 – tends to use her/his client's narration both as an element functional to raising the client's awareness 'about what happened and in which ways' and as a tool for acquiring precise information about the case. When drawing up a written narration of the events, clients not only remembers and reconstructs the facts, but also go about a process of somehow elaborating their own emotional experience. For example, Viviana heads her reports with the title "memories". In addition to constructing a theory of the case that involves the client actively in the process of qualifying the facts (mobbing or dequalification?), Laura's attorney, meanwhile, makes strategic use of the narration to model the interaction between the client and her employer (i.e. via e-mail). In Chapters 8 and 9, which describe the experiences of foreign clients (in Italy and Switzerland), the attorney's relationship with the client is presented in more complicated terms. Since the client is unfamiliar with the context of hospitality, her relationship with her attorney is perhaps unlikely to be reciprocal in nature. For example, in the case of Margaret (discussed in Chapter 9), a multiplicity of factors intervenes in the construction of the story, starting with the role played by the cultural mediator who has to negotiate the meaning of the story in both linguistic and cultural terms.

Moving from the examples offered in this book, we can certainly confirm that storytelling is a tool for lawyering and for engaging with clients and developing a lawyer-client relationship, as announced in Chapter 2. In any case, these examples themselves illustrate the existence of a lack of awareness about the functions of narrative in law by lawyers. Any increase of this awareness requires the development of conceptual as well as practical skills for clinical lawyering.

This educational goal, which is most typical of US law schools, require clinical teaching to be extended towards some crucial topics, such as 1) making law students aware that clients are human beings and that facts must be connected not only to legal elements, but also to broader stories; 2) creating settings for listening adequately to the client's story; 3) framing the lawyer-client relationship in terms of reciprocity rather than in term of asymmetries, thereby involving clients as channels in the case theory as well as in the solution of the case; 4) increasing law students' awareness of multicultural issues, including gender, race and inequality.[1]

5. Towards new directions of action research: including powerless voices in legal discourse

One of the questions tackled in this book concerns the possibility of considering narration as a fully-fledged legal category. I have shown how in certain fields of the law, such as that of international protection (Chapter 9), the criterion of truth is replaced in practice by that of verisimilitude, of the consistency and plausibility of the story. In the absence of proof in the classical sense of the term, the client's narration plays a vital role in the procedures of international protection hearings. From criteria typical of literary narration, consistency and plausibility

1 For a conceptual framework as well as the practice of supervision in lawyering, see Shalleck and Aiken (2014).

now become evidence of a legal story's verisimilitude. Hence the direct invitation to practitioners to learn how narration can be employed to support not only their everyday professional practices, but also their clients' 'performance', so as to mediate between their positions and society.

The adoption of a dynamic narrative approach to including excluded voices (Daiute, 2014) helps us understand that supporting powerless voices requires an understanding of the 'other' voices that make up the narrative patchwork, such as that of the lawyers, the judge, public officials and so on. Consequently, in order to enhance the different points of view through which the story takes shape, I propose the creation of a 'socio-clinical legal space', in the form of a storytelling workshop, where stories are told and cases are discussed in collaboration with researchers, clients, lawyers, social workers and other professionals (Daiute and Kreniske, 2016). Originally created by the psychologist Daiute (2014) to favour the inclusion of minorities in pedagogical programmes in Eastern Europe, in the framework of my proposal, the storytelling workshop would put clients at the core of the case reconstruction in a dialogue with other actors involved in the story. The aim of this collective storytelling would be to understand how and whether diverse stakeholders' narratives interact, clash and might come into better contact. In fact, the storytelling workshop is designed not to socialise laypersons to the culturally consistent narrative, but to introduce tensions which then transform what is or might be the culturally consistent legal narrative. In the storytelling workshop, clients, lawyers and other members of society could work together to increase awareness (Merry, 2003; Silbey, 2014) about the ways in which the law operates in daily life, in administrative practices as well as in court proceedings. Case by case, lawyers, judges, public officials and civil servants would be invited to tell their versions of the story, as previously narrated by the client from her/his point of view, highlighting rules, procedures and practices. This process would allow clients' perspectives about their cases (and about themselves) to change and a 'new narrative' to take shape that would take the all participants' perspectives into account, so as then to see which story works in which contexts and for which audiences. Discussing all these narratives in a socio-clinical legal space with shared competences among lay and expert actors (included researchers and students) would enable us to understand the case 'as a whole', providing a deeper understanding of how best to listen to clients' stories, the context within which the problem has arisen and the ways the stories are understood and interpreted by others, thereby achieving forms of collaborative lawyering and justice and expanding legal culture toward new topics, dealing with race, gender and inequalities.

References

Amsterdam, A.G. and Bruner, J.S. (2000). *Minding the Law*. Cambridge, MA: Harvard University Press.

Bennett, W.L. and Feldman, M. (1981). *Reconstructing Reality in the Courtroom. Justice and Judgment in American Culture*. New Brunswick: Rutgers University Press.

Bruner, J.S. (1991). The Narrative Construction of Reality. *Critical Inquiry*. 18(1): 1–21.

Bruner, J.S. (2003). *Making Stories*. Cambridge, MA: Harvard University Press.

Daiute, C. (2014). *Narrative Inquiry: A Dynamic Approach*. Thousand Oaks, CA: Sage Publications.

Daiute, C. and Kreniske, P. (2016). Hopes, Misunderstandings and Possibilities of Narrating for Inclusive Education. In: Surian, A. (Ed.). *Open Spaces for Interaction and Learning Diversities*. Rotterdam: Sense Publishers. 53–67.

Ferraris, M. (2012). *Manifesto del Nuovo Realismo*. Roma-Bari: Laterza.

Frank, J. (1949). *Courts on Trial*. Princeton, NJ: Princeton University Press.

Gaakeer, J. (2017). The Perplexity of Judges Becomes the Scholar's Opportunity. In: Olson, G. and Reimer, F. (Eds.). *German Law Journal. Special Issue Law's Pluralities*. 18(2): 233–440.

Merry, S.E. (2003). Rights Talk and the Experiences of Law: Implementing Women's Human Rights to Protection from Violence. *Human Rights Quarterly*. 25: 343–381.

Shalleck, A. (2015). *Toward a Jurisprudence of Clinical Thought: Investigating the Contours, Urges and Trajectories*. Manuscript on file with the author.

Shalleck, A. and Aiken, J.H. (2014). Supervision: A Conceptual Framework. In: Bryant, S., Milstein, E.S. and Shalleck, A. (Eds.). *Transforming the Education of Lawyers: The Theory and Practice of Clinical Pedagogy*. Durham, NC: Carolina Academic Press. 169–203.

Sherwin, R. (1994). The Narrative Construction of Legal Reality. *Vermont Law Review*. 18: 681.

Silbey, S.S. (2014). The Courts in American Public Culture. *Daedalus, the Journal of the American Academy of Arts & Sciences*. 140–156.

Index

For Product Safety Concerns and Information please contact our EU representative GPSR@taylorandfrancis.com
Taylor & Francis Verlag GmbH, Kaufingerstraße 24, 80331 München, Germany

www.ingramcontent.com/pod-product-compliance
Ingram Content Group UK Ltd.
Pitfield, Milton Keynes, MK11 3LW, UK
UKHW022011180926
475701UK00003B/309

* 9 7 8 0 3 6 7 7 2 6 9 3 5 *